An Ethical Evaluation *of* Lethal Functions
in Autoregulative Weapons Systems

An Ethical Evaluation *of* Lethal Functions
in Autoregulative Weapons Systems

———————————

NICOLE KUNKEL

☞PICKWICK *Publications* • Eugene, Oregon

AN ETHICAL EVALUATION OF LETHAL FUNCTIONS IN AUTOREGULATIVE WEAPONS SYSTEMS

Copyright © 2024 Nicole Kunkel. All rights reserved. Except for brief quotations in critical publications or reviews, no part of this book may be reproduced in any manner without prior written permission from the publisher. Write: Permissions, Wipf and Stock Publishers, 199 W. 8th Ave., Suite 3, Eugene, OR 97401.

Pickwick Publications
An Imprint of Wipf and Stock Publishers
199 W. 8th Ave., Suite 3
Eugene, OR 97401

www.wipfandstock.com

PAPERBACK ISBN: 979-8-3852-1447-1
HARDCOVER ISBN: 979-8-3852-1448-8
EBOOK ISBN: 979-8-3852-1449-5

Cataloguing-in-Publication data:

Names: Kunkel, Nicole, author.

Title: An ethical evaluation of lethal functions in autoregulative weapons systems / Nicole Kunkel.

Description: Eugene, OR : Pickwick Publications, 2024 | Includes bibliographical references.

Identifiers: ISBN 979-8-3852-1447-1 (paperback) | ISBN 979-8-3852-1448-8 (hardcover) | ISBN 979-8-3852-1449-5 (ebook)

Subjects: LCSH: Military weapons—Law and legislation. | Military weapons—Technological innovations—Moral and ethical aspects. | Robotics—Law and legislation. | Weapons systems. | War—Moral and ethical aspects. | Arms race—Moral and ethical aspects.

Classification: U163 .K86 2024 (paperback) | U163 .K86 (ebook)

12/28/24

Scripture taken from the New King James Version®. Copyright © 1982 by Thomas Nelson. Used by permission. All rights reserved.

This book was submitted and approved as a dissertation at Humboldt-University Berlin in 2023.

Contents

Acknowledgments | vii

1 Introduction | 1
    1.1 The Phenomenon: Autoregulation in Weapons Systems | 1
    1.2 The Input This Study Provides | 7
    1.3 Overview of the Argument | 10

2 Autonomy and Moral Agency in Humans | 17
    2.1 Connecting Humans and Machines: Transcendental Technologies | 18
    2.2 Terms of Autonomy: Autonomy in Philosophy and Theology | 22
    2.3 Humans as Moral Agents | 31
    2.4 Conclusion | 33

3 Autonomy and Moral Agency in Machines | 35
    3.1 Defining Technological "Autonomy" | 36
    3.2 How Machines Do (Not) Operate: On AI and Machine "Learning" | 39
    3.3 Reckoning and Judgment: The Problem of "Intelligent" Machines | 43
    3.4 Machines: Autoregulative, Not Autonomous | 47
    3.5 Artificial Entities as Moral Agents | 53
    3.6 Artificial Entities as Moral Patients | 58

Contents

    3.7 The Implementation of Moral Behavior into Robots | 63

    3.8 Conclusion | 79

4 Human–Machine Interaction | 84

    4.1 Joint Cognitive Systems | 85

    4.2 Implications of Automatization | 90

    4.3 Implementations of Automatization | 101

    4.4 Meaningful Human Control | 105

    4.5 Conclusion | 113

5 The Ethical Framing: Peace Ethics | 116

    5.1 Absolute Pacifism and Peace Studies | 120

    5.2 Just War Tradition | 153

    5.3 Contingent Pacifism | 187

    Excursus: Approaches Among Jewish Traditions | 249

    5.4 Conclusion | 267

6 Violence Without Guilt: Transferring the Decision Between Life and Death to Machines | 281

    6.1 Legal Framework | 283

    6.2 Revisiting the Ethical Discourse on Autoregulation in Weapons Systems | 291

    6.3 Finding Just Peace After Violence: *Jus post bellum* | 295

    6.4 Redistributing Risk | 297

    6.5 Responsibility | 313

    6.6 Waging War Without Guilt | 339

7 Conclusion | 351

Bibliography | 361

Acknowledgments

WRITING THIS BOOK WOULD not have been possible without the help and support of many colleagues and friends.

I would like to express my deepest gratitude to my doctoral advisor Torsten Meireis for his continuous support, patience, motivation, and for sharing his expertise from the initial to the final stage of this work. I am also deeply indebted to the dissertation committee, especially to Notger Slenczka and Traugott Jähnichen for providing valuable and auxiliary feedback. Thanks should also go to the members of the *Forschungskolloquium* to whom I presented parts of this work time and again for their encouragement, insightful comments, and intellectual guidance—especially Florian Höhne, whom I must mention here by name. Many thanks should also go to my colleagues, namely to the members of the *Arbeitskreis Theologische Wirtschafts- und Technikethik* and the Network for Theology and AI for their feedback and encouragement—the latter was especially important for meeting up virtually during the Covid-19 pandemic. Special thanks also to Volker Stümke for organizing a panel discussion with different members of the *Bundeswehr* so I could talk over my argument and examine whether my thoughts were valid.

I could not have undertaken this journey without the funding and support of the *Evangelisches Studienwerk Villigst e.V.*, who not only gave the financial resources, but also provided a network of colleagues. Moreover, winning the *Humboldt-Preis* for dissertations in 2023 helped to fund the printing and revision of this project, along with the generous financial support of the *Alfred-Loges-Stiftung* and the *Protestant Military Chaplaincy*.

Thanks should also go to Mairi Bunce, Felix Fischer, Fiona Bender, Maria-Magdalena Pruß, Omer Malik, and Itamar ben Ami, who helped me deal with writing this book in English, for their revisions, support, and many corrections.

Acknowledgments

I would be remiss if I did not mention Kilian and Eunike, who remind me constantly that there are more important things in life than writing a dissertation, and Tabea for her unwavering love and support. If it were not for the nature of topic, I would have dedicated this book to them.

1

Introduction

1.1 THE PHENOMENON: AUTOREGULATION IN WEAPONS SYSTEMS

THIS BOOK BRINGS TOGETHER two of the most important ethical topics of our day, which are the ethics of artificial intelligence (AI) and peace ethics, materialized in so-called lethal autonomous weapons systems or, as I propose to call them more adequately, autoregulative functions in weapons systems.[1] It does so from an outright religious perspective, which is the idea that in creating humans, God did not intend violent conduct but rather a peaceful attitude, meaning that Christians—and not only Christians—are called to act nonviolently. However, as long as violence is part of humanity's practices, the way violence is conducted must not be ignored by Christian ethics.

In March 2021, the United Nations (UN) Security Council reported for the first time on the potential deployment of such a system, called *STM Kargu-2*, in Libya. The report reads,

> Logistics convoys and retreating HAF [Haftar Affiliated Forces] were [...] hunted down and remotely engaged by the unmanned combat aerial vehicles or the lethal autonomous weapons systems such as the STM *Kargu*-2 [...] and other loitering

---

1. I will spell out this term in full throughout this thesis. Some quotations, however, might use common abbreviations, such as AWS or LAWS, which means (lethal) autonomous weapons system.

An Ethical Evaluation of Lethal Functions in Autoregulative Weapons Systems

munitions. The lethal autonomous weapons systems were programmed to attack targets without requiring data connectivity between the operator and the munition.[2]

Even though it is not exactly clear whether the device has indeed been deployed autoregulatively, it shows that the existence of autoregulative functions in weapons systems are no longer mere fiction but already constitute part of reality. This new reality poses a dire and pressing question: Is it appropriate that a rule-based machine makes the most intimate decision to kill a human being? The aim of this book is to address this question by asking whether this phenomenon can be approved of and what exactly the problem might be from a Christian perspective.

What technology exactly is this book about? Autoregulative functions in weapons systems come in two divergent modes of operationality. For one thing, there is a single device operating without human control and supervision in real time, such as STM Kargu-2. For another thing, there is a network of the same or of different devices operating side by side and linked to each other in real time, the former called *swarm*, the latter *system of systems*. The three following examples ought to demonstrate how a weapons system with autoregulative functions operates.[3] Since autoregulation is software that can be implemented into various kinds of technological systems, I attempt to introduce different kinds of weapons systems here. First, there is *Super aEgis II*, which is a sentry weapon that can be deployed stationary or mobile by installation on different platforms. Further, there is the drone *Harpy*, which is a loitering weapon that searches for a certain radio-signature and attacks the origin thereof, if it finds its target. Finally, there is the system of systems *Future Combat Air System (FACS)*, which is currently under development.

Among them, Super aEgis II was invented by the company DoDAAM (South Korea) as a sentry weapons system. Once installed, the system can operate on its own. The thermal sensor, color camera and laser range finder provide the necessary environmental input, so the system can detect people within the range of three kilometers by day and 2.2 kilometers by night. The remote targeting system will target

---

2. United Nations Security Council, "Final Report of the Panel of Experts on Libya Established Pursuant to Security Council Resolution 1973," 17.

3. A very detailed and broad overview of weapons systems with a special take on autoregulation is given by Vincent Boulanin and Maaike Verbruggen in their book *Mapping the Development of Autonomy in Weapons Systems*. The first two examples are taken from this book.

Introduction

them and even check if the detected individual is friend or foe, according to their clothing.

For engaging targets, the system can be deployed in three different modes: When operating in the *human-in-the-loop mode*, a human has to key in a password in order to deploy the weapon; when operating in the *human-on-the-loop mode*, humans supervise the machine as it does its job and can disrupt the target cycle in case of need; while in the *human-out-of-the-loop mode*, the system will operate without any human supervision in real time but according to some predetermined factors.[4] It is particularly this last out-of-the-loop mode that is of interest here, even though the other two modes also pose severe ethical problems, as will be discussed below.[5]

As a second example, the loitering drone IAI Harpy is a device that operates autoregulatively with the aim of destroying foreign air defense. Its subsequent versions, Harop and Harpy NG, can also be deployed in a human-in-the-loop mode. Once the weapon is launched, it loiters in a certain area and upon detecting the enemy's radar emitters, it will destroy them. It is also possible to preprogram a list of potential targets and to prioritize them, thereby making it possible for the weapon to engage a secondary target if a prioritized target is not in sight. If the system operates in a human-in-the-loop mode, the operator in a ground control station can abort the attack as well as order the system's self-destruction, return the device to loitering, or command it to return to its base. If the system is deployed out-of-the-loop, it will operate without any human oversight.

Finally, and as an example of a network of devices, the Future Air Combat System (FCAS) is a program launched by France, Germany, and Spain in order to develop an airborne weapons system by 2040, designed as a system of systems. As such, FCAS will be composed of heterogeneous kinds of aircraft, such that already exist and such that are currently under development, combined to operate together.[6] More importantly, crewed and uncrewed technology, as well as remote carriers, ought to operate together with the help of the Air Combat Cloud, providing the

---

4. See Boulanin and Verbruggen, *Mapping the Development of Autonomy in Weapons Systems*, 44–47.

5. See 4.4 Meaningful Human Control.

6. See Bundesverband der deutschen Luft- und Raumfahrtindustrie e.V., "Positionspapier," 6.

necessary data in real time. Besides that, autoregulative functions and AI[7] are also expected to be part of this undertaking.[8]

As the codeveloper of the system Wolfgang Koch puts it,

> In the future, conflicts will be fought more automatically than ever before. Within the framework of the Future Combat Air System FCAS, unmanned, artificially intelligent and technically autonomous aircraft will accompany manned fighter jets of the latest generation as loyal *wing men*. In the event of an attack, they will protect the pilot and divert attention from them. In combat missions, they fly far ahead as remote carriers, reconnoitering in a coordinated manner and engaging enemy targets. Other air defense components are also networked by FCAS as systems-of-systems: the Eurofighter, military transports, guided missiles or AWACS [airborne early warning and control systems, i.e., flying radar systems]. Thus, it is clear that artificial intelligence and technological autonomy must play a key role in FCAS.[9]

While the exact configurations and devices are still awaited, it is worth noting that the developers of the system emphasize the crucial role of humans while simultaneously maintaining that the system will consist of "comprehensive automation."[10] They also wish to implement moral and legal guidelines directly into the system, holding that responsibility is more fundamental than the differentiation between human-in-the-loop and human-on-the-loop, whereas it might be reasonable to resort to automated decision-making on the grounds of human-based rules in scenarios where humans cannot react appropriately.[11]

Before I turn to the input this book provides, some clarifying remarks are needed. This is because the question of whether this technology indeed exists depends to a high degree on the definition. The approach I take follows the definition brought forward by the US Department of Defense (DOD), characterizing such systems as weapons that

---

7. I refer to technologies that use so-called artificial intelligence with the abbreviation *AI*. For further information on the term and the methodologies used, see 3.2, How machines do (not) operate: On AI and machine "learning."

8. See Bundesverband der deutschen Luft- und Raumfahrtindustrie e.V., "Positionspapier," 11.

9. Koch, "FCAS—Herausforderungen für Sensordatenfunktion und Ressourcenmangement," 8–11. My translation, my emphasis.

10. Keisinger and Koch, "Defence and Responsibility."

11. See Keisinger and Koch, "Defence and Responsibility," 2.

Introduction

select and engage targets without human supervision in real time.[12] In addition, there are definitions that emphasize the use of AI in weapons systems. From that perspective, such a system would be a weapon that can interact with its environment, learn by itself, and asses the fulfillment of its tasks on its own.[13] While the former systems do exist, the latter do not. This is also because in the latter case, the definition of so-called *machine autonomy* depends on what exactly is to be understood as AI, as I will demonstrate. Ethically important, however, is the critical function of target selection and engagement, which is the scope of the DOD's definition—though this does not mean that AI does not play an important role in the technological architecture of the device. On the contrary, AI and the algorithmic infrastructure are crucial because autoregulation, even if embodied in a lethal device, is still software.[14] Yet, it is not the major focus the ethical emphasis is put on: The ethical issue at stake is rather whether it is justified to apply potentially lethal force with the help of technology that is no longer directly controlled, nor supervised by any human in real time. This also rules out any functions that do not serve a lethal purpose, such as takeoff and landing of an aircraft or autoregulative driving. In prioritizing the lethal function, peace ethical questions come to the fore so that the technological issues are put into perspective. It is exactly this angle that my work attempts to address.

Definition problems also concern the term "AI" because there are not only different technological procedures this term can designate but also different ideas connected to it, mainly depending on how strongly humans are seen to be the role model "intelligence" is built after. This is an inherent challenge within the discussion because AI easily becomes a catch-all term instead of being used as a concrete description for a specific technological procedure. Moreover, the term "AI" is fundamentally oriented toward the human role model when referring to intelligence. Yet, the technological procedures are by no means comparable to human

12. This definition is in line with the definition used by the US Department of Defense and the International Committee of the Red Cross. See US DOD, "Directive 3000.09," 13; Davidson, "Legal Perspective," 5–6.

13. See Altmann, "Zur ethischen Beurteilung automatisierter und autonomer Waffensysteme," 796; US DOD, "Unmanned Systems Integrated Roadmap," 17.

14. Although it is not the topic of my contribution, this is important to note because it yields major challenges for arms control regimes. This is because, in contrast to previous forms of arms control, software is hard to quantify, on the one hand, and can easily be up- and downloaded from a specific device, thereby making it hard to trace its deployment, on the other hand.

intelligence, as I will demonstrate below. For that matter, there are attempts to replace this term, but none of them seems persuasive.[15] Similar discussions pertain to the closely connected technological procedure of so-called *machine learning*. Again, humans are the role model in the machine's learning abilities, while the technological processes differ categorically from a human being's ability to learn.[16] Since I cannot find any better terms, however, I will use the abbreviation "AI" for algorithmic procedures that apply bottom-up approaches and "machine learning" for such algorithms that

> allow a program to 'learn' based on data collected from previous experiences. Programmers do not need to write the code that dictates what actions or predictions the program will make based on a situation, but instead, the system takes appropriate action based on patterns and similarities it recognizes from previous experiences.[17]

The same holds true for the term "autonomy" in machines. I will explain in the course of this book in great detail why I deem this term problematic, especially when applying it to machines used in ethically sensitive contexts.[18] At this point, it suffices to say that the technological procedures differ categorically from humans' capabilities. I will therefore refer to autoregulation instead of autonomy, replacing the anthropomorphic description with a more technological one and simultaneously hinting at the fact that autoregulative systems depend on autonomous entities, which are humans.

---

15. AlgorithmWatch, for instance, proposes the use of the term "automated decision-making instead." See AlgorithmWatch, "Automating Society." This term, however, is not only extremely vague but also still refers to the human role model when using the term "decision-making." This is because a machine does not make a decision but only reckons certain parameters and probabilities. See 3.3 Reckoning and Judgment.

16. See Steil, "Roboterlernen ohne Grenzen?"

17. Dignum, *Responsible Artificial Intelligence*, 3. Although I refer to this definition, I must add that it still uses anthropomorphized language when referring to previous "experiences" a machine cannot have and that might be described more accurately as "sensor-mediated data input."

18. See 2 Autonomy and Moral Agency in Humans; 3 Autonomy and Moral Agency in Machines.

Introduction

1.2 THE INPUT THIS STUDY PROVIDES

With these examples in mind, this book aims to evaluate whether the technology of autoregulation can be approved of from a peace ethical and Christian perspective. The stance I adopt, which is called just peace, is rooted in Christian thought and inspired by the biblical promise of peace, which deems violence and war inherently problematic and precarious. However, since violence is part of human life and history, questions regarding the use of force need to be addressed. Yet, at least from a theological perspective, violence cannot stand for itself but is perceived as a precarious phenomenon that one aspires to overcome.[19] This means that both justice and peace are closely intertwined with each other. That said, just peace theory not only rejects the notion of just war—in the sense that war could ever be an appropriate means to achieve a (political or legal) goal—but also emphasizes that whenever justice decreases, peace is endangered as well. This view is mirrored in the alteration of a Latin adage, *si vis pacem, para pacem* (if you want peace, prepare for peace), instead of *si vis pacem, para bellum* (if you want peace, prepare for war).[20] However, the use of force is not ruled out categorically, but expounded within the framework of a law-sustaining force (*rechtswahrende Gewalt*),[21] giving criteria for the assessment of violence and violent means, such as autoregulative functions in weapons systems.

With respect to the latter, the scholarly debate mainly focuses on technological, legal, and political aspects.[22] Even though there are some explicitly ethical approaches in philosophical thought, they are either

---

19. See Meireis, "Liebe und Gewalt," 36–37.
20. See EKD, "Live from God's Peace," 75.
21. See EKD, "Live from God's Peace," 98–103. There has been the proposal to substitute the term "law-abiding force" (*rechtserhaltende Gewalt*) used in the peace memorandum with "law-sustaining force" (*rechtswahrende Gewalt*), a term that is more open because it refers to international law, emphasizing the idea of human rights more appropriately in contrast to positive, established law. See Reuter, "Kampfdrohnen als Mittel rechtswahrender militärischer Gewalt?" 41; Meireis, "Der gerechte Frieden und die Ambivalenz rechtswahrender Gewalt," 150. Therefore, I prioritize the term "law-sustaining force," even though it differs from the terminology used in the peace memorandum.
22. This can be seen in several contributions that claim to elaborate the ethics of autoregulation in weapons systems but spend only little space and effort on this in comparison with other topics. See, for example, Dahlmann and Dickow, "Preventive Regulation of Autonomous Weapon Systems"; Federal Foreign Office, "Lethal Autonomous Weapons Systems."

confined to just war thinking[23] or discuss single arguments of the debate, such as human dignity or responsibility,[24] detached from an overall (peace) ethical perspective, such as contingent pacifism.[25] Moreover, there are no scholarly ethical assessments of autoregulative functions in weapons technology from a Christian point of view.

This book turns to exactly this gap. This entails mainly that the focus of the question of whether autoregulative functions in weapons systems can be approved of or not from a legal or ethical point of view changes to the question of whether and to what degree such weapons can contribute toward just and sustaining peace. This is because the conventional question of whether these weapons can make warfare safer or contribute to a stronger adherence toward international humanitarian law (IHL) principles, such as discrimination and proportionality, fades from the spotlight, while the issue of how to establish and maintain peace after the use of such weapons comes to the fore. In other words, in order to gain an overall viewpoint, and therefore a fully-fledged peace ethical framing, an approach is needed that takes account of whether such weapons might help or hinder the establishment of peace for reasons of commencing, conducting, and ending wars. My account attempts to do so by addressing matters of risk, thereby asking whether autoregulative functions in weapons systems increase or decrease the (moral) risk to participants in a violent scenario in a problematic way. It is mainly the

---

23. See Bustamante, "Robotisierung der Kriegsführung"; Misselhorn, *Grundfragen der Maschinenethik*. Leveringhaus points out that in an (absolute) pacifist view, a weapon could never be a legitimate means to achieve one's political goal, thereby taking into account other stances as well. He also concedes that this does not necessary mean that both theories—that is, just war and pacifism—are completely opposed to each other and that there are thinkers intersecting both ideas, referring to David Rodin, for instance. He also refers to contingent pacifist ideas in the course of his book. See Leveringhaus, *Ethics and Autonomous Weapons*, 21–22, 101. Nevertheless, his approach can hardly be seen to be a fully-fledged approach within (contingent) pacifism because of two remarks.

24. See Birnbacher, "Are Autonomous Weapons a Threat to Human Dignity?"; iPRAW, "Focus on Ethical Implications for a Regulation of LAWS"; Zawieska, "Ethical Perspective on Lethal Autonomous Weapons Systems."

25. The only exception thereof is the approach taken by Koch and Rinke, who refer to just war verbatim but for pragmatic reasons only, thereby making use of the gist of the theory to confine but not to justify violence—an objective that seems very close to contingent pacifism. See Koch and Rinke, *Ethische Fragestellungen im Kontext autonomer Waffensysteme*, 29. In their study, however, they hint at an outright research gap with respect to a *jus post bellum* perspective toward autoregulation in weapons technology. See Koch and Rinke, *Ethische Fragestellungen im Kontext autonomer Waffensysteme*, 155–56.

Introduction

question of how the nature of warfare is changed by new technological means which I will take into account here, so that participation in violent scenarios where such systems are deployed is morally problematic from the outset. I will do so while keeping in sight the crucial issue of whether this technology serves the intended purpose of achieving peace. When addressing issues of responsibility and guilt, a focus on just and sustaining peace seems much more straightforward, since I suggest that for matters of reconciliation in the aftermath of a violent undertaking, the issue of who is to blame for a certain lethal deed is decisive. This is because, if it should turn out that the assignment of responsibility is inherently problematic, this would make the case against deploying such systems in the first place.

Another point I want to make is that the framing of technology with the help of anthropomorphized terminology is troubling. This perception is not new to the debate but has been recognized several times, for instance, in the fields of technological autonomy,[26] AI,[27] and machine learning.[28] With respect to autonomy, authors are usually aware of the different meaning this term has in philosophical thought and that it is not coextensive to the technological process. They therefore hint at the difference somewhere in their accounts. In my opinion, however, the problem remains, as referring to autonomy with respect to machines still means that metaphoric language is used, and in doing so we "talk and, potentially, think about something in terms of something else."[29] In this case, it means that we talk and think about technology in terms of humans and apply human characteristics to machines. This, however, is a misperception of technology that reckons rather than judges, a distinction brought forward by the philosopher Brian Cantwell Smith with regard to AI.[30] For that matter, I want to propose talking about technology in terms of technology, thereby using the word "autoregulation" instead.

A third point I want to make brings humans and machines closer together and is decisive for the framing I want to propose here. Referring to

26. See, for example, Leveringhaus, *Ethics and Autonomous Weapons*, 32–33; Grünwald and Kehl, *Autonome Waffensysteme*, 36.

27. See, for example, Charbonnier, "Wahrnehmen, entschieden, handeln"; Fuchs, "Menschliche und künstliche Intelligenz"; Smith, *Promise of Artificial Intelligence*.

28. See, for example, Steil, "Roboterlernen ohne Grenzen?" All of these procedures are addressed in van Oorschot, "Einleitung."

29. Semino, *Metaphor in Discourse*, 1.

30. See Smith, *Promise of Artificial Intelligence*. I depict his approach in greater detail below. See 3.3 Reckoning and judgment.

An Ethical Evaluation of Lethal Functions in Autoregulative Weapons Systems

Bruno Latour's account of actor-network theory and Mark Coeckelbergh's transcendental approach toward technology,[31] I maintain that humans and technology are indissolubly linked to each other, co-shaping forms of life.[32] This, however, does not mean that the characteristics of humans and machines should get mixed up by using anthropomorphized language or design. It rather means that the way humans perceive technology and interact with machines deeply influences the way we perceive ourselves, as it is this technology that shapes the ways humans interact as well.

Thus, my objective with this piece of work is threefold. Primarily, it is my aim to assess autoregulation in weapons technology against a contingent pacifist backdrop, maintaining that, from an ethical perspective, autoregulation in violent contexts might pose severe problems. This does not mean that the technology can be ruled out definitively. There might be cases where deploying autoregulative functions in weapons systems is conceivable, while the majority of cases are surely not of such character. In making that argument, I (second) strongly criticize the anthropomorphic langue used when addressing technology because, in using anthropomorphic terms, humans and machines become mixed up, thereby threatening an appropriate collaboration of humans and machines. Third, however, this does not mean that humans and technology are not closely connected. On the contrary, both are entangled; collaborating, interacting, and co-shaping the worlds of life in which we live.

1.3 OVERVIEW OF THE ARGUMENT

In order to address the assessment of autoregulation in weapons systems, I begin by establishing the notion that humans and machines are connected intimately and that technology can be seen as transcendental rather than as a simple means (2.1). Within this frame, I will then elaborate on the philosophical and theological ideas connected to autonomy and moral agency (2). I will therefore draw on Martin Luther's idea of free will, which forms the foundation for Kant's approach toward autonomy, and finally present the thoughts of Harry Frankfurt, a contemporary philosopher elaborating on autonomy in humans (2.2). In a

31. See 2.1 Connecting Humans and Machines; Latour, *Pandora's Hope*; Coeckelbergh, *Using Words and Things*.

32. With this term, I refer to Coeckelbergh's interpretation of Wittgenstein, designating the social and cultural background to which language and technologies refer. See 2.1 Connecting Humans and Machines; Coeckelbergh, *Using Words and Things*, 32.

Introduction

second step, I will turn to the philosophical concept of moral agency in humans (2.3) and finally draw the conclusion that humans typically envision themselves to be autonomous and moral agents, thereby becoming intertwined with technology (2.4).

In my third chapter, I will then address the very same concepts, namely autonomy and moral agency, in machines, elaborating on the definition of technological autonomy (3.1) and describing which technological procedures are involved when talking about AI or machine learning (3.2). This serves the intent of showing that the procedures in humans are barely similar to the technological procedures, a point I will illustrate with the distinction between technological processes of reckoning and humans' ability to judge (3.3). Against this backdrop, I propose to talk about autoregulation instead of technological autonomy (3.4). I then turn to the question of whether and to what degree an artificial entity can be seen as a moral agent or a moral subject (3.5), or even a moral patient or addressee (3.6), arguing that both ideas pose severe ethical problems. Nevertheless, there are ideas to implement moral procedures into machines, and I will demonstrate several attempts to do so with reference to three proposals made in the discussion (3.7). From that, I conclude that ascribing autonomy and moral agency to machines constitutes a crucial mistake because anthropomorphic capabilities are assigned to the machine without noticing that the machine does not have the very same characteristics; it only simulates them. For that matter, the question of how to implement morals into machines can be rephrased into the issue of how we deal with and deploy technology in a way that endorses the overall performance of the human–machine system, so humans can contribute their moral agency to the system. To address this issue, I elaborate on the interaction of humans and machines in the fourth chapter.

The fourth chapter turns to the subject of human and machine interaction, thereby mainly harking back to the paradigm of *joint cognitive systems*, which perceives humans and machines to be cognitive systems with different features, each of them contributing their specific characteristics to the overall system. As for control, however, humans need to actively maintain control because the machine in itself lacks the ability to set itself goals and it therefore remains dependent on humans in that regard (4.1). For delving deeper into the technological nature of such systems, I will address several aspects that come into play when interacting with technology, which are first and foremost the crucial role of control, closely connect to trust (4.2.1); the so-called out-of-the-loop performance problem, which is the problem that a human collaborating with a heavily automated machine typically experiences a loss of skill as well as fatigue (4.2.2) in conjunction with *automation bias*, which is the phenomenon that humans tend to overtrust machines, even if they know better (4.2.3). In addition, there is an aspect that commonly accompany the use of AI, which is the problem that it is hard to tell how a certain algorithm reaches its outcomes, thereby enabling the occurrence of unintended side effects (4.2.4). Another aspect is algorithmic bias, referring to the fact that algorithms reproduce the societal biases underlying the data they are trained with, thereby favoring racism, for instance (4.2.5). One way to at least mitigate some of these aspects is adaptive or adaptable automation, which means that the level of automation can and should be adjusted toward the workload of the humans collaborating with the system. In situations of high pressure, the level of automation could then be increased in order to relieve humans or to put their focus on the most important tasks, while in situation without much pressure, the automation level could decrease (4.3). What becomes clear though, is that human control is crucial because only humans possess the knowledge to judge the world and to set an objective for the human–machine system. For that matter, I will take into account the idea of *meaningful human control*, a term that originated in the political discussion of autoregulation in weapons systems (4.4), concluding that the autoregulative system remains dependent on the autonomous agent, who in turn needs to yield control, otherwise the system as a whole lacks agency, autonomy, and control (4.5).

Having thus laid the philosophical and ethical groundwork in terms of technology, I turn to the discussions within peace ethics proper in chapter 5. My aim is to depict the peace ethical discussions leading to the development of a contingent pacifist approach, such as just peace. I therefore discuss these two strands within the ethics of war and peace that are next to contingent pacifism, which is absolute pacifism, on the one hand (5.1), and just war thinking, on the other hand (5.2). Within the middle ground between both approaches, contingent pacifist concepts evolve (5.3). For the matter of introducing the gist and logics of the respective theories, I will provide a historical sketch in the beginning of each section, highlighting the most important theories and developments that led to today's formation of the respective theory (5.1.1; 5.2.1; 5.3.1), while I conclude with the perspective of the respective theory toward autoregulative functions in weapons systems (5.1.3; 5.2.3; 5.3.4).

Introduction

I will commence my depiction with absolute pacifism and the study of peace because the concept of peace forms the very basis of peace ethics, therefore covering what peace means and entails at the beginning (5.2). I then turn to the different concepts within absolute pacifism, classified according to the question of whether an approach harks back to a religious institution, such as the Protestant Church of Baden (5.1.2.1), or to an individual author, such as Judith Butler's account (5.1.2.1). My attempt is to discuss theories from different angles, showing that the addressee of absolute pacifism is either a certain political collective or the individual, while there are no approaches bridging the gap between individual and collective. As for just war tradition, my recollection of *bellum iustum* serves the intent of showing that there is no single authoritative theory of just war but rather a bundle of approaches that developed over the course of time. Within the English-speaking world, just war saw a revival around the time of the Vietnam War, searching for ethical approaches toward war and peace. Michael Walzer's account gained particular momentum at this time and has highly influenced the following discussions (5.2.2.1). A newer phenomenon is the revisionist critique of just war, discussing mainly whether *jus ad bellum* and *jus in bello* can be seen to be separate categories, as Walzer maintains. Revisionist thinkers mainly call into question whether it is possible that a certain war can be for a just cause on both belligerent sides. Holding that this is not true, these thinkers maintain that only these combatants—and not noncombatants—are legitimate targets that indeed contributed to a certain war, be it with or without gunfire (5.2.2.2). Yet, these theories have been disputed by thinkers following Walzer (5.2.2.3). In a third step, I turn toward contingent pacifism, where I maintain that this theory aims to strike a balance between absolute pacifism and just war thinking, finding that there might be situations where use of force is the lesser evil, while this does not justify its use generally. Moreover, just peace thinking is not confined to warfare but assess the use of force in general, be it in the frame of police work, self-defense, or warfare. In the preliminaries to this section, I discuss historical and conceptual accounts that influenced the development of this account. I hereby maintain a specific focus on just peace thinking as proposed by the Protestant church in Germany in their peace memorandum in 2007, as it is the stance I argue from when assessing autoregulation in weapons technology (5.3.1). I then present Larry May's account of *contingent pacifism* because this philosophical approach focuses on *jus post bellum*, showing what exactly contingent pacifism means and why *jus post bellum* is an important and missing category in the current discourse (5.3.2). Subsequently, my aim is to depict the Christian account of just peace. Since Dietrich Bonhoeffer's theories form the foundation for current just peace thinking, I commence by elaborating on the peace ethical stance of this German Protestant theologian (5.3.3.1) and depict the Roman Catholic development in tandem (5.3.3.2) before elaborating in greater detail on the Roman Catholic stance toward just war (5.3.3.2.1) as well as the Protestant stance (5.3.3.2.2). Finally, I provide an excursus, illustrating how the issue of autoregulative functions in weapons systems is discussed within Jewish-halachic approaches to broaden the scope of my viewpoint with another religious and ethical perspective. In my conclusion I find that contingent pacifism is a concept worthy of consideration with regard to autoregulation in weapons technology (5.4). This is mainly because it changes the viewpoint from asking whether autoregulation in weapons technology is in line with existing legal frameworks toward the question of whether it hinders or helps in establishing just and sustaining peace, a question I turn to in chapter six.

In my sixth chapter, I zoom in on the specific discussion of autoregulation in weapons technology from a contingent pacifist point of view. I prepare the ground by showing what legal issues are at stake and what scholarly discussions are taking place within the field of legal studies (6.1), before recollecting the ethical discourse on this topic in greater detail (6.2). On those grounds, I turn to my own account, which is arguing from a contingent pacifist point of view, showing how—couched in terms of just war—*jus ad bellum, jus in bello,* and *just post bellum* are closely intertwined (6.3). I then discuss the argument of risk (6.4), finding that risk is a multifarious concept that is hard to apply to one argumentation only. While technological risk pertains to the issue of how an autoregulative device can operate safely with means of reckoning only (6.4.1), moral risk refers to the uncertainty that a morally unjust person will be harmed in a violent undertaking, especially when considering the ideas of revisionist just war thinking (6.4.3). The main theoretical problem here is that a paradoxical situation is created where the risk of the people deploying the device practically vanishes, while the addressee bears the cost. This is especially problematic if the right to use force is somehow connected to self-defense—a phenomenon a technological device does not need (6.4.2). Most important, then, is how risks are perceived and interpreted because the (technological) numbers do not simply speak on their own

Introduction

but are always embedded into an interpretative framework (6.4.4). For my second argument, I turn to the crucial issue of responsibility (6.5), commencing with an introduction to the concept and an idea connected thereto, and especially the fundamental role of agency (6.5.1). I find that it is questionable to disconnect agency and responsibility, as critical posthumanist thinkers maintain, while I nevertheless approve of the interconnectedness of humans and nonhumans in that regard (6.5.2). The most important ethical question with respect to autoregulation, however, is whether it entails the occurrence of responsibility gaps. For that matter, I argue that a diffusion of responsibility is very likely to happen but might be solved through legal means. The major problem is rather an outright gap in moral responsibility, which might occur if control is no longer maintained by humans. Therefore, control is the most decisive issue in terms of responsibility (6.5.3). Subsequently, I address the idea of forward-looking responsibility, which entails that the human part(s) of the human–machine collaboration need to be aware of the system's characteristics and flaws and therefore are the first addressee of responsibility (6.5.4). Finally, I conclude that responsibility and risk need to strike a balance (6.5.5). From a more theological perspective, I again turn to the ethics of Bonhoeffer and his account of responsibility (6.6), which is closely connected to the willingness to become guilty (6.6.1). Harking back to Berman's Jewish-halachic account, I make the argument that autoregulation in weapons technology can be seen as a means to eschew responsibility, but that this comes at the cost of incurring even more guilt (6.6.2). Put differently, such technological means can also be seen as a way of achieving *cheap grace* because it is an attempt avoid the guilt and responsibility that comes with targeting people lethally (6.5.5).

In my conclusion, I propose that the deployment of autoregulative functions can be assessed according to two vectors, which are clarity on the one hand and controllability on the other hand. As for clarity, I advocate that an autoregulative function within a violent scenario can be deployed only in very clear scenarios where the technological device can safely reckon its way through. In or on the deep sea might be such a scenario, while an urban fighting scenario is clearly off-limits given the technological development. With respect to controllability, I argue that humans can decide to resort to autoregulative functions only in cases where the human part of the collaboration is indeed under the control of humans. Adaptive or adaptable automation might help humans to remain in control of the most important features in such cases, even though it might not solve the general problem. In addition, it is not only the operator that needs to be addressed. If the device fails, the companies and people who trained the device need to be addressed, while flaws in design will come back to the engineers and designers. If a certain violent undertaking is not justified in the beginning, the political entity that started the war will also have to bear the blame for using a certain form of technology. In any case, it is decisive that there is a human entity, be it individual or political, shouldering responsibility for the harm done when force is used autoregulatively.

2

Autonomy and Moral Agency in Humans

AUTONOMY AND AGENCY ARE key terms in anthropology, describing the human ability to act on behalf of their intentions[1] and to govern those actions freely, especially in issues of moral concern.[2] Both conceptions, however, have been applied to technology, thereby merging anthropological ideas with technological patterns. Before turning to the concrete issue of autoregulative functions in weapons systems, it is therefore my objective to scrutinize whether this transfer holds true. To do so, I will first depict how closely humans are connected to their technology, making use of Latour's actor-network theory as well as Coeckelbergh's transcendental account[3] (2.1), before I analyze the concept of autonomy (2.2) and then turn to moral agency (2.3). This serves to introduce the anthropological concepts transferred to technology in order to grasp the philosophical meaning standing behind these terms.

One disclaimer needs to be made at the outset, though, which is that I cannot cover a holistic approach toward agency and autonomy but rather outline some very general and broad conceptions within philosophical and to some degree also theological thought. This is because the main interest of this study is the transfer of these concepts from humans to machines and not the concepts in themselves. To provide such a broad perspective would go beyond the scope of this book; the focus of

1. See Schlosser, "Agency."
2. See Christman, "Autonomy in Moral and Political Philosophy."
3. See Latour, *Pandora's Hope*; Coeckelbergh, *Using Words and Things*.

my depiction is rather on ideas attempting to implement autonomy and morality into machines and on the implications such an idea brings in its wake, especially with regard to violent applications.

2.1 CONNECTING HUMANS AND MACHINES: TRANSCENDENTAL TECHNOLOGIES

In his approach, called *actor-network theory*, Latour depicts that humans and nonhumans—among them technological artifacts—are closely connected. For that matter, he refers to humans as agents and to nonhuman as *actants*.[4] In his view, humans do not only use their tools in order to establish a goal but they themselves are transformed by interacting with these nonhumans. He illustrates his point by referring to a person holding a gun. In holding the gun, the person themselves changes. The gun, however, changes as well, leading to both gun and person being fundamentally different together. If cooperating, they constitute a very new actor with new goals. Moreover, Latour states that in dealing with an artifact, humans who are in touch with the artifact do not simply make use of this very specific object but, in doing so, are connected to the humans who built it, invented it, and planned it as well. This process can be seen as the "folding of time and space,"[5] as humans who can be separated from each other over long distances and times become connected via an artifact.[6] Using the gun metaphor again, this means that there are people who built the gun—not only this gun in particular but also the inventors of the concept of a gun. These people made up this tool for a certain reason, and that is also why they gave it special mechanics and a certain design. That means that in the moment a human carries a gun, they are simultaneously connected with the mechanisms and ideas standing behind that artifact. In that way, it is plausible to say that the nonhuman that humans are dealing with embodies a certain aspiration. In this sense,

---

4. This thought is part of a larger picture where Latour explicates that the sharp distinction between subject and object, epistemology and ontology, or human and plain artifact is artificial and unnecessary. He therefore proposes a new terminology for a number of the common sociologist's nomenclatures. Since I rely on this argument only, it is not my aim to cover actor–network theory in general, so I do not want to go into great detail here. For the sake of readability, I will not resort to the language actor–network theory uses. For further reading, see Latour, *Pandora's Hope*; Latour, *Reassembling the Social*.

5. Latour, *Pandora's Hope*, 183.

6. See Latour, *Pandora's Hope*, 176–93.

the gun "wants" to shoot, the knife "wants" to cut, and the car "wants" to drive. To be clear, this does not mean that the artifacts, or nonhumans, have a will of their own but that they are interconnected with the human world in a much broader way and to a deeper level than is usually assumed. To put it differently: By making use of an artifact, connections are established and, at least in the moment of use, both distinct entities become one for the sake of the action. From this, it can be inferred that the design, interface, and function of an artifact all have to be manufactured in a very exacting way at all stages of development because they influence the people collaborating with this technology. Consequently, the advent of new technologies changes the humans working with them on a small scale, while it also changes society on a large scale.[7]

It is mainly this point of Latour's work that Coeckelbergh builds on in his book *Using Words and Things* (2017), where he develops a transcendental account of technology that links language, technology, and humans. To make this argument, Coeckelbergh harks back to Wittgenstein's theory of language games. According to Wittgenstein, language is always embedded into a certain sociocultural background, into specific forms of life. By using a language, humans simultaneously refer to the background, meaning the forms of life the language is part of. Wittgenstein calls this phenomenon of mutual dependency "language games."[8] According to Coeckelbergh, these interdependencies are not only to be found within language but also within technology, since technology is always embedded into a certain sociocultural context.[9] As Coeckelbergh puts it, "Technologies are embedded in forms of life and cultures, and their use is shaped and constrained by those cultures."[10] From that perspective, humans are not only involved in language games but also in "technology games."[11]

Coeckelbergh then proceeds to demonstrate that language and technology both are transcendental in the sense of conditional for our agency, forming the foundation for our shared worlds of life because "it shapes our prior understanding of things."[12] For that matter, humans

---

7. See Latour, *Pandora's Hope*, 193–98.
8. See Coeckelbergh, *Using Words and Things*, 27–28.
9. See Coeckelbergh, *Using Words and Things*, 30–31.
10. Coeckelbergh, *Using Words and Things*, 35.
11. Coeckelbergh, *Using Words and Things*, 29.
12. Coeckelbergh, *Using Words and Things*, 25. Coeckelbergh uses the term "transcendental" himself and explains in this quote what he refers to with this term. Later

cannot do without language in the same way they cannot do without technology. Both transcendentals, however, shape our forms of life, and we influence them on our part by shaping narratives and technology. That way, humans, technology, and language are indissolubly linked to each other. As Coeckelbergh puts it:

> Using the metaphor of speech, we can formulate a more integrative view as an answer to the question: Who or what speaks? When we speak through technologies, language and technology also speak; when we use words, language and technology also speak; when technologies and language speak, humans speak.[13]

If Coeckelbergh is right, the given sociocultural background in language and technology presets humans' ability to act freely, thereby not only influencing how humans are able to act but simultaneously predisposing the ways humans are able to think. This entails that technology might also be used to nudge people toward certain behavior, which might then turn out to be a challenge to human freedom, as Coeckelbergh describes in his book *Green Leviathan or the Poetics of Political Liberty* (2021).[14]

Therefore, it is decisive to underline that the idea of a separate technological device and a separate human being, working apart from each other while humans use the technological tool in an instrumental way, might be misguided. This is, nevertheless, the standard approach taken within the political and ethical discourse.[15] As I have shown here, humans and technology might rather interact in the form of technology games, thereby co-shaping forms of life. This has implications for the attitude toward technology: If technology is perceived to be a mere tool, it only carries weight if humans use it. Moreover, it is then part of the *adiaphora*, meaning it is neutral from an ethical point of view. If this was true, the use of a certain tool would be decisive. For instance, a knife can be used for both cutting bread and killing a human being. The way in which the knife is used depends solely on the human being. This rather simple bill

---

in his book, he shows that such an account amounts to "postphenomenology," in combining phenomenology and transcendental ideas, thereby combining material and empirical notions of phenomenology with the idea that language and ideas constitute our worlds of life. Accordingly, Coeckelbergh writes, "Our speaking about *technology* is made possible by conditions that are linguistic *and* material in nature. Both language and technology frame our way of speaking about technology." Coeckelbergh, *Using Words and Things*, 125. Emphasis original.

13. Coeckelbergh, *Using Words and Things*, 273.
14. See Coeckelbergh, *Green Leviathan*.
15. See Schwarz, "Autonomous Weapons Systems," 55.

might, however, not entirely grasp the situation. Knives can be designed differently—enabling the cutting of bread, on the one hand, but ensuring the safety of people, on the other hand. Put differently: The knives used for cutting are usually not intended for harming people and are designed along this rationale. Alex Leveringhaus calls attention to a similar point when he elaborates on the importance of design. Even though nearly everything can be used as a weapon, "weapons are distinctive, because they have been specially designed in order to harm others."[16] This also means that the use of a weapon does not fit the definition of *adiaphora*, because something designed in order to harm is not neutral from an ethical point of view. Weapons might be used for preventing even more harm, and just peace theory, for instance, leaves room for deploying weapons in that way when establishing the theory of law-sustaining force. Yet, even this use of weaponry is inherently deficient because harming others cannot be separated from incurring guilt.[17]

I want to push things even further: It is not only that technology might not be neutral from an ethical point of view, but that we relate to technology more closely than we realize. This entails that technology does not only have an influence on us, but that it rather shapes the way the world looks, and that in doing so it affects the way we do things. Coming back to the example used by Latour, a human holding a gun is not only a human plus a gun, but a human-gun-assemblage. The gun opens up new possibilities that have not been there before and gives rise to ideas that have not been there before either. This is even more extreme if the gun is replaced by a machine gun or a nuclear weapon because, in such cases, the design of the specific weapon can cause nothing but harm and even more harm. Consequently, resorting to weapons technology is a measure that is always and inherently problematic in nature. This entails, first, that we must ethically discuss autoregulative weapons technology apart from civic deployments of autoregulation because in combining a certain technology with the intention to do harm, the whole framework changes. This does not mean that the difficulty of dual use—meaning that a certain technology such as autoregulation might be developed and deployed in civic society and is then transferred into the military field—ceases to persist. But it does mean that civic means of autoregulation need to be assessed on different terms. As for weapons technology, this

---

16. Leveringhaus, *Ethics and Autonomous Weapons*, 39.

17. See EKD, "Live from God's Peace," 103; 6.6.1 The Acceptance of Guilt in Responsible Action; 5.3.3.1 On Bonhoeffer's Account of War and Peace.

entails that the ethical framework is the ethics of war and peace or, taking a broader approach, ethical questions pertaining to the use of force in general. Therefore, the main question must, second, concern how to contain violence and how to minimize the use of this specific technology. Given that weapons technology is only one piece of the technology and language games we are part of, other and less troubling means of our sociocultural forms of life, such as diplomacy, come to the fore. Finally, even though the ethical discussion of autoregulative weapons systems must be addressed apart from civic means, the impact of this certain technology on the whole technology game we play must not be sidelined. This means that using a certain technology in the military sector usually affects other forms of life as well. And in this matter, weapons technology in particular is neither neutral, nor do I expect its deployment in the military sector to have no repercussions on the civic sphere.[18]

What becomes clear in my approach is that human social and cultural forms of life cannot be imagined without technology. Technology deeply influences the ways humans interact and relate to one another and is therefore by no means neutral. Given the interdependence of humans and nonhumans, the question of how humans and machines are distinct arises, especially if classical anthropological ideas such as agency and autonomy are applied to machines. Is the agency ascribed to machines in any way similar to the agency humans hold? In what way does technological autonomy resemble the autonomy of humans? In order to address these questions, I will briefly outline what the philosophical concepts of autonomy and agency typically entail and how algorithmic processes, especially so-called AI, differ from anthropological concepts.

2.2 TERMS OF AUTONOMY: AUTONOMY IN PHILOSOPHY AND THEOLOGY

Autonomy is a philosophical term defined in *The Stanford Encyclopedia of Philosophy* (hereafter *SEP*) as follows:

> Individual autonomy is an idea that is generally understood to refer to the capacity to be one's own person, to live one's life

---

18. That this development is already on the way can be seen in a decision made in San Francisco that paved the way for deploying lethal functions in autoregulative weapons systems within the police. See Beuth, "Polizei von San Francisco darf künftig Roboter zum Töten einsetzen."

according to reasons and motives that are taken as one's own and not the product of manipulative or distorting external forces.[19]

Following this definition, the concept of autonomy is closely linked to other central philosophical concepts such as volition, freedom, agency, responsibility, and morality. All of these terms have one thing in common: They have only been applied to humans so far.[20] Consequently, when speaking of an autonomous machine, autonomy can only be understood in a figurative sense. This poses an elemental problem. When transferring a fundamental philosophical concept to another area—for instance, from humans to machines—we transfer not only a single idea but a whole universe of connected theories. When speaking about autonomy in machines, we therefore think about them as moral agents acting in accordance with reason and based on the notion of an inherent free will. That this instance is not merely a case of philosophical pedantry can be illustrated with reference to machine learning or artificial intelligence. In general, people often either over- or underestimate the capabilities of machines and ascribe human features to them,[21] such as intelligence, the ability to learn, or autonomy. Without doubt, technology has evolved rapidly in the course of recent decades. However, technological conceptions of "intelligence," "learning," and "autonomy" differ rapidly from that of humans. This is also the reason why I will refer to technological autonomy as autoregulation, thereby pointing to the technological quality of the procedure.[22]

It is the aim of this chapter to provide the philosophical background for the understanding of autonomy and agency in classical philosophical thought in order to distinguish those anthropological phenomena from the functioning of machines. To do so within the limits of this study, I will concentrate on paradigmatic concepts and authors, such as the concept of autonomy brought forward in the ethics of Kant.[23] Kant's ideas, in

19. Christman, "Autonomy in Moral and Political Philosophy."

20. The question of the extent to which animals share similar states of consciousness may arise but goes beyond the scope of this book. However, it is beyond doubt that animals also have basic emotions and—at least to some extent—a "conscious mental life." Yet, that does not mean that they share the same capability to oversee their actions as humans do. See Allen and Trestman, "Animal Consciousness."

21. See Steil, "Roboterlernen ohne Grenzen?" 32.

22. I explain the terminology in greater detail below. See 3.4 Machines: Autoregulative, Not Autonomous.

23. See Christman, "Autonomy in Moral and Political Philosophy."

turn, are based on concepts drawn from Christian theology, mainly Martin Luther's *On the Freedom of a Christian* (1520). In order to illustrate the way Kant transforms the theological concept of Christian freedom into philosophical thought,[24] I will commence my discussion with a sketch of Martin Luther's concept of Christian freedom, continue by introducing Kant's understanding of autonomy, and then show how Harry Frankfurt, as one contemporary philosopher, makes use of this concept.

2.2.1 Martin Luther's Idea of Christian Freedom

Martin Luther opens his treatise *On the Freedom of a Christian* with a twofold assumption, reading,

> A Christian is a free lord of all things and is subject to none.
> A Christian is a dutiful servant in all things and is subject to everyone.[25]

I will try to unravel Luther's paradoxical-sounding idea. First, Luther distinguishes between the inner, new, and spiritual *(innerer, neuer, geistlicher)* nature of the person on the one hand and the corporal, older, and outer *(leiblicher, alter, äußerer)* nature on the other.[26] With respect to the inner, spiritual person, Luther deems it free from all outer influences. This is because a Christian believer's main purpose is to believe in God and, within this belief, to trust in salvation by faith. By that, Luther states that by faith alone *(sola fide)*, not by deeds, the believer will be justified in front of God. Therefore, believers are free to do whatever pleases them because no good works will help them to obtain salvation.[27] However, with regard to the outer nature of the person, followers of Christ are motivated by two types of reason. First, there is thankfulness for God's grace. Second, there are two obligations to do good works: One the one hand, Christians have to bring the body under the subjection of the Holy Spirit, on the other hand, Christians are called to establish good relationships with other human beings. If a person does good works for the sake of others or in order to subject their own body

---

24. See Caygill, "Autonomy," 88.
25. Luther, *On the Freedom of a Christian*, 18.
26. See Luther, "Die Freiheit des Christenmenschen," 283.
27. See Luther, "Die Freiheit des Christenmenschen," 287.

to God's will, they do these deeds freely, to please God (*aus freier Liebe umsonst, um Gott zu gefallen*).[28]

Accordingly, freedom in Luther's definition is not just negative freedom, meaning freedom from external restraints, but it implies in addition an inclination to act freely in order to obey God's law. It is this specific definition that Kant refers to and transforms into a philosophical concept.[29]

2.2.2 Kant or Autonomy as Rational Agency

Kant develops his concept of autonomy throughout a number of writings, mainly his *Groundwork of the Metaphysics of Morals* (*Grundlegung zur Metaphysik der Sitten*, hereafter *GMM*, 1785). Other works of Kant deal with this issue, too, for instance, the *Critique of Practical Reason* (*Kritik der praktischen Vernunft*, 1788) or *The Metaphysics of Morals* (*Metaphysik der Sitten*, 1791).[30]

In Kant's view, autonomy is a crucial term in practical philosophy and moral thought. His objective in the *GMM* is to establish pure (i.e., *a priori*) moral thought without any regard to empirical arguments,[31] thereby creating a formal, universal law or maxim: the categorical imperative (CI).[32] Since there is an indissoluble relationship between autonomy and moral will—because for Kant, autonomy is the condition for morality—one can deduce that an agent who acts autonomously is a moral agent.[33] This necessitates that the agent requires the reasonable capability to act morally in an autonomous way, and accordingly, reason

28. See Luther, "Die Freiheit des Christenmenschen," 301.

29. See Caygill, "Autonomy," 88.

30. See Johnson and Cureton, "Kant's Moral Philosophy." Since the Kant's approaches in his various works differ slightly, I will hold to the *Groundwork* as often as possible and only take other works into consideration if necessary. For a more detailed description of the term "autonomy" in the different works of Kant, see Düsing, "Ethische Freiheit, Autonomie und Selbstbewusstsein bei Kant mit einem Ausblick auf Fichte."

31. See Kant, *AA*, 4:387–88. When quoting Kant, I refer to the pages of the *German Akademieausgabe* (*AA*). The English edition I use is provided by Cambridge University Press and refers to the *German Akademieausgabe* as well, which is why I only quote the *AA* for the sake of simplicity.

32. The categorical imperative is delivered in different varieties, the most common among them can be found in the *GMM* and is stated as follows: "*Act in accordance with a maxim that can at the same time make itself a universal.*" Kant, *AA*, 4:437. Emphasis original.

33. See Taylor, "Kant's Theory of Freedom," 325.

and autonomy are mutually entangled with each another.[34] This provides the background for the following definitions:

> Autonomy of the will is the property of the will by which it is a law to itself (independently of any property of the objects of volition).[35]

Later in the same text, Kant defines free will as autonomy:

> What, then, can freedom of the will be other than autonomy, that is, the will's property of being a law to itself?[36]

In these passages, Kant holds that through autonomy, an agent provides their very own laws to themselves. This is in agreement with the literal sense of the Greek words αὐτός and νόμος, meaning "self"[37] and "law, legal norm,"[38] combined with αὐτόνομος, meaning "governed by one's own laws, independent."[39] In doing so, Kant's concept exceeds negative freedom, because the laws agents give to themselves extend the aforementioned basic notion thereof. In Kant's view, moral agents who act autonomously are acting for reasons they give to themselves. This is what Kant calls positive freedom, in addition to negative freedom.[40] These self-given laws are essential and have to be followed. Due to the universal law (i.e. the categorical imperative), which takes the shape of duties (Greek: δέον), the ethics resulting from this concept are called *deontological*. Since human agents are imperfect agents and are therefore drawn by desires and inclination, they sometimes fall short of their self-given laws. Once that happens, the agent acts arbitrarily and loses—strictly speaking—their autonomy, for they do not obey their own reasonable given law but are governed by their desires, thus acting under the rule of heteronomy.[41] Finally, Kant lends substance to the decision-making itself,

---

34. See Kant, *AA*, 4:452–453.
35. Kant, *AA*, 4:440.
36. Kant, *AA*, 4:446.
37. See Montanari et al., *Brill Dictionary of Ancient Greek*, αὐτός, 346.
38. See Montanari et al., *Brill Dictionary of Ancient Greek*, νόμος B, 1404.
39. See Montanari et al., *Brill Dictionary of Ancient Greek*, αὐτόνομος, 345.
40. See Kant, *AA*, 4:446. The relation between freedom and autonomy is discussed intensely at the moment. It suffices to say here that Kant deems them strongly bound together. "Freedom and the will's own lawgiving are both autonomy and hence reciprocal concepts." Kant, *AA*, 4:450. For more insight into this debate, see Ameriks, "Kant on Freedom and Autonomy."
41. See Johnson and Cureton, "Kant's Moral Philosophy." There is an ongoing

thereby refuting theories that underline the outcome of an act (namely utilitarianism or consequentialist thinking).[42] This is important to note because the act of decision-making is the main moral action the agent puts into practice. In doing so, the agent needs to listen to their inner voice, namely their conscience.[43]

Following the definition of the term "autonomous" in a Kantian philosophical, deontological tradition, it is possible to determine who counts as an autonomous agent. So far, it is already clear that such an agent needs to have free will and that they must have the reasonable as well as the moral capability to act autonomously. Kant defines such an agent as a person in contrast to a thing (*Sache*). In *The Metaphysics of Morals*, he writes,

> A *person* is a subject whose actions can be *imputed* to him. *Moral* responsibility is therefore nothing other than the freedom of a rational being under moral laws (whereas psychological personality is merely the ability to be conscious of one's identity in different conditions of one's existence). From this it follows that a person is subject to no other laws than those he gives to himself (either alone or at least along with others).
> A *thing* is that to which nothing can be imputed. Any object of free choice which itself lacks freedom is therefore called a thing (*res corporalis*).[44]

Although Kant does not use the term "autonomy" directly, the definition is in accordance with the picture illustrated above because in defining the term "person," Kant uses the same ideas and concepts as when speaking about autonomy. This will become clearer in the following: Kant differentiates a person from a thing by several characteristics. With respect to the very nature of them, he states that a person is a subject and therefore acts as an agent, for it is the cause of (its own) actions. A thing, by contrast, is an object that has no agency whatsoever. Another characteristic, and for my inquiry the most essential one, is the notion of freedom. A person has freedom of will or autonomy, while a thing is under the rule of arbitrariness.[45] That way, freedom equates with autonomy

---

debate about the extent to which an agent still acts freely and responsibly, especially if they fall short of their duties, but this question is beyond the scope of this book.

42. That is why this position is also called nonconsequentialist thought.
43. See Taylor, "Kant's Theory of Freedom," 321; Taylor, *Sources of the Self*, 363–67.
44. Kant, *AA*, 6:223. Emphasis original.
45. Although freedom of the will and autonomy can be examined separately, at

because the definition that a person may follow no rule other than the one they give to themselves is the very same definition used in the quote above with regard to autonomy. From that, it follows that a person, which is a rational moral agent, can be held accountable for their actions while a thing cannot. To sum up, according to Kant, it is safe to say that everyone who gives themselves universal moral laws is a person. Therefore, they are accountable agents, endowed with an autonomous will. Most interestingly, Kantian moral agents, according to the aforementioned characteristics, are not simply coextensive with human species. Put differently: Not every human being is a rational agent and therefore considered to be an autonomous person. Accordingly, Kant can imagine rational autonomous agents that are not humans, such as extraterrestrial lifeforms.[46] That way, autonomy is not confined to humanity but rather to morality and rationality. This becomes clearer in another work by Kant, his *Anthropology from a Pragmatic Point of View* (*Anthropologie in pragmatischer Hinsicht*, 1798). Here, Kant differentiates between three different modes of being. At the bottom of the hierarchy, animals constitute a first level, followed by humanity—meaning all entities belonging to *homo sapiens,* including entities that are not (yet) able to think in the manner demanded. At the top, a human person is the highest form of being.[47] Consequently, Kant defines every person as a human, though not every human as a person.[48]

To summarize, according to Kant, an autonomous agent is a person who is typically human and acts for formal reasons they gave themselves

---

least for Kant, they basically correspond with each other. See Guyer, "Freedom, Will, Autonomy," 86.

46. See Kant, AA, 7:331; Seen in Gutmann, *Würde und Autonomie.*

47. See Kant, AA, 7:127; Caygill, "Person," 316.

48. There is an ongoing discussion of whether and to what extent every human being holds autonomy and therefore dignity. As Gutman argues, at least people who lack moral agency such as infants, people suffering from dementia, or people with severe mental disabilities would be ruled out. See Gutmann, *Würde und Autonomie,* 8. On the other hand, thinkers as Forst, Höffe, Honnefelder or Spaemann have pointed out that dignity is bestowed on every member of humanity because of their opportunity to act autonomously as well as morally. See Forst, *Das Recht auf Rechtfertigung,* 78–79; Honnefelder, "Die Frage nach dem moralischen Status des menschlichen Embryos," 82–88; Höffe: "Menschenwürde als ethisches Prinzip," 127–33; Spaemann, "Menschenwürde und menschliche Natur," 40. In a similar way but with respect to society and the participation in society, Nussbaum points out that every member of humankind does have "freedom and equality," but Kant allocates infants and people suffering from dementia or with disabilities a passive role in society. This means that even though they cannot support themselves sufficiently, they are cared for by others because of their status as human beings. See Nussbaum, *Frontiers of Justice,* 51–53.

by moral reasoning. Even though a formal duty may provide a general guideline, Kant provides no clearly defined pattern for repetition in a particular situation. Autonomy in this sense is based on a maxim that is universal to the extent that everyone needs to decide afresh in every new situation how to act.[49]

2.2.3 Harry Frankfurt and the Autonomy of Love

Not every philosopher agrees with Kant's concept of autonomy.[50] Harry Frankfurt's account poses a contemporary critique of Kant's ideas and might also be enlightening with respect to the issue of ethics and technology.[51] To do so, I am focusing here on Harry Frankfurt's *wishes of the second order* and his definition of autonomy: Frankfurt's concept of the freedom of the will is built on the notion that every person has the ability to form so-called wishes of the second order. By that, Frankfurt means the ability of an agent to (self-)reflect on their own wishes. A person does not carry out every wish they have, Frankfurt argues, because they are able to reflect on these wishes and subordinate them to more important wishes they have. This idea can be illustrated with the example of a drug addict who is not irredeemably lost to their addiction but can establish the wish to quit drugs. In this case, the second-order volition not to be addicted would determine the self of the person, regardless of whether the agent succeeds in quitting drugs eventually.[52]

In addition to Kant's understanding of autonomy as moral self-government, Frankfurt defines autonomy as in tandem with love, recurring to the parent's unconditional and selfless love toward their children. The love they have therefore holds an underlying authority regarding the loving person. A parent cannot help but love their child.[53] This entails acting in accordance with what is in the best interest of the beloved, even if this

---

49. See Wood, "How a Kantian Decides What to Do," 284.

50. Under the critics, philosophers such as Hegel, Kant, or Nietzsche argue that this concept is too formal and therefore negligible or even tyrannical. See Caygill, "Autonomy," 89.

51. See Leveringhaus, *Ethics and Autonomous Weapons*, 108–11.

52. See Frankfurt, "Freedom of the Will."

53. Frankfurt does not deem this assessment to be empirical or descriptive in nature. He rather talks about obligations and volition, so the idea of loving parents is a normative idea rather than a descriptive reality. See Frankfurt, "Autonomy, Necessity and Love," 129–30.

may not be in line with the self-interest of the loving person. Hence, the lover is constrained by the object of their love, meaning that they cannot do anything other than act for the sake of the beloved. The reason is that the loving person identifies with the love they hold. Every action at variance with the benefit of the beloved would amount to self-betrayal and thus destroy the unity of the self.[54] Frankfurt's approach toward autonomy consequently has two main features. First, it is in accordance with the main claim of deontological thought, defining autonomy as rational, *a priori*, and universal. Second, Frankfurt introduces an additional concept, which is based on love and in consequence contingent, personal, and to some extent irrational. Both conceptions have in common that they are unconditional. Violation of a self-given law or betrayal of a beloved would compromise the very self of the person. Frankfurt's understanding of autonomy rests on that notion.

With regard to the agent holding both the freedom of the will defined in terms of second-order volitions and autonomy as law and love, it is clear that Frankfurt has human agents in mind, as these concepts rest on the notion that there is a self—an identity underlying (moral) reasoning and agency.[55] For that matter, Frankfurt establishes a link between the very essence of a person—that is, what makes a person a person—and their substantive constraints, which he identifies as love. The distinctive marker between humans and nonhumans, in Frankfurt's view, rests on the notion that humans are able to reflect their own will, thereby laying the groundwork for autonomous love. In consequence, only humans have the ability to act freely and autonomously.

My very brief introduction to these main thinkers who have historically defined the term "autonomy" served the purpose of providing a grasp of what is meant when referring to autonomy in this day and age. As demonstrated above, deontological tradition puts the stress on the process of decision-making itself and is less interested in the outcome. Autonomy also provides the essence of what constitutes a person. Vice versa, this rules out some individuals who do not share these characteristics, without providing room for a middle ground: Either somebody

54. See Frankfurt, "Autonomy, Necessity and Love," 129.

55. According to the rationale of Steil, who criticizes the term "machine learning" because it indicates that the way machines acquire data is somewhat similar to what humans do in learning, it is exactly these second-order desires a machine is not capable of because it cannot have the kind of metaprocesses second-order desires would entail. See Steil, "Roboterlernen ohne Grenzen?" Even though Steil does not use Frankfurt's terminology, he describes the same idea.

is autonomous or not. Autonomy in the history of this debate, consequently, has been closely linked to identity and used to define a person in contrast to animals and things. Moreover, autonomy constitutes an inherently ethical term describing the moral capacities of agents. To put it simply: It is autonomy that enables an agent to be a person in the full sense of the word. For that reason, autonomy, agency, and personhood cannot be separated. An autonomous agent is by definition a person and—vice versa—a person is necessarily autonomous. Therefore, I now turn to the concept of (moral) agency.

2.3 HUMANS AS MORAL AGENTS

In the context of robot or machine ethics, the concept of agency typically refers to a gradual concept, which means that there are different forms of agency that can be described. However, the human being clearly serves as a prototype.[56] It is, however, important to understand what is classically referred to when conceptualizing agency.

Moral agency pertains to the ability of an agent to act morally or, more precisely, the ability of an agent to act according to their intention in matters of moral concern. Classically, agency—and especially agency in moral issues—has been applied to humans only, as only humans are seen to have these inner capabilities.[57] This is due to agency being indissolubly linked with conceptions such as "desires, beliefs, and intentions,"[58] as well as responsibility and autonomy: While autonomy forms the foundation for counting as a (moral) agent,[59] responsibility is classically assigned toward (moral) agents.[60]

As for a rather classical approach, Harry Frankfurt, for instance, argues that the possibility of having second-order desires is decisive for being an agent, a characteristic pertaining to humans only.[61] Charles Taylor adds to that thought but expands it even further. In doing so,

---

56. This is the case in Misselhorn's *Grundfragen der Maschinenethik*, as van Oorschot proves, as well as in Moor's concept, which will be discussed below. See van Oorschot, "Alles Technik oder was?"; 3.5 Artificial entities as moral agents.

57. See Schlosser, "Agency."

58. See Schlosser, "Agency."

59. See Loh, *Roboterethik*, 71.

60. See Loh, *Roboterethik*, 133; Taylor, "What Is Human Agency?" 28. I discuss this below. See 6.5.2 Responsibility without agency?

61. See Frankfurt, "Freedom of the Will," 12.

Taylor draws a differentiation between weak and strong evaluations. Whereas weak evaluations pertain to outcomes, strong evaluations pertain to "the quality of our motivation"[62] or the qualitative worth of a desire. The notion of strong evaluations has more weight in that regard because it makes it possible to reflect and articulate why a certain course of action has been taken by orienting oneself to certain values. Taylor outlines this thought:

> It must be clear that an agent who could not evaluate desires at all would lack the minimum degree of reflectiveness which we associate with a human agent, and would also lack a crucial part of the background for what we describe as the exercise of will.[63]

What stands out in this approach is that agency cannot be separated from qualitative evaluations, which in turn enable an assessment of individual choices. And, in being an evaluation, agency pertains to the realm of morality.[64] Since humans can typically do these reflective processes, the issue of whether or not they are genuine moral agents is out of the question: They simply are,[65] even if this does not mean that there cannot be other moral agents than humans. Yet, classically, moral agency has been considered with regard to humans only.[66]

These brief remarks must suffice, and at least sketch out what moral agency entails philosophically. It should have become clear that the general and classical modern understanding of humans is dependent on moral agency, which in turn is indissolubly linked with autonomy as well as responsibility. In any case, it seems important that a moral agent is able to relate to the world in a reflective and evaluating way, so the question arises of whether an artificial system is altogether able to develop such characteristics, an issue I will address in chapter three.

---

62. Taylor, "What Is Human Agency?" 16.
63. Taylor, "What Is Human Agency?" 28.
64. See Taylor, "What Is Human Agency?" 28. And, in turn, second-order desires.
65. See Taylor, *Quellen des Selbst*, 55.
66. See Schlosser, "Agency." This, however, does not mean that the question of whether nonhumans can count as agents is not considered. Rather, the standard theory does not pertain to this question. Yet, with respect to nonhuman entities, the qualifications necessary are too high. Here, different and weaker forms thereof need to be taken into account, as I will discuss below. See 3 Moral agency and autonomy in machines.

2.4 CONCLUSION

My brief revision of the concept of autonomy and moral agency served the purpose of demonstrating how humans typically envision ourselves—as autonomous agents acting morally—and demonstrated that the transfer of these typically human characteristics threatens this perception because it might produce a reductive picture of humans. This, however, must not entail that humans and machines are not closely knit together. As Latour holds, humans and nonhumans form assemblages, where artificial entities influence our forms of life as well. As for Coeckelbergh, technology might even be transcendental. This, however, must not mean that artificial entities hold the very same characteristics humans do. In technology labeled as autonomous, however, the line between machine and human is blurred in a troubling way because the technology is indeed envisioned to be autonomous and independent. While these technological implications will be dealt with in the following two chapters, I want to highlight that a way of speaking that conceals rather than clarifies the inherent characteristics of an entity endangers adequate dealing with these entities.

With respect to the term "technological autonomy," this transmits the idea of technology taking on a life of its own, but in a different way than Latour describes. When Latour seeks to remove the line between human and nonhuman, he wants to show that both entities influence each other and that an artifact may open completely new possibilities. He writes, "You wanted to injure but now, with a gun in your hand, you want to kill."[67] As for technological autonomy, one tends to think and speak of such devices as "self-guiding" or "self-acting," thereby mixing up the abilities humans and machines have. To put it clearly, this means that in labelling such a device with the anthropomorphic term "autonomous," all of the implicit anthropomorphic characteristics are implied. Yet, this imagination is flawed given the system's capabilities. What it does, though, just as any other artifact, is open up new possibilities through the way it operates. This means that terminology very much affects the way we, as humans, think about and make use of artifacts. This again emphasizes the significance of the way we talk about technology, and the question of if we use the adequate language for describing it.[68]

---

67. Latour, *Pandora's Hope*, 178–79.

68. Similarly, the digital memorandum of the Protestant church in Germany hints at these differences between human and machine, while simultaneously proceeding on

An Ethical Evaluation of Lethal Functions in Autoregulative Weapons Systems

To do so, Latour offers a way of describing humans and artifacts in a close relationship without confusing them. Every time a human acts with the help of an artifact, both human and artifact form one entity. This does not change with the introduction of autoregulation, even though these processes become more concealed because the collaboration might cross the lines of time and space, as the very definition of autoregulation is to operate without human influence in real time. However, the fact that human and nonhuman do indeed *co*llaborate, even if separated by time and space, becomes even less clear. This might be illustrated once again with the image of a gun. The actor who holds a gun has the opportunity to shoot. The gun might also be used as a hammer, or in another way, but the main idea a human gets when they see and hold a gun is to shoot. This means that the human being who invented the gun—the one who designed it—had the idea of using it for shooting. Now, if I take up the gun, I get the same impression. This does not mean that I have to shoot— I can do otherwise as well.[69] But the general idea that goes with guns is shooting. This thought can be transferred to the use of an autoregulative device. Here, I do not simply take up the gun and then think about what to do. Instead, I make up my mind in advance about which occasions a gun could be of use and then program it to do so—or least set an objective, predetermine the parameters of the undertaking, and provide the necessary data. Accordingly, the focus rests on the decision-making previous to the event. Hence, what makes an autoregulative device different from a device manually operated is the fact that a human either needs to predict every single possible event or program the device to do so.

Against this backdrop, I want to introduce the way in which agency and autonomy is conceptualized with regard to machines and then proceed to discuss contemporary engineering proposals that shape the collaboration between human and machine.

---

the assumption that digital, as well as any other technological devices, are by no means ethically neutral because they preset a certain course of action and in the process of design and development, ethical decisions are already made. That way, they increase as well as decrease freedom at the same time. The inherent anthorpomorphization, however, is a misperception of the underlying technology. See EKD, *Freiheit Digital*, 25–34.

69. As has been shown with respect to humans and autoregulative weapons by Leveringhaus. See Leveringhaus, *Ethics and Autonomous Weapons*, 89–117.

3

Autonomy and Moral Agency in Machines

WITHIN THE PHILOSOPHICAL DISCOURSE on technology, the possibility of technological devices acting in any sense similar to human beings is discussed under the term "artificial moral agency," while "technological autonomy" refers to the possibility of deploying a technological device without human supervision in real time. Closely connected to this issue is the question of whether the artificial system depends on humans, especially regarding moral decision-making. There is an immense amount of research conducted in this field.[1] This chapter discusses the phenomenon in a broader sense, taking a viewpoint not necessarily attached to machines designed to use force. My question is rather whether the idea of implementing morality into machines makes sense from an ethical point of view, and what this means for the deployment of lethal machines. I will argue that the depicted philosophical concept of moral agency and autonomy is in no way similar to the algorithmic procedures in machines, but that by transferring these ideas into the realm of technology, a metaphoric anthropomorphization takes place that might hinder rather than support a successful collaboration between humans and machines. In order to avoid such a misperception, I propose to refer to autoregulation instead of technological autonomy and to provide some examples for implementing technological procedures that emulate human moral thinking into machines. To do so, I will commence by defining and elaborating on what I have in mind when talking about technological "autonomy"

---

1. I will introduce some of the concepts in this chapter.

An Ethical Evaluation of Lethal Functions in Autoregulative Weapons Systems

(3.1), as well as AI and machine "learning" (3.2). Subsequently, I will hark back to a differentiation brought forward by Brian Cantwell Smith, who makes a distinction between technological reckoning and human judgment (3.3), before I explain why exactly I prefer the term "autoregulation" over "technological autonomy" and what I mean by that (3.4). I then discuss and refute philosophical concepts maintaining that artificial entities can count as moral agents (3.5) before I turn to the issue of artificial entities as moral patients, meaning the question of whether machines might be addressed as morally relevant entities (3.6). The final section of this chapter serves to demonstrate how morality is expected to be implemented into machines, depicting three different proposals to do so (3.7), before I draw a conclusion (3.8).

3.1 DEFINING TECHNOLOGICAL "AUTONOMY"

As mentioned earlier,[2] the definition of "autonomy" with regard to weapons systems is still disputed, just as there is no universally accepted definition of artificial "intelligence."[3] With respect to "autonomy," a differentiation is made between automatic and "autonomous" weapons. To begin with, it is important to note that "autonomy" in this context is related to the interaction between a human operator and the machine. A system operating without immediate human influence is called automatic. "Autonomy," however, is a much more wide-ranging concept because it implies the ability of the machine to interact with the environment, as well as certain forms of machine "learning."[4] Sometimes, "autonomy" is also applied to refer to the machine's anticipated ability to pursue its own objectives. This, however, is still a very vague and anticipated concept.[5] For the remainder of this book, I will refer to technological "autonomy" in the latter sense, while I characterize the former as autoregulative.[6]

The most common way to describe how machines operate with regard to humans is the tripartite classification of in-the-loop, on-the-loop, and out-of-the-loop. While a system operating in-the-loop is operated by

2. See 1.2 The Input This Study Provides.
3. See Ertel, *Grundkurs Künstliche Intelligenz*, 1–3.
4. See Altmann, "Zur ethischen Beurteilung automatisierter und autonomer Waffensysteme," 796; US DOD, "Unmanned Systems Integrated Roadmap," 17.
5. See Funk, "Drohnen und sogenannte 'autonom-intelligente' Technik im Kriegseinsatz," 170.
6. For further details, see 3.4 Machines: Autoregulative, Not Autonomous.

a human, a machine on-the-loop operates without direct human intervention, while a human supervises it. Finally, machines that are neither operated nor supervised by a human are called out-of-the-loop systems. Discussions about autoregulation usually refer to such out-of-the-loop systems.[7] The generality of this approach poses an essential problem because it does not specify in which regard machines are defined as autoregulative, since autoregulation can be generated within different parts of the system. A machine could, for example, navigate autoregulatively, but the process of targeting something or somebody and engaging a target might still be operated by a human being. Likewise, autoregulation could be implemented in the machine's ability to collect and assess data, but for engaging a target, the machine would need a command from a human operator. The ethical concerns dealt with in this book focus particularly on the process of targeting and target engagement. For that reason, I need to narrow down autoregulation solely to autoregulation in critical functions, such as targeting and target engagement. This is exactly what the definition of the US DOD emphasizes—a definition into which the International Committee of the Red Cross joined. Within this frame, a lethal autoregulative weapons system is defined as "a weapon system that, once activated, can select and engage targets without further intervention by a human operator."[8] Since this is exactly what I deem to be the issue at stake in this book, I will therefore orient myself to this latter definition. In contrast to that, there are definitions focusing more on the technological nature of "autonomy," such as the definition of the United Kingdom's Ministry of Defense, comparing automation with "autonomy." In this framework, an automated system follows "a predefined set of rules" and is therefore "predictable," while an "autonomous" system "is capable of understanding higher-level intent and direction." Moreover, it is "capable of deciding a course of action, from a number of alternatives, without depending on human oversight and control," therefore "individual actions may not be [predictable]."[9] Even though this definition may focus on technological terms, it is again based on an anthropomorphic misunderstanding of the technology by using words such as "decide," "understand," or "being capable" because such terms refer to humans.

---

7. See Boulanin and Verbruggen, *Mapping the Development of Autonomy in Weapon Systems*, 5–6.

8. US DOD, "Directive 3000.09," 13. The definition of the International Committee of the Red Cross is given in Davison, "Legal Perspective," 5–6.

9. United Kingdom Ministry of Defence, "Joint Doctrine Publication 0–30.2," 13.

An Ethical Evaluation of Lethal Functions in Autoregulative Weapons Systems

Moreover, it does not zero in on critical functions, such as target selection and engagement.

In addition to such definitions, scholars have developed more sophisticated classifications, such as Noel Sharkey, who proposes a five-level classification system. On the first level of Sharkey's concept, a human operates the machine (by remote control) meaning that the human operator themselves decides how the machine should select as well as engage the target. On the second level, the system suggests different targets, while humans choose which one to attack. In the remaining levels, the program always selects the target, but on the third level humans approve the attack, in the fourth the operator has the opportunity to intervene within a certain time frame, while in the fifth level the machine operates by itself and engages without any human involvement whatsoever.[10] Yet another proposal to shed light on the different varieties of autoregulation in weapons systems is called *Multidimensional Autonomy Risk Assessment* (MARA) and has been developed by the *Stiftung Wissenschaft und Politik* (SWP).[11] It was designed to assess autoregulation in weapons systems and takes into account more general features as well. These features are grouped into five vectors, ranging from physical characteristics, armament characteristics, human relevance, and information processing / situational awareness to exposition. The vectors are then subdivided into different categories so that, altogether, fourteen characteristics are defined. Each of these characteristics receives a certain amount of autoregulation in the respective field. Proceeding from this, an average is computed as a percentage. MARA in particular shows that the transition between automation and autoregulation is actually fluid. Generally, an automatic system, such as a land missile, would score low on MARA, while a more autoregulative system, such as Phalanx or Harpy, would reach a higher score.[12] However, there is no clear-cut line that could be drawn between automatic and autoregulative. This may even be subordinate for addressing ethical issues because the machines' operation without actual human involvement raises the question of accountability for life and death decisions.[13] It is not the technical

10. See Sharkey, "Staying in the Loop," 27.

11. See Alwart et al., *First Steps Toward a Multidimensional Autonomy Risk Assessment (MARA) in Weapons Systems*.

12. See Alwart et al., *First Steps Toward a Multidimensional Autonomy Risk Assessment (MARA) in Weapons Systems*, 18.

13. See Geiß, "Die völkerrechtliche Dimension autonomer Waffensysteme," 7; 6.5 Responsibility.

degree of automation that might be important with respect to the critical functions concerning life and death, but the human involvement in these decisions. As long as the process of targeting and the target engagement is done without any human involvement, the system poses ethical and legal issues that need to be addressed.[14]

To draw a conclusion, with regard to the discussion in this book, there is no urgent need to define exactly what is technologically meant by autoregulation in weapons systems. However, it is important to narrow down the debate to weapons that select and engage their target without human involvement. Since automation and autoregulation are difficult to distinguish from each other and the technical definition of autoregulation is contested, it does not seem plausible to me to employ the term "autonomy" in its technological perspective. The most decisive point from a peace ethical perspective is rather whether a system is programmed and designed to target people lethally without human control, intervention, and oversight in real time. Additionally, the most important issue regarding terminology is that the anthropomorphic description of technology is flawed, and the remainder of this chapter serves to show why this is the case.

Finally, a short disclaimer is necessary. First, this contribution does not elaborate on uncrewed technology as long as some critical functions are (remotely) controlled, as this kind of technology operates with a human subject who controls the device and is therefore not in the range of automation that operates without human influence or supervision in real time. Neither will the discussion presented here cover very basic automated weapons, such as anti-personnel landmines. Although these pose serious ethical concerns, they are less advanced and therefore outside the scope of my inquiry.[15]

3.2 HOW MACHINES DO (NOT) OPERATE: ON AI AND MACHINE "LEARNING"

The mechanical basis for autoregulation is generally provided by AI-driven algorithms. Definitions of this term pose several problems,

---

14. See Davidson, "Legal Perspective," 5–6; Schörnig, "Automatisierte Kriegsführung," 29.

15. Within the frame of MARA, every weapon that scores less than 50 percent is not considered to operate autoregulatively. Antipersonnel landmines score only 42 percent and are therefore not taken into consideration. See Alwart et al., *First Steps Toward a Multidimensional Autonomy Risk Assessment (MARA) in Weapons Systems*, 18.

similar to the problems the term "autonomy" poses. First, they take humans as their role model, defining AI to be "a computational artefact built through human intervention that thinks or acts like humans, or how we expect humans to think or act."[16] Second, there is no single, clear-cut definition of the term, but several thereof. Next to the already quoted definition, there is also the rather vague description that AI is a system that "processes information in order to do something purposeful."[17] A third example would be the rational agent approach, which Stuart Russel and Peter Norvig bring forward in their coursebook on AI. This states that "A *rational agent* is one that acts so as to achieve the best outcome or, when there is uncertainty, the best expected outcome."[18] Here, the rationality as well as the consequences are emphasized, so the implicit human role model is still present. Third, there is a major difference between narrow (or weak) and general (or strong) AI. Whereas the first refers to the ability of current technology to operate within a very clear and narrow domain, the latter refers to the idea that machines might be able to combine these different fields of applications, thereby resembling human intelligence. Despite the significant public and philosophical interest strong AI arouses,[19] research has only made significant progress with regard to weak or narrow artificial intelligence so far. In this concept, computers exceed human skills in limited computational tasks—such as in computing itself or image analysis,[20]—but they cannot, for instance, transfer their knowledge to another domain. Rather, a *deep neural network* trained on a specific set of data reaches a certain state, and if it is then trained on a new set of data, the former training will be completely erased and concomitant interference with the original data will become impossible—a phenomenon referred to as *catastrophic forgetting*.[21] Fourth, and in connection to this, AI is often used as a catch-all term for a wide range of diverse technical approaches, from what is called *good old-fashioned artificial intelligence (GOFAI)* and *deep neuronal networks*

---

16. Dignum, *Responsible Artificial Intelligence*, 9. This is also what van Oorschot criticizes. See van Oorschot, "Alles Technik, oder was?"

17. Dignum, *Responsible Artificial Intelligence*, 9.

18. Russel and Norvig, *Artificial Intelligence*, 4. Emphasis original.

19. See Kehl and Coenen, "Technologien und Visionen der Mensch-Maschine-Entgrenzung," 32; Bostrom, *Superintelligence*.

20. See Dickow and Jacob, "Das globale Ringen um die Zukunft der Künstlichen Intelligenz," 2.

21. See Kemker et al., "Measuring Catastrophic Forgetting in Neural Networks."

to *neural Turing machines*.[22] Since these all operate differently, there is a need to specify which precise method is used in any given device. Despite the different characteristics, the human brain and its artificial counterpart reach similar capacities in certain domains. However, "even with a computer of virtually unlimited capacity, we still would not know how to achieve the brain's level of intelligence."[23] In spite of these shortcomings, I will continue to use the term "AI" for lack of a more adequate definition.[24]

In order to understand the ways in which an algorithm can be trained, I will additionally, and briefly, introduce the three main approaches used for machine learning,[25] which are supervised and unsupervised methods as well as methods using reinforcement. Although other approaches exist as well, these three stand out. When programming an algorithm in a supervised method, the data is already labeled, so the system can sort it by this default labeling. A spam filter is the classic example of this. In contrast, unsupervised methods do not resort to already labeled data, but make use of unclassified data, so the system itself should find recurrent patterns or collocations. This kind of data structuring is used when the outcome is not determined, and an overlapping pattern has to be discovered. Finally, methods using reinforcement are mainly important in robotics. The environment here is much more complex, since robots are not confined to virtual surroundings. This method is based on the notion of trial and error: The technological device is confronted with a certain task and prompted to find a solution by trying different moves. A famous example of this kind of machine learning is the algorithm AlphaGo, which beat a human player at the game Go in 2016.[26] All of these approaches can be combined with each other in order to create new constellations. One of those constellations is called a neural network. The term indicates a method of machine learning modeled on the human

22. See iPRAW, "Focus on computational methods in the Context of LAWS," 9; Misselhorn, *Grundfragen der Maschinenethik*, 21–26.

23. Russel and Norvig, *Artificial Intelligence*, 12.

24. Since this is not the focus of my work, as the problems autoregulation poses are to some degree detached from the exact way a particular algorithm operates, I will not go in any greater detail here.

25. I must add that similar problems occur with regard to machines learning, which needs to be defined more precisely because there are different approaches here as well. In addition, the term "learning" also points to a similarity in humanity. This, however, is not exactly the case. See Steil, "Roboterlernen ohne Grenzen?"

26. See Ertel, *Grundkurs Künstliche Intelligenz*, 137, 370–73.

brain: More frequent procedures are reinforced while fewer common moves are diminished.[27]

In that context, robots pose a somewhat specific problem because they operate in the real world and are not limited to virtual surroundings. In order to interact with the environment, robots do not predominantly need to label data or find patterns, but rather have to perceive, move toward, and interact with living beings. Not every use of robots needs to involve methods of machine learning, but with respect to heavily automated uses, such as autoregulative driving, these methods are said to be inevitable.[28]

One major difference between plain software and robotics with regard to their training is that the robot cannot easily refer to a vast amount of data—as provided by the internet—but has to test every move in the field, which takes a lot more time than running a virtual program. After this kind of training, the robot would be able to perform one task using specific devices and interacting with one human being. If that human being is replaced by another one who does not have the exact same constitutions, the devices they work with change, or the procedure could be different, then the robot needs to be trained again to accommodate those changes.[29] Even though a robot could be connected to a server and trained on data provided by the internet, it still would need to be trained on a very specific or new task. Likewise, if the robot does not have sufficient computing ability, it needs to be trained in the aforementioned way. Moreover, real-life scenarios entail theoretically infinite possible incidents and therefore necessarily pose conditions that cannot be foreseen, which means that the robot cannot be trained for every single circumstance beforehand. Yet, despite these difficulties, robots already form an important part of our lives and will become even more important in the near future.[30]

---

27. See Ertel, *Grundkurs Künstliche Intelligenz*, 321–33; Dignum, *Responsible Artificial Intelligence*, 27–28.

28. See Hertzberg and Chatila, "AI Reasoning Methods for Robotics," 207.

29. See Steil, "Roboterlernen ohne Grenzen?" 21–23.

30. See Siciliano and Khatib, "Introduction," 1; Steil, "Roboterlernen ohne Grenzen?" 21.

3.3 RECKONING AND JUDGMENT: THE PROBLEM OF "INTELLIGENT" MACHINES

As already mentioned, the role model for creating AI, machine learning, and autoregulation is humans, so the question of if, and to what degree, the technological procedures indeed resemble the ones of humans arises. This is exactly the issue the philosopher and cognitive scientist Brian Cantwell Smith ponders in his book *The Promise of Artificial Intelligence: Reckoning and Judgment* (2019), drawing a sharp differentiation between a human's and a machine's cognitive abilities, referring to the former as "judgment," and the latter as "reckoning." Smith's account refers to the term "intelligence" but can easily be transferred to the concepts of autonomy and agency as well. For Smith, the main difference between both entities is that humans reason in a wholesale way, including awareness of the situation, while machines are unable to do so in a similar manner: They rather calculate, compute, and recognize patterns. He writes,

> I use judgment for [...] a form of dispassionate deliberative thought, grounded in ethical commitment and responsible action, appropriate to the situation in which it is deployed.[31]

This contrasts with the cognitive processes of machines:

> I use the term reckoning for the types of calculative prowess at which computers and AI systems already excel.[32]

The main difference for Smith is the way both entities perceive the environment. He holds that this is not only a qualitative difference, which might be overcome in due time, but that it is a categorical distinction marker: Machines will never be able to judge, and therefore are not intelligent in any way similar to humans.[33] To make his argument, Smith lists seven characteristics that intelligence consists of. He argues, first, that intelligence includes *orientation*, meaning that the respective entity relates from within toward a certain object. Second, he holds that it needs to differentiate between *reality* and *appearance*: "The system must recognize [...] that the object is different from its representation of it."[34] Third, this entails that a system can differentiate between matter and concept,

---

31. Smith, *Promise of Artificial Intelligence*, xv.
32. Smith, *Promise of Artificial Intelligence*, xv.
33. See Smith, *Promise of Artificial Intelligence*, xiii.
34. Smith, *Promise of Artificial Intelligence*, 85.

understand that objects are different from ideas, and thus grasp what is *at stake*. Fourth, intelligence entails *legibility*, which means that the object in question can be categorized along known and common parameters.[35] Smith, fifth, refers to the concepts of *actuality*, *possibility*, and *impossibility*, meaning that the system needs to differentiate between what is true, what is false, and what is impossible—an ability important for acting within this world. Sixth, since all the aforementioned differences are relevant, it is crucial that the system cares about them and shows *commitment*, which means that there is some sort of existentialism. This, finally, leads Smith to argue that an entity, in order to be intelligent, needs a *self*. Only then it is perceived as other and as accountable.[36] For Smith, these seven criteria result in perceiving the world as a unity:

> Everything we believe, everything we take in, everything we represent and are committed to, must be something we can understand as being in a single world—the world that both we and it inhabit.[37]

In summary, Smith holds that machines cannot make the distinction between a virtual, a real, and a cognitive principle and then combine all of them to represent a common and unified world within their self. Consequently, they are not intelligent.

Smith then goes on to discuss what he means by understanding the world as unified, which entails, on the one hand, that an entity can be held accountable and, vice versa, that the world is accountable for "hosting the object."[38] This amounts to Smith's main thesis that only objects that perceive the world in a wholesale way, that "make sense of the world as world,"[39] are intelligent in an anthropological sense. Since machines are not capable of doing that, Smith deems the term "intelligence" with respect to machines to be a severe misunderstanding.[40] In other words, the acting entities inhabiting the world need to understand themselves as living in one shared world. This necessarily entails that each of them understands the world in a similar way. Only entities that share a similar understanding of this world are perceived to be meaningful and accountable

---

35. See Smith, *Promise of Artificial Intelligence*, 87.
36. See Smith, *Promise of Artificial Intelligence*, 82–94.
37. Smith, *Promise of Artificial Intelligence*, 97.
38. Smith, *Promise of Artificial Intelligence*, 97.
39. Smith, *Promise of Artificial Intelligence*, 102–3.
40. See Smith, *Promise of Artificial Intelligence*, 110.

agents: If an entity does not understand what it is doing, it can hardly be called intelligent. At the same time, this world gives credit to entities that are called intelligent, autonomous, and accountable. Such entities are expected to behave in a certain understanding and caring way. But if there are entities that we credit as being intelligent and behaving in a meaningful way without them being able to live up to these expectations, this might harm the way we understand our common world and ourselves.

Even though Smith focuses on the idea of intelligence, his insights hold true for agency and autonomy as well because these concepts are also based on the notion that there is an agent that understands the world as a whole, judging and evaluating their position in the world rather than reckoning.

Smith is not the only researcher arguing that way. Similarly, the roboticist Noel Sharkey draws a differentiation between the abilities of a human and a machine, arguing that while machines are better at calculating numbers, searching large data sets, and performing repetitive tasks, humans exceed them in perceiving novel patterns, metacognition, and inductive and deliberative reasoning.[41] Sharkey also draws the conclusion that humans and machines do not share the same capacities and that machines therefore cannot be deployed apart from humans.[42] Moreover, the roboticist Jochen Steil demonstrates that the learning procedures within robots are by no means comparable with the leaning mechanisms of humans, even though the phrase "machine learning" seems to indicate exactly that,[43] while the philosopher Thomas Fuchs has objected strongly to addressing AI as intelligence, arguing that the procedures of the technology are in no way coextensive to the procedures of humans because mere appearances of consciousness are not enough.[44]

41. Without questioning Sharkey's argument as a whole, I must point out that his enumeration might not match the current technological achievements and trends. As for indictive reasoning, for instance, the whole idea of neuronal networks can be seen as an attempt to reproduce exactly these processes.

42. See Sharkey, "Staying in the Loop."

43. See Steil, "Roboterlernen ohne Grenzen?"

44. See Fuchs, "Menschliche und Künstliche Intelligenz." Fuchs's main argument is that the procedures of the technology are in no way coextensive to the procedures of humans because appearances of consciousness are not enough. Even though Fuchs is certainly right in his conclusion, his argumentation seems to overstate the problem. This is because Fuchs not only essentializes artificial entities but also perceives technology in a very idealized way, picturing artificial entities looking and behaving like humans. The main problem, however, is that Fuchs seems to lose sight of the existing intimate relationship between humans and machines.

An Ethical Evaluation of Lethal Functions in Autoregulative Weapons Systems

As for theology, Ralph Charbonnier and Frederike van Oorschot hold comparable positions. While Charbonnier admonishes not to anthropomorphize technology in terms such as AI,[45] van Oorschot argues that AI is a "bullshit word," which means that it does not correspond to the expectations it conveys. This is because the word catches the gist of an *imitative imagination* oriented toward human characteristics, thereby neglecting the technology's capabilities. This entails that by using the word "intelligence" with respect to technology, the link toward human intelligence is already there and intelligence similar to that held by humans is imagined.[46]

All of these approaches share the concern that by using words that stem from the particularly human sphere—such as intelligence, autonomy, or learning—it is not only that the expectations that accompany these ideas are flawed but that the reassignment of this term toward humans leads to an anthropomorphic misperception. As the philosopher Bernhard Koch puts it,

> It is not implausible that we will interpret and explain our conduct in the future rather with respect to machines than in the genuine human self-realization [*Selbstvollzug*], having its source in ourselves, and thus being assigned to us, and which we are responsible for.[47]

Similarly, Florian Höhne demonstrates that such a misperception leads to a shift within anthropology because humans are reduced to their ability to make decisions based on being informed about a certain risk. This entails two different developments. Since technology seems to be better suited for risk-assessment, it makes sense, on the one hand, to compute these procedures, thereby driving digitization and automatization. On the other hand, this reduces humans to exactly these procedures of risk-informed-decision-making, concomitantly transforming anthropology.[48]

The gist of my argument here is to critically call attention to the technological development and the social perception thereof, as the inherent anthropomorphic misunderstanding of the technology might not only lead to its misuse but also to a misperception of humans in the long run. Within the field of peace ethics, this might entail that lethal decisions

---

45. See Charbonnier, "Wahrnehmen, entschieden, handeln."
46. See van Oorschot, "Alles Technik, oder was?"
47. Koch, "Maschinen, die uns von uns selbst entfremden," 118–19. My translation.
48. See Höhne, "Bilder des Menschlichen."

are outsourced to machines, while machines do not have the necessary means to make any (moral) decisions at all. In addition, humans might perceive themselves to be inferior in such decision-making because a machine reckons more quickly and more reliably, thereby blurring the difference between judgment and reckoning, which then reduces the process of judgment altogether. This is why it seems important to reflect on the potential reduction of anthropology that comes with mixing up anthropomorphic with technological concepts.

3.4 MACHINES: AUTOREGULATIVE, NOT AUTONOMOUS

Over the course of the last century, due to progress in the field of AI, the term "autonomy" was adapted from ethics for use in computer science, where it was initially applied to describe "an abstract system or a physical network" that is "independent of, or not subject to, external influences or controls."[49] Later, its meaning shifted again when it was applied to machines in general, where autonomy came to signify the capability "of carrying out, without supervision, tasks typically performed by humans."[50] This shift indicates a metaphorical use[51] and, thereby, an anthropomorphism or personification.[52] By metaphor, I refer to the linguistic phenomenon "whereby we talk and, potentially, think about something in terms of something else."[53] With an anthropomorphism, we accordingly apply something nonhuman to a typically human action or characteristic.[54] We therefore talk and, potentially, think about something nonhuman in terms of humans.[55] The metaphors used to describe machines seem to be conceptual, meaning that there is a shared source domain (humanity) that is brought in line with a target source (i.e. machines). By that, I mean

---

49. Oxford English Dictionary, "Autonomous."
50. Oxford English Dictionary, "Autonomous."
51. Recurring to Semino's "metaphor identification procedure," I will briefly demonstrate that autonomy in reference to machines is indeed a metaphysical use of this term: While in the lexical and ethical sense, autonomy describes the ability of an agent to give themselves laws, a machine lacks this kind of freedom. Despite the gap between lexical understanding and current metaphorical use, this term is understood as described above. For further details regarding methodology and background, see Semino, *Metaphor in Discourse*.
52. See Koch, "Maschinen, die uns von uns selbst entfremden," 100.
53. Semino, *Metaphor in Discourse*, 1.
54. See Krennmayr, "Metaphor and Parts-of-Speech," 172–73.
55. Oxford English Dictionary, "Anthropomorphism."

that the whole cosmos of technology is structured by anthropological metaphors.[56] Moreover, this use could imply a frame, which is used to sideline certain meanings while others are underscored.[57] With respect to autonomy and machines, for example, self-governed behavior seems to be highlighted, while the process of programming is ignored. This not only describes a phenomenon in a biased way, but also leads to certain expectations within this field.[58] This means that something different is connected to the idea of an autonomous agent than to a programmed entity. Research conducted in this context indicates that, at least in politics, metaphorical framing is more convincing than nonmetaphorical framing and therefore could lead to strong assumptions.[59]

With that in mind, I want to ask two questions. First, is this description solid? To put it differently, are the phenomena described by the terms "autonomous" machines or "autonomous" weapons systems similar or comparable to the autonomy that humans hold, and, if so, in which regard and to what extent? If this question can be answered in the affirmative, it indicates a valid use of this metaphor. If not, another term would be more appropriate.

With regard to the first issue, the question is whether a machine can "act" and "decide" autonomously in the full sense of the word ascribed to this philosophical term. I argued above that, in my opinion, autonomy is first in line with self-government or love. This ethical and philosophical definition has much in common with personal identity and selfhood. Machines, however, lack such capabilities, as Smith has pointed out. A technological device neither follows morally informed, self-given laws, nor acts out of love. And even if the outcome of such morally informed decisions could be implemented in machines and human decisions emulated, the whole perception of the algorithm remains in a mode of reckoning, omitting processes of judgment. However, that is what autonomy, in its ethical sense, is mainly about. Similar problems arise when using the terms "AI" or "machine learning" because they indicate

---

56. See also van Oorschot, "Alles Technik, oder was?"

57. See Semino et al., "Integrated Approach to Metaphor and Framing in Cognition, Discourse, and Practice," 268.

58. See Semino et al., "Integrated Approach to Metaphor and Framing in Cognition, Discourse, and Practice," 267.

59. See Brugman et al., "Metaphorical Framing in Political Discourse," 19. I will elaborate on anthropormophization in the context of robots below in greater detail. See 3.5 Artificial entities as moral agents.

features machines inherently lack.[60] As shown above, the intelligence attributed to machines is not similar to the intelligence humans possess. Rather, intelligence in machines merely indicates the capability to search through and label data. This is similar to the learning of machines, which is applied when speaking about gathering and classifying data instead of gaining an understanding of the world. The same argument holds true for autonomy, since a machine, even though it can gather and classify data unsupervised, is always dependent on the information provided and, especially, does not give itself goals. It can sort and label data in a more or less accurate way, but it cannot make sense of the things it collects. Making sense of the things around us, however, is one essential characteristic of autonomy in its moral sense, as it is essential for making sound moral decisions.

If autonomy in humans and autonomy in machines do not share the same features, though, what is meant by this metaphor? Technological autonomy refers to the capability of a machine to do something without a human operating or supervising it in real time. It regulates itself for the task it was ordered to do. Expressed technologically, such a device is no more than a heavily automated machine. For those reasons, I would rather abstain from using anthropomorphized language in that regard and propose to use the term "autoregulation" instead. I take this term from a contribution from Lucy Suchman and Jutta Weber, who differentiate between biological and technological development, which they call *self-regulation*, and the philosophical term "autonomy." For Suchman and Weber, both terms are entwined with each other in the idea of "autonomous" machines.[61] I will attempt to dissolve this connection here.

Following the Oxford English Dictionary, I define autoregulation as the "regulation of a system or process by itself or from within, especially in such a way as to maintain a stable state."[62] Historically, the term describes "the ability to manage or control one's own behavior, emotions, work, learning, etc."[63] Following this, it has been applied to organizations, industry, and the like, describing the capability of an organizational structure to "regulat[e] itself without intervention from external bodies."[64] It has been especially important in cybernetics, where the

60. See also van Oorschot and Fucker, "Einleitung, 7."
61. See Suchman and Weber, "Human-Machine Autonomies," 79–80.
62. Oxford English Dictionary, "Autoregulation."
63. Oxford English Dictionary, "Self-regulation."
64. Oxford English Dictionary, "Self-regulation."

classic example for an autoregulative system would be a thermostat that adjusts the temperature in a room according to given parameters, but does so independently. Another typical example would be an autopilot in an aircraft.[65] Given the complexity of current systems, this rather basic notion needs to be extended so that adaptations to changing environmental influences are provided as well. The main advantage of this term is that the emphasis remains on a technological level, thereby avoiding a flawed imagination invoked by the anthropomorphic metaphor.[66] That way, the difference between the technological process of autoregulation and the human capacity of autonomy becomes distinct. As Francis Heylighen and Cliff Joslyn put it in their definition, "Artificial systems, such as thermostats and automatic pilots, are not autonomous: their primary goals are constructed in them by their designers."[67] The main difference is that humans, because they are able to judge the world as it is, are also able to define primary objectives, for instance, in assigning a device to play chess or in constructing an autoregulative car with the goal of driving safely. In doing so, the algorithm adjusts to new surroundings and circumstances without the need for instantaneous external governance, so—next to demarcating the difference between autonomous agent and autoregulative device—the independence of an external influence in real time remains.

In contrast to *heavy automation*, though, the term embraces the notion that the phenomenon indeed designates an (ethical) threshold because the technological device adjusts to its surroundings and even determines secondary goals according to its primary goal, which is not exactly what one would expect from an automated device.[68]

One objection to this change of terms could be that referring to autonomy poses no major problem because it is common knowledge that autonomy in machines is not coextensive with human autonomy. People can generally tell the difference between a robotic vacuum cleaner or even human-shaped robots such as Sophia from Hanson Robotics on the

---

65. See Heylighen and Joslynn, "Cybernetics and Second-Order Cybernetics," 165.

66. Since the term already exists within the natural sciences, my extended reinterpretation of the concept of autoregulation is certainly not without issue. Nevertheless, I see a considerable gain in a rather technologically oriented way of speaking. Therefore, I will use this terminology within this book to describe so-called technological autonomy.

67. Heylighen and Joslynn, "Cybernetics and Second-Order Cybernetics," 165.

68. See Altmann, "Zur ethischen Beurteilung automatisierter und autonomer Waffensysteme," 795–96.

one hand[69] and a human being on the other. However, the term implies an anthropomorphization and, as Sören Krach and Frank Hegel have demonstrated, people tend to treat robots as if they were human beings, especially if they look anthropoid.[70] Talking about machines in anthropomorphic terms entails that people also tend to think about them the way they tend to think about humans, thereby attributing similar capabilities to them.[71] As Nicholas Epley, Adam Waytz, et al. put it:

> Metaphors that might represent a very weak form of anthropomorphism can still have a powerful impact on behavior, with people behaving toward agents in ways that are consistent with these metaphors.[72]

Given this finding, there is a strong likelihood that the person dealing with the device ascribes an inner self to the machine that they would also ascribe to humans: a self that acts for reasons or out of love, a self that can connect one idea to another, a self that expresses itself and bears the power of imagination. These are all characteristics machines currently lack, and it is unlikely that they will ever be able to achieve these qualities.[73] Eventually, this leads to an overestimation of robots and their qualities in general. Research conducted by M. R. Endsley and E. O. Kiris indicates that people readily cede responsibility to machines they believe are better at specific tasks. Connected to this handover of responsibility, however, is the loss of a certain competence in the long run because the person operating the machine no longer has full control of its task.[74] This creates at least two problems. First, if the machine fails to do its job for whatever reason, the operator cannot take over the task because they lack the necessary competence. Second, the human operator no longer understands what the machine is doing and why and could easily overlook mistakes.[75] Especially in contexts that resort to using force, both

69. See Hanson Robotics, "Sophia."
70. See Krach et al., "Can Machines Think?"
71. Similarly, Koch, "Maschinen, die uns von uns selbst entfremden," 100. I will elaborate on the process of anthropomorphization below in greater detail. See 3.6 Artificial entities as moral patients.
72. Epley et al., "On Seeing Human," 867.
73. See Decker, "Robotik," 376.
74. See Endsley and Kiris, "Out-of-the-Loop Performance Problem and Level of Control in Automation"; de Greef, *ePartners for Dynamic Task Allocation and Coordination*, 23.
75. I will elaborate on that issue in greater detail below. See 4.2.2 The out-of-the-loop performance problem.

consequences pose severe ethical problems. Moreover, as I have already pointed out, ascribing anthropomorphic terms to machines will also have an impact on the way we think of humans because experiences with machines could be ascribed to humans as well, with the result that people might begin to think about humans as if they were machines.[76]

On the other hand, by overemphasizing the similarities between humans and machines, there is a risk of under- or at least misestimating robots—as Jochen Steil has pointed out—as unexpected problems that often arise escape notice because they emerge in areas not under scrutiny if this anthropomorphic misinterpretation is in place. One major problem, for instance, is surveillance. Imagine a surgical robot that assists in performing a surgery. The surgeon operates the robot with the help of a console. The slightest movements are transferred to the machine and the entire data of the operation saved in its database. The whole process is under video surveillance and the system tracks the patient's vital signs.[77] In this example, the system needs to measure the pressure of the operator's hand in order to operate correctly, and it might compare this parameter with another one perceived earlier. That way, the system not only passes on the impulse information but is simultaneously capable of sensing a trembling of the muscles or even the slightest difference in the operator's heartbeat. Yet, the employer could use such information about the employee's state of health and then base employment decisions on information they are not entitled to have. The same would be true for assisted or autoregulative driving, since a self-driving car needs to collect data not only from other (autoregulative) vehicles but also from pedestrians, animals, or plants surrounding it—and not least from the passengers as well.[78] From that, the question of how the collected data should be dealt with arises. Who should be allowed to access it? Who should interpret it?[79] The main problem here is that in order to operate properly, the robot requires a vast amount of data, so surveillance

---

76. See 3.3 Reckoning and Judgment. For the linguistic use of such metaphors in this context, see Semino, *Metaphor in Discourse*, 154. With regard to philosophy, see Koch, "Maschinen, die uns von uns selbst entfremden." For a feminist perspective within science and technology studies, see Suchman and Weber, "Human-Machine Autonomies," 79–80.

77. See Steil, "Roboterlernen ohne Grenzen?" 28–29.

78. See Broggi et al., "Intelligent Vehicles," 1178.

79. See Steil, "Roboterlernen ohne Grenzen?" 27–28.

is an inherent issue if humans and machines collaborate.[80] This entire problem, however, might disappear from sight if machines are perceived anthropomorphically.

3.5 ARTIFICIAL ENTITIES AS MORAL AGENTS

In conjunction with the question of whether the concept and term "technological autonomy" is suitable, the idea that artificial entities might be moral agents is of importance too because both concepts are closely linked. I have already outlined the philosophical concept of agency, emphasizing that agency is classically attributed to humans only because it is indissolubly linked with intentionality.[81] I have also made clear that I have severe reservations regarding agency in machines, referring to the theory of Brian Cantwell Smith.[82] In this section, I will delve deeper into these problems, introducing proposals to address the issue and suggesting, with Deborah Johnson's approach, that we think of machines as "moral but no moral agents."[83]

There are several proposals to qualify agency along a line, whereby humans are typically perceived to be fully fledged moral agents, and several kinds of technology have degrees thereof according to their technological equipment. A very famous classification is the one brought forward by James Moor, ranging from ethical impact agents, implicit ethical agents, and explicit ethical agents to full ethical agents.[84] While an ethical impact agent has moral qualities only *en passant* (such as robots in the working sphere changing the working situation), implicit ethical agents have an implicit ethical value (such as banking software), because they need to be constructed along safety and reliance parameters that imply a certain kind of morality. An explicit ethical agent, then, is a device that is programmed to be explicitly ethical, such as the ethical system Ronald C. Arkin proposes to implement in autoregulative weapons[85] or the web

---

80. See Steil, "Roboterlernen ohne Grenzen?" 30–31.
81. See 2.4 Conclusion; Schlosser, "Agency."
82. See 3.3 Reckoning and Judgment.
83. Johnson, "Computer Systems."
84. I adopt the terms here from Moor. Given the definitions of ethics and morality I refer to, however, it is highly questionable whether the term "ethical" should be replaced by the term "moral" here. For further information on that, see 3.7 The Implementation of Moral Behavior into Robots.
85. See 3.7.2.1 Arkin's Artificial Ethical System.

tool Ask Delphi[86], which is designed to give answers to moral questions. Finally, for Moor, an "average human adult"[87] is a full ethical agent.[88]

Alongside Moor, there are several other proposals to define artificial agency, such as the suggestions brought forward by Luciano Floridi and J. W. Sanders[89] or the approach taken by Wendell Wallach and Colin Allen.[90] As for research on that topic, the authors are mainly interested in what Moor calls an explicit ethical agent, so artificial moral agency would be accomplished if a system operated on behalf of internal moral-like structures. All of these approaches share the idea that artificial agency is based on autoregulation, which is then constructed according to bottom-up processes, thereby ensuring that the machines are to some degree independent of their programmer.[91] Moreover, all of them perceive the human—or to be more precise the "average human adult"[92]—to be the ultimate aspiration of the technological endeavor, thereby again attempting to imitate human behavior. In doing so, such authors quantify morality in humans and nonhumans along a perceived line,[93] which is in contrast to the approach of Smith, for instance, who marks a categorial difference between human intelligence and technological processes. The main difference, then, is that according to Smith, morality cannot be programmed for general reasons, while this seems possible in the approaches discussed in this chapter. An autoregulative car, for instance, is expected to deal with the trolley problem. In this thought experiment, a dilemma situation is presented where an autoregulative car can either run over a child or a group of adults, for instance. Both situations would be problematic, so the impression of a dilemma is created. Even though situations such as this are very unlikely to happen in real life—and if they do, they do not pose an ethical issue for the human driver, as they will act instinctively rather than with ethical deliberation—they gain momentum

---

86. See Allen Institute for AI, "Ask Delphi."
87. Moor, "Nature, Importance, and Difficulty of Machine Ethics," 20.
88. See Moor, "Nature, Importance, and Difficulty of Machine Ethics," 19–20.
89. See Floridi and Sanders, "On the Morality of Artificial Agents." Furthermore, Misselhorn brought forward an approach toward that topic in Misselhorn, "Robots as Moral Agents?" My list here is taken from Loh, *Roboterethik*, 48–71.
90. See 3.7.2.2 Wallach and Allen's Artificial Moral Agents.
91. See Loh, *Roboterethik*, 71.
92. Moor, "Nature, Importance, and Difficulty of Machine Ethics," 20.
93. See Loh, *Roboterethik*, 72. This assumption is inherently different to that of Smith, who argues that there is no qualitative but rather a categorial distinction.

Autonomy and Moral Agency in Machines

with regard to autoregulative driving. Within an autoregulative system, such incidents can be foreseen and the device's operations programmed.[94] In such situations, the machine is expected to make explicit moral decisions. The same is true with regard to autoregulation in weapons systems: When Arkin proposes that the system itself is equipped with an advisor for maneuvering lethal situations, moral reasoning is handed over to the machine. These approaches, therefore, proceed on the assumption that moral reasoning can indeed be programmed into the machine. Yet, as I have already shown above, autonomy and agency cannot justifiably be expected. Thus, it appears fallacious to suggest moral reasoning from a machine. What can be programmed is rather a set of certain concrete parameters and rules, such as Arkin suggests, for instance.[95]

Yet, there is a major difference between driving and killing, which is that driving means to follow certain rules, and as long as autoregulative driving follows these explicit rules, the automatization of driving seems to pose no considerable problems. If, however, situations are more complex and unforeseeable, it is hard to prepare the system for all the eventualities that might occur. Accordingly, and with respect to autoregulative driving, for instance, engineers are confident that driverless cars will be able to drive safely on motorways or specially designed roads, while they are less sure about driving in inner cities—mainly because the whole driving situation is much more complex.[96] Yet, fighting wars mainly concerns unexpectedness and dealing with unclear situations that are hard to predict. It therefore seems hard to implement such rules into a technological device.

In the bigger picture, the still implicit human role model stands out, so a question arises: Why should an inferior ethical deliberation, as the technological solution clearly seems to be, be adopted if humans constitute a full ethical solution? The answer given by proponents of the technology would clearly be that the ethical processes within the system are superior to those of humans because humans fall short of their ethical aspiration due to being humans, such as when they react in anger and frustration or for reasons of self-protection.[97] Clearly, time and information processing are an important issue in that regard because the

---

94. See Brändle and Grundwald, "Autonomes Fahren aus Sicht der Maschinenethik," 285–86.
95. See 3.7.3.1 Arkin's Artificial Ethical System.
96. See Broggi et al., "Intelligent Vehicles," 1191–95.
97. See Arkin, "Governing Lethal Behavior," 29.

machine exceeds humans in processing vast amounts of information in a short amount of time. This, however, is not coextensive with moral agency because processing information, which is done by reckoning methods, is not the same as judging moral situations according to moral agency. Yet, the question remains whether artificial moral agency might exceed human moral agency, as the proponents argue, and in which regard.

This question, however, is flawed for several reasons. First, from a theoretical standpoint, to take the human role model and then deem it inferior to artificial agents that purportedly share this characteristic only to a minor degree is clearly a *contradictio in adiecto* because the role model can hardly be inferior. Second, given Smith's differentiation between judgment and reckoning, there is simply no way the technology could ever meet human standards, especially when moral characteristics are concerned. Because of the number of characteristics typical for humans only that form the foundation for agency, such as autonomy, the technology can never achieve this goal. For that matter, reckoning processes are simply not sufficient, and understanding the world we live in and the forms of life we—humans and nonhumans—share is of greatest importance. As long as the technology cannot do that, there is simply no reason to assume that artificial entities will ever reach that goal.[98] Finally, within the data that drives the algorithm, humans and their social world are mirrored due to phenomena such as algorithmic bias, which I will depict below.[99] There is simply no objective data but only data that mirrors human forms of life because it is taken thereof. Therefore, humans and their standards, ideas, and procedures are still in place, even if the machine seems to operate on its own.

I, therefore, contend that artificial entities cannot be said to be outright moral agents. Yet, this does not mean that they are not part of the moral realm. In that regard, Deborah Johnson marks a difference, finding that computers are "moral but no moral agents."[100] Taking this stance means to repudiate two possible misunderstandings, which are first the view that "computer systems [are] independent, autonomous

---

98. This is also no question of quality, which would be that the artificial entity at some point reaches the state of general artificial intelligence, thereby connecting different subareas. The step is rather categorial, as in order to be an agent and to be autonomous, the entity has to gain consciousness. This, however, is a step purported by posthumanist thinkers that is not foreseeable right now. See Puzio, "Über-Menschen," 115.

99. See 4.2.5 Algorithmic Bias.

100. Johnson, "Computer Systems."

Autonomy and Moral Agency in Machines

moral agents,"[101] and second the idea that such systems "are outside the domain of morality."[102] Johnson here takes a middle ground, arguing that artificial systems are not simply ethically neutral, but at the same time cannot be said to share a human being's capability to act. She does so for reasons of intentionality, arguing that only entities that have mental states and intentionality can be said to be agents in a reasonable way. Yet, Johnson holds that artificial entities are not completely devoid of intentionality, though the intentionality laid in them is not theirs. She writes, "Computer systems and other artifacts have intentionality, the intentionality put into them by the intentional acts of their designers."[103] From there, she contends that artificial systems inherently depend on humans, since it is humans who provide their intentionality. Yet, if once turned on, some machines can operate without human control, oversight, and intervention because of the already introduced intentionality, which again hinges on the human being that put their intentionality into the device. To put it bluntly: Machines can only have intentionality to the degree that the human designer and programmer put their intentionality inside the device. They cannot have intentionality on their own, while they surely relate to the intentionality of their human inventor. This also entails that these machines are close to being moral agents without actually being such. That way, artificial systems are part of the moral world because they affect it.[104] She finally points to the ramifications of dismissing the interweaving of machines and humans by stating,

> I believe that attributing independent moral agency to computers is dangerous because it disconnects computer behavior from human behavior, the human behavior that creates and deploys the computer systems. This disconnection tends to reinforce the presumption of technological determinism, that is, it reinforces the idea that technology has a natural or logical order of development of its own and is not in the control of humans. This presumption blinds us to the forces that shape the direction of technological development and discourages intervention.[105]

The consequences Johnson marks underscore the impact technology has on our forms of life and, most importantly, it shows why the

---

101. Johnson, "Computer Systems."
102. Johnson, "Computer Systems."
103. Johnson, "Computer Systems," 201.
104. See Johnson, "Computer Systems," 202.
105. Johnson, "Computer Systems," 204.

detached perception of humans and machines might hinder people perceiving the realm of technology to be an area of (social) influence. I will elaborate on that perspective more intensely below by discussing the idea of meaningful human control.[106] Now, I will turn to another perspective within the discussion of technology, which is the question of how to address ever more advanced technology ethically.

3.6 ARTIFICIAL ENTITIES AS MORAL PATIENTS[107]

Next to the issue of whether artificial entities can be said to be moral agents, another strand within philosophical thinking points out positively the ability of humans to anthropomorphize, and argues the other way around. The rationale here is rather that because humans anthropomorphize technology, it is important to grant certain moral or even juridical rights to the technology for the sake of the humans concerned.[108] This viewpoint ignores the question of moral agency, or is more optimistic in that regard, because the importance authors such as Brian Cantwell Smith put on consciousness, self-awareness, or reality is sidelined. The point in question here is rather whether artificial entities can and should be regarded as moral patients, which are addressees of moral behavior. The underlying assumption is based on the thought that the differentiation between reality and appearance is not a necessary condition for treating an entity as moral entity. Harking back to Thomas Nagel's article *What is it Like to Be a Bat?* Coeckelbergh argues,

> If intelligent autonomous robots were able to produce the appearance of being moral—including the appearance of emotions—and behave in ways that contribute to the moral life, we would have a good reason to be more optimistic about living with them (or at least to be as optimistic as we are about living with other humans). Thus, it would be unfair or at least inconsistent to require that robots must have real mental states, real consciousness, or real emotions in order to be moral.[109]

---

106. See 4.4 Meaningful Human Control.

107. This section harks back to two articles of mine: Kunkel, "Programmierte Autonomie?"; Kunkel, "Am Grab meines Roboters," although I do not draw the same conclusions here.

108. With respect to moral rights, see, for example, Gunkel, *Robot Rights*; Nyholm, *Humans and Robots*. Juridical Rights are demanded by Mamak, "Should Criminal Law Protect Love Relation with Robots?"

109. Coeckelbergh, "Moral Appearances, Emotions, Robots and Human Morality," 241.

Autonomy and Moral Agency in Machines

According to this rationale, even though artificial entities such as robots can only simulate having a moral life, they nevertheless can—and should—be treated as moral entities.

In that regard, the research of Julie Carpenter is of interest. In her study on the relation between humans and robots in militarized spaces, she focuses on bomb disposal robots. She finds that working with such robots hinges on the respective situation as well as the cultural background, which entails that the relation between humans and machines is not fixed but rather dynamic. Moreover, this relation can change if the situation changes, moving from a situation where the robot is perceived as a tool to a situation where it is seen as an extended self. This transition is dependent on the design of the robot, among other things:

> For instance, customizing a teleoperated robot to appear especially fearsome in a war situation may bolster the operator's assertiveness, which could lead to either helpful or overconfident or risky behaviors.[110]

Such a finding is of great importance for the discussion of building and deploying autoregulation in weapons technology because design might be key. The reason is that humans tend to anthropomorphize, thereby ascribing the object in question human-like capacities, as I have already pointed out.[111] Epley, Waltz, et al., for instance, find in their study that the way people perceive an object, meaning if they deem it to have moral characteristics or not, depends on whether they perceive the entity to be human. This perception then influences how they will behave toward that entity. They write,

> Treating agents as human versus nonhuman has a powerful impact on whether those agents are treated as moral agents worthy of respect and concern or treated merely as objects, on how people expect those agents to behave in the future, and on people's interpretations of these agents' behavior in the present.[112]

Yet, this does not mean that humans anthropomorphize nonhumans in every situation to the same extent. How strong such an anthropomorphization is depends on several factors, such as the knowledge of humans, the motivation to be an agent themselves, and the wish for

---

110. Carpenter, *Culture and Human-Robot Interaction in Militarized Spaces*, 129.
111. See 3.4 Machines: Autoregulative, Not Autonomous.
112. Epley et al., "On Seeing Human," 864.

social interactions. Autistic people, for instance, and people who do not build relationships with other people easily, tend to anthropomorphize to a lesser extent.[113] To put it bluntly: The person longing for interaction with other people will, in case of need, make up this interaction by anthropomorphizing objects.[114] Metaphors can serve this end as well.[115]

This is exactly the case with metaphors such as artificial intelligence, machine learning, or technological autonomy. The moment metaphors refer to humans, humans also ascribe the entity human-like capacities via anthropomorphization. What is important here is that by changing the viewpoint toward a social interaction with the technology, where the respective machine is perceived to be human-like, the technology assumes the quality of being an agent. And it does so not because it embraces this quality, but because humans attribute it toward the technology, an effect that might be espoused by human-like design but that does not necessarily depend on it. This means that the design of the robot and the perception of humans working with the machine influences whether the operator will be prepared to take risks or will rather eschew them. This is exactly what Carpenter found when interviewing the operators of bomb disposal robots: The robots can be perceived to be an adequate teammate, so the robots are given names, for instance. This does not mean that every distinction between human and machine is done away with, but it entails that the robot is no simple tool used for the task of bomb disposal. Hay, one of Carpenters interviewees, depicts his feeling after a robot broke:

> During a mission in Iraq 2006, I lost a robot that I had named "Stacy 4" (after my wife who is an EOD [explosive ordnance disposal] tech as well). She was an excellent robot that never gave me any issues, always performing flawlessly. Stacy 4 was completely destroyed, and I was only able to recover very small pieces of the chassis. Immediately following the blast that destroyed Stacy 4, I can still remember the feeling of anger, and lots of it. "My beautiful robot was killed . . ." was actually the statement I made to my team leader. After the mission was complete and I had recovered as much of the robot as I could, I cried at the loss of her. I felt as if I had lost a family member. I called my wife that night and told her about it too. I know it

113. See Epley et al., "On Seeing Human," 865.

114. See Epley et al., "On Seeing Human," 867, 875–76. At this point, the authors refer mainly to pets and religious entities.

115. See Epley et al., "On Seeing Human," 867.

sounds dumb, but I still hate thinking about it. I know that the robots we use are just machines and I would make the decisions again, even knowing the outcome. I value human life. I value the relationships I have with real people, but I can tell you that I sure do miss Stacy 4, she was a good robot.[116]

This example clearly shows that Hay, the human operator, draws a distinction between a fellow human and the robot he is working with. He does, however, feel the loss, which might indicate that before exposing his favorite robot to danger, he might think twice and perhaps even deploy another robot.

These thoughts can be pushed even further. Coming back to the philosophical debates on whether an artificial device can and should be addressed morally, the philosopher David Gunkel sees no logical reason why this should not be the case,[117] and Sven Nyholm, modifying Kant's categorial imperative, holds that to the amount an entity appears to be human, it needs to be treated as such. His modification of the categorial imperative also includes artificial entities, such as human-shaped robots. His revised categorial imperative reads as follows:

> Always treat the humanity in each person as an end in itself, and never as a means only—and out of respect for the humanity in each person, also treat the apparent humanity in any person (or robot!), never merely as a means, but also as an end in itself.[118]

According to that rationale, artificial entities also need to be addressed as moral patients because humans dealing with them perceive them to be human. This, again, is not because of the robot itself but the humans dealing with the robot, who transgress the moral imperative by not addressing the artificial entity morally. In not treating the human-shaped robot with respect and dignity, humans fall short of their own morality.

With respect to autoregulation in weapons technology, this debate is important because arguing from a standpoint where the robot is perceived to be the addressee of moral rights also entails that robots in the battlefield might benefit from such rights. This would be especially true if these robots were given the shape of humans, but even if this is not the case, this discussion is still relevant given the notion that the human-like

---

116. Carpenter, *Culture and Human-Robot Interaction in Militarized Spaces*, 117.
117. See Gunkel, *Robot Rights*.
118. Nyholm, *Humans and Robots*, 187.

shape of a robot might not be decisive for the process of anthropomorphization. From this perspective, two conclusions could be drawn with regard to autoregulation in weapons systems. First, proponents of this argument might infer that autoregulative weapons systems can and should be treated as moral patients because otherwise the person working with them betrays their moral integrity. This might entail thinking twice about whether it is appropriate to deploy a robot in the battlefield—because it might be destroyed. Second, it might mean that the people targeting a (foreign) robot need to make sure that the moral entitlement of this entity is not harmed. Both implications do not make much sense, though. Particularly with regard to lethal machines, the difference between humans and machines and the vulnerability of humans comes to the fore. In this field of deployment, it is therefore crucial to prevent processes of anthropomorphization and identification. According to the study of Eply, Waytz, et al., it might help to increase the knowledge, which means training the operators in advance. In any case, it seems imperative not to deploy weapons systems that have a human-like shape because this increases the possibility of identification with the robot. That way, human combatants might be tempted to revenge the robot or protect it as if it were a human and the purported advantages might be removed.[119] For that matter, anthropomorphic metaphors might also add to such an identification process. It therefore seems crucial, especially with regard to lethal functions of autoregulative technology, to avoid metaphorical speech and to address the technology as technology, adopting terms such as "autoregulation."

To conclude, I deem it important to take the characteristic human tendency to anthropomorphize seriously because it makes a difference to how a certain system is deployed. As research indicates, operators do not simply follow the rationale that they use a tool for a certain end; they, at least at some points, identify with the object, feel the loss if it is broken, and get attached to it. This means that these identification processes need to be reflected on and minimized in scenarios of high risk because their effects could cost lives and inflict harm.[120] This, very importantly, means that a weapons system should never take a human shape, because this will impede the performance of the human–machine collaboration.

119. See Arkin, "Governing Lethal Behavior," 29–36.
120. This might be different in other fields of deployment, such as in social care, where anthropomorphizing and identification processes might help to increase the desired result.

3.7 THE IMPLEMENTATION OF MORAL BEHAVIOR INTO ROBOTS

Regarding the possibility of implementing outright moral deliberation into machines, there are several proposals to do exactly that. The general idea of these concepts is easy to grasp: Moral reasoning ought to be implemented into algorithmic procedures resembling more or less the moral reasoning processes of the human. These suggestions make use of a decision-making loop that attempts to formalize how moral decisions are made. In that regard, some scholars argue for the formalization of ethical deliberation. Having recourse to the differentiation between ethics and morals I introduced above,[121] such a proposal seems to make the mistake of anthropomorphizing technology. This is because ethics refers to the process of deliberation and judgment of a certain situation, while morality rather refers to the inclusion of operationalized rules. While it might be possible to implement the latter into machines, the former is not possible.[122] For the sake of this chapter, I will first depict two such decision-making loops, the OODA-loop and F2T2EA, thereby showing that processes of automation are highly dependent on preceding information and states and influence subsequent information and states, as well (3.6.1). I then will briefly define how I use the terms "morality," "ethos," and "ethics," and then dwell upon three proposals for implementing moral agency into machines, as made by Ronald C. Arkin, Wendel Wallach and Colin Allen, and Derek Leben (3.6.2).

3.7.1 From OODA to F2T2EA

In order to implement moral procedures into machines, there first needs to be a way to formalize decision-making. There are several proposals to find such a way, with the aim being to make clear how decisions are made in detail and to automate at least some parts thereof. The general idea is that the decision-making process can be broken down into several steps, which are then carried out one after another and revised in the process (by a human operator). It is important to note that though each step as well as the process as a whole can be iterated, one step builds on another,

---

121. See 1.3 Overview of the Argument.

122. Also, the term "decision-making" is clearly an anthropomorphization because machines cannot make decisions.

An Ethical Evaluation of Lethal Functions in Autoregulative Weapons Systems

with the result that the outcome always and necessarily depends on the preceding steps.

One proposal to illustrate the procedures involved in automated decision-making has been brought forward by R. Parasuraman, T. B. Sheridan, et al. It is a quadripartite approach that consists of acquisition of available information, analysis of perceived information, selection of what to do or how to decide, and implementation of the decision taken. Since automation is a dynamic process rather than a fixed format, every step within this loop can be automated to a greater or lesser degree, from no automation at all up to autoregulation. Within the first step, which is information acquisition, this may include automatically moving sensors or detectors toward objects that are in the range of interest, or even highlighting some objects that may be of special interest. With respect to the analysis of the information, automation can help to compute an anticipated trajectory, which might then be put into relationship with other (flying) objects. Regarding the decision-making itself, automation could present a list of possible actions and rank them according to preset configurations. Referring to the last step, the decision taken is put into action. An automated system could implement what has been ranked highest before, while a less automated system would wait for the operator's veto at least for a certain amount of time, while a nonautomated system would need the approval of the operator in order to put the decision into action.[123]

This basic idea has been adopted by the military in what is called the OODA loop, which spelled out means orient, observe, decide, and act.[124] In addition to this, various forms of this approach exist, most famously the target cycle of the US Air Force, called F2T2EA, which means find, fix, track, target, engage, and assess.[125] Here, the single steps are broken down into a series of six sequences and are specially modeled to engage a target. In the first step, a potential target is found on the basis of given parameters, while this potential target is (in-)validated in the second step. In the next step, the object is tracked, which includes permanent

---

123. See Parasuraman et al., "Model for Types and Levels of Human Interaction with Automation," 286–98.

124. See de Greef, *ePartners for Dynamic Task Allocation and Coordination*, 31; Scharre, *Army of None*, 23–25: Boulanin and Verbruggen, *Mapping the Development of Autonomy in Weapon Systems*, 61.

125. See iPRAW, "Focus on Technology and Application of Autonomous Weapons," 12.

surveillance as well as tracing it back to its original source. Subsequently, the operator targets the object in question, thereby factoring in possible side effects as well as scenarios that would forbid the use of force. If the target passes this test, it is engaged. The last step of this sequence, namely the assessment, is carried out in addition to the aforementioned four-step approach. In this stage, the whole venture is reviewed to check if the desired objective has been achieved by appropriate means.[126] This step is particularly important with regard to automation because autoregulative machines would need to assess their actions and gain knowledge for another strike.[127]

No matter which decision-making cycle is referred to, it is important to note that automation might occur at every single stage of this chain in various forms. Even if the first steps are carried out in an autoregulative mode, the last steps might be controlled manually or vice versa. This raises the general question of whether there are single steps that might be more problematic to automate than others from an ethical point of view. According to my observations, the current discussion focuses on the plain decision-making process itself, which is only one step in the target cycle. This gives rise to the question of whether the manually given order to engage a target can sufficiently ensure that the operator knows about the selections that have been made earlier. This can be exemplified with reference to a system where the first steps are autoregulative, meaning that the system has already classified some objects as suspicious and prioritized those that are most likely to become dangerous. Based on this, the system presents a list of the targets in question to the human part of the collaboration, who then they has to decide how to deal with it in a certain time frame. To me, the problem seems to be that if there is a bug in the already given list, there is nothing the operator can do about it, which means that they must trust the system to make the right classification before they make their own. Another concomitant problem is automation bias, meaning the overreaching trust the operator puts into

---

126. See United States Air Force, "Doctrinal publication 3–60," 45–47. Another enlightening explanation based on this document is given in iPRAW, "Focus on Technology and Application of Autonomous Weapons."

127. The F2T2EA approach has the major advantage in adding this final step because an evaluation of whether the intended outcome has been achieved properly is important for the conduct of a following similar task as well as for the ascription of responsibility. This is because the actual outcome is compared to the intended outcome and a possible deviation would need to be justified.

their automated machines.[128] If there is, however, a suspicious target that turns out to be harmful and there are no unintended side effects to be apprehensive of, the operator will (have to) engage the target, so—down the road—the outcome will be the same regardless of who made the decision or classification. This implies that the major (ethical) problem might not be the single life-and-death decision but the process as a whole, or the question of which single step could and should be automated and to what degree.

3.7.2 How to Implement Morals

In order to deal with these complex questions, authors have rightly pointed out that ethical consideration is necessary at some point. Some, namely Robert C. Arkin, Wendell Wallach and Colin Allen, and Derek Leben, have proposed to do so in a technological manner. I have already critically discussed the philosophical questions of machine autonomy and agency in this chapter, so I can now present some concrete suggestions made so far.

First, however, there is a need to define the way I use to the terms "morality," "ethos," and "ethics" because they are defined differently by different authors. All of these terms pertain to the question of how to conduct life, but each of them alludes to a different level. Confusingly, different philosophers and ethicists use these terms to describe different things, which is why I will briefly introduce the definitions I will use.

"Morality" refers to the underlying normative and shared convictions of humankind differentiated by right and wrong or good and evil in the sense of *common morality*. The term "ethos" is either related to a group holding the same moral convictions (*objective ethos*) or to an individual's moral beliefs and characteristics. Finally, "ethics" pertains to the reflexive deliberation of morality and ethos.[129]

When it comes to machines, the idea of implementing morality into a technological device is faced with the question of which morality to implement. In that regard, authors usually refer to contemporary applied ethics, which can generally be categorized into three different approaches: *top-down*, *bottom-up*, and a *coherentist* approach merging

---

128. See 4.2.3 Automation Bias.

129. The definitions are taken from Beauchamp and Childress, *Principals of Biomedical Ethics*, 1–5; Reuter, "Grundlagen und Methoden der Ethik," 14–18.

Autonomy and Moral Agency in Machines

both of the aforementioned conceptions.[130] These approaches form the foundation for the following debate.

A top-down approach entails ethics that apply one general rule to a particular case, such as the categorical imperative or the golden rule.[131] This general rule is then divided into more concrete guidelines, which are again subdivided into even more explicit rulings.[132] However, the theologian Hans-Richard Reuter demonstrates three problems with this paradigm. First, in real life, rules may conflict with each other, meaning that from one principle, a person can come to different explicit rulings.[133] Second, in a modern, pluralistic world, one cannot simply refer to some shared general rules and values. By way of contrast, general rules are sometimes opposed to each other, so there needs to be a discussion about the rule in question first. Third, since this theory does not consider the context of the single decision but merely requires compliance with the general rule, it is not clear to what extent a general rule can be applied directly to a real-life scenario at all. With respect to computer science, the bottom-up approach in ethics should be differentiated from information-processing techniques that solve large tasks by dividing them into smaller tasks, though they are called the same.

On the other hand, bottom-up approaches focus on a specific situation. Here, biological preconditioning (genes) and the environment both enable the individual to develop their own moral self, as in the development of a child or the biological evolution of an organism.[134] In a similar way, a bottom-up approach is used in computer science, where no general rules are implemented but a task is specified, such as winning a game.[135] These procedures are referred to when calling an algorithm *self-learning*, or artificially intelligent. In contrast to top-down approaches, bottom-up approaches seem much more dynamic and might therefore be more in line with the complexity of decision-making. At the same time, as Reuter notes, this advantage could turn out to be disadvantageous because there is no major rule that could guide the decision-making, but the common

---

130. See Reuter, "Grundlagen und Methoden der Ethik," 95.
131. See Wallach and Allen, *Moral Machines*, 84.
132. See Reuter, "Grundlagen und Methoden der Ethik," 95.
133. This is also mentioned by Wallach and Allen. See Wallach and Allen, *Moral Machines*, 84.
134. See Wallach and Allen, *Moral Machines*, 80, 99.
135. See Wallach and Allen, *Moral Machines*, 80.

sense may be biased one way or another.[136] With regard to machines used in sensible contexts, this entails that there are no general rules that could adjust the performance of the machine, even though these rules might turn out to be flawed. Moreover, this kind of approach is hard to implement in complex scenarios and can only be used safely if the goal and environment is very clear.[137]

Finally, a third approach—called *coherentism* by Reuter—combines both of the aforementioned techniques. From an ethical perspective, every moral agent can be described as a combination of top-down and bottom-up approaches: The agent neither solely applies general rules to a specific scenario nor develops rules in a casuistic way, but they decide according to their overall moral thought either with respect to a problem or with respect to an argumentation.[138] John Rawls is one of the most influential scholars who has brought forward the thought that both normative principles, as well as intuitions, strike a balance in what he calls *reflective equilibrium*.[139] There are several debates related to this issue, such as the question of whether intuitions or coherence are to be seen as the most constitutive part of the reflective equilibrium.[140] Another debate concerns the issue of whether the reflective equilibrium only needs to be in coherence with the individual's moral reasoning (weak reflective equilibrium), as Rawls states, or in line with the moral beliefs of others too, as the American philosopher Norman Daniels holds.[141] Reuter concedes two main problems associated with coherentism, though, which are particularism and conservatism. With particularism on the one hand, he refers to the problem that, at least in the case of weak reflective equilibrium, the validity is confined to a group holding the same moral convictions or even an individual, with the result that there is no way to achieve universal normative principals. Conservatism, on the other hand, describes the issue that only preexisting principles and intuitions matter, while norms that exist only theoretically are ruled out at the outset. This is a problem as theoretical norms might offer a critical potential

---

136. See Reuter, "Grundlagen und Methoden der Ethik," 98.

137. See Wallach and Allen, *Moral Machines*, 113–14.

138. See Reuter, "Grundlagen und Methoden der Ethik," 98.

139. See Reuter, "Grundlagen und Methoden der Ethik," 99; Daniels, "Reflective Equilibrium"; Rawls, *Theory of Justice*, 48.

140. In favor of intuition, see McMahan, "Moral Intuition," 111. In favor of coherence, see Rawls, *Theory of Justice*, 48.

141. See Rawls, *Theory of Justice*, 48; Daniels, "Reflective Equilibrium."

regarding an actual situation. Yet, this potential could never be actualized within this frame.[142]

Finally, there is no single ethical procedure that can elucidate the structure of moral decision-making comprehensively, but rather a variety of different approaches with their own advantages and disadvantages. It is therefore crucial to consider whether it is even fundamentally possible to implement structures of ethical deliberation into machines and what outcomes can be reasonably expected.[143] In that vein, the following pages will explore how different authors suggest implementing ethics into a technological system.

3.7.2.1 *Arkin's Artificial Ethical System*

The roboticist Ronald C. Arkin addresses this issue by proposing to implement different steps of moral and mainly legal considerations. His main assumption is that autoregulation can help to reduce the infliction of harm in general, and with regard to noncivilians in particular, because he argues that machines do not fail due to typical human behavior that is anticipated to result in mistakes, such as fatigue, revenge feelings, fear, or distress. He states that "it is a design goal of this project to be able to produce autonomous system performance that not only equals but exceeds human levels of capability in the battlefield from an ethical standpoint."[144] His objective is therefore to build a program that can avoid human flaws and at the same time apply the relevant legal (and moral) norms. The underlying thought is, first, that war is part of the human condition and can therefore not be overcome, though he indicates that peaceful solutions are preferable.[145] Second, he assumes that a method to reduce harm in belligerent scenarios is to be adopted because every method that is able to decrease the number of victims and reduce the harm they suffer should be embraced.[146] Third, within this frame, he assumes that autoregulation in lethal weapons will gain currency and understands his contribution as a way to reign in the process already

---

142. See Reuter, "Grundlagen und Methoden der Ethik," 100–101.
143. For further information, see 3.7 The implementation of moral behavior into robots.
144. Arkin, "Governing Lethal Behavior," 120.
145. See Arkin, "Case for Ethical Autonomy in Unmanned Systems," 332–41.
146. See Arkin, "Ethics and Autonomous Systems," 1780.

underway.[147] Fourth, though Arkin systematically talks about ethical implementations, he rather seeks to implement legal principles such as rules or laws by considering *rules of engagement* or *laws of war*.[148] This is important to note because, strictly speaking, Arkin does not mean that the machine deliberates ethically but that some basic legal boundaries are implemented.[149] He therefore proposes to construct a system that determines which actions are permissible within a certain situation. The aim is to ensure that only legitimate actions are carried out, while forbidden activities are suppressed. Consequently, a cemetery or a hospital, for example, could be determined as a prohibited target, while a military camp would pose a legitimate target.[150] If the autoregulated device detects the signal it is programmed to attack, such as the radio signal of an anti-missile system, it would check the preprogrammed legal parameters and, according to them, either attack the legitimate target or refrain from attacking the illegitimate one. The same would apply to wounded or surrendering soldiers. However, the extent to which the targeted side could use these fixed parameters in their interests remains an open question.[151]

For establishing his theory, Arkin draws on former evolutionary biologist Marc Hauser and adopts one of his proposed models for moral reasoning that revolves around deliberation as the basis for a moral decision.[152] He deems Hauser's approach promising because it is mostly in line with the idea of expressing moral reasoning in a formal, logical manner.[153] Five steps must be considered before a system could engage a target. First, the responsibility needs to be handed over from humans to the machine. Second, military necessity is to be considered. Third, the target needs to be identified as a legitimate target, thereby applying rules

147. See Arkin, "Governing Lethal Behavior," 5, 36.

148. With respect to the laws of war, see Arkin, "Governing Lethal Behavior," 71–80, with respect to rules of engagement, 81–91.

149. As I noted above, this is especially confusing, since ethical deliberation would entail judging and reflecting on the decisions made, a process machines are unable to undertake. A more appropriate terminology would be the reference to morality. But even if making this distinction, Arkin's attempt remains to implement *legal* norms.

150. See Arkin, "Governing Lethal Behavior," 155–76.

151. It seems very easy to trick this kind of pattern, for example, in providing every fighting soldier with a white sheet in order to signify that they are surrendering, while they are in fact still playing an active role in combat. Similarly, it would be easy to construct military infrastructure within areas that are forbidden to attack, such as hospitals or cemeteries, thereby potentially worsening the situation.

152. See Arkin, "Governing Lethal Behavior," 118.

153. See Arkin, "Governing Lethal Behavior," 118.

of discrimination between combatant and noncombatant, ensuring that force is used only against military targets. Fourth, potential harm to civilians needs to be taken into consideration, so it is reduced to a minimal amount in applying the principle of double intention. Finally, the weapons and firing patterns are selected according to proportionality, thereby ruling out undue weapons in general and employing an appropriate use of force in particular.[154] Arkin then fleshes out his general remarks with specific recommendations for design, where he attempts to factor in as many aspects as possible and opts for a quadripartite design. A first part of this ethical system is called *ethical governor*, and it commences its operations when the system computes to engage a target.[155] If this were to happen, it would first verify the permission to use force in general. The objective is to double-check the use of force by some preset parameters—for example, moral reasoning as in deontic thought—in order to rule out behavior restricted by law or to avoid a situation that is not appropriate due to discrimination or proportionality. However, Arkin admits that control at this level remains an open question.[156]

In the second device, called *ethical behavioral control*, the overall behavior of the system is taken into consideration with the aim of ruling out immoral actions, following the rationale that a machine, not capable of acting immorally in general, would act morally in every single situation. Such a rationale could be implemented, in the author's view, by engineering basic rules of engagement—bearing in mind that it is a machine and not a human carrying out the lethal decision. This means, for instance, that while a soldier would be allowed to use force for the reason of defending themselves, a machine would not have to respond in the same way.[157]

A third component is called *ethical adaptor* and serves to update the machine's presets, but only in a more restrictive way after, or concomitant with, a lethal action. Its aim is to operate according to moral emotions or intuitions such as guilt or remorse, according to the theory of moral intuitions provided by the psychologist Jonathan Haidt. This entails two

---

154. See Arkin, "Governing Lethal Behavior," 121–23.

155. The "ethical governor," as well as the "responsibility advisor" Arkin proposes to implement entail an anthropomorphism, because they seemingly refer to a human's rank (governor), in the first case, and a human's ability (to advise), in the second case. Both, however, are characteristics the machine does not have.

156. See Arkin, "Governing Lethal Behavior," 127–33.

157. See Arkin, "Governing Lethal Behavior," 133–38.

options. First, in the process of analysis, a lethal decision already taken is reevaluated after the event and then restricted in the aftermath for further similar situations. Second, a course taken is overwritten in real time by the *ethical adaptor* because it is assessed inappropriate mainly because of unintended effects. In the first case, which would occur ideally in the training process, a human operator would intervene and tighten the programmed rules, while in the second case the system regulates itself. If an unintended effect occurs and thereby a certain threshold is passed, the system automatically terminates its lethal action.[158] Such a system has been criticized because it would lack the ability to identify with a human and would not be able to exert compassion, whether to a (non-)combatant or to a civilian.[159] Arkin admits that this is true, but points out that the existing rules in fact imply some compassion "for civilians, the wounded, civilian property, other noncombatants, and the environment."[160] Since his aim is to implement these prevailing rules, he infers that compassion is already part of his proposal.

The final part of Arkin's moral system is called *responsibility advisor*, and it serves to ensure that a human bears the responsibility for the machine's actions. In order to provide this responsibility, Arkin proposes that the use of lethal force needs to be authorized in advance by a human operator. This operator needs to be aware of the system's general settings and be able to adjust them in line with the current mission. They need to prove that they have the proper training to handle the system, permit the uses of force that they would like to exert one at a time, probably update the system on the grounds of recently gained knowledge that the system has not been trained in yet, and finally give the approval for the system's use.[161] Within this paragraph, Arkin considers the possibility of overriding moral constraints because, referring back to Walzer, it might sometimes be necessary to disregard prevailing rules for the sake of military necessity. Arkin strongly advises against such an overriding and concludes that the system would then no longer act in an autoregulative fashion but "as an extension of a human soldier,"[162] meaning that the soldier who removed these constraints would also be personally responsible for the deeds of the technological device.

158. See Arkin, "Governing Lethal Behavior," 138–43.
159. See Human Rights Watch, "Losing Humanity," 38.
160. Arkin, "Governing Lethal Behavior," 143.
161. See Arkin, "Governing Lethal Behavior," 143–49.
162. Arkin, "Governing Lethal Behavior," 150.

At first sight, Arkin's proposal seems to be sophisticated and feasible to a high degree. There are, however, some issues that pose severe problems. First, the author's tone is rather legalistic, following the rationale that if an actor applies the given rules correctly to the situation, then the actor will act morally. Although this seems convincing at first glance—especially with respect to deontic thought, which is mainly concerned with rules—it might turn out to be flawed. This is because deontic thought is not only about applying rules correctly but also about somebody's intentions when acting, and the application of rules to a given situation affords a correct assessment, which in turn is built on processes of judgment.[163] Strictly speaking, a device that has no intentions cannot apply any rules whatsoever. Still, if we put aside these mere theoretical objections, some issues remain. A second problem belonging to the same topic is the fact that it might sometimes be necessary not to play by the rules, not only from a tactical but also from a moral point of view. This is closely linked to compassion. It is true that within the rules and norms already existing, there is some compassion encoded, for instance, when sparing the wounded and civilians. One very commonly depicted scenario in (philosophical) literature about autoregulative weapons systems, however, is a situation where a child reaches for a gun, thereby becoming a legitimate target. An autoregulated weapons system would shoot without hesitation, at least if this situation would pose a threat to the soldiers it is programmed to protect, while a human soldier might at least think twice or even refrain from pulling the trigger.[164] Two more unresolved issues come with the terms "control" and "responsibility." Arkin himself admits that these topics are not sufficiently accounted for.

3.7.2.2 *Wallach and Allen's Artificial Moral Agents*

In another approach, Wendel Wallach and Colin Allen suggest introducing artificial moral agents (AMAs) into all kinds of autoregulated systems. In contrast to Arkin, they do not confine their scope to their use within weaponry, but focus on civic uses of autoregulation, such as

---

163. See 3.3 Reckoning and Judgment.

164. See Leveringhaus, *Ethics and Autonomous Weapons*, 89–94; similarly, Scharre, *Army of None*, 2–4. The problem with this example is that it can be interpreted in two opposing ways. Leveringhaus and Scharre depict a situation where the child does not pose any threat because it does not shoot. If the child were to harm a lot of people, though, the system's course of action seems to be more appropriate.

the care of elderly or disabled people. Their main concern is that ever more automated technology will be in use soon and that while a lot of effort went into making machines more independent, the question of the moral adequacy of machines received less attention. Accordingly, their aim is to promote the moral factor in line with growing automation.[165] Furthermore, they want to endorse moral decision-making in general, which they couch in the following terms: "Future [artificial] moral agents may consider a broader array of proposals, objections, and supporting evidence than a human agent can, and thereby, perhaps, select a more satisfactory course of action than many humans."[166] Unlike Arkin, who has a very narrow scope for what he calls ethical behavior, Wallach and Allen attempt to factor in the complexity of ethical deliberation, as well as what they call *suprarational faculties*, meaning moral emotions and intuitions. They attempt to merge both top-down and bottom-up approaches in particular. Wallach and Allen reach the conclusion that a top-down approach is not a feasible solution to the question of how to implement ethics. On the other hand, a bottom-up approach with regard to machines in areas of ethical decision-making entails that there are no general rules that could stop the machine, even if its operations might be harmful. Moreover, this kind of approach is hard to implement in complex scenarios and can only be used safely if the goal is very clear.[167] For that reason, Wallach and Allen propose to merge both of the paradigms into one comprehensive, virtue ethical complex.[168] In the authors' view, virtue ethics does blend in well with connectionism or artificial neural networks because both theories put the stress on the actual training within a concrete situation rather than on developing abstract rules. The overall idea is that robots could learn to simulate moral behavior analogous to that of humans.[169] In contrast to Arkin, they attempt to focus on an analogue to human deliberation and decision-making and concentrate on an artificial agent called *learning intelligent distribution agent* (LIDA), a model of cognition that has been presented by

---

165. See Wallach and Allen, *Moral Machines*, 25–36.
166. Wallach and Allen, *Moral Machines*, 185.
167. See Wallach and Allen, *Moral Machines*, 113–14.
168. See Wallach and Allen, *Moral Machines*, 117–24. This is not the most common way to unite these two theories, which can be seen with regard to my description above. See 1.3 Overview of the argument.
169. See Wallach and Allen, *Moral Machines*, 117–24.

computer- and neuroscientists.[170] So far, the system has been developed on a theoretical level only and attempts to resemble human but not necessarily moral thinking, thereby referring to the idea of what is called general AI. In order to engage with its environment and to decide, the system passes through a cycle in which it determines what is situated in its surroundings. In the process of doing so, so-called *attention codelets* scan the environment and influence the artificial neural network to focus on some of the objects in its surroundings according to some preset (or by-training-gained) data. One of the objects eventually stands out and thus gains LIDA's attention. Then, other attention codelets bring their findings to the system's attention. According to the system's memory and the strength of the input, the system passes through several cycles to determine the most important influence, on which basis it plans a certain course of action. Subsequently, the system takes this action with respect to this very object. This model is based on the theory of mind developed by William James, who holds that humans make decisions by deciding between several options, a process through which they weigh up the pros and cons of every possibility and, after having ruled out unwanted possibilities, decide on one course of action.[171] Each attention codelet serves to represent one of these single negotiation processes, which in the end produces one decision. Wallach and Allen then propose to use LIDA to implement not only plain decision-making but also moral reasoning to some degree. The morally relevant information should be brought to the attention of LIDA as part of the existing attention codelets. In this context, the bottom-up approach, resembling the moral intuition of humans, is exerted by reference to a memory feature LIDA holds. That way, trained operations could be reinforced, while unusual operations would be suppressed. Nevertheless, the system can be trained in that way in new operations. Concurrently, top-down approaches could be implemented to set some general guidelines for the system, which come back to the system's attention via the attention codelets. In order to perform a strict imperative or prohibition, however, they need to be reinforced on a higher level. Moreover, as for the act of killing somebody, for instance, the system needs to be aware of the situation in which somebody could be killed and needs to differentiate between homicide, killing in warfare,

---

170. See Wallach and Allen, *Moral Machines*, 172.
171. See Wallach and Allen, *Moral Machines*, 176.

and killing in order to protect somebody from greater danger. Here, the attention codelets serve the purpose of depicting the specific context.[172]

In contrast to Arkin, who seems to have a more static procedure in mind, Wallach and Allen concentrate on bottom-up approaches to a higher degree. Consequently, their proposal seems more dynamic and adaptable to various situations. They aim to develop systems that resemble human thinking but aim to avoid errors humans usually make. However, as research indicates, AI might not be as impartial as is seems either: It all hinges on the underlying data. If the data represents biases, that is exactly what the system will reproduce.[173] Another problem that can be brought up here is that, even if the artificial neuronal network is trained in a very sensible way and biases in the data could somehow be reduced to a minimal amount, the question of whether the artificial device would operate in a way that can be anticipated by the operator still remains due to effects such as the black box phenomenon or unintended side effects.[174]

Yet another issue can be seen when James's work is reconsidered because in his study, James differentiates between five types of decision-making, whereas the procedure described above is only one, which he calls *reasonable type*. It is made when all arguments are clear and the agent has weighed every option. In the other cases mentioned by James, decisions lack this kind of quality either because of a scarcity of time or because this comprehensive deliberation could not clearly mark one option.[175] The question of what happens if LIDA does not properly finish its process of "deliberation" arises. On what basis could LIDA act then?

3.7.2.3 *Derek Leben's Moral Algorithm*

Yet another proposal has been made by the philosopher Derek Leben, who argues that contractarianism is the most promising philosophical thought to be implemented in autoregulative systems. Leben proceeds on the assumption that moral judgments are not arbitrary but follow some underlying universal rules, similar to grammatical rules, a thesis

172. See Wallach and Allen, *Moral Machines*, 182.

173. See Noble, *Algorithms of Oppression*. One example is the chatbot "Tay," that became a racist within only hours. See Graff, "Rassistischer Chat Roboter." I depict this problem in greater detail below. See 4.2.5 Algorithmic Bias.

174. See 4.2.4 Black Boxes and Unintended Side Effects.

175. See James, *Principles of Psychology II*, 522–35.

presented by John Mikhail, harking back to John Rawls's linguistic analogy.[176] He calls these underlying moral rules *moral grammar* because they are present in every moral decision-making process, just as grammar is present in every use of language without being considered consciously. This moral grammar exists in basic assumptions (such as "harm," "agent," "intend," etc.) that form greater patterns (such as *harmful battery*), which are then incorporated into legal norms.[177] Leben then recollects Darwin's evolutionary theory and zeroes in on the idea that moral thought is a by-product of human cooperation. Since there are algorithms that are able to play cooperation games and have therefore gained the ability to cooperate, it is likely that machines will also be able to infer moral rules because, as Leben states, "morality is cooperation."[178] The author then analyzes existing philosophical theories that have been considered to coincide with (moral) algorithmic decision-making, such as utilitarianism, libertarianism, deontic thought, and virtue ethics. In his view, all of them fall short of resolving moral issues sufficiently, while only contractarianism would be an appropriate solution because it strikes a balance between top-down and bottom-up approaches and might therefore avoid the blind spots the other theories retain.[179]

According to Leben, contractarianism contains three main parts: *self-centered players* who have to cooperate with each other; *primary goods* that every player equally longs for, such as life, opportunity, health, and essential resources; and the so-called *maximin*, which is the way the players decide to distribute their equally wanted goods by optimizing the worst outcome.[180] In a next step, the author merges philosophical thought with technology, referring to a chess engine. With the help of a decision tree, the possible decisions and their outcomes are elucidated in order to determine which decision would entail which outcomes. Then, the single outcome is evaluated to ascertain the best result. Leben admits that it might not be easy to quantify primary goods, so they can only be estimated and need to be updated by the single player according to their current individual state.[181] With regard to a moral dilemma in autoregulative driving, for example, an approach favoring contractarianism would

176. See Mikhail, *Elements of Moral Cognition*.
177. See Leben, *Ethics for Robotics*, 7–24.
178. See Leben, *Ethics for Robotics*, 25–41.
179. See Leben, *Ethics for Robotics*, 42–58.
180. See Leben, *Ethics for Robotics*, 59–75.
181. See Leben, *Ethics for Robotics*, 76–96.

select a course that optimizes the worst harm-scenario. This means that, as the author poses, not only the mere sum of harm is added (as it would be in utilitarianism) but the circumstances, as the need for protection of the single traffic participant is taken into account so that more fatal collisions could eventually be avoided.[182] Finally, Leben turns to autoregulative systems used in the police and military. His main argument is that machines could help to bypass the bias humans have and therefore might save lives. Autoregulative weapons systems in service of the police, which he calls police bots, he imagines to be inactive until somebody uses a kind of buzzword to wake them up. The system would then figure out who did what to whom and prevent the wrongdoer from performing their action. The bot would have to use as little violence as possible, according to the rule that it should harm the wrongdoer only to the same degree that they are to harm the victim. This is in line with contractarianism because the basic goods would be guaranteed to the perpetrator as well, at least as long as they did not take them from the victim. Leben is confident that a system equipped with sufficient data would be able to determine who was the wrongdoer and who was the victim. It would also not need to gather too much data from its environment because it would be inactive until it was activated by the particular buzzword.

With respect to autoregulative functions in military context, the author is much more tenuous, since there has already been a lot of public criticism regarding that topic. However, he advocates for autoregulation at least to a certain degree because he expects that more lives would be spared. This pertains not only to the lives of the soldiers who no longer need to attend the battlefield or risk their mental health by operating lethal drone strikes but also to the lives of enemy soldiers and civilians because autoregulative systems might be better at determining potential threats and neutralizing enemy soldiers without taking their lives. He exemplifies this with weapons that would refuse to kill when directed to a civilian or noncombatant. In that way, he concludes, massacres could be warded off.[183]

Leben's approach stands out because he attempts to apply one philosophical concept, namely contractarianism, to machines. This is convincing to the extent that he makes clear why he presumes contractarianism to be the most promising philosophical approach and that he illustrates

---

182. See Leben, *Ethics for Robotics*, 97–115.
183. See Leben, *Ethics for Robotics*, 130–45.

how this thought could be implemented. However, there are some basic assumptions that seem highly controversial. First, it is very unclear how an anticipated police bot could manage to find out who did what to whom because it lacks this kind of situational awareness. If, for the sake of the argument, we assert that it would be able to differentiate between wrongdoer and victim, the wrongdoer could still argue to the contrary and the system would not be able to discern the truth. The bot would only have the chance to find out what really happened if it had perceived the situation prior to the emergency call. This, in turn, would be opposed to the principle of not gathering an extensive amount of data. His assessment of autoregulative functions in the military also seems unconvincing because the assumption that such a system would spare the lives of civilians is profoundly questionable, since it is currently unclear how the system might be able to differentiate between civilians and soldiers. In summary, Leben's proposal is elaborated with respect to contractarianism, but is less compelling regarding the possibilities (autoregulative) machines pose. In my opinion, it is also unclear who would have need of a weapon that denies its own purpose for moral reasons in the case of an emergency. Although this sounds like a very judicious thought, I doubt that anybody would be interested in such a weapon from a tactical point of view, at least in violent scenarios such as war.[184]

3.8 CONCLUSION

All things considered, the described considerations are proposals to deal philosophically, and to some degree technologically, with the problems autoregulative systems raise, namely that they cannot deliberate and act ethically and that moral thinking should be integrated into the decision-making processes of the machine at the same time. They do so on a very different level, though. While anthropomorphic language can be seen as an attempt to bridge the gap between humans and machines in linguistic terms, the idea that artificial entities can indeed be seen as artificial moral

---

184. While this seems an odd proposal in military and even police contexts, it might be helpful for regulating private uses of weapons. Accordingly, a hunting gun could be programmed only to shoot when directed at deer, but when a person was targeted, it would overwrite this input. This seems not only reasonable but also feasible because a technical device can already distinguish humans from animals, as can be seen at DoDAAM's Super aEgis II. See Boulanin and Verbruggen, *Mapping the Development of Autonomy in Weapon Systems*, 44–47. Some movie plots, however, would need to be rewritten under such circumstances.

agents addresses this difference but disregards it. The idea of implementing moral behavior into machines, finally, aims at emulating human ethical deliberation technologically. In doing so, the various proposals approach this problem in different manners. While Arkin zeroes in on military uses and concentrates on the implementation of relatively narrow operational rules, Wallach and Allen and Leben are broader in their scope or even hold back regarding autoregulative functions in weaponry but assume some sort of moral reckoning capability in machines.[185] From all of this, the following conclusion can be drawn.

First, I am very doubtful about the moral capabilities of machines. Even if it were possible to implement basic moral or legal rules, that would not mean that the device itself could act morally, or rather ethically, especially with regard to deontic thought where the focus rests on the person's intentions.[186] The observation made by Deborah Johnson stands out in that regard, namely that machines are indeed moral because they are part of and influence our forms of life. They have, however, no actual moral agency because they cannot act in the proper sense of the word.[187] This is also the reason why I propose to use the term "autoregulation" instead of technological "autonomy." In that way, the (still) remaining difference between humans and machines is highlighted, and at the same time, it points to the circumstance where an autoregulative device is still dependent on an autonomous agent. The particular merit a human has in contrast to an algorithm is that they can deliberate profoundly, taking into account not only somewhat narrow (preset) patterns but a comprehensive picture of the whole scenario with at least some of its political, legal, or ethical consequences. Yet, taking into account the anthropomorphic connotations that terms such as technical "autonomy," artificial "intelligence," and machine "learning" conjure up, there is a high chance that humans project their own capabilities—that is, ethical reasoning—onto machines. Since machines compute and reckon in a very different way than humans think and judge, there is no reason to believe that machines can come to ethically sound decisions on their own terms.[188] This, however, does not mean that the basic rules humans perceive as moral cannot be implemented into technology. In fact, there

185. See Leben, *Ethics for Robotics*, 6.
186. See 2.2.2 Kant or Autonomy as Rational Agency.
187. See Johnson, "Computer Systems."
188. See 3.3 Reckoning and Judgment; Nida-Rümelin and Weidenfeld, *Digitaler Humanismus*, 82–89.

Autonomy and Moral Agency in Machines

are always moral issues connected to technological devices. The design of a device, for example, is not confined to mere aesthetics, perfection, and simplicity[189] but also has an important impact on its use, as Alex Leveringhaus has demonstrated.[190] This serves to indicate that technology cannot only be used in a more or less appropriate way, but also that the design of the device has an impact on its use. That also entails that ethics is already part of the undertaking, even if it may not be there in a very reasonable way.[191]

Given the findings that humans can be seen as agents and autonomous and artificial entities cannot —at least not to the same degree— the claim for human agency in a human–machine collaboration seems decisive. This thought is also encapsulated in an argument Alex Leveringhaus brings forward in his book *Ethics and Autonomous Weapons* (2016). His argument is built on the notion that artificial agency is not coextensive with human agency, mainly because humans have the option "to do otherwise,"[192] which in the context of weaponry means not to shoot. He writes:

> Unless re-programmed, the machine *will* engage the targeted person upon detection. Killing a person, however, is a truly existential choice that each soldier needs to justify before his own conscience. Sometimes it can be desirable not to pull the trigger, even if this means that an otherwise legitimate target survives. Mercy and pity may, in certain circumstances, be the right guide to action.[193]

What is of importance in this argument is that Leveringhaus makes the case against artificial agency because humans are oriented toward norms and virtues, while the machine is not. This applies the argument made by Taylor as he distinguished between human and artificial agency:[194] Because humans orient themselves to greater goals, they might change their course of action even in war. Leveringhaus has backed away

---

189. Against Sarah Spiekermann's description of the values Steve Jobs represents with Apple. See Spiekermann, *Digitale Ethik*, 59.

190. See Leveringhaus, *Ethics and Autonomous Weapons*, 34–38.

191. A lot of contemporary ethics take into account precisely that problem, see for example: Spiekermann, *Digitale Ethik*; Hancock, "Teleology for Technology."

192. Leveringhaus, *Ethics and Autonomous Weapons*, 89.

193. Leveringhaus, *Ethics and Autonomous Weapons*, 92.

194. Taylor, "What Is Human Agency?" I refer to Taylor in 2.3 Humans as Moral Agents.

from his own argument in a subsequent article, pointing out that the operator of a system is already very distanced from the battlefield and in an overall situation where reconsideration and alteration are hard to carry out. From that perspective, maintaining agency seems to be a problem not only pertaining to autoregulation but also to less automized technology.[195] However, even though the problem does not refer solely to autoregulative devices, this does not mean that human agency can be done away with. In my opinion, therefore, the argument of human agency is still a valid point. This is not so much because the battlefield is the most plausible place to show mercy but rather because artificial entities cannot act in the full sense of the word. This entails that the idea of deploying an autoregulative device in order to make warfare more humane and moral is flawed from the outset. Returning to the argument Leveringhaus brought forward against his own reasoning—meaning that the situation in the battlefield hinders processes of reflection and reconsideration—it is possible to turn the question on its head: What would be necessary to maintain (human) agency in the battlefield, and how can technologies contribute to that?

Two conceptual aspects stand out in that regard. On the one hand, there is the crucial question of the ways in which human control can and should be exercised over the system in order to maintain (moral) agency. I will elaborate on this problem in the next chapter and with regard to the collaboration of humans and machines. On the other hand, and in close connection to this, there is the issue of how responsibility for the outcome of a (lethal) attack can be ensured, a problem I will also address below.[196]

As for the idea that morality might be implemented into machines, I want to mention three concluding thoughts before turning to the interaction of humans and machines. First, even though the idea of implementing a moral decision by means of a decision-making loop seems feasible at first glance, problems arise when we take a closer look. This is because the cycle itself is made of different decisions, so the single life-and-death decision constitutes the result of the target cycle as a whole. If one part of this decision-making chain is biased or flawed, the overall result is also flawed. For that reason, it is important that humans not only react according to the machine's suggestion but that they have insight into how this decision has been made and on what basis the machine

---

195. See Leveringhaus, "Morally Repugnant Weaponry?" 484.
196. See 6.5 Responsibility.

targets a specific objective. This is crucial for technological reasons because the machine lacks real-life experience and might therefore misconstrue the behavior of a specific target. Here, the perception of both entities—human and machine—might enhance the overall performance qualitatively because the machine can gather more information than a human could and therefore factor in issues humans might overlook, while only humans can make sense of this information. Concerning moral decisions, this is even more important because morality is about how to conduct life and therefore a certain understanding of what life is seems to be indispensable at each step of the decision-making-cycle. In practice, however, there might hardly be enough time to consider every single piece of information, so there might be an imperative to automate at least some of these steps.

Second, and with regard to the implementation of moral boundaries into machines, it is still unclear to what extent a device that has no intentional understanding of a situation could be tricked into a certain pattern of behavior. This means that if a morally trained weapons system refrained from attacking graveyards, hospitals, or kindergartens, the other side could simply install their headquarters and military devices in such places and could not be defeated.

Third, as has already been seen with the three examples of implementing morality into machines, morals cannot easily be used in the singular, meaning that morals and systems of morality abound and that different people or groups hold different moral opinions. Of course, there are existing norms and laws of war that could be implemented in an autoregulated device, as Arkin proposes. However, different parties might use distinctive legal norms that could either be opposed to each other or, in the worst case, prey upon the fixed rules an autoregulated system holds and play the system, so eventually an ethical deliberation device of any kind, even if it existed, would turn out to be detrimental. This might lead to a situation where the system is overwritten in the moment of its deployment by a human and is then no longer constrained by any ethical rule: a situation where neither control nor responsibly would be exerted.

To conclude, the main question is not that of how we can implement morality into machines but of how we can deal with and deploy technology in a way that endorses the overall performance of the human–machine system so that humans can contribute their moral agency. To answer this question, the interaction of machines and humans needs to be addressed, an issue I will turn to in the following chapter.

4

Human–Machine Interaction

EVERY DAY, HUMANS PERFORM tasks that involve the use of complex technology, and the world we live in relies on technology to a very high degree. An extensive body of research is done in order to scrutinize the ways in which humans and machines interact and what this entails.[1] In this chapter, it is my objective to determine how the human–machine interaction emerges in the case of autoregulative weapons systems in order to determine the normative scenarios and consequences if force is used that way. To accomplish this goal, it is crucial to delineate how humans and machines work together and what influences their collaboration. I will argue, first, that human–machine interaction is crucial for the problem under consideration and that, second, this interaction is characterized by several severe shortcomings that make the deployment of autoregulative weapons systems problematic from an ethical perspective. In doing so I will, as I depicted below,[2] take a stance that puts humans and machines in a very close relationship.

This might not be apparent at first glance because the very definition of an autoregulative device seems to rule out human interference. This thought, however, is flawed due to an anthropomorphic

---

1. There is a whole research area of science and technology studies, for instance, dedicated to such questions on a societal level, researching the nexus between research, technology, and society. See Niewöhner et al., "Einleitung," 9. On a more individual level, the research area of human–computer interaction draws mainly on four divergent disciplines, which are human factors/ergonomics, information systems, computer science, and library and information science in order to find out how humans and machines collaborate successfully. See Grudin, "Introduction," xxviii.

2. See 2.1 Connecting humans and machines.

misunderstanding of the technology. A machine cannot operate completely on its own because somebody has to provide data for algorithmic systems, even if they operate unsupervised. Primarily by determining the aim of the systems task, the human interferes with the device in an eminent way, even if it might not be in real time. Accordingly, there is human involvement from the outset and thus a machine that operates in an autoregulative mode is still part of a human–machine interaction. This is even more the case if we consider not the single autoregulative device but rather autoregulative functions that might be deployed within a system of systems or a swarm. This raises the issue of the extent to which it is safe, reasonable, and responsible to employ machines in an autoregulative fashion. Vice versa, the artifact used by humans also influences humans themselves, for instance, because humans have different options for employing the device, which might also influence their volition.[3] This, in turn, calls into question what influences humans to act in which way and how it is possible to raise their situational awareness via the artifact. I will navigate through this topic by, first, introducing the paradigm of *joint cognitive systems,* which is one approach in the field of cognitive systems engineering, as I critically review the aims and methods of this approach in general (4.1) and describe generic problems that go hand in hand with increasingly automated technology (4.2). Subsequently, I will introduce a possible answer to these problems called adaptive or adaptable automation (4.3), until I turn the issue of human control (4.4), and finally draw a conclusion (4.5).

4.1 JOINT COGNITIVE SYSTEMS

The interaction between humans and machines is part of the overall discussion of how a human collaborates with other parts of a system, addressed mainly in the field of *ergonomics and human factors.* It therefore consists of three main interacting factors, which are physical, organizational, and cognitive. Classically, the interaction between human and computer is situated between organizational and cognitive factors.[4] The concept of joint cognitive systems is based on that assumption and defines cognitive systems as follows:

    3. See Latour, *Pandora's Hope,* 178–80.
    4. See International Ergonomics Association, "What Is Ergonomics?" Additionally, to the extent that robots have to interact with humans on a physical level, such physical factors will also have to be considered.

> A cognitive system produces "intelligent action," that is, its behavior is goal oriented, based on symbol manipulation and uses knowledge of the world (heuristic knowledge) for guidance. Furthermore, a cognitive system is adaptive and able to view a problem in more than one way. A cognitive system operates using knowledge about itself and the environment, in the sense that it is able to *plan* and *modify* its actions on the basis of that knowledge. It is thus not only data driven, but also concept driven. Man is obviously a cognitive system. Machines are potentially, if not actually, cognitive systems. An MMS [Man-Machine-System] regarded as a whole is definitely a cognitive system.[5]

Following that, a machine is not a cognitive system in itself but only in combination with a human. The machine part can enhance or impede the overall performance because it may collaborate with humans in a more or less successful way. However, it cannot perform an action or set an objective from within.

The concept of joint cognitive systems serves the purpose of this book, as it is based on the assumption that humans and machines can work together effectively for the sake of solving convoluted tasks. It is a special approach associated with systems engineering.[6] In contrast to other models of engineering, the approach of joint cognitive systems emphasizes dynamic collaboration between humans and machines as well as the outcome of such a joint venture. Accordingly, the focus is put on humans and machines as a joint system. This necessitates that the machine is more than just a tool of humans. In working together, machines and humans influence each other, reshape patterns of behavior, adapt, and are altogether entwined with one another. Bearing this in mind, technology has a strong social impact because humans are not only working with a specific device but are also present in various stages of a machine's existence, from the first development, its verification, and its use for a certain purpose, to maintenance,[7] while all of these factors influence how humans finally interact with the machine.

---

5. Hollnagel and Woods, "Cognitive Systems Engineering," 589.

6. This method does not restrict its view to the use of a certain artifact but takes into account a larger scale, thereby integrating different "elements, or parts," such as "people, hardware, software, facilities, policies, and documents." NASA, *Systems Engineering Handbook*, 3.

7. See Hollnagel and Woods, *Joint Cognitive Systems*, 3.

Human–Machine Interaction

Considering the aforementioned critique of the term "autonomy" and its anthropomorphic implications, a disclaimer needs to be added right at the outset. While some scholars within the framework of joint cognitive systems tend to call the computational side of the collaboration the e-partner or agent,[8] I will refrain from using this terminology because it again invokes an anthropomorphism. One objective of this thesis, however, it is to mark the difference between both entities so that the joint venture is not jeopardized by a flawed imagination. I will therefore call the technological part of the collaboration "machine," or "computational/technological (part of the) system." Nonetheless, what is intended is the image of a close collaboration between machine and human, which goes beyond regarding the machine as the mere tool. In its transcendental character, it rather co-constitutes the way humans interact with the machine.

That said, I will now turn to the concept of joint cognitive systems, which was introduced by Erik Hollnagel and David D. Woods in the 1980s. Since then, research has scrutinized the role human and machine play in collaboration and how they influence each other.[9] The primary objective within this frame is to depict the ways in which humans and machines interact, and in which humans relate to machines, in more detail and thus more accurately. Joint cognitive systems are therefore in disagreement with several features of what the authors call the classical view.[10] In this classical perspective, humans and machine are considered as distinct entities that are related by an interface through which they communicate. The focus is on the single device or human and their discrete actions, which are seen mainly as reaction in the wake of an input-output model that underlies both human and machine functionality. Applying such a model also leads to a mechanistic image of humans because humans and machines are then described in similar terms. Yet, such a model ultimately blurs the difference between both entities, even though they are described distinctly.[11] In contrast, the joint cognitive systems approach puts the stress on the joint performance, thereby regarding the single action as connected to a flow of interrelated actions by humans and operations by the machine serving a certain end. Most

---

8. See de Greef, *ePartners for Dynamic Task Allocation and Coordination*; Neerincx and Grant, "Evolution of Electronic Partners."
9. For example, de Greef, *ePartners for Dynamic Task Allocation and Coordination*.
10. See Hollnagel and Woods, *Joint Cognitive Systems*, 16–18.
11. See Hollnagel and Woods, *Joint Cognitive Systems*, 42.

importantly, machines and humans are not merely seen as separate entities; their concerted action is considered. Among the resulting consequences, I want to highlight two that are most relevant for my discussion, which are cognition and control. While scholars of the classical perspective have been concerned with the problem of the extent to which a technical system can be called cognitive,[12] this problem is sidelined with the perspective of the joint cognitive systems approach. In this concept, the emphasis is put on the joint action, and since there is a human involved, cognition is included.[13] This also pertains to the discussion of the anthropomorphic misconception of technology going hand in hand with the use of advanced technology, as I depicted above,[14] and seems to be a viable solution because there is no need to describe in detail the respect in which technology can be "intelligent" or "autonomous"; it simply takes these characteristics from the human part(s) of the joint action.

The same remains valid regarding control and therefore liability. If the focus is on the joint action and the consequence of it is decisive, it is clear from the outset that humans have to be in charge, since they set the purpose, the rules, and the objective of a joint action.[15] Yet, this should not hide the fact that the outcome of such a collaboration is unpredictable to some degree. This is due to human involvement but also to more and more complex technology that can result in unintended side effects.[16] For the purpose of this book, this means that a machine is always integrated into some kind of human–machine interaction, though some functions may operate autoregulatively. While a human can act autonomously, set their own purpose, and determine their way of achieving a certain objective, a machine lacks this kind of freedom and relies on the autonomy of humans. It is therefore important to ensure that humans maintain their control (in general), otherwise the system would not be able to work safely.

---

12. Such as the view of the physical symbol system theory, which Newel and Simon suggest. They hold that humans and machines work by similar patterns of intelligence, thereby producing, destroying, and modifying these patterns. Therefore, a machine can be called intelligent. See Newel and Simon, "Computer Science as Empirical Inquiry." Another view, expressed by Haugeland, has similar implications, thereby risking the reduction of humans to some sort of computational system. See Haugeland, *Artificial Intelligence*.

13. See Hollnagel and Woods, *Joint Cognitive Systems*, 22.

14. See 3 Autonomy and Moral Agency in Machines.

15. See Hollnagel and Woods, *Joint Cognitive Systems*, 23.

16. See Hollnagel and Woods, *Joint Cognitive Systems*, 23.

Before going into greater detail with respect to individual conditions that could jeopardize human control, it is important to understand the ways in which humans and machines work in order to comprehend the ways in which they collaborate effectively. This is crucial, and within the scope of the joint cognitive systems approach, because otherwise we risk misunderstanding what humans and machines are able to accomplish, and such a misjudgment could compromise the joint action.[17] In that regard, machines lack procedures of judgment, because they only have the means to reckon.[18] In order to maintain control of a system, however, the human part of the system needs to judge the situation, including anticipating possible incidents. Even though programs may suggest different possible actions more quickly, they cannot critically review them and find the most auspicious option.[19] To put it differently, in order to obtain the desired outcome, a joint system needs to build collaboration on the capabilities of each member, be it machine or human, using them in the most efficient way. Bearing in mind that humans develop artifacts for their purposes and use them to accomplish goals they develop in advance, it seems obvious that humans should be in control of the joint system, though this may exclude particular (computational) operations in which the machine surpasses humans. Control, within this scope, can be defined as "the ability to direct and manage the development of events, and especially to compensate for disturbances and disruptions in a timely and effective manner."[20] This entails having the capability to influence the outcome in a desired way, but also having the necessary means to get the system back on track.

At this point, the question of what happens if human loses control and "the machine controls the human" arises.[21] Such a situation might occur due to "lack of time, lack of knowledge, lack of competence, [or] lack of resources."[22] A system is out of control if there is not (sufficient) time to engage with occurring problems; if the system does not know how to cope with an upcoming situation; if the operator is unable to deal properly with an event—either because they were not trained for it or because they simply do not know how to handle such an event; or if, for

17. See Hollnagel and Woods, *Joint Cognitive Systems*, 67.
18. See 3.3 Reckoning and Judgment.
19. See Hollnagel and Woods, *Joint Cognitive Systems*, 46.
20. Hollnagel and Woods, *Joint Cognitive Systems*, 136.
21. Hollnagel and Woods, *Joint Cognitive Systems*, 23.
22. Hollnagel and Woods, *Joint Cognitive Systems*, 75.

An Ethical Evaluation of Lethal Functions in Autoregulative Weapons Systems

whatever reason, the system is short of supply. Vice versa, an adequate availability of these conditions would provide a situation where a joint system can work properly. In order to do so, all of the conditions need to be fulfilled. If there is not sufficient supply or the knowledge to deal with a problem, one could have an eternity and still not be able to deal with the situation properly.[23] This can be encapsulated from the operator's view in two opposing situations. In the first case, there is too much information for the given amount of time (information input overload). In the second case, too little information is in place (information input underload). Instead of just reducing the complexity of a situation and thereby forcing the real world into a research lab that does not exist, it seems more promising to deal with a complex scenario as it is, since otherwise the human part(s) of the system no longer understand what the machine part does and have therefore lost—at least to some extent—their control. This can be done by providing enough time to cope with a certain situation or by producing alternatives relevant to a particular action within a certain time frame.[24]

4.2 IMPLICATIONS OF AUTOMATIZATION

In addition to control in terms of time, knowledge, competence, and the relationship a human establishes with a nonhuman, their attitude toward the technological system is crucial. In the following section, I will delve into some details that human–machine interaction and autoregulative technology necessarily entail. This section serves to depict some of these characteristics. In doing so, I will show that technology is by no means objective, but deeply influenced by the biases it gains from the data that stem from human culture and forms of life. Moreover, I will demonstrate that humans are deeply influenced by the technology they work with and the imagery they use to make sense of that technology, so the issue of control is conceptualized in a bigger picture. To do so, I will first depict the importance of trust in a human–machine collaboration (4.2.1), before I turn to two intricate problems within this interaction. These problems are the out-of-loop performance problem (4.2.2), referring to the human being's inability to interfere with the machine in case of need, on the one hand and automation bias (4.2.3), meaning the tendency of

---

23. See Hollnagel and Woods, *Joint Cognitive Systems*, 75–78.
24. See Hollnagel and Woods, *Joint Cognitive Systems*, 78–91.

humans to follow the technological system's advice even against their better judgment, on the other hand. Subsequently, I will turn to two problems connected to AI and autoregulation. The first is the occurrence of unintended side effects due to the black box problem, meaning that humans cannot know for sure what output the algorithm produces from a certain input, especially if neural networks of deep learning are concerned (4.2.4). Second, I will elaborate on algorithmic bias, meaning the mirroring of humans' social biases in the algorithm (4.2.5).

4.2.1 How to Maintain Control? The Crucial Role of Trust

That being said, the amount of trust an operator places in the machine might affect the way they collaborate with the machine. This is because trust will guide the reliance of an operator,[25] while reliance is decisive for dealing with a machine. In other words, an operator needs to rely on a machine in order to collaborate with it. If they do not rely on the machine at all or if they rely on it insufficiently, they will *disuse* it. If, on the other hand, they rely on the machine too much, they will *misuse* it.[26] Both scenarios entail different consequences. If humans disuse a machine, they simply do not adopt the chances the (proper) use of a device entails, often due to experiencing a malfunction earlier.[27] Misuse will lead to several consequences that might interfere with the overall performance of the joint system and, in the worst case, cause a lack of control.

 Before I focus on these negative effects, I want to dwell on the crucial role of trust in automation and describe what factors influence the attitude of humans toward a machine with respect to trust. I will therefore refer to an article brought forward by John D. Lee and Katrina A. See. The authors proceed on the assumption that trust between humans is, at least to some degree, similar to the trust humans put in machines. However, there also happen to be three important differences between the two relationships. First, regarding human–human relationships, intentionality is a main aspect. If somebody behaves in a way that tells another human they are loyal, hold similar values, and so on, this will deeply influence

---

 25. See Lee and See, "Trust in Automation," 76. Trust is this context is defined as follows: "Trust [...] is the attitude that an agent will help achieve an individual's goal in a situation characterized by uncertainty and vulnerability."

 26. See Parasuraman and Riley, "Humans and Automation."

 27. See Lee and See, "Trust in Automation," 71–72; Parasuraman and Riley, "Humans and Automation," 244.

their trust in each other. A machine has no such inner qualities or virtues, therefore trust will be established in a different way. Second, a relationship between humans is symmetrical. This is especially important when it comes to responsibility. While an interpersonal team is expected to split their responsibility for a joint task equally, the responsibility for a human–machine collaboration would rest with the operator alone or at least to a higher degree than with the machine. This is in line with a study where people preferred to delegate a task to a human if they thought themselves not to be trustworthy (enough).[28] Third, relationships between humans and relationships between humans and machines evolve differently. In the first case, the relationship commences with a phase of reliability, then evolves to a stage of dependability, until it finally develops into a phase of faith. In comparison, a human–machine relationship might also occur the other way around.[29] This is important to note because a human might start their collaboration with a new machine with a very high level of trust, which is then lost if the machine turns out to have a flaw. This entails that working with a new device influences the level of trust and might lead to mis- or disuse.

Although it might not be possible to transfer all the knowledge gained from the study of interpersonal trust, some general insights may produce parameters to determine an appropriate level of trust. Three criteria with respect to the human collaborating with the machine stand out, which are *calibration, resolution,* and *specificity*. While calibration scrutinizes whether the machine's capabilities meet the human being's trust, resolution refers to the operator's ability to differentiate different modes of automation, and specificity describes the trust of the operator in a subset of an automated device. This can be summed up as follows:

> Good calibration, high resolution, and high specificity of trust can mitigate misuse and disuse of automation, and so they can guide design, evaluation, and training to enhance human-automation partnerships.[30]

This means that if the trust of the operator must be in line with the capabilities of the system, the operator has to differentiate between different modes of automation and know about different subsets of functions and modes. In order to achieve these outcomes, they have to be

---

28. See Lee and See, "Trust in Automation," 65–67.
29. See Lee and See, "Trust in Automation," 65–67.
30. Lee and See, "Trust in Automation," 56.

considered while designing a system, their impact needs to be evaluated, and the human needs to be trained properly in advance.[31] In addition to this, trust is not only guided by the machine itself but also relies on a human's personality traits, such as their self-confidence or their organizational and cultural background.[32]

Focusing on the machine, See and Lee mention three main factors influencing the level of trust, which are *performance*, *process*, and *purpose*. Performance refers to what an automated device does, while process identifies how it works, and purpose describes why it was developed in the first place. Therefore, an operator tends to trust that a machine that performs its task reliable, processes information in a way that is understandable, and serves a purpose communicated to the operator by the designer. If performance, purpose, and process are made sufficiently clear and meet the aim the operator wants to achieve, the operator will find the device trustworthy.[33]

Now, it becomes clear that trust in machines plays an eminent role in collaboration with the system but depends on parameters such as the machine's performance, process, and purpose, and also the operator's trust—more precisely, their trust's calibration, resolution, specificity, and some personal traits. In order to deal with this complex situation, researchers insist that approaches need to be developed to adjust the different influences of machines and humans. This means, on the one hand, constructing systems that operate reliably and transparently and whose objective given by the designer is clear and, on the other hand, training operators properly so they develop suitable calibration, high resolution, and high specificity of trust.

For the remainder of this section, I want to focus on some consequences misguided trust in machines can have, a topic broadly discussed in the scholarly debate.[34] Since it is beyond the scope of this book to

31. See Lee and See, "Trust in Automation," 55–56.
32. See Lee and See, "Trust in Automation," 56–58.
33. See Lee and See, "Trust in Automation," 59–60.

34. While Parasuraman and Riley discuss the role of the possible (mis-)uses of automation, Endsley and Kiris describe problems that entail the use of ever more automated technology as the out-of-the-loop performance problem, which is rooted mainly in the passive role to which the operator is assigned. Yet another proposal has been made by Sheridan and Parasuraman, in which the problems are clustered around possible incidents and accidents, while Sarter et al. focus on problems that have not been considered in the design phase. See Parasuraman and Riley, "Humans and Automation"; Endsley and Kiris, "Out-of-the-Loop Performance Problem"; Sheridan and

dwell at length at every proposal that has been made, I want to focus on two main problems that have been described as core problems in the wake of increasingly automated technology: the out-of-the-loop performance problem and automation bias.

4.2.2 The Out-of-the-Loop Performance Problem[35]

Research indicates that the automation of actions once solely undertaken by a human might entail an ongoing loss of competence as well as a reduced understanding of the processes of automation by which the program runs. Consequently, humans operating with the machine lose their ability to do so properly and, down the road, are operated by the machine instead of operating it.[36] Endsley and Kiris have described three implications that revolve around situational awareness and that constitute the out-of-the-loop performance problem. Situational awareness is defined by Endsley and Kiris as "the perception of elements in the environment within a volume of time and space, the comprehension of their meaning, and the projection of their status in the near future."[37] By this definition, situational awareness is crucial for collaborating with and maintaining control of a machine. A loss of situational awareness implies three problems. First, vigilance decreases while complacency increases. Second, the role of the operator shifts from performing an action actively to being a passive observer, which, third, results in a loss of competence and skills.[38] Here, the increased feeling of complacency is especially closely linked to the trust an operator puts in the system, meaning that if a human trusts a system to a high degree, they are inclined not to watch it vigilantly—all the more so if systems tend to operate very reliably.[39] Complacency re-

---

Parasuraman, "Human-Automation Interaction"; Sarter et al., "Automation Surprises." Described in: Bahner, "Übersteigertes Vertrauen in Automation."

35. The same problem was mentioned for the first time under the term "ironies of automation" by Lisanne Bainbridge as early as 1982. In her account, she describes that even highly automated systems still need human supervision and that supervising a machine is a highly demanding task, making the human operator prone to forget how to fulfill the work manually. See Bainbridge, "Ironies of Automation." The problem is still unresolved. See Baxter et al., "Ironies of Automation."

36. See de Greef, *ePartners for Dynamic Task Allocation and Coordination*, 22.

37. Endsley and Kiris, "Out-of-the-Loop Performance Problem," 382.

38. See Endsley and Kiris, "Out-of-the-Loop Performance Problem."

39. See Bahner, "Übersteigertes Vertrauen in Automation," 37; Mouloua et al., "Human Monitoring of Automated Systems," 19; Lee and See, "Trust in Automation."

sults from an overreliance on a system while monitoring. Moreover, this indicates that a human who might be good at executing tasks manually might be a poor passive observer, or at least that the passive task might be as onerous as the same task executed actively. This is counterintuitive to the idea that more automation helps the operator to do their task and leads to the assertion that "human operators of automated systems may have to work as hard or even harder, for they must watch the computers to do their work."[40] Furthermore, this whole process might lead to a situation where the operator loses their manual skills because there might be no need to keep practicing the manual performance. This is even more critical if new operators of systems are not even trained to handle the required manual task properly in the first place. As a result, the operator cannot take over the task in the case of a systems failure as easily as if they were used to doing the same task manually.[41] These effects need to be taken into consideration when automating highly complex systems.

4.2.3 Automation Bias

Another effect of overreliance and overtrust in automated systems is automation bias. It is closely linked to complacency[42] and occurs while working with an assistant system.[43] It can be defined as "the tendency to use automated cues as a heuristic replacement for vigilant information seeking and processing"[44] and carries with it *omission* and *commission* problems. While omission refers to a situation where an operator overlooks a flaw in the system that has not been explicitly reported by the program, commission is linked to the compliance to the system's advice, which then turns out to be false.[45] Automation bias has been described in many research fields, and its primary source rests upon trust and self-confidence.[46] While operators with low self-confidence and high trust in the machine tend to rely too much on the machine, operators with

---

40. Mouloua et al., "Human Monitoring of Automated Systems," 2.
41. See Endsley and Kiris, "Out-of-the-Loop Performance Problem," 281–384.
42. See Goddard et al., "Automation Bias," 121–22.
43. See Bahner, "Übersteigertes Vertrauen in Automation," 40.
44. Mosier and Skitka, "Human Decision-Makers and Automated Decision Aids," 205. Seen in Bahner, "Übersteigertes Vertrauen in Automation," 40.
45. See Bahner, "Übersteigertes Vertrauen in Automation," 40.
46. See Goddard et al., "Automation Bias."

high self-confidence and little trust tend to do so less.[47] Another factor can be seen in multitasking demands. While exerting multiple tasks simultaneously, the operator tends to rely on the automation to a higher degree than if their only task is to monitor a system.[48] A study conducted by Michelle Yeh and Christopher. D. Wickens concerned with assisted targeting indicates that the operator tends to rely excessively on the technology, thereby not only overlooking possible flaws but also showing riskier behavior. Furthermore, operators tend to trust automation despite knowing that it is not reliable.[49] This finding has been observed in another study by Jennifer Elin Bahner, who found that commission faults do not only occur due to insufficient verification of information but can also be the result of informed decision-making, meaning that the operator is aware of the flaw, but still follows the system's advice.[50]

In summary, automation bias and the out-of-the-loop performance problem constitute serious issues regarding progressing automated technology. These issues need to be addressed and considered when developing, designing, and working with heavily automated systems that include autoregulative features. This is because an operator would have to decide when to use autoregulation, or at least monitor whether the use of an autoregulation mode by the automation had been deployed correctly.

4.2.4 Black Boxes and Unintended Side Effects

Another major problem when it comes to AI and autoregulation is the problem of the algorithm making use of the data by itself in finding patterns. These processes are very complex and not easily understandable for humans because they simply do not know for sure how the algorithm "learns" from the data—for instance, to differentiate cats from dogs—and on what features the algorithm bases its operations. This is also why it is hard or even impossible to explain what the algorithm is doing there, a problem referred to as *black box phenomenon*.[51] This is also the reason why nobody, not even the operator, can know for sure why the algorithm comes to a certain conclusion. To mitigate that problem, procedures to

---

47. See Lee and See, "Trust in Automation," 70–71.
48. See Lee and See, "Trust in Automation," 71.
49. See Yeh and Wickens, "Display Signaling in Augmented Reality."
50. See Bahner, "Übersteigertes Vertrauen in Automation," 145.
51. See Dignum, *Responsible Artificial Intelligence*, 29.

Human–Machine Interaction

explain how a certain outcome has been achieved have been introduced, such as in the *explainable artificial intelligence* approach. The idea is that even a layperson can understand how an algorithm trained with the help of machine learning produces a certain outcome.[52] Even though the exact definitions are under discussion, the main idea is that the algorithm reveals the procedures that lie behind a certain output to humans, so the humans working with the device can assess the value of this information. The problem, however, might still be that the algorithm does not understand any of the information it produces, and therefore the explanations, strictly speaking, do not explain but rather show how a certain output has been produced without giving an explanation of why.[53] Taken together, this means that in machine learning networks, not even the programmer of the algorithm can tell for sure how the machine reaches a certain outcome and that processes to mitigate that problem, such as the Explainable AI approach, conceal rather than weaken the issue. This is because they give ostensible explanations, while they in fact only show a causal chain.

On those grounds and connected to the problem that the algorithm has no understanding of the overall world they are part of, unintended side effects might occur. Such effects occur if a technological system does not apply the data it is trained on correctly to a certain scenario. To make clear what this entails, Nick Bostrom invented his paperclip thought experiment. He writes,

> It [...] seems perfectly possible to have a superintelligence whose sole goal is something completely arbitrary, such as to

---

52. See Vilone and Longo, "Notions of Explainability and Evaluation Approaches for Explainable Artificial Intelligence," 89. According to Vilone and Longo, there is an abundance of approaches attempting to solve this issue, which entails that there is no clear-cut definition of what exactly explainable AI is and what it entails. They, therefore, point to the need to define what exactly explainable AI must entail in their metaresearch and find that explainability can refer to two divergent approaches: On the one hand, there are approaches focusing on objective markers, such as transparency, correctability, efficiency, etc., while, on the other hand, there are approaches centering on humans, whose feedback is involved in assessing explainability. Here, as a rule, "explanations are effective when they help end-users to build a complete and correct mental representation of the inferential process of a given model," 97. Since understanding the technological procedures turns out to be decisive for working together with complex technology, explaining to the user how the algorithm produces a certain outcome is key, even though no conclusive definition and method exists so far. Yet, Vilone and Longer underscore that considering humans here is focal, because humans ultimately need to collaborate with the system, 89.

53. See Grünwald and Kehl, *Autonome Waffensysteme*, 61.

manufacture as many paperclips as possible, and who would resist with all its might any attempt to alter this goal. [...] This could result [...] in a superintelligence whose top goal is the manufacturing of paperclips, with the consequence that it starts transforming first all of earth and then increasing portions of space into paperclip manufacturing facilities.[54]

While this example describes a rather unlikely scenario, is makes the point very clearly: Since an algorithm does not understand what it is doing, it might operate in unanticipated ways. Indeed, similar problems occur when real algorithms are deployed, for instance, for detecting skin cancer. Generally, such an application is highly useful and already well established within medicine,[55] but some incidents have been described where the algorithm did not apply the data in the intended way, diagnosing rulers instead of cancer. This is due to the pictures the algorithm was trained with having a ruler next to the melanoma in order to show its size, while the same was not true for the healthy skin cells.[56] The problem is that the algorithm depends on the data on which it is trained. And if this data is flawed in a way humans cannot perceive of, then these flaws have repercussions on the trained algorithm. A similar problem pertaining to the underlying data is the problem known as algorithmic bias.

4.2.5 Algorithmic Bias

Another topic that has been discussed broadly in academia and in public discourse[57] is algorithmic bias, that is, the underlying biases an algorithm has resulting either from the data it is trained on, some underlying inherent malfunctions, or careless programming. In this sense, (algorithmic) bias "refer[s] to computer systems that *systematically* and *unfairly discriminate* against certain individuals or groups of individuals in favor of others."[58] The phenomenon has been known since 1976 when Joseph

---

54. Bostrom, "Ethical Issues in Advanced Artificial Intelligence."
55. See Dildar et al., "Skin Cancer Detection."
56. See Narla et al., "Automated Classification of Skin Lesions."
57. For the scholarly debate, see, for example, Friedman and Nissenbaum, "Bias in Computer Systems"; Lambrecht and Tucker, "Algorithmic Bias?"; Brayne, "Big Data Surveillance." For the public debate, see, for example, Condliffe, "Algorithmic Bias is Bad"; Dastin, "Amazon Scraps Secret AI Recruiting Tool that Showed Bias Against Women."
58. Friedman and Nissenbaum, "Bias in Computer Systems," 332. Emphasis original.

Human–Machine Interaction

Weizenbaum insinuated these kinds of processes when writing about the relation between the programmer and their program:

> A computer's successful performance is often taken as evidence that it or its programmer understand a theory of its performance. Such an inference is unnecessary and, more often than not, is quite mistaken. The relationship between understanding and writing thus remains as problematical for computer programming as it has always been for writing in any other form.[59]

The quote indicates that, similar to a text that contains the author's thoughts and biases, a computational program contains the programmer's thoughts and biases. The problem can be illustrated with respect to policing: A human who is more likely to be under surveillance due to socioeconomic factors for instance, is more likely to be caught committing a crime. This will again raise their likelihood of being and staying under surveillance. In contrast, a similar human from another socioeconomic background might not be caught because the policing algorithms are simply not aware of these people or groups, thereby building a "self-perpetuating circle."[60] Especially when combined with autoregulative technology, such underlying patters pose severe problems because nobody could stop the system from making errors with fatal consequences in a very short amount of time. That is why it is crucial to address this topic and look for means of mitigating or even preventing this effect.

Algorithmic bias occurs for several reasons. First, it follows from preexisting biases that exist in society or institutions that infiltrate the algorithm, for example, when an algorithm is trained with data resulting from real-life scenarios that are already biased.[61] This is a severe problem because the algorithm has no flaw but operates in the way it should. The bias of the algorithm simply reflects an existing bias.[62] In a similar way, an algorithm might be biased by its designer, for instance, by choosing an already biased variable or by not taking into account data that contradict the designer's view, maybe even through intentional omission.[63] Biases might also occur with respect to the technology, for example, with regard to limits hard- and software pose or when data is transferred from the

---

59. Weizenbaum, *Computer Power and Human Reason*, 110–11.
60. Brayne, "Big Data Surveillance," 997.
61. See Friedman and Nissenbaum, "Bias in Computer Systems," 333–35.
62. See Baer, *Understand, Manage and Prevent Algorithmic Bias*, 51–57.
63. See Baer, *Understand, Manage and Prevent Algorithmic Bias*, 59–68.

societal world to computers, thereby shifting from quality to quantity. Finally, biases might occur when technology emerges and users get in touch with the algorithms, for instance, due to changing social background knowledge or values.[64]

Against this backdrop, it becomes clear that algorithms are neither objective nor unbiased, as they operate according to data that mirrors humans' forms of life, and they are programmed or designed by a human who transfers their own biases down into the technology. With respect to lethal technology, this might be a severe problem because different algorithms might target different objectives depending on the quality and quantity of data they are trained on as well as on the person that supervised the training. These underlying potential biases due to data, designer, or emergence need to be found and eliminated as far as possible in order to ensure the appropriate use of autoregulative functions. The human–machine interface is especially important in this respect because the operator might detect possible biases or even influence the machine to adopt their own biases.

It is possible to take several precautions in order to mitigate algorithmic bias. First, it is important that the operator of a system is aware of the fact that an algorithm might be biased and takes this into account when making a decision. This also applies to the operator deciding whether an autoregulative device is to be used. Humans working with the algorithm should bear in mind some general insights—such as the fact that algorithms operate more reliably if more data is provided, which means that in cases where there is not much data, it might be better to resort to other methods of decision-making.[65] The main challenge, however, seems to be how to generate data that is less biased. With regard to this, transparency is important because it is only possible to verify the operating principle in order to criticize and enhance it if an algorithm and its data are made transparent.[66] Another important suggestion is to include people from diverse social and cultural backgrounds in the development of an algorithm, as this might help to mitigate the implementation of biases into the algorithm.[67] Moreover, it might be helpful to establish (international recognized) regulations complying with the

---

64. See Friedman and Nissenbaum, "Bias in Computer Systems," 335–36.
65. See Baer, *Understand, Manage and Prevent Algorithmic Bias*, 115–16.
66. See IEEE: "Ethically Aligned Design," 183.
67. IEEE: "Ethically Aligned Design," 190.

aforementioned suggestions.[68] This is crucial because if an algorithm can be developed in a way that operates (almost) unbiased, it might also help to mitigate bias in human decision-making.[69] That way, an algorithm might be a useful means of reviewing the decision-making process and, together with a human mind, provide a sound groundwork for a (joint) decision. However, a biased algorithm in combination with automation bias might reverse this effect to the contrary because in such a case the operator would become the system's puppet. It is therefore important to note that both entities—humans and machines—may have biases and that a biased human might make decisions that are worse than the decisions requested by the machine. Moreover, it seems that introducing people from diverse backgrounds and transparency in the development phase, as well as the operator's vigilance toward these phenomena, might reduce the effects algorithmic biases have. This effect, however, does not necessarily occur, and a biased autoregulative algorithm equipped with lethal force and making decisions much faster than a human might wreak havoc if operating unsupervised.

That said, I consider algorithms to pose a great opportunity to enhance less biased decision-making in addition to human reasoning. This entails that the perception an algorithm contributes can be helpful to check a human-only decision, thereby potentially reducing bias. However, especially when lethal force is involved, the hazards might outweigh potential benefits, raising the question of what can be done to maintain control. One suggestion to alleviate this kind of difficulty is *adaptive automation*, a model I will discuss subsequently.

4.3 IMPLEMENTATIONS OF AUTOMATIZATION

As has been clarified above, a human collaborating with increasingly automated machines is prone to the out-of-the-loop performance problem, thereby risking becoming complacent, losing their manual skills, and following the machine's advice blindly. Research indicates that these problems decrease if phases of active control and manual task performance are embedded,[70] and adaptive or adaptable automation can be

---

68. IEEE: "Ethically Aligned Design," 199.

69. IEEE: "Ethically Aligned Design," 216; Baer, *Understand, Manage and Prevent Algorithmic Bias*, 118.

70. See Mouloua et al., "Human Monitoring of Automated Systems," 17.

seen as one way to address this problem. In his dissertation, Tjerk de Greef discusses how a joint cognitive system can collaborate when operating under high pressure. Particularly in hazardous contexts when humans work under a lot of stress, it is important to reduce ambiguity to a minimum. In scenarios of this kind, for example, when searching for survivors after an urban calamity such as an earthquake, human rescue workers tend to lose track of the buildings they have already searched, thereby losing precious time. By introducing a computer program, coordination and productivity might rise because the joint system stays on top of the situation.[71] Research conducted regarding aviation automation shows that mounting automation makes flying more safe, more reliable, and has positive effects on economy as well as comfort.[72] Based on this, de Greef seeks to install a setting where humans and machines collaborate dynamically. That means that, despite doing the same procedure in the same roles over and over again, the procedure should vary constantly depending on the circumstances and especially on the condition of the humans involved. In other words, under normal circumstances, humans would be in control of as many of the system's features as possible, while with mounting pressure, the system would take over more and more functions, so the human part(s) of the collaboration can concentrate on the most important tasks, a process labeled adaptive automation. The same would occur if the machine perceived that the human part(s) of the collaboration were no longer able to control the situation. The aim is to ensure that the joint action will be performed properly, notwithstanding extraordinary circumstances. Nevertheless, due to continuous training, the human operator should be able to take over the machine's tasks if it fails to operate correctly or if the pressure is high.[73] Such an undertaking also seems advisable for lethal contexts on the grounds that the demand for highly-trained personnel is constantly growing because, first, belligerent settings are becoming more and more asymmetric[74] and therefore more complex and, second, fewer people are employed due to staff reductions.[75]

Adaptive automation thereby incorporates the idea that automation is not simply twofold—meaning that there is an automated mode,

---

71. See de Greef, *ePartners for Dynamic Task Allocation and Coordination*, 18.
72. See Billings, *Human-Centered Automation Aviation*, 90.
73. See de Greef, *ePartners for Dynamic Task Allocation and Coordination*, 198.
74. See Münkler, *Die neuen Kriege*.
75. See de Greef, *ePartners for Dynamic Task Allocation and Coordination*, 73.

a manual mode, and nothing in between—but rather a continuum of intermediate stages that can be used for different tasks. That is why different tasks are automated to various degrees in a flexible way and in real time.[76] Mark Scerbo defines it as follows:

> In adaptive automation, the level or mode of automation or the number of systems that are automated can be modified in real time. Further, *both* the human and the machine share control over changes in the stage of automation.[77]

This definition is ambiguous to the extent that it does not determine who is in control of the actual stage of automation because two cases are possible. In one case, it is the machine controlling the degree of automation based on the information it gathers from its environment, while in the other case, it is the human deciding which level of automation is to be used according to the degree of their self-reflection. Therefore, it is preferable to differentiate between two approaches: adaptive and adaptable automation.

> Adaptive automation refers to an approach that dynamically divides work between humans and machines based on a machine decision to reallocate work," while "adaptable automation refers to a mechanism where a human decides on the reallocation of tasks.[78]

Both paradigms face different challenges and will be depicted in turn. Adaptive automation can be described as follows. First, humans and machines have a different approach to a special environment or event. This is represented with the help of an interface such as a screen. While humans observe the machine's "view" and the environment, whether with their own eyes or by means of a camera, the machine perceives the setting with the aid of its detectors. In addition, it monitors humans, ascertaining their physical situation. In a second step, the two representations of the scene are compared to each other. If they are consistent, the machine could react to them with autoregulation, while objects that are not assessed in the same way by both entities would remain under the direct control of humans. This procedure might vary depending not only on the context of the situation—such as air or sea—but also

---

76. See Mouloua et al., "Human Monitoring of Automated Systems," 16–17.

77. Scerbo, "Theoretical Perspectives on Adaptive Automation," 108. Emphasis original.

78. de Greef, *ePartners for Dynamic Task Allocation and Coordination*, 22.

An Ethical Evaluation of Lethal Functions in Autoregulative Weapons Systems

according to individual preassigned parameters. Adaptive automation is thus meant to provide a formula that copes with the out-of-the-loop performance problem as well as with an operator's overload.[79] In order to do so, the system needs to determine the degree to which humans need computational support. De Greef addresses this topic with a hybrid model that adapts to the operator's performance due to their response time as well as their overall view of the situation and to the operator's cognition, meaning the mental work they are expected to accomplish in a special scenario. This implies that an operator is anticipated to need less cognition to deal with a clear situation—for example, if all or nearly all of the combat units screened are classified as friendly—and that they are expected to be in need of a higher degree of cognition if the screened units are suspicious or even hostile. These aspects are factored in to determine the effective workload and to adjust the suitable amount of automation.[80] These assumptions are then validated under real-life circumstances within their context.[81]

One major problem connected to adaptive automation is the observation or even surveillance of the operator. To determine whether the operator's workload is adequate, the system needs to keep track of the operator, which can be done either by evaluating their overall performance, by determining levels of workload in advance, or through biopsychometrics.[82] Each of these approaches entail their own technological problems, which is why de Greef favors a hybrid model. One issue remains, though, which is the surveillance function the system needs to exert in order to perform its tasks. This means that the system constantly gathers all sorts of data to determine the operator's workload, be it biopsychometrics or response time. This data can then be compared not only in various scenarios but also with different operators. This might lead to a situation where a great amount of the operator's corporal data was revealed to the machine. Therefore, everyone who could access the data could gain knowledge about the operator and would be able

---

79. See de Greef, *ePartners for Dynamic Task Allocation and Coordination*, 30–53.

80. See de Greef, *ePartners for Dynamic Task Allocation and Coordination*, 55–69.

81. See de Greef, *ePartners for Dynamic Task Allocation and Coordination*, 71–94. In the remainder of his thesis, de Greef addresses the problem of teams that work together but are separated by time and space and suggests a special type of observability display as solution to this problem. Since this issue is not in the focus of my interest, I will refrain from illustrating it.

82. See Scerbo, "Theoretical Perspectives on Adaptive Automation," 108–9.

to compare them to other operators. This entails the question of what should be done with the data gathered.[83]

Another crucial subject is who maintains control of the overall system if the task and workload of the human part(s) of the collaboration are determined by a machine.[84] For that reason, the implementation of adaptable automation has been proposed. The general mode of operation does not change radically within adaptable automation, but the system does not necessarily need to gather as much data about the operator and the control would remain by the controller unambiguously. Although this seems reasonable at first glance, research indicates that this approach might not solve the problem because, in times of high workload, the operator might not be able to determine their own workload appropriately or they might simply be too busy to hand over control to the system.[85] Accordingly, it seems reasonable—at least from an engineering point of view—to transfer this kind of control in certain scenarios to the machine, for instance, in cases where the resources of the human part(s) of the collaboration would not meet the required capabilities, such as if time and knowledge were too limited.[86]

To sum up, even though adaptive or adaptable automation might seem to be a reasonable way to mitigate the problem of human control, it still faces the conceptual issue that a machine cannot judge but only reckon and that the computational part of the human–machine collaboration remains dependent on the human part. Accordingly, the problem of control is still unresolved even by means of adaptive or adaptable automation.

4.4 MEANINGFUL HUMAN CONTROL

Since 2014, representatives of several countries participate in an expert group, the Group of Governmental Experts (GGE), hosted by the Convention of Certain Conventional Weapons (CCW) at the UN in Geneva in order to discuss the development and deployment of autoregulative weapons systems. It is not my objective to unravel this intricate process

---

83. With respect to robots, this has been addressed by Steil, see Steil, "Roboterlernen ohne Grenzen?"
84. See Scerbo, "Theoretical Perspectives on Adaptive Automation," 110–11.
85. See Scerbo, "Theoretical Perspectives on Adaptive Automation," 110–11.
86. See Inagaki, "Automation and the Cost of Authority," 169.

with its political implications, motivations, and ramifications for the different players. It is rather my intent to wrap up the status of the current debate and to introduce the term and concept of meaningful human control, which has not only proven to be the focus of the political debate but was also incorporated into other fields of research as well, even though an international binding solution with regard to autoregulative functions in weapons systems has not been reached so far.[87]

In 2013, the NGO Article 36 brought forward the concept of meaningful human control.[88] Heather M. Roff and Richard Moyes have made clear what is meant by this concept by fleshing out what constitutes the basis for their premises, which are

> 1. That a machine applying force and operating without any human control whatsoever is broadly considered unacceptable.
> 2. That a human simply pressing a "fire" button in response to indications from a computer, without cognitive clarity or awareness, is not sufficient to be considered "human control" in a substantive sense.[89]

For the authors, this entails predictability, reliability, transparency, the certainty that the user has all the information needed, the certainty that the human acts in a timely manner and has sufficient time to react, and that accountability is guaranteed.[90] In 2018, the International Panel on the Regulation of Autonomous Weapons (iPRAW) extended this concept by assessing the role of IHL because taking precautions depends highly on context, which means it cannot be done by the machine on its own.[91] Therefore, this group demands that humans make the target decision, whereby they yield control technologically, meaning by design, as well as operationally, meaning in use. This entails that the system allows humans to monitor both the environment and its own functions (control

---

87. For further information on the idea and its development, mainly within the political debate, see 1.1 The Phenomenon: Autoregulation in Weapons Systems.

88. See Dahlmann, "Militärische Robotik als Herausforderung für das Verhältnis von menschlicher Kontrolle und maschineller Autonomie," 176–77.

89. Roff and Moyes, "Meaningful Human Control, Artificial Intelligence and Autonomous Weapons," 1.

90. See Roff and Moyes, "Meaningful Human Control, Artificial Intelligence and Autonomous Weapons," 2–3; Dahlmann, "Militärische Robotik als Herausforderung für das Verhältnis von menschlicher Kontrolle und maschineller Autonomie," 177.

91. See iPRAW, "Focus on Human Control," 11.

by design) and that humans have the authority over the system, so they can be held responsible (control in use).[92]

This proposal, however, seems to be a maximal demand in the discussion. Wolfgang Koch, in contrast, seems to deem it appropriate when the operator turns the machine on or presets some parameters.[93] For Florian Keisinger, campaign manager at FCAS, meaningful human control also does not seem to exclude every form of autoregulation in the targeting process.[94] Moreover, some state actors involved in the GGE, namely the US and Israel, disagree with the terminology and propose to use another term, which is *appropriate (levels of) human judgment*, whereby the term "appropriate" indicates that the level of human involvement has to be flexible according to the situation, the system, and the specific function.[95]

Given the different terms in use and the unclear and disputed definition of the term, meaningful human control is a concept that is hard to flesh out because, depending on who is talking, meaningful human control can imply everything from pressing the on/off button to making every target decision.[96] But even within every minimal or maximal demand, one needs to take a deeper look at what precisely is demanded because it makes a difference if a highly trained, informed, and vigilant operator presses the on/off button or a complacent, uninformed, and poorly trained operator follows the machine's advice in every single target decision.[97] Moreover, as Rebecca Crootof concludes, the definition of meaningful human control might become problematic if human control becomes more important than the risk to which combatants and non-combatants are exposed.[98] With this in mind, the question behind the exact definition and the (political) debate boils down to the question of whether human control in itself constitutes such an essential value that it needs to be exerted in every single case, also outweighing the (potential)

92. See iPRAW, "Focus on Human Control," 12.
93. See Koch, "Künstliche Intelligenz—Technische Autonomie," 46.
94. See Keisinger and Koch, "Defence and Responsibility."
95. See Human Rights Watch, "Killer Robots and the Concept of Meaningful Human Control"; United States of America, "Human-Machine Interaction in the Development, Deployment and Use of Emerging Technologies in the Area of Lethal Autonomous Weapons Systems."
96. See Crootof, "Meaningful Floor for 'Meaningful Human Control.'"
97. See Crootof, "Meaningful Floor for 'Meaningful Human Control,'" 56.
98. See Crootof, "Meaningful Floor for 'Meaningful Human Control,'" 62.

benefits for the soldiers' and civilians' security. If this question can be answered in the affirmative, an autoregulated device needs to be forbidden from the outset and under all circumstances. However, if this is not the case, more detailed parameters—including the extent to which human oversight in real time in every single case needs to be maintained—need to be defined, under which circumstances the deployment of an autoregulated device would potentially be possible.

As for the ethical debate, my previous finding that an autoregulative device cannot judge a situation and is not an actual moral agent is of great importance for this topic, as it emphasizes the part of the human being in the human–machine collaboration. Elke Schwarz is one of the scholars who addresses meaningful human control in autoregulative weapons technology from a stance that perceives humans and machines as intertwined in a human–machine complex. In her view, the relationship between human and machines is "co-constitutive,"[99] thereby reshaping each other. In contrast to the classical and instrumental view, where the structure for ascribing agency and responsibility seems very clear (only humans can deploy a device and therefore shoulder responsibility), the relations within such a co-constitutive complex are rather dynamic and not so easy to define.[100] Schwarz further finds that some prerequisites are of importance for maintaining control, such as understanding oneself to be a moral agent, having adequate knowledge of the foreseeable consequences, and understanding the ethical relevance of a situation. Yet, "for actions and outcomes that are mediated through machine learning and computational processing, this awareness might well be obscured."[101] Schwarz identifies two limitations in that regard: cognitive limitations, on the one hand, and temporal and epistemic limitations, on the other hand.

With respect to cognitive limitations, she refers to a theory brought forward by Daniel Kahneman, who differentiates between two main cognitive systems within humans: one that "operates automatically and quickly, with little or no effort and no sense of voluntary control"[102] and a second that "allocates attention to the effortful mental activities that demand it, including complex computations."[103] The second system—

99. Schwarz, "Autonomous Weapons Systems," 57.
100. See Schwarz, "Autonomous Weapons Systems," 56–57.
101. Schwarz, "Autonomous Weapons Systems," 63.
102. Kahneman, *Thinking, Fast and Slow*, 29.
103. Kahneman, *Thinking, Fast and Slow*, 30. Schwarz does not refer to Kahneman explicitly but to a report given by Sharkey, who seems to draw on the findings of Kahneman.

or, as Kahneman puts it, "System 2"—is exactly what we identify with "agency, choice, and concentration."[104] Kahneman extensively describes that usually, and especially in situations where decisions need to be taken quickly, people tend to make decisions based on what System 1 offers. This, however, often entails jumping to conclusions instead of deliberating an issue carefully. This is because deliberating issues carefully, as we do with the help of System 2, takes time, concentration, and mental effort, so in situations with only limited time, we tend to take a shortcut via System 1. This entails, among other things, answering complex questions rather heuristically, for instance, by replacing the intricate question of "How much would you contribute to save an endangered species?" with the simpler question, "How much emotion do I feel when I think of dying dolphins?"[105] Kahneman's book is full of examples that I do not want to unravel here. The gist of his account, however, is clear: System 1 is good for making quick decisions based on heuristics and intuition, while System 2 is what makes us human because it endows us with rational deliberation and therefore agency and morality.

The problem, however, is that in cooperating with machines, System 1 is targeted rather than System 2 due to phenomena such as automation bias.[106] Moreover, this phenomenon is accompanied by anthropomorphization in the sense that the human counterpart attributes to the machine what they would attribute to the human collaborator as well: intentionality. If the machine then becomes more and more an expert in a certain field, an untrained human seems to lose their entitlement to a say in certain actions.[107] Taken together, this might very easily lead to a situation where the human operator can hardly be perceived to be the moral agent within the human–machine complex because "the human operator might not have enough time to process the information required to exercise control."[108] Eventually, human control might be eliminated even when humans seem to be in the loop because they merely pro forma operate the system.

---

104. Kahneman, *Thinking, Fast and Slow*, 30.
105. Kahneman, *Thinking, Fast and Slow*, 98.
106. For further details, see 4.2.3 Automation Bias; Schwarz, "Autonomous Weapons Systems," 64.
107. See Schwarz, "Autonomous Weapons Systems," 65.
108. Schwarz, "Autonomous Weapons Systems," 66.

An Ethical Evaluation of Lethal Functions in Autoregulative Weapons Systems

Concerning epistemic and temporal limitations, Schwarz argues that compared to automated decision-making and algorithmic learning procedures, decision-making and learning for humans takes time. They need time to process the information, to determine the ramifications of a certain decision, and to anticipate its outcome. Algorithmic counterparts are much quicker in doing so but face a number of challenges such as algorithmic bias, unintended side effects, or potentially incomplete data. Yet, to the extent that military operations rely heavily on the time factor, humans' time frame to intervene decreases, thereby simultaneously eliminating human control.[109] Against this backdrop, Schwarz draws the conclusion that "in the LAWS human–machine complex, technological features and the underlying logic of the AI system progressively close the spaces and limit the capacities required for human moral agency,"[110] so that ultimately "conditions that would safeguard or indeed promote human moral agency cannot be ensured with LAWS."[111] This however, constructs a paradox situation because in attempting to mitigate risk and ensuring morality on the battlefield with the help of technology, we might lose our moral ability in the very same process.[112] That way, morality—which is said to be enhanced with the advent of new technology—becomes detached from humans and is handed over to machines, which have no means to calculate this. As a consequence, moral agency vanishes. This is because in the human–machine complex, it is humans who maintain morality, even though the data is perceived with the help of technological devices.

This brings into focus the paradigm of joint cognitive systems because it takes an approach where human and machine work together for the sake of a joint task while each of them carries out the single function they can do best,[113] which is processes that entail reckoning with respect to the algorithm and tasks that require judgment with respect to humans. This means that processes that only need reckoning might be automated. In that context, it is imaginable to define certain scenarios within a greater task that could do without human judgment and could thus be decided with the help of algorithms alone, while there might be others that are off-limits and need to be under the (full) control of

109. See Schwarz, "Autonomous Weapons Systems," 66–69.
110. Schwarz, "Autonomous Weapons Systems," 55.
111. Schwarz, "Autonomous Weapons Systems," 69.
112. See Schwarz, "Autonomous Weapons Systems," 69.
113. As described above. See 4.3 Implementations of Automatization.

humans. It is possible, for instance, that the deployment of autoregulation in the deep sea could be approved of, while its use in an urban fighting scenario could not. This is because the overall situation in the deep sea is relatively clear—meaning that there are no human targets to be expected and, if so, they are very likely to pose military targets.[114] An urban fighting scenario, on the other hand, is obscure, hard to keep in overview, and constantly changing, so the machine cannot compute its way through the scene safely. Moreover, it would need to make moral decisions it is not equipped to make. One situation in which a possible automatization of scenarios might be possible, therefore, is the clarity of an anticipated scenario and the absence of humans within it because the better algorithms can operate, the clearer the scene is, and they would need moral judgment to make moral decisions such as targeting people. This, however, does not do away with the issue of speed. As for human control, Hollnagel and Woods emphasize that control can only be exercised if there is enough time, knowledge, competence, and resources.[115] While the operator of a system might obtain knowledge and competence by sufficient and purposeful training and adequate resources might be provided, the issue of time is the most imminent here.

In this case, dynamically allocating the tasks to human and machine, such as with adaptive automation, might at least mitigate the problem to some degree. Tasks that might entail less judgment can thus be automated if the pressure in a situation is high so that more time and resources are available for the human operator. If the time frame is narrow, though, there might still not be enough room to deliberate a lethal decision carefully. In such a situation, no agency and therefore no control would be applied, even though a human was in place, thereby creating an agency gap. In contrast to dilemma situations in driving, which are expected to pose an exception, this loss of agency within weapons systems might be a rather common situation because it occurs due the growing speed of warfare, which is a result of accelerating technologies. This loop of growing technological speed and deceasing human agency

114. Even though the sea is an area that is easier to deal with by means of autoregulative functions weapons systems, this does not mean that the sea does not pose any problems. This is because humans depend on their vessels to stay alive, so the necessity of coming to the rescue in the case of an emergency at sea is decisive. It might be an imperative to program autoregulative devices at sea to do so. For further detail, see Sparrow and Lucas, "When Robots Rule the Waves?"

115. See Hollnagel and Woods, *Joint Cognitive Systems*, 75. As described above, see 4.1 Joint Cognitive Systems.

is the core issue that meaningful human control needs to face. But this seems considerably difficult to implement, to say the least: What would be a sufficient time frame here? Is thirty seconds enough, two hours, or a day? How much time is needed to decide the death of another person? These questions seem inadequate because it is a kind of quantification of the life-and-death decision that cannot do justice to the person targeted or to the moral integrity of the person targeting. Nevertheless, in order to cooperate with machines, such time frames must be set. I cannot resolve these issues here; only hint at them. What should be clear from this, however, is that autoregulation in weapons technology is out of bounds on ethical grounds to the extent that processes of judgment are concerned because the human–machine complex hinges on humans in that regard. If a device is nevertheless deployed or if humans do not have sufficient time to deliberate, the system lacks any kind of (moral) agency. It simply does away with ethics and morality entirely so that, ultimately, humans might lose their agency in the process.

That said, I am doubtful whether, from an ethical perspective, the idea of meaningful human control can be more than a political catch-all phrase.[116] This is because it is not clear what exactly it should entail and, moreover, the issues at stake do not pertain to out-of-the-loop decisions only. Every situation that would not provide sufficient time to ponder a moral decision cannot be said to be a morally considered decision. In that regard, there is no difference between a human in-the-loop making a (quick) decision based on the machine's assessment, a human out-of-the-loop not intervening into the machine's lethal course, or the system operating out-of-the-loop without human oversight in real time: All the scenarios are out of moral control and all pose a severe threat to human agency. What is decisive is a design that includes humans in-the-loop in the sense that they are aware of the way the system operates, they understand the courses of actions it offers and can assess their consequences, and they have sufficient time to process and deliberate that information. Since the concrete design is not my concern here, I can only hint at the importance of designing machines ethically from the beginning.

---

116. The same might be true for the field of the law. See Marauhn, "Meaningful Human Control and the Politics of International Law." This, however, does not mean that the term has no political importance. In the political discourse on the banning of regulating autoregulative functions in weapons technology, the term plays a significant role, and its importance must therefore not be underestimated.

4.5 CONCLUSION

To sum up what has been discussed so far, it can be said that two somewhat diverging phenomena are coming to the fore. First, ever more complex scenarios where violence can occur, in combination with redundancy, accelerate the quest for (sophisticated) technology that is able to support or even to replace humans. Second, there is the task of maintaining control of the system. With that in mind, the central problem regarding technology is how to maintain control in increasingly complex scenarios.

For the purpose of this book, I have introduced the paradigm of joint cognitive systems because it puts the stress on a *co*llaboration, with the aim of performing a joint task in the safest and most reliable way. One of my basic assumptions here is that a machine never operates without an operator, though it might seem that way because it is not supervised by a human in real time. Rather, the aim of a machine—or the joint action, the data provided, and the frame of the whole venture—is human shaped. Therefore, control needs to rest with humans. This is also why an evaluation of an autoregulative device that focuses on the technical implications can sideline the general concern of whether or not a human should be involved in the decision-making process: they just are. Therefore, more detailed questions arise, such as that of how a joint action can be performed in the safest and most reliable way. This entails that there might be scenarios where the actual control or authority seems safer with the machine, for instance, in an emergency driving situation where humans might be too slow to react no matter what.[117] The major goods that need consideration here are the safety/reliability of the joint performance on the one hand and the control of the system on the other hand. Bearing in mind what has been said above, it might be naive to demand that the actual control of the system has to be with humans in every moment because this might result in uncontrollable situations, as can be illustrated easily with an emergency driving situation. To put it differently, anybody who wants to resort to increasingly automated technology will have to deal with situations where the machine is superior simply because it can process more information in a shorter amount of time and react faster. Yet, this does not mean that the machine should maintain the overall control or authority over a joint venture simply because it has advanced qualities in certain areas, or that maximizing the efficiency can be seen as

---

117. See Flemisch et al., "Toward a Dynamic Balance Between Humans and Automation," 5–11.

an excuse for using autoregulation. Even though it might be possible to implement some basic legal guidelines—such as prohibiting the machine from engaging a target placed on a hospital—ethical decision-making and an overall perspective of the situation can only be gained by a human because machines (still) lack this kind of insight.[118]

This means that, also from a technological point of view, the crucial features of a system must stay with humans, such as determining an overall goal and predefining the parameters for the collaboration. Within the collaboration, it is humans ensuring that the joint system accomplishes the joint task *better* than humans could alone. That way, both entities work together beneficially because they actualize their inherent possibilities. Humans maintain control and, within their control, use an autoregulative mode wisely in situations where it is clear the operator cannot react appropriately, similar to avoiding an emergency driving situation. Yet, this still entails that the operator does their best to directly control the machine either manually or by supervising it vigilantly. To do so, operators need to be trained in advance to mitigate the out-of-the-loop performance problem, as well as automation bias. Furthermore, the design of the display ought to help the operator to yield their control.[119]

Keeping that in mind, criteria need to be developed for situations where the transfer of authority and control to the machine is appropriate. According to the sliding scale of automation, it might be possible to clarify diverse levels of automation within different scenarios that oscillate between autoregulation and manual operation dynamically.[120] If this should be done, the ramifications of trust toward machines, the out-of-loop-performance problem, automation bias, unintended side effects, and algorithmic bias need to be addressed and considered. This entails that in situations where overall pressure on the human part of the collaboration is relatively low, they should take over procedures from the machine. In that line of argumentation, however, it needs to be taken into account that even if there might be less problematic tasks that can be handed over to the machine in case of need—for instance, the analysis of an image—this might lead to a flawed evaluation of the system, giving erroneous advice. If only the final step of the decision-making loop, meaning the target decision, is decided by a human, it might seem as if humans exert control and bear responsibility, while they in fact rely

118. See 3.3 Reckoning and Judgment.
119. See Mouloua et al., "Human Monitoring of Automated Systems," 15–16.
120. See 4.3 Implementations of Automatization.

on the whole decision-making procedure and might not know how this decision was achieved. They would have the option not to follow the system's instructions, but they would not know why. In my view, this cannot be what is meant by control. However, if the human already cooperates with the machine in the beginning of the target cycle, it might not matter who took the actual decision to shoot in the end because the outcome would be the same. For that reason, the questions of which steps can be automized to what degree need to be scrutinized very carefully. For that matter, procedures such as adaptive automation might also help to include the human operator in the different stages of the decision-making loop, at least if the workload is not too high.

As for the deployment of autoregulation in weapons systems, the violent framework is decisive and must be elaborated on. This is because the ethics of violent means is not coextensive with civic means of this technology, so peace ethics constitutes the ethical frame for pondering this specific technology, a topic I will turn to now.

5

The Ethical Framing

Peace Ethics

IN THIS CHAPTER, IT is my objective to scrutinize the normative ethical framework within which matters of war and peace, such as weapons systems, are addressed. As Michael Allen Fox describes, war and morality can be linked in various ways reaching from absolute pacifism to the moral valorization of war, whereas the moral permissibility of war increases along a conceived line. Along this line and next to absolute pacifism, moderate or contingent pacifist approaches are located, followed by approaches of just war. Subsequently, there are so-called realistic positions, where war is conceived to be one political option among others, even though it might not be favored.[1] Finally, positions that perceive war as a heroic and morally good undertaking complete the picture.[2]

---

1. The professed "realism" consists of a number of controversial assumptions, assuming that war is inevitable, or a plausible political means within a framework where the political actors compete with each other overpower in an ever more disorganized world. See Reuter, "Der internationale Rechtsfrieden zwischen Realismus und Idealismus," 151.

2. This classification harks back to Fox, *Understanding Peace*, 107. The main framework that discusses matters of war and peace, especially within the Anglo–American context, however, is just war thinking. This also means that pacifist paradigms, such as contingent pacifism, have little saying within the current discourse and this is the reason why scholars who have another viewpoint, such as Koch and Rinke, nevertheless couch their account in terms of just war for pragmatic reasons. I provide an overview of the state of the debate in my introduction. See 1.4.2 The Ethics of War and Peace.

The Ethical Framing

As for my own approach, I proceed on the assumption that war does not simply happen by itself but is a socially chosen undertaking that must not be taken for granted. As Robert L. Holmes puts it:

> We have to deplete natural resources in order to live. But we do not have to kill other human beings. We have to cope with conflict in order to live socially. But we do not have to wage war. However much we wrap our rationalization in the language of necessity, we *choose* to do these things. And as with all our choices, these are subject to moral assessment.[3]

In line with Holmes's assumption, I will therefore confine myself to these contemporary approaches that render the use of force precarious in nature and therefore seek to confine violence. This also entails a disclaimer: I will not cover theories indicating that war is just one political means among others. This is a realistic position, famously represented by Clausewitz, that I reject right at the outset. Similarly, I disapprove of positions that valorize war as a heroic or morally good undertaking. This selection is due to my own background in theological ethics and my conviction that peace is not a "nice-to-have" condition but rather essential and indispensable, a belief based on Scriptures found in the Old as well as the New Testament. It is stated, for instance, in Psalm 34:14, "Depart from evil and do good; seek peace and pursue it," and in the Sermon on the Mount, "Blessed *are* the peacemakers, for they shall be called the children of God" (Matt 5:9). However, the exact significance of such a normative premise and the conclusions I draw from it form the essence this chapter aims for. I will therefore scrutinize in greater detail those approaches that contribute to my standpoint, which are absolute and contingent pacifism as well as just war tradition.

While absolute pacifist approaches deem the use of force illegitimate per se and under all circumstances, contingent pacifism and just war tradition both perceive war as a last resort constituting an exemption of the ordinary. Yet, both approaches differ in the amount to which the use of force is morally permissible: Within just war tradition, on the one hand, this is done carefully, based on several criteria. War, however, can sometimes be legitimized here. Contingent pacifism, on the other hand, puts a stronger emphasis on peace and therefore considers the idea that peace can be brought about by means of war inherently problematic. Yet,

---

3. Holmes, *On War and Morality*, 3.

there might be situations so severe that refraining from violence would cause even more harm.[4]

Hereby, just war tradition and absolute pacifism are well established theories whose roots can be traced back thousands of years.[5] Contingent pacifism, which has several varieties such as legal pacifism[6] or pragmatic pacifism,[7] is an ostensible new phenomenon, at least regarding its designation. Nevertheless, as will be shown below, contemporary contingent pacifist approaches are very well in line with the historical developments of just war thinking that seek to confine violence to a minimal amount. Moreover, since contingent pacifism attempts to strike a balance between the well-established theories of absolute pacifism and just war tradition by focusing on peace while also considering the possibility of cases where the use of force is the lesser evil, it is a paradigm worth scrutinizing.

With that said, I will present several current conceptualizations of absolute pacifism, just war thinking, and contingent pacifism, putting a focus on the question of how their contribution depicts and discusses the issue of autoregulative functions in weaponry. The sequence of my account is oriented toward the insight that just and sustaining peace is the main goal peace ethics seeks to establish and that this goal has been a strong impetus to develop and adapt just war tradition. Therefore, I will first introduce these two theories—including some of their current conceptualizations and reviews—commencing with absolute pacifism, as all of the following approaches aim at peace (5.1). I will then continue with just war thinking, thereby focusing on the critique this approach has been exposed to by scholars who seek to revise this kind of approach (5.2). Against this backdrop, I will then elaborate in greater detail on contingent pacifist approaches, intertwining the results of the preceding considerations (5.3). Within the respective approaches, I will, one at a time, address the assessments these approaches have taken so far toward autoregulation in weapons technology.

My own approach, however, is rooted within Western Protestant thought and therefore refers in great measure to Western Christian tradition. This entails that my depiction of absolute pacifism refers to Christian traditional literature such as the New Testament and introduces current concepts that have been developed within the Protestant and

4. This classification is oriented on Fox, *Understanding Peace*, 107.
5. See 5.1.1 Historical Sketch; 5.2.1 *Bellum iustum*: History of Ideas.
6. See Brücher, "Rechtspazifismus."
7. See Müller, "Pragmatischer Pazifismus."

The Ethical Framing

Roman Catholic churches (5.1.2). As for just war thinking, I especially consider its historical Christian background (5.2.1) and scrutinize its rediscovery in the context of the Vietnam War (5.2.2.1). For the majority of Christian approaches toward war and peace, World War II represents a complete break in just war thinking, which eventually led to its reconceptualization in terms of just peace. Yet, the concept of just peace is a variety of contingent pacifism rather than just war, because war is deemed an undertaking that can never be justified by any means but is inherently precarious in nature (5.3.3).

This brief classification shows likewise that Christian thought is woven into Western moral approaches toward war and peace and vice versa. This becomes especially clear when approaches that stem from other religious contexts are taken into account. As for the Jewish-halachic approaches I refer to in this book, this classification is not as easy to apply, as these concepts reject pacifism but also renounce (Christian) just war thinking in order to provide an account of their own.[8] Yet, Jewish-halachic propositions address and assess autoregulation in weapons technology as well and are worthy of consideration. I will therefore cover Jewish approaches within an excursus.[9]

With a final remark here, I need to point toward the over- and underrepresentation of my own perspective within the current discourse. On the one hand, moral assessments from a just war and therefore Western point of view toward autoregulation in weapons technology abound. Nearly all of the ethical approaches I laid my eyes on in the course of this research have been written by scholars resorting to just war tradition in one of its variants, which hints at the imbalance of the discourse. To a certain degree, my account also adds to that imbalance, because it is exactly this Western perspective I consider. On the other hand, my approach takes a different stance, because it aims to contribute a particular Christian perspective drawing on to the inner-Christian discourse

8. I distinguish Jewish-halachic approaches from approaches stemming from Jewish authors but rooted in just war thinking. For that matter Walzer, who is the contemporary main protagonist in just war thinking, and Benbaji and Statman, who I will discuss below, share a Jewish background. Yet, neither Walzer nor Benbaji and Statman argue with respect to Jewish traditional literature, which is why I will discuss these authors within the current of just war thinking that is deeply influenced by Christian thought and delimit halachic approaches thereof. I will address these approaches separately in an excursus.

9. Nevertheless, the possibility to arrange the topic differently and to come to different solutions within another framework hints at the preliminary nature and contextuality of my own view within Western Christian thought.

within peace ethics and explicitly referring to these theories—a perspective strongly underrepresented in the contemporary discussions.[10] By the same token, theories that stem from other religious backgrounds, such as Jewish traditions, are of great interest as well. Yet, since I studied Protestant theology, I can only perceive these contributions from an outsider's point of view.

5.1 ABSOLUTE PACIFISM AND PEACE STUDIES

Peace is the defined goal that absolute pacifist approaches aim for. Such theories proceed with the assumption that violent means are inherently wrong, and therefore war must not be carried out for any reason. There is an ethical obligation to do without violence and it needs to be fulfilled by any means necessary. This includes the restriction against interfering violently in an ongoing conflict, even if this means tolerating victims. The basic idea of this rationale is that the use of violence in order to impede more violence cannot be justified: It is merely a logical contradiction. Having this argumentation in mind also means that such an approach is rather normative in nature. Since violence is wrong, war must not be fought. In several cases, absolute pacifism is in line with a certain religious belief, for instance, in the teachings of Gandhi. But with respect to Christianity, pacifism has also been connected to Christian Scripture.[11] Concerning the latter, the Sermon on the Mount in particular, with its obligation to love one's enemy (Matt 5:44.; Luke 6:27.), is highlighted, as well as the request for nonviolence (Matt 5:39–41; Luke 6:29–31.).[12]

In the following paragraph, I will consider several approaches that stem from various backgrounds in order to show the broad range within this approach and the diverse backgrounds against which an absolute pacifist viewpoint can be adopted. In the abundance of positions, exemplary treatment is called for. To represent paradigmatic positions, I follow a typology depicting theories that stem from institutional sources, such as the approaches taken from the Roman Catholic or the regional

---

10. There are some scholars who introduce a Christian perspective toward autoregulation in weapons technology, though, such as von Schubert and Bernhard Koch. I will illustrate their positions below. Yet, their contributions are either orientated rather toward just war tradition—at least apparently—or relate to autoregulative functions in weapons systems quite superficially or inexplicitly.

11. See Fiala, "Pacifism."

12. See Hofheinz, "Radikaler Pazifismus," 416.

The Ethical Framing

Protestant Church of Baden (5.1.3.1). In this line of thought, I will also address the theory developed by Stanley Hauerwas and Samuel Wells because their account is deeply rooted within ecclesiological thought and therefore refers to the Church as an institution. In addition, I will depict notions that stem from individuals, such as the suggestions from Judith Butler, Michael Allen Fox, and Robert L. Holmes (5.1.3.2). Another selection criterion is the issue of who is addressed. Generally, there are approaches that put the emphasis on the individual, such as the accounts of Butler and Hauerwas, while others focus on society and politics, such as the perspectives taken by the Protestant Church of Baden and Michael Allen Fox. Yet, before diving deeper into the details of the single approaches, I will make some brief remarks on the historical dimension of such an approach, indicating that pacifism is a concept rooted in a long-standing tradition (5.1.1). Subsequently, I will comment on some rather descriptive and theoretical insights within peace theory, attempting to move toward a classification of peace that I can work with (5.1.2).

I will, however, not go into great detail concerning the historical dimensions as descriptive and theoretical classifications, because my main interest is normative in nature, examining which approaches could be taken from the respective point of view toward autoregulation in weapons systems and against which backdrop (5.1.4).

5.1.1 Historical Sketch

Regarding Western Christian thought, a strong pacifist tradition is rooted in the New Testament, which has existed throughout Christian history. Most famously, Tertullian—one of the church fathers—stood for this tradition next to Origen or Lactancius.[13] However, this account needs to be put into perspective because the ancient reason for arguing to withdraw from the miliary service, as the church fathers maintain, cannot be seen to be coextensive with today's understanding and mainly deals with being enlisted in an army that is perceived to have idolatrous practices. The reason for a pacifist standpoint is therefore religious and not moral or ethical in nature. Accordingly, the problems Tertullian describes are based on religious observance within the army, such as taking the military oath that binds the soldiers "unconditionally to the emperor and its supreme

---

13. See Looney, "Augustinus," 226.

commander"[14] and engaging in Mithraism. The main focus here is therefore not the issue of fighting and killing in war but rather the religious and idolatrous practices that come with enlistment.[15] Similarly, Origen perceives the main problem not to be bloodshed in war, but rather the entanglement in the world's affairs. This is because Christians are already concerned with "spiritual combat"[16] and should thus be exempt from warfare just as the Roman priests are. By the same token and among others, the works of Lactantius, Eusebius of Caesarea, or Cyprian could also be mentioned here, so John Haugeland draws the conclusion that

> For the church Fathers of the first three centuries [. . .] there was no such thing as an early church pacifism. Whatever objections to enlistment there were, and there were not many, were based on the nature of the observances of the official and unofficial religions in and surrounding the legions.[17]

In the Middle Ages, absolute pacifism was also upheld, famously by Francis of Assisi or the Unity of the Brethren. In the thought of Erasmus of Rotterdam and Thomas Morus, pacifism obtains a utopian and humanist character, as the authors urge for a renewal of humanity according to the life and teaching of Christ. Peace within this context is an antithesis to the world the authors live in and becomes an unattainable goal. In contrast to this utopian conception, the peace churches developed a version of pacifism where nonviolence is the main tenet and becomes a political attitude over time.[18] Pacifistic ideas, however, are not confined to Christian or religious thought; they have also been reconstructed within a philosophical frame, for instance, by Fox. In his book, he emphasizes that the focus when thinking about peace needs to be put on peace and not on war. He writes,

> We first have to get past being captivated by thoughts about war. The second step is to try seeing the world from the standpoint of peace rather than war. This amounts to an epistemological and ethical reversal of sorts, inasmuch as we must not only foreground peace as the norm in human life and war as the aberration, but also seek to define the positive attributes of peace,

---

14. Helgeland, "Christians and the Roman Army," 151.
15. See Helgeland, "Christians and the Roman Army," 152.
16. Helgeland, "Christians and the Roman Army," 153.
17. Helgeland, "Christians and the Roman Army," 156.
18. See Hofheinz, "Radikaler Pazifismus," 418–22.

placing it in the position of primacy, instead of viewing peace as merely the negation or derivative opposite of war.[19]

Fox means changing the viewpoint from a perspective where war is an essential part of our world toward an attitude where peace is the starting point as well as the angle of thinking. Thereby, the focus changes from the question of the extent to which going to and conducting war can be justified to the question of what means are necessary in order to establish peace. Different questions arise, including: What is the meaning of peace? What contributes to peace? And what might help to maintain peace? These questions also constitute the basis for peace (and conflict) studies, a field that researches peace in its political meaning.[20]

5.1.2 Definition(s) of Peace

Within peace (and conflict) studies, several attempts have been made to define peace, but up to this point, no single one has gained overall acceptance. One main disagreement is the question of whether peace is more than the absence of war. This points back to the essential distinction Johann Galtung has drawn between negative and positive peace. While negative peace denotes the absence of personal (direct) violence, positive peace designates the absence of structural (indirect) violence, thereby providing the foundation for social justice. This indicates that structural violence can still be in place in situations where there might be no personal experience of violence. Accordingly, both schemes of violence are interconnected, and through that connection, a narrow understanding of peace—meaning solely the absence of war—is ruled out. For that reason, peace research is closely connected to conflict and development theory alike because it refers not only to the mere use of violence but also to its social contexts.[21] While the difference between positive and negative peace is cogent, the understanding of violence that comes with it is not self-evident because there is an inherent difference between physical violence (*violentia/vis*) on the one hand and structural violence (*potestas*), or power, on the other hand, as Torsten Meireis argues.[22] Harking back to Wolfgang Lieneman, Meireis defines violence as a coercive physical

---

19. Fox, *Understanding Peace*, 4.
20. See Werkner, "Zum Friedensbegriff in der Friedensforschung," 20.
21. See Galtung, "Violence, Peace and Peace Research," 183.
22. See Meireis, "Liebe und Gewalt," 37.

violation of somebody's will and freedom, which must be differentiated from other and different kinds of (economical) oppression and contempt.[23] That way, the severeness of harming somebody violently is taken into account, while at the same time the issue of structural harm is acknowledged. Against this backdrop, a question needs to be asked: To what extent peace can be more than the absence of war? Scholars such as Wolfgang Huber and Hans-Richard Reuter have clarified that the absence of war is already one essential ingredient of sustaining peace.[24] Yet, they have also made clear that peace is not confined to the rejection of violence alone but likewise entails "the *promotion of freedom and cultural diversity* and the *alleviation of want.*"[25]

Since peace, understood in that way, is a very broad concept, it is important to find at least a rough definition of what is meant, otherwise peace might become a catch-all term—a danger already inherent in Galtung's definition of positive peace.[26] For that reason, Christian Davenport, Erik Melander, and Patrick M. Regan suggest thinking about peace along a continuum of qualified peace, where the negative part entails that there is no peace at all—as in "utmost political violence, or more specifically, war and genocide"—and the positive, opposing end of the scale would mean that there is "political mutuality," which "entails a quality of respect and fundamental good will between relevant actors."[27] Though the term "political mutuality" needs further definition, the idea of defining peace along a continuum, which does not only leave the dichotomous possibilities of peace and no peace, seems convincing. In addition to this approach toward peace, which clearly aims at the political status of whole societies, it is possible to differentiate peace within three main dimensions: first, small-scale approaches that focus on individual endeavors; second, medium-scale approaches that concentrate on single societies; and third, large-scale approaches examining systematic conditions.[28]

23. See Meireis, "Liebe und Gewalt," 37–38.
24. See Huber and Reuter, *Friedensethik*, 22.
25. EKD, "Live from God's peace," 29. Emphasis original.
26. See Davenport et al., *Peace Continuum*, 29. Galtung's approach has been critiqued. Ines-Jacqueline Werkner makes clear, for instance, that it might not be distinctive enough and might be outdated in the contemporary international situation. See Werkner, "Zum Friedensbegriff in der Friedensforschung," 26–27. I therefore refer here to an adapted approach that nevertheless mirrors the insights Galtung has brought to attention.
27. Davenport et al., *Peace Continuum*, 2.
28. See Werkner, "Zum Friedensbegriff in der Friedensforschung," 26–27.

Pacifist thought, focusing on peace in the described broad sense, needs to strike a balance between all three of these levels, which again can be qualified as a continuum rather than an absolute state. These attempts to organize the different implications and connotations of peace form the foundation for my subsequent assessment of different and contemporary proposals to conceptualize absolute pacifism.

5.1.3 Concepts of Absolute Pacifism

5.1.3.1 Conceptions Bound to Institutions

STANLEY HAUERWAS AND SAMUEL WELLS

In *The Peaceable Kingdom* (1983), Hauerwas develops his view that "nonviolence is the hallmark of the Christian moral life."[29] The center of Hauerwas's thought is Jesus and his nonviolent and forgiving example: In imitating Jesus' deeds, Christians learn to forgive and not to fear one another. Normally, to encounter another person is a challenge, as every human is a possible threat. "Only when my self—my character—is formed by God's love, do I know I have no reason to fear the other."[30] This is exactly what hospitality is about and why it is key in Christian ethics. Following that thought, the Christian community—namely the church—becomes the role model for politics because it embodies the possibility of accepting the other as other and living together peacefully. Therefore, "the gospel is a political gospel."[31] Hauerwas elaborates on that account further in his book *Performing the Faith* (2004), which is primarily a review of Dietrich Bonhoeffer's pacifist account, which he interprets in line with John Howard Yoder to be absolute pacifist in nature.[32] Hauerwas's view entails that the individual is prepared to encounter the world in a peaceful way, a culture Christianity calls "faith," when developing the necessary virtues of peace and justice informed by the role model of Jesus as passed down by Scripture in its multifaceted way.[33]

---

29. Hauerwas, *Peaceable Kingdom*, xvi.
30. Hauerwas, *Peaceable Kingdom*, 91.
31. Hauerwas, *Peaceable Kingdom*, 99.
32. I will discuss and interpret Bonhoeffer's account of peace in greater detail below, objecting to Hauerwas's interpretation. See 5.3.3.1 On Bonhoeffer's Account of War and Peace.
33. See Hauerwas, *Performing the Faith*, 17. As Hauerwas makes sure, this does not mean that this development of peaceful virtues necessarily needs to take place within

Because this is an ongoing process, "theology is never finished."[34] This means that Christians and the church cannot withdraw from the world: Only in being visible in the social and political sphere is the church able to perform peace publicly.[35] In doing so, the church exemplifies the way in which Christ interferes with the world. To put it in Hauerwas's terms: "As Christ was in the world so the Church is in the world."[36] By the same token, the church cannot claim that it simply knows what violence, nonviolence, and peace mean, since the qualities of Christian life exceed mundane circumstances. From that perspective, peace has an ontological problem: It is more than nonviolence, but at the same time it does not coincide with the peace humans find in Christ. To Hauerwas's mind, it might even be impossible to find an overarching definition of pacifism. This is because Hauerwas's pacifist notion cannot be separated from his ecclesiological, Christological, and eschatological thinking.[37] In order to understand peace, what is needed is therefore not a cogent theory but rather a "practice of peace," which Hauerwas identifies within everyday Christian practices such as "praying and singing the hymns."[38] Christians are therefore not pacifists per se but first and foremost "disciples of Jesus Christ."[39] Therefore, Hauerwas writes,

> "Pacifism" names the ongoing form of habituation necessary to force our imagination to discover forms of life otherwise unknown, or, if imagined, too often described by those who think there is no alternative to violence as "unrealistic."[40]

Within such socioethical framing, Hauerwas describes peace as a virtue, which he sees as closely connected to friendship: Both attributes are "interdependent virtues."[41] This classification has far-reaching consequences because, even though Hauerwas describes peace as a virtue, it is not individualistic, meaning that one person alone cannot live peacefully

---

the church. But since the narrative of the church is based on that assumption, it is much more likely to happen here.

34. Hauerwas, *Performing the Faith*, 17.
35. See Hauerwas, *Performing the Faith*, 44.
36. Hauerwas, *Performing the Faith*, 46.
37. See Hauerwas, *Performing the Faith*, 170–72.
38. Hauerwas, *Performing the Faith*, 26, 21.
39. Hauerwas, *Performing the Faith*, 26.
40. Hauerwas, *Performing the Faith*, 26–27.
41. Hauerwas, *Performing the Faith*, 181.

just as one person alone cannot live in a friendship. Therefore, peace is always interpersonal and radically different from concepts such as (self-) awareness, which solely focus on the individual.[42] For that reason, Hauerwas links this virtue to the social dimension of the church, which consists of individuals but exceeds an individualistic account by providing the ground for interpersonal, peaceful relationships. This is important to note because in approaching peace that way, it is situated somewhere between a small-scale and a middle-scale approach, focusing on each person's virtue but simultaneously exceeding the limits of this small-scale domain toward interconnected groups.

In another contribution called *Breaking Bread: Peace and War* (2011), Hauerwas, in conjunction with Wells, focuses on another point by drawing on the imaginary of liturgy, thereby making very clear the implications of Hauerwas's thinking. The authors open their article with the following remark:

> War is a counter-liturgy to worship of God. War is a sacrifice designed to take away sin. Except it does not take away sin. War is thus, for Christians, a parody of the cross and a parody of the Eucharist. It is a technology and an idol that rivals and obscures the grace of salvation.[43]

Such an imaginary is crucial because it informs the way people develop their virtues, so, eventually, narrative and imaginary affect the way people interact with each other. Having this in mind, the authors reconstruct war within a liturgical language, meaning that war is a liturgy that serves secular reasons. From that point of view, war is an undertaking that requires the belief that there is something worth dying for. In Wells's words, "this war must be about something more important than life, otherwise these beloved men and woman would not be dead."[44] War's altar is the nation; the sacrifice consists of the people who leave their lives for their nation's sake. In doing so, a nation constitutes itself. It obtains a foundation and an identity: "The sacrifice of those who have died must be received by the community for which they died in a manner that reinforces the community's justifications for why it is a body of people worthy of sacrifice."[45] Furthermore, their sacrifice needs repetition to assure that

---

42. See Kernberg, *Liebe und Aggression*, 29.
43. Hauerwas and Wells, "Breaking Bread," 415.
44. Hauerwas and Wells, "Breaking Bread," 416.
45. Hauerwas and Wells, "Breaking Bread," 420.

their deaths have not been in vain. That way, "war becomes an endlessly repeated spiral of meaning."[46] That is why war serves an end for the specific community that fights it. It is therefore imagined as an inevitable ingredient of contemporary societies, which entails that we are used to perceiving war in this function. This default view, however, is contested by the liturgy of the cross represented in the Eucharist. This is because Jesus is the end of sacrifices. Moreover, Jesus himself did not answer force by counterforce, but died at the cross. Therefore, at least to the extent that Christians are concerned, nonviolence must be the default position and ignites the hope to give an example of peace to their non-Christian surroundings that seems worthy of imitation.[47] Accordingly, pacifism entails a "counter-liturgical" regarding of the secular idea of war.[48] Positively, what is needed—at variance with a liturgical imagination of warfare—is reconciliation, which is apparent in the sacrifice of Christ and revived in the Eucharist.[49]

Hauerwas's pacifist stance stands out, as he combines the virtue of peace, which is connected to a single person, with a greater community, namely the church. In doing so, peace does not linger within the boundaries of the individual but becomes a social practice that can be habituated and emanates from the Christian community to the society in which it is situated. Since peace, friendship, and reconciliation are always interpersonal, these characteristics are necessarily social in their nature and thereby exceed the individual. This is important because war, as a joint and therefore social endeavor, surpasses the single person, and pacifism needs to relate to this social dimension of war and violence.

There are, however, several problems associated with Hauerwas's approach, revolving mainly around his ecclesiology and his pacifist interpretation of Bonhoeffer. While I will review his interpretation of Bonhoeffer in greater detail below,[50] I concentrate on his ecclesiological view here. The main problem in that regard is that his description of

46. Hauerwas and Wells, "Breaking Bread," 421.

47. See Hauerwas and Wells, "Breaking Bread," 423.

48. In between these ideas, a Christian account of pragmatic pacifism or just war tradition also articulates a critique on the liturgy imagination of war because its aim is to remove the liturgical character of warfare. While pragmatic pacifism emphasizes the practical benefit of peaceful solutions to violent scenarios, just war tradition, in the eyes of Hauerwas and Wells, "legitimize[s] sacrifice but without resort to liturgy." Hauerwas and Wells, "Breaking Bread," 423.

49. See Hauerwas and Wells, "Breaking Bread," 424.

50. See 5.3.3.1 On Bonhoeffer's Account of War and Peace.

The Ethical Framing

the church is rather normative with regard to the existing communities, a finding Birgit Rommel uncovered.[51] Subsequently, a question arises: What happens if the normative framework and the empirical ramifications do not strike a balance and the church falls short of this peaceful framing, thereby giving a bad example to the world? Clearly, the theological answer would be repentance and reconciliation, but the inherent tension remains and is then closely connected to the relation between mundane and ecclesiastical law. In other words: To what extent can and should mundane law outperform the church's law? In Hauerwas's concept, severe failures of the church can hardly be addressed sufficiently. This entails the possible occurrence of situations where the imitation model operates better the other way around, so the world gives an example for the church. Against such a strong normative ecclesiological model, it seems more persuasive to differentiate various dimensions within the church. Hans-Richard Reuter, for instance, draws a distinction between the dimension of faith, practice, and law. The dimension of faith pertains to the dogmatic concept, meaning that the way the gospel is preached proves itself to be true for individuals and as a result forms the foundation for a community, visible and invisible at the same time, because both aspects are interrelated. What is most important here, however, is the idea that the objective of the church is oriented at the gospel, while it does not coincide with it. This is because the church, in its dogmatic dimension, does foreshadow the kingdom of God in the way the church ought to demonstrate the reconciliation of God with humanity, and as a consequence, the reconciliation among individuals. It does so, however, in a rather symbolic, provisional way.[52] Reuter then relates the dimension of practice to an ethical idea, which is the way the Christian community engages practically by representing itself in worship and liturgy, on the one hand, but also in taking part in the affairs of the world by providing education, by practices of justice, and by assistance in case

---

51. Rommel criticizes Hauerwas mainly for his incoherent historicism. She shows that Hauerwas, on the one hand, maintains that theological knowledge is always situated in a certain context and tradition, while he, on the other hand, argues that there is truth within this knowledge that in itself is not contingent on the historical context. See Rommel, *Ekklesiologie und Ethik bei Stanley Hauerwas*, 275. This practically makes Hauerwas's account hard to reconcile with pluralistic notions, and, as she convincingly shows, is also the reason for an inherent androcentrism and sexism. See Rommel, *Ekklesiologie und Ethik bei Stanley Hauerwas*, 266–74.

52. See Reuter, *Botschaft und Ordnung*, 33–40.

of need, on the other hand.[53] Finally, the juridical dimension refers to the organizational structure of the church, enabling it to carry out its tasks and organizing the structure of ministry and membership.[54] When assessing Hauerwas's concept in terms of Reuter, the ways in which the different dimensions are blurred becomes very clear. The idealistic concept Hauerwas develops would then rather constitute a dogmatic description that does not necessarily have ethical and juridical implications. Reuter's thought that the dogmatic character of the church is considerably symbolic is particularly decisive here: The kingdom of God is not simply realized within the Christian community but constitutes an aspiration, which the particular community can live up to or not. Consequently, the dogmatic character of the church performs the task of being a signpost rather than embodying the reality lived. If these two aspects are blended into each other, there is no way to critically reflect on whether the church realizes its aspiration or not.

Based on that criticism, two other issues need to be addressed, which are, first, Hauerwas's political framing and, second, his purported inability to define peace in theory. With respect to the former, Hauerwas emphasizes the interpersonal role of peace but confines its performance to rather small communities of religious character, from where they might emanate into the political sphere. For that reason, everything done within these communities is political in nature. I certainly deem Hauerwas's idea of a narrative that informs people to act accordingly and that then might emerge from this small context into a greater context astute. Yet, I perceive a tension in matters of international affairs that needs to be addressed in politically and legally binding terms. Here, the distinction between dogmatic, ethical, and juridical dimensions, as described above, seems to be helpful: While the church can set an example in the ways in which it meets the gospel's standards, this does not entail that these standards apply to the remainder of society correspondingly. It does not even necessarily entail that they apply in the same way externally as they apply internally, since in a pluralistic world, the beliefs and persuasions of the addressee need to be taken into account as well. Accordingly, to the extent that autoregulation in weapons systems is a matter of international regulation, I doubt that the recourse to a pacifist narrative that might enforce a pacifist virtue is sufficient. Even if the pacifist notion within the Christian community makes

---

53. See Reuter, *Botschaft und Ordnung*, 40–44.
54. See Reuter, *Botschaft und Ordnung*, 45–55.

the case against such weapons technology, there will be a need to address this refusal in legal terms, factoring in other perspectives as well.

Finally, and with respect to my latter point, Hauerwas argues that it is impossible to define peace theoretically because peace is rather a virtue following from a certain narrative that is therefore indissolubly linked to its respective ideological roots, while the practice of peace is of greater interest. Related to concrete questions of political range, however, this account is highly vague and might rather impede the possibility of finding concrete solutions or measuring achieved outcomes. This must not necessarily mean that a conclusive and exhaustive definition of peace can and must be found, but rather that certain conditions and ramifications are clear. If such implications are not evident, it is hard to address questions such as: What does peace entail? What measures must be taken to achieve which goal? Or might it be possible to use force in order to at least reach a truce?

THE PROTESTANT CHURCH OF BADEN

In 2018, the Protestant Church of Baden developed an approach that favors an absolute pacifist model, and it does so on a large, political-institutional scale under the heading *Rethinking Security: From Military to Civil Security* (*Sicherheit neu denken. Von der militärischen zur zivilen Sicherheitspolitik*, 2018). The authors make use of the so-called scenario technique where a possible positive, middle, and negative future scenario is developed. They then focus on the positive scenario, where civic peacekeeping means would be achieved by 2040.

Their vision is based on a resolution taken in 2013 within the Protestant Church of Baden to become a just peace church.[55] In this resolution, the Church of Baden contests the just peace approach as proposed in the peace memorandum (2007) by criticizing its contingent version of pacifism, favoring just policing over law-sustaining force and prioritizing an absolute pacifist notion.[56] They do so on the basis of the Scripture,

---

55. See Evangelische Landeskirche in Baden, "Richte unsere Füße auf den Weg des Friedens."

56. See Evangelische Landeskirche in Baden, "Richte unsere Füße auf den Weg des Friedens," 8–9. I only mention the peace memorandum of the Protestant church in Germany here, without going into greater detail, for this will be discussed more broadly below. See 5.3.3.2.2 Peace Memorandum of the Council of the Protestant Church in Germany.

which they interpret to indicate "active nonviolence" (*aktive Gewaltlosigkeit*) as a primary way of solving conflicts, thereby highlighting the essential role of the Sermon on the Mount.[57]

The resolution from 2013, on the one hand, focuses on some general peace ethical remarks and makes suggestions to elaborate on their interpretation of just peace as an absolute pacifist approach within the boundaries of the church, such as educating Christians to become nonviolent actors. *Rethinking Security*, on the other hand, takes a broader, political stance. The authors couch their vision in the following terms:

> Shared security means, for the sake of our own security, adopting appropriate lifestyles and developing an economy, which uses the Earth's ecological resources only in proportion to our share of the world's population, and which also leads to global trade and economic relations which are ecologically and socially just. [...] This scenario entails the diversion of all financial resources from military security to civilian prevention and management of conflicts by 2040. [...] A (reformed) UN is the central institution which regulates the peaceful coexistence of peoples and nation states.[58]

This quote illuminates the thrust of the argument: Civic, nonviolent means can be accomplished within an international frame, namely the UN, by redistributing financial resources from the military sphere to the civic sphere. This is possible mainly through economy. If nations are bound up with each other by trade, and they do so in relation to their share in the international community, more just international relations will develop. Here, international peace becomes closely connected to economic and social factors. Proceeding from these assumptions, the authors identify intermediate goals—for instance, the withdrawal of arm export guarantees in 2021,[59] a papal encyclical for the promotion of peace in 2023,[60] or a peace process with Russia.[61] These steps will finally lead to a complete disarmament, so the German *Bundeswehr* will become expendable and can be incorporated into the International

---

57. See Evangelische Landeskirche in Baden, "Richte unsere Füße auf den Weg des Friedens," 6. This does not mean that the whole church favors this approach unanimously, but the gist of the discussion can be seen in this vote for an absolute pacifist notion.

58. Evangelische Landeskirche in Baden, "Rethinking Security," 6–7.

59. See Evangelische Landeskirche in Baden, "Rethinking Security," 10.

60. See Evangelische Landeskirche in Baden, "Rethinking Security," 11.

61. See, for example, Evangelische Landeskirche in Baden, "Rethinking Security," 13.

Agency for Technical Relief.[62] In this process, the UN forces will also be reorganized as police forces[63] and nonviolent resistance will replace violent means thereof.[64]

In contrast to that prior positive scenario, the authors also briefly discuss an ongoing trend toward militarization, which not only entails a continuing merging of police and armed forces but also the collapse of several African states, leading to increasingly more refugees and rising sea levels, which makes some countries uninhabitable.[65] In a final negative trend, the authors see the world "close to the abyss."[66] Here, additionally, national borders are reinstated within the EU, armed drones are deployed by the Bundeswehr, and nuclear conflict between the NATO and Russia becomes imminent.[67]

I discuss this proposal here because it develops an institutional, large-scale approach by contesting the contingent version of just peace. While the latter will be discussed in greater detail below,[68] I focus on the large-scale dimension of this approach here. Combined with the aforementioned resolution, a bigger picture comes into view. On the basis of their interpretation of the Scripture, underlining the biblical imperative to nonviolence and pacifism, the Protestant Church of Baden demands training individuals to resolve conflicts peacefully but also delineates an institutional approach to peace. This is important because the positive scenario addresses the intricate area of peace and security in a way that shows that international peace might be possible if the relevant actors would make a determined effort to overcome war. This, however, should not distract from the major problems of this account. First, the basis of the normative implications of why peace should be embraced internationally is not made sufficiently clear. If the previously mentioned resolution is also taken into account, the nexus between a biblical interpretation and the demand for international peace hinges on the relationship between justice and peace, which does not naturally entail an absolute pacifist approach, as the peace memorandum of 2007 shows. This theoretical

---

62. See Evangelische Landeskirche in Baden, "Rethinking Security," 14.
63. Evangelische Landeskirche in Baden, "Rethinking Security," 20.
64. Evangelische Landeskirche in Baden, "Rethinking Security," 22–23.
65. See Evangelische Landeskirche in Baden, "Rethinking Security," 26–28.
66. Evangelische Landeskirche in Baden, "Rethinking Security," 29.
67. See Evangelische Landeskirche in Baden, "Rethinking Security," 29–31.
68. See 5.3.3.2.2 Peace memorandum of the Council of the Protestant Church in Germany.

imbalance then leads to two divergent proposals: Either, in the case of the resolution, to focus on the education of individuals or, in the case of the scenario study, to concentrate on (international) politics. Admittedly, these contributions do not have the objective of deliberating the topic comprehensively but of outlining a certain vision. These vacancies, however, pose a difficulty that needs to be addressed. Second, the negative as well as the trend scenario merely seem to serve the purpose of contrasting the positive scenario. In doing so, the authors give the impression that the world will be destroyed if the international community does not take the steps described in the positive scenario, thereby mainly provoking fear of such a devastating scenario. The problem here is mainly that, from that perspective, all of the scenarios turn out to be deeply biased, following a normative and not a descriptive rationale. Clearly, the normative principle is to construct (international) peace. But again, to the extent that the normativity of the principles is not sufficiently made clear, such an undertaking seems hardly convincing. Finally, the political suggestions seem rather utopian and naive. While a utopian account is not problematic per se, and might even release the necessary vigor to fulfill an undertaking, a naive proposal is indeed questionable because it is hard to take its ideas seriously. For instance, the idea of achieving an international and sustaining peace is surely a goal worth pursuing—and with a high effort, at that. But when put into a certain time frame, thereby assuming some vague and rather random developments in international politics, such as national borders being reinstated within the EU, the approach loses its cogency. Here, the focus on certain years and dates seems especially precarious, even if these make the approach vivid.

Taken together, the gist of the approach, which is to discuss peace as a matter of international affairs thereby addressing political means to achieve those goals, serves as a good starting point. The normative basis for this demand and its concrete implementation, however, needs further (re-)consideration.

THE ROMAN CATHOLIC NONVIOLENCE INITIATIVE OF PAX CHRISTI INTERNATIONAL

Among the Roman Catholic initiatives advancing nonviolence, Pax Christi International stands out. It currently represents 120 international member organizations and promotes peaceful ways of resolving conflicts.[69] It was founded in the late days of World War II, taking root in the resistance against Nazi Germany's persecution of Jews within France, where the founding figure of the organization, Bishop Pierre Marie Théas, wrote a pastoral letter in 1942 declaring the shared humanity of all people, as all of them "are brothers and sisters created by the same God."[70] In 1944, the Gestapo arrested Théas and held him captive for several months. He then met Marthe Dortel-Claudot in 1945, who was also an opponent of Nazi ideology. Together, they decided to bring an initiative called Pax Christi into existence. The objective of this movement was to pray for Germany thereby performing Jesus' command to love one's enemy. This served as the starting point for a movement aiming to reconcile Germans and the French, whose first international congress was held in 1948 in Kevelaer, a German town near Aachen.[71] In 2020, the organization brought forward its own absolute pacifist approach within the Catholic Nonviolence Initiative in the book *Advancing Nonviolence and Just Peace in the Church and the World* (2020). This contribution refers to the papal encyclical *Laudato Si* that constantly emphases the nexus between justice and peace as well as the importance of the common good, which "calls for social peace, the stability and security provided by a certain order which cannot be achieved without particular concern for distributive justice; whenever this is violated, violence always ensues."[72] Against this backdrop, it is the aim of the Catholic Nonviolence Initiative to foster "a culture of peace, disarmament and development."[73] Basically, the authors interpret the gospel to proclaim an ethics of nonviolence and perceive nonviolence to include more than pacifism and the rejection of violent means. Moreover, they expect nonviolence to foster peaceful means to resolve conflicts.[74] For that matter, the authors address four different dimensions. These are, first, the experiences of people living under violent circumstances yet refusing to answer them violently. Second, they scrutinize the church's tradition of nonviolent approaches, thereby developing a "theology of nonviolence."[75] In a third dimension, the focus is

69. See Pax Christi International, "Catholic Nonviolence Initiative."
70. See Pax Christi International, "Our History."
71. See Pax Christi International, "Our History."
72. Francis, "*Laudato Si*," 157.
73. Berger et al., *Advancing Nonviolence and Just Peace in the Church and the World*, 9.
74. See Berger et al., *Advancing Nonviolence and Just Peace in the Church and the World*, 20.
75. Berger et al., *Advancing Nonviolence and Just Peace in the Church and the World*, 25.

put on the implications and ramifications of nonviolent methods within certain historical circumstances until, fourth, the authors articulate how they expect the church to engage within ongoing conflicts in a nonviolent way.[76] For the sake of my contribution, I will concentrate on the theological explanation underlying this approach, which the authors unfold primarily in the end of the second dimension. Here, the initiative states that the world was initially created by God in an inherently good and nonviolent way. The same is true for humanity, which is made in God's image and therefore bestowed with a special responsibility for creation. Humanity, however, has fallen into sin, which not only affects individual humans but social structures as well. Humans are nevertheless called to challenge these sinful structures in nonviolent ways.[77] With respect to Christology, the authors interpret Christ to be an example of nonviolent behavior. They write,

> The entire drama of the incarnation and the redemption operates with a nonviolent logic of kenosis; rather than use power to overcome resistance coercively, God empties Godself and turns the logic of power on its head, absorbing the violence of the world rather than perpetuating the cycle of retribution.[78]

This means that Christ deliberately decided to forgo his godly power and chose to die instead of using violence. This, in turn, is the groundwork for reconciliation and forgiveness not only for the individual Christian but also between different people and peoples, thereby emphasizing the shared humanity of all humans.[79] These processes are made possible by "the creative power and guidance of the Holy Spirit."[80] Finally, the initiative emphasizes the church's part within nonviolent approaches. Both paragraphs, as well the anterior elaborating on the Holy Spirit and the posterior revolving around the church, draw back mainly to *Lumen gentium*, a document that originated in the Second Vatican Council and

---

76. See Berger et al., *Advancing Nonviolence and Just Peace in the Church and the World*, 25–26.

77. See Berger et al., *Advancing Nonviolence and Just Peace in the Church and the World*, 127.

78. Berger et al., *Advancing Nonviolence and Just Peace in the Church and the World*, 128.

79. See Berger et al., *Advancing Nonviolence and Just Peace in the Church and the World*, 127–41.

80. Berger et al., *Advancing Nonviolence and Just Peace in the Church and the World*, 142.

represents the dogmatic constitution on the church. Referring to both *Lumen gentium* and Scripture—especially Paul's concept of the charisms given by the Holy Spirit—the authors of the Nonviolence Initiative argue that the charisms are directed "toward the good not only in the Church but in the world as well."[81] This angle is then combined with the eschatological notion of God's reign in Matthew 25:31–46, where people's works are works of mercy done out of love for other people. Changing the viewpoint toward the church, the authors state that, "As followers of the Prince of Peace, the Church is called to be nonviolent."[82] From that perspective, the purpose of the church is to imitate Christ in acting nonviolently.[83] For that matter, the church is a sacrament for the world. In the initiative's words:

> It can be said that Christ is the sacrament of God, and the Church is the sacrament of Christ. The Church concretely manifests this claim when it is faithful to the nonviolent witness and teachings of Christ, who came to inaugurate the Kingdom of God.[84]

In the course of this section, the authors also turn to just war tradition but repudiate this strand of theory because they deem all forms of violence to stand against Christ's teachings.[85]

In summary, this approach is an attempt to review the church's tradition critically and to follow its nonviolent paths. While this approach is coherent in rereading traditional texts in the light of an absolute pacifist approach, it simultaneously omits some strands of tradition that do refer to violence. For instance, the question of the reasons for which violent and gruesome texts within Scripture are passed down is simply not addressed. In line with this argumentation is also the redefinition of just peace theory within an absolute pacifist approach, thereby repudiating every form of violence. For that matter, the general critique of absolute pacifist approaches applies here too, which is that there might be

---

81. Berger et al., *Advancing Nonviolence and Just Peace in the Church and the World*, 147.

82. Berger et al., *Advancing Nonviolence and Just Peace in the Church and the World*, 152.

83. See Berger et al., *Advancing Nonviolence and Just Peace in the Church and the World*, 153.

84. Berger et al., *Advancing Nonviolence and Just Peace in the Church and the World*, 154.

85. See Berger et al., *Advancing Nonviolence and Just Peace in the Church and the World*, 163.

situations where a strict denial of any violent means whatsoever might facilitate even more suffering and pain.

5.1.3.2 Noninstitutional Conceptions

JUDITH BUTLER

In the book *The Force of Nonviolence: An Ethico-Political Bind* (2020), Judith Butler develops an own approach to nonviolence. Even though Butler does not use the terms "pacifist" or "pacifism," Butler's account revolves around the categorical renunciation of violence, which is the reason for addressing it here. Butler's monograph aims primarily at the large-scale dimension of peace, and the main interest is to zero in on violence in its structural and systemic impact. In order to do so, Butler highlights the formative role of social relations between humans, thereby constituting each other, be it harmfully or helpfully. The text reads,

> For if the one who practices nonviolence is related to the one against whom violence is contemplated, then there appears to be a prior social relation between them; they are part of one another, or one self is implicated in another self. Nonviolence would, then, be a way of acknowledging that social relation, however fraught it may be, and of affirming the normative aspirations that follow from that prior social relatedness. As a result, an ethics of nonviolence cannot be predicated on individualism, and it must take the lead in waging a critique of individualism as the basis of ethics and politics alike.[86]

This quote reveals Butler's objective, which is to demonstrate that people are always interrelated, and by using force against another person, they eventually use force against themselves. Moreover, the claim brings to the fore that this individual approach has no individualistic outcome but relates to politics and ethics in a normative way. For that reason, this account can be interpreted as not only covering the large-scale dimension of nonviolence but also considering minimal and medium-scale issues: Because humans (and other living beings) are interrelated from the outset, they also need to build their ethical, political, and social lives according to a rationale of nonviolence. To make that point, three presuppositions concerning (non-)violence are expressed. First, violence does not occur detached from any social context and, accordingly, comes

---

86. Butler, *Force of Nonviolence*, 12.

The Ethical Framing

with an interpretation, which marks a difference between good and bad violence, whereas good violence is mainly seen as the violence needed to uphold a certain government. Second, Butler casts doubt on the rationale that nonviolence is an individualistic moral standpoint. This can be seen with regard to the role of the self and its boundaries as well as the crucial question of the extent to which different selves within a certain society have different social standings and are thus seen to be more or less important to defend. The latter point is made clear with reference to the issue of which lives are considered to be grievable and which are not—and are therefore considered expendable. Third, having recourse to Walter Benjamin's account of violence, Butler raises the question of whether violence can simply be seen as a tool or rather needs to be regarded as a social practice. While in the first case, humans use violence as any other means for their own terms, the second case defines violence as an existing social practice that becomes operative on its own, thereby (re-)shaping the social sphere in a violent way. Butler clearly advocates for the second understanding, emphasizing the need to develop nonviolent social practices.[87] Against the argument that nonviolence is an unrealistic goal to pursue, Butler strengthens the necessity of raising the issue of "what counts as reality" in order to create a new "political imaginary."[88]

In the course of the book, the author then fleshes out the arguments. At the outset, the idea of the state of nature is criticized because not only is an individual adult male imagined—thereby disregarding nonmale humans—but also a person that has no social bonds whatsoever. He is independent in the sense that he is not subordinated to any instance but also—and this is even more important—he is deprived of any relationship, as if he has never been young. This depiction of independence embodied in the idea of individualism is the focus of Butler's critique because "no one is born an individual, [but rather] born into a condition of radical dependency."[89] The intention, consequently, is to develop an account that

---

87. See Butler, *Force of Nonviolence*, 14–15.

88. Butler, *Force of Nonviolence*, 13. Butler's term here mainly harks back to Lacan and Castoriades. Both refer to the term "imaginary," but Castoriades clearly exceeds and criticizes the meaning Lacan has in mind. Lacan, on the one hand, refers to the individual as being constituted via an imagined relatedness to oneself as another in the mirror stage. See Pagel, *Jaques Lacan*, 30–31. For Lacan, the imaginary is therefore inherently bound to the individual and to their private self-perception. Castoriades, on the other hand, refers to the political dimension thereby applying the individual notion of Lacan toward society. See Castoriades, *Gesellschaft als imaginäre Institution*, 174–75.

89. Butler, *Force of Nonviolence*, 26.

factors in these dependencies and rejects the idea of a solitarily existing individual. For instance, Butler proposes regarding equality not as an individual right but as a basis of interdependent relations, thereby making a social claim: "Equality is thus a feature of social relations that depends for its articulation on an increasingly *avowed* interdependency."[90] Having made this clear, the character of self-defense as an undisputed exception to the rule is questioned. Besides the issue that an ostensible self-defense might turn out to be an offensive, aggressive act, Butler highlights the problem that making this exception entails that a distinction is drawn between people who are worthy of protection and others who are seen as legitimate targets, so the tantamount issue is the question of what distinguishes one group from the other. This distinction, however, eventually leads the way to divergent forms of group identities, following a "war logic"[91] that assumes that the lives of a certain group are more valuable and, accordingly, more worth fighting for than the lives of the others. In contrast to that rationale, Butler puts forward the demand for a "radical equality of the grievable,"[92] arguing that a life that is grievable needs to be protected. This opens up a utopic perspective because potentially everything can be grieved for. By the same token, Butler addresses the imbalance between grievable persons who "*would be* mourned if their lives *were* lost," while "the ungrievable are those whose loss would leave no trace, or perhaps barely a trace."[93] Since mourning is an interpersonal practice, it exceeds the single individual: It is structured "dyadic"[94] and has social and political implications and therefore leads to an "egalitarian approach to the value of life"[95] that does not distinguish between expendable and indispensable lives. Yet, this rationale seems inscribed into the consideration of "collateral damage"[96] in order to achieve a military objective. To address this issue, Butler raises a question: "What leads any of us to seek to preserve the life of the other?"[97] To the author's mind, the answer to this question is best given with reference to grievability: All lives share the quality of grievability and are worth securing, hence the

90. Butler, *Force of Nonviolence*, 28. Emphasis original.
91. Butler, *Force of Nonviolence*, 35.
92. Butler, *Force of Nonviolence*, 35.
93. Butler, *Force of Nonviolence*, 42. Emphasis original.
94. Butler, *Force of Nonviolence*, 42.
95. Butler, *Force of Nonviolence*, 42.
96. Butler, *Force of Nonviolence*, 46.
97. Butler, *Force of Nonviolence*, 38.

practice of nonviolence must be embraced. Butler elaborates further on that, regarding the tradition of psychoanalysis, namely Sigmund Freud and Melanie Klein. Recurring to Freud, it is stated that aggression and destructiveness, even if they might be morally contained, still play an integral part in a person's psychic life. Yet, drawing on Klein, they can be transformed when identifying positively with the other: In doing something good for the other, the person in question themselves copes with their own losses and guilt.[98] That way, both are closely intertwined and need each other to live their lives.[99] By destroying the other, however, a person also destroys themselves. Butler then attempts to transfer this concept to the political realm by taking into account the category of grievability in a normative way, meaning that every life "*ought to be grievable*,"[100] thereby making room for a utopic perspective. For that reason, referring to Foucault's concept of biopolitics as well as Fanon's notion of racism, it is first argued that a certain population only becomes relevant if it is seen as grievable. That way life is given or taken.[101] In a second step, Butler scrutinizes law's violence, hereby mainly interpreting Benjamin. The gist of his contribution, according to Butler, is that Benjamin unveils that violence is embedded into an interpreted framework, and we can only understand the characteristics of this framework, its boundaries, and its end if we come to see what violence entails and how it is constituted. That way, we can understand that framing a certain behavior to be a violent act (of resistance) against an existing government is done to indicate that this action is an assault on the overall (violent and racist) framework.[102] At variance with this, Butler suggests becoming aware of our inter-relatedness, thereby emphasizing the constitutive role of equality.

Finally, Butler shifts the focus to Freud and his idea of destruction, stating primarily that humanity does not become more cruel, but emerging technologies enable destruction on a larger scale. Subsequently, Butler turns to Freud's account of love, which is ambivalent in character,

---

98. See Butler, *Force of Nonviolence*, 49–50.

99. Klein's idea is that the child is always in close relation to their parents and, growing up, reenacts these relations over and over again with other people, thereby either recreating the love of a parent shown to this person or straightening out feelings of loss, guilt, and despair. See Klein, Liebe, *Schuldgefühl und Wiedergutmachung*, 86.

100. Butler, *Force of Nonviolence*, 57. Emphasis original.

101. See Butler, *Force of Nonviolence*, 57–63.

102. See Butler, *Force of Nonviolence*, 70–71.

meaning that love is "structured by the oscillation between love and hatred."[103] This ambivalence, however, can only be seriously considered if transferred to an ethical practice that knows about its own destructiveness. This is an effort Butler sees as opposed to ideas that merely appeal to somebody's conscience in order not to use violent means. What the author ultimately has in mind is to transfer our own hatred and aggression against violence itself according to the norm of equality and directed against anything that undermines it.[104]

In summary, Butler approaches the topic of nonviolence from two different directions. First, the author draws on a small-scale approach, where the individual and their relations form the foundation for a new imaginary of equality, following the rational: Because I know that I depend on you, I have to secure your life as you secure mine. Second, Butler elaborates on a large-scale approach, where it is emphasized that legal and political institutions and structures of violence hinge on their interpretation. By reacting nonviolently to violence, this framework of interpretation is exposed, thereby revealing whose lives are seen as grievable and whose are not, an act that ultimately discloses who is given the right to live and who is not. The problem arises, however, when the two theories meet. Butler can show cogently how persons are interdependent from a psychoanalytic point of view, and illuminates the given social framework in which people are incorporated. Butler fails, however, to explain sufficiently how these two realms are bound up with each other. Thus, it is eventually not clear how the dependent individual should advocate for minorities or suppressed groups they do not know. Moreover, even though a new egalitarian imaginary is demanded, it is not made clear how this is about to happen. The hint at the nonviolent possibilities of subaltern groups or persons does still not explain how these persons can make themselves understood in a world that does not care about them. With regard to their suffering, Butler's demand to act seems rather cynical.[105]

What is convincing in that account, though, is the call for the need for a new political imaginary that takes the power of nonviolence seriously. This is in line with the preeminent role of pacifist authors such as

103. Butler, *Force of Nonviolence*, 85.
104. See Butler, *Force of Nonviolence*, 89–90.
105. Dorlin has addressed exactly this issue in her book about self-defense, where she describes the subaltern groups that can hardly defend themselves, even more so nonviolently. See Dorlin, *Selbstverteidigung*.

Fox or the Protestant Church of Baden, who highlight how they consider pacifism. Here, nonviolent means are granted the power to make room for a new narrative and a new imaginary that ultimately might change social and political practices. Additionally, Freud's remark—that the cruelty of humans did not change but the possibilities—is worthy of consideration, as it shows that technology has an impact on how humans act out their cruelty toward one another, an undertaking inherently different if done by means of sticks and stones, guns and knives, bows and arrows, or autoregulative weapons systems.[106] When both of these ideas are combined, the ongoing development of technology within a bellicose framing comes into view.

Michael Allen Fox

The American/Canadian/Australian philosopher Michael Allen Fox provides one of the most straightforward contemporary—and cosmopolitan—pacifist accounts. In his understanding, peace needs to be the center of attention. He discovers, for instance, in historical descriptions of war, biased narratives that focus on the violent aspect of human history only while ignoring peaceful episodes and concurrently presenting themselves as "objective."[107] At variance with such a description, Fox, having recourse to Foucault, holds that historical descriptions of war are closely linked to questions of power and are very likely to be influenced by a certain political interest.[108] He thus aims to emphasize peaceful and nonviolent episodes in history, writing,

> To the extent that we characterize the past as the product of violent acts, so too shall we be likely to project this as our image of the present and future. There is therefore a pressing need to highlight nonviolence in history in order to counteract this imbalance of perspectives and open up the possibility of a different kind of future.[109]

This means that the way historians describe our past affects the way we perceive ourselves as human beings. If, on the one hand, the past is depicted in a violent way, we also perceive ourselves violently and

---

106. See Butler, *Force of Nonviolence*, 77.
107. Fox, *Understanding Peace*, 46.
108. See Fox, *Understanding Peace*, 48–51.
109. Fox, *Understanding Peace*, 51.

imagine our future to evolve in violent ways. If, on the other hand, peaceful periods in history are zeroed in on and nonviolent means leading to political solutions are highlighted, we gain the potential to experience ourselves as peaceful and might imagine our future to be nonviolent.

In order to imagine ourselves and our future peacefully, however, one of the most eminent questions is whether war is part of the human condition or not. Fox seeks to uphold that it is not, yet (pre-)historical studies can neither confirm one assumption nor the other due to lack of evidence. He does, therefore, refer to the malleability of humans, meaning that they are predisposed to be neither peaceful by nature nor belligerent but can be influenced one way or the other.[110] He endorses his point with reference to the cropping up of more and more literature that highlights peaceful ways to achieve (political) goals within societies.[111] Even though this bulk of material does not mean that humans are peaceful by nature, it casts doubt on the default assumption that war is part of the human condition. Yet, peace needs to be endorsed just like other social achievements. "In other words, peace, like violence and war, is a product of cultures and the dynamics of reinforcement or social learning that are prominent in them."[112]

From that standpoint, he then criticizes just war thinking. One of his main concerns is that just war tradition states an extraordinary yet expedient case, which essentially expels some groups like war combatants from the "moral community."[113] Recurring to Camus, he emphasizes that violence can only be overcome if politics relinquishes it from its political toolbox. He then seeks to endorse his stance with a twofold argument. First, in a syllogism borrowed from Diana Francis and focusing on human well-being, if human dignity is a moral concept forming the foundation for morality and war annihilates this fundamental concept, then war is a threat to our moral reasoning. If further morality is essential for the well-being of humanity and the individual, then war is in opposition

---

110. See Fox, *Understanding Peace*, 80.

111. See Fox, *Understanding Peace*, 80–85. Another publication within this field of interest is Tomasello, *Natural History of Human Morality*. Against Tomasella, however, I agree with Fox that the possibility of reconstructing prehistorical societies in a cooperative and peaceful way is far away from proving that prehistorical societies really conducted their lives that way and that morality necessarily evolved naturally by cooperation.

112. Fox, *Understanding Peace*, 86.

113. Fox, *Understanding Peace*, 111.

The Ethical Framing

to our well-being.[114] Second, he argues in a broader sense including other forms of life: If humans interrelate with other species and interrelated beings share a common fate, then humans share their fate with other beings. Consequently, the moral realm of humans expands into other species too. Further, if war contrasts with the well-being of life in general, then war is also contrary to "moral obligations."[115] This means that, according to Fox, "war is the most profound kind of wrongdoing, and as such, should never be fought,"[116] at least from his ethical standpoint.[117]

In a next step, he then scrutinizes the role of peace carefully, commencing with the focal point of nonviolent means, which entails avoiding harm but can also be a way to strategically plan a political undertaking.[118] In doing so, he admits that nonviolent methods might not be the most promising way to achieve a certain (political) goal. They are, however, the better approach to pursuing such goals and should therefore be favored. Moreover, nonviolence is not only the (negative) absence of violence but also entails striving for "improving the conditions of human life."[119] For that matter, Fox needs to define peace and nonviolence as very close to each other, for both of them share a negative and a positive connotation where the positive side is hard to define, as "any end-state, if there is one, is so remote as to be merely hypothetical in character."[120] They are not entirely coextensive with each other, though, for peace necessarily entails nonviolence, while the same is not true the other way around. As Fox puts it:

> *There can be nonviolence without peace, but not peace without nonviolence prevailing.* Another way of putting this point is to say that nonviolence is a necessary, but not a sufficient condition for peace to be realized.[121]

---

114. See Fox, *Understanding Peace*, 118.

115. Fox, *Understanding Peace*, 122–23.

116. Fox, *Understanding Peace*, 125.

117. Fox further notes that war is also wrong from a legal point of view and backs this argument with reference to the Kellog-Briand Pact. He, however, does not elaborate on this idea on detail, so I will not cover this line of argumentation here. Fox, *Understanding Peace*, 129–30.

118. See Fox, *Understanding Peace*, 167.

119. Fox, *Understanding Peace*, 183.

120. Fox, *Understanding Peace*, 183.

121. Fox, *Understanding Peace*, 184. Emphasis original.

Accordingly, peace exceeds the dimensions of nonviolence. It also interweaves an inner subjective and an outer objective dimension, where the subjective dimension refers to the inner state of the individual and the outer dimension points to the political sphere.[122] Fox then links these dimensions to the idea of positive and negative peace and holds that, regarding negative peace, the inner dimension means security, while the outer dimension refers to a state's stability, including the protection against hostilities. With regard to positive peace, however, the field is broader. Next to an inner dimension, which is mainly a "state of well-being," and an outer dimension, which refers to "goal" and "process," Fox adds the dimension of a cosmic peace, which entails the "unity with a larger whole" and the prescriptive/visionary dimension, which serves as a "guiding principle."[123]

This categorization forms the foundation on which Fox asks for the chance to achieve peace. The individual account and the individual's daily cooperation with other individuals serves him as a starting point for deliberating the crucial role of compassion, which he reconstructs regarding virtue ethics and having recourse to the teachings of Buddha. In his understanding, compassion is imperative, as it primarily means an "awareness of the suffering of another coupled with the wish to relieve it"[124] and is therefore in close relation to peace by definition. Yet, what is needed is the will to act peacefully, which Fox recognizes as having the character of a personal trait knit together with such concepts as self-awareness.[125] This is Fox's starting point for enlarging the scope to society, since an individual can only live a peaceful life in peaceful surroundings.[126] For that reason, peace is a bottom-up as well as a top-down approach, meaning that it involves the individual and society equally. Against this backdrop, he then considers diverging violent scenarios such as terrorism, the arms trade, and nuclear weapons, which he deems

---

122. See Fox, *Understanding Peace*, 184–87. The terms I refer to here are Fox's terms. I am somewhat skeptical about whether the political outer dimension coincides with a purported objective dimension, especially with regard to peace, which is very open in its definition and therefore highly dependent on cultural predispositions. I therefore prefer the term "outer dimension."

123. Fox, *Understanding Peace*, 193.

124. Fox, *Understanding Peace*, 195. Fox quotes this definition from the *American Heritage Dictionary*.

125. See Fox, *Understanding Peace*, 201.

126. See Fox, *Understanding Peace*, 197.

The Ethical Framing

to be "obstacles to peace."[127] He further criticizes the default assumption that conflict is a universal phenomenon. Even though this is true on a basic level because conflicts occur on all stages of human interaction between individuals, groups, and societies, this does not naturally entail that conflict cannot be transformed.[128] Therefore, a framework is needed that takes the other and their dignity seriously. This attitude then ought to be transferred to the societal realm, so society as a whole benefits.

Finally, Fox suggests three main principles that might help to establish a peaceful (world) community. First, the acceptance and affirmation of the other, as well as the recognition of their universal human rights. Fox reconstructs the gist of these human rights in close connection to the Human Rights Declaration of the UN and argues that "as autonomous agents, all people deserve to be treated with dignity, respect, and justice."[129] Further, he emphasizes,

> The suggestion being made here is not that these are alternatives to involvement with international issues, but that we should avoid merely pointing the finger elsewhere and also realize, once again, that *peacebuilding starts wherever we are situated*.[130]

Second, he widens the scope from human relationships to animals and the environment by including them in the moral community.[131] Fox, third, highlights the crucial role of education with regard to peace, which means giving preference to nonviolent means, reflecting on the connection between masculinity and violence, giving rise to education programs, and endorsing women and girls.[132]

In summary, three aspects stand out. First, it is important to note that Fox makes extensive recourse to religious sources in order to establish his pacifist approach. He often refers to Gandhi,[133] several times to Buddha,[134] Zen,[135] the biblical concept of שלום (*shalom*),[136] and to some

---

127. Fox, *Understanding Peace*, 209.
128. See Fox, *Understanding Peace*, 235.
129. Fox, *Understanding Peace*, 254.
130. Fox, *Understanding Peace*, 256. Emphasis original.
131. See Fox, *Understanding Peace*, 257.
132. See Fox, *Understanding Peace*, 259–67.
133. See Fox, *Understanding Peace*, 56, 154, 159–67, 194.
134. See Fox, *Understanding Peace*, 196, 177.
135. See Fox, *Understanding Peace*, 189.
136. See Fox, *Understanding Peace*, 182.

passages within the New Testament.[137] Also, Muslim tradition is mentioned within this context.[138] This is insightful because even though Fox's attempt is clearly to approach pacifism from a philosophical stance, he deems religion to be decisive for pacifist thought. To do justice to his approach, he discusses different historical accounts that aim at reconstructing history with respect to peace, even to the degree that he factors in prehistorical times. He does, however, admit that this is very hypothetical and can be reconstructed differently. Therefore, his main sources with regard to peace as a normative framework are indeed religious sources.

Second, and rather critically, even though Fox's main focus is peace on a global scale, he almost entirely considers it on an individual level, reducing his solution to a small-scale approach. This is because Fox's pacifist stance is within virtue ethics and therefore focuses on the individual. This is also in line with cosmopolitanism, to the degree that the focus here is put on the individual being that bears universal rights. He then, rather simplistically, postulates that this individual account can be transferred to the societal level without explaining the thought on which he bases this assumption in detail. In fact, he admits that this does not necessarily guarantee society to be an entirely peaceful entity, but claims that this is very probable.[139] The problem here is that it does not seem entirely clear whether and to what degree individual traits and behavior can be transferred to society at large because, as Fox himself argues, "any whole is more than the sum of its parts."[140]

Third, however, his approach is cogent with regard to his call to consider peace within a pacifist framework that prefers peace over war, as he elaborates on peace and its establishment on a very broad scale while reflecting war and violence within this view to a minor degree. The main problem, however, is that while Fox makes very clear that the individual can and should live a peaceful and nonviolent life, the issue of violence within war or the police exceeds the individual's standpoint. This entails that the soldier and the police-officer are socially entitled to use violent means, even if this is not true for the individual.

---

137. See Fox, *Understanding Peace*, 120, 182.
138. See Fox, *Understanding Peace*, 107.
139. See Fox, *Understanding Peace*, 197.
140. Fox, *Understanding Peace*, 197.

The Ethical Framing

Robert L. Holmes

The philosopher Robert L. Holmes dedicated several contributions to the question of war and peace, elaborating on a technically contingent pacifist standpoint. However, with respect to the practical outcome, the theory seems to rather fit within the scope of an absolute pacifist stance. In his book *On War and Morality* (1989), Holmes already argued that "not all wars under all conceivable circumstances are morally impermissible" but that "war is impermissible in the world as we know it,"[141] meaning that not every historical or fictional war needs refuting but rather contemporary forms of war. In his book *Pacifism: A Philosophy of Nonviolence* (2016), he presents an even stricter argument within a theory he calls existential pacifism. The argument goes as follows:

> 1. Killing persons is presumptively wrong. 2. War entails killing persons, hence entails the performance of presumptive wrongs. 3. Thus war is presumptively wrong. 4. Unless that presumption is defeated, war is morally impermissible. 5. That presumption has not been defeated. 6. Therefore: War is morally impermissible.[142]

In order to make his argument, he focuses on the nexus between war and morality, asking if there are circumstances that authorize the use of force and concluding that if certain wars are seen to be permissible, this entails "that the world is *morally better* with them than without, that there is no available alternative that would be morally preferable."[143] This however, does not seem convincing: Since warfare involves killing, it is simply wrong.[144] He then scrutinizes the metaethical premise that underlies these assumptions, which is basically a differentiation between individual and collective ethics. In cases of conflict, either individual or collective ethics overrides the other. Yet, Holmes contests this view. He writes,

> To impute to collectivities a macroethics is to commit a category mistake. It is to transfer moral concepts that are meaningful in one category, that of human actions, to another category to which they do not belong, that of the so-called actions of states.[145]

---

141. Holmes, *On War and Morality*, 14.
142. Holmes, *Pacifism*, xviii.
143. Holmes, *Pacifism*, 23. Emphasis original.
144. See Holmes, *Pacifism*, 52.
145. Holmes, *Pacifism*, 63.

This quote unveils Holmes presuppositions: Since morality refers to humanity's realm only, it cannot be transferred to the institutional level at all. Therefore, there is no such thing as social ethics but only individual ethics. This does not preclude any form of ethical evaluation of the institution and politics, though; it rather means that questions of collective interest are subordinated to matters of individual concern and need to be assessed from that viewpoint.[146] For that reason and with respect to warfare, "it is the lives and well-being of individual persons that is of greatest moral importance."[147] With this argument, he also rejects political and moral realism, theories that stress the importance the other way around.

In a next step, Holmes turns to just war tradition, commencing with Augustine, whom he interprets as having prepared the ground for "mainstream Christianity's course from pacifism to warism"[148] because Augustine did not constrain the participation in warfare sufficiently.[149] Further, the general notion of just war tradition cannot confine war comprehensively because just war tradition is interested in a partial perspective exclusively, since its objective is to evaluate the use of force for only one (belligerent) party. Moreover, the individual criteria, such as last resort or proportionality, are subject to interpretation. This is especially important when assessing the role of self-defense, which traditional just war approaches generally permit. Yet, harking back to David Rodin and his refutation of this view (which will be presented below[150]) Holmes argues that individual self-defense is not on a par with collective self-defense, which is in line with Holmes's rebuttal of collective morality in general.[151]

Holmes then scrutinizes modern wars and concludes that neither the Vietnam War, the Gulf and Iraq Wars, nor the intervention in Kosovo can be regarded as just wars, even when considering just war tradition standards.[152] Against this backdrop, Holmes then spells out his own notion of pragmatic pacifism, meaning "opposition to war on moral grounds. [Pragmatic pacifism] asks whether war, understood as whole

---

146. See Holmes, *Pacifism*, 64.

147. Holmes, *Pacifism*, 65.

148. Holmes, *Pacifism*, 93.

149. Although Holmes reconstructs Augustine's thought that way, there are different possibilities to put Augustine into context. One of them will be shown below when considering the history of just war tradition. See 5.2.1 *Bellum iustum*: History of Ideas.

150. See 5.2.2.2 Revisionist Just War Thinking.

151. See Holmes, *Pacifism*, 143–44.

152. See Holmes, *Pacifism*, 165–234.

war, is ever morally permissible in the modern world and answers that it is not."[153] Even though pragmatic pacifism is based on a moral theory, it is essentially not a theory but a "moral judgment"[154] and therefore at variance with just war tradition, which Holmes deems to be a theory. Consequently, both approaches exclude each other because if just war tradition is right, then at least some wars can be justified, which pacifism negates. Therefore, any version of contingent pacifism must be ruled out. With regard to humanitarian intervention, Holmes does not preclude such an undertaking to be impermissible per se but only the violent forms thereof.[155] By the same token, Holmes rejects violent means of countering terrorism. He instead advocates for rediscovering "the humanity of all persons, friends and adversaries alike."[156]

Finally, Holmes comes to the conclusion that what is needed is "existential pacifism," an account he defines as follows:

> Existential pacifism represents a commitment to a micro perspective. An existential pacifist refuses, as a matter of conscience, to kill other human beings on the order of others or in the service of causes defined by them. A country as a whole can be committed to pragmatic pacifism, but it cannot be committed to existential pacifism. At most, it can consist of individual persons who are existential pacifists, who associate freely and respectfully with the minimum of pressure and coercion. Ideally, they would live in small communities. Such communities would not concentrate military, political and economic power in the hands of a few people. Their relations among one another would be the product of education that stresses from the earliest age the values of nonviolence.[157]

This means that if every individual is educated rightly and pacifistically and grows up within a (small) community that would favor nonviolent means to solve conflicts, there would not be any need to resort to war. Holmes stresses again his individual notion: Since only individuals are moral agents, there is no reason to attribute moral agency to collectives or institutions such as states. Accordingly, the individual and their personal pacifist or nonpacifist stance is decisive.

153. Holmes, *Pacifism*, 268.
154. Holmes, *Pacifism*, 269.
155. See Holmes, *Pacifism*, 298.
156. Holmes, *Pacifism*, 309.
157. Holmes, *Pacifism*, 330.

Holmes's concept stands out because his objective is to bring together morality and warfare, thereby taking into account war and warfare as a whole. This entails that he is not so much interested in a certain state's or individual's motives to go to war but in assessing war as a comprehensive phenomenon with its beginning and its side effects. Furthermore, he does so within an outspoken individual frame. From that perspective, an absolute pacifist stance seems compelling. Holmes's approach is cogent to the degree that he succeeds in demonstrating the paradox of the general assumption that killing is generally wrong combined with the exception of warfare. Problematic, however, is his rejection of collective ethical approaches, for it is not clear how the individual with their pacifist stance can influence the collective view. Even more importantly, this notion might indicate that peace in its large-scale dimension is out of focus here, because large-scale peace focuses on the collective, political notion of peace. This thought is backed by Holmes's summary, where he suddenly changes his viewpoint from questions of political and institutional interest—such as terrorism, humanitarian intervention, or the Vietnam War—to the single individuals growing up in small communities that favor nonviolent means. Pacifism is certainly the morally superior approach to questions of war and peace, and in a world where all individuals hold a pacifist stance, resorting to war might be implausible. In the real world, however, the morality of collective institutions might differ from the moral ideas of individuals.[158] Moreover, if violence is already part of an ongoing undertaking and the lives of humans are threatened to an enormous degree, to further insist on nonviolent means seems implausible, even dangerous. An illustration of this is World War II, a war that has, in its overall performance, not been a just war. The Allies' entrance into this particular war, however, averted an even greater evil, which shows that, sometimes, resorting to war might save lives. Accordingly, an absolute pacifist stance might very well remove political and institutional agency.[159]

5.1.4 Absolute pacifism and autoregulation in weapons systems

With respect to the question of the extent to which violent means in general, and autoregulative weapons in particular, can be integrated into an

---

158. See Niebuhr, *Moral Man and Immoral Society*.

159. This is in line with the critique of just war thinking, as Walzer, for instance, argues. See Walzer, *Just and Unjust Wars*, 329.

absolute pacifist view, the answer can be given very quickly and easily: Since weapons and weapons systems do not pose peaceful means, this standpoint sees no way to endorse the development and use of autoregulative weapons systems.

Yet, the majority of the approaches discussed here do not address this topic explicitly. Only Fox does so, and he deems the development of autoregulation in weapons technology troubling. Even though he approves of the possible protection of humans in dangerous scenarios, he holds back regarding ever more sophisticated weapons technology, also due to the possible arms race they might facilitate and the lack of control that is to be expected with their wake.[160] He concludes that

> The focus here, however, is on the negative implications of pursuing inventions and discoveries that, so far as can be judged, have no apparent goal other than to expand the repertoire of violent and harmful means to achieve political ends. And the worry is whether we will decide (or perhaps at a later stage, even can decide) to control them.[161]

5.2 JUST WAR TRADITION

Just war—or, in its Latin phrasing, *bellum iustum*—is the most important and influential idea concerning the issue of war and peace in history and today. Its branched roots can be dated back to the ancient world, and the concept has been represented by various thinkers in different traditions and forms ever since. This also means that there is nothing like *the* just war theory that can be referred to in the singular, but rather a collection of diverging theories with different impacts and outcomes. Moreover, just war has been enshrined in international humanitarian law and has therefore been expressed in in juridical terms as well.[162]

In order to understand the gist of just war tradition and its background, I will first provide an overview of this idea's historical development and then delve into contemporary discussions by introducing some of the main figures of the ongoing discourse. My aim is not to conduct an exhaustive study on the current debate, but rather to illustrate the central theories of different thinkers and, by doing so, to show the ideas that

---

160. See Fox, *Understanding Peace*, 72–74.

161. Fox, *Understanding Peace*, 74.

162. The juridical appearance, however, is not in the focus of the following study. I will refer to this aspect only occasionally.

form the foundation for these theories and how they can be clustered. This is important because, as will be shown, the assumptions authors make in their version of just war tradition are accompanied by other presumptions, be they political or ethical.

5.2.1 *Bellum iustum*: History of Ideas[163]

As indicated beforehand, today's ethics of war and peace are rooted in the doctrine of *bellum iustum*. This concept dates back to idea(s) brought forward by classical Greek philosophy, mainly Plato and Aristotle,[164] who sought to answer the question of the purpose of state and law, thereby elaborating the subject of war and peace,[165] prioritizing peace, and deeming war to be evil.[166] Their basic assumption is that humankind is social in nature (Aristotle: ζῷον πολιτικόν) and that the appropriate way to organize cohabitation is by law, thereby educating people to act peacefully.[167] What is applied to the individual is then transferred to the state. Accordingly, Plato holds "τό γε μὴν ἄριστον οὔτε ὁ πόλεμος οὔτε ἡ στάσις [. . .] εἰρήνη δὲ πρὸς ἀλλήλους ἅμα καὶ φιλοφροσύνη [. . .]"[168] ("The highest good, however, is neither war nor civil strife [. . .] but peace one with another and friendly feeling"). Aristotle, on the other hand, is the first author to combine the terms "just" and "war" to "just war" (δίκαιος πόλεμος), even though he describes something different than the modern reader has in mind.[169] Furthermore, he claims that war can be fought for

---

163. With regard to political and juristic development, as well as some main figures throughout the history, I will mainly draw on a dissertation by Jensen published in 2014 addressing the development of just war tradition with a focus on international law. See Jensen, *Krieg um des Friedens willen*.

164. Plato and Aristotle are not the only ancient Greek philosophers dealing with this subject. Thucydides, Herodotus, or Isocrates could also be quoted as examples. Still, Plato and Aristotle can be seen as the most famous and important sources and are therefore addressed here.

165. See Ricken, "Krieg und Frieden," 204.

166. See Jensen, *Krieg um des Friedens willen*, 19.

167. See Ricken, "Krieg und Frieden," 211.

168. Plato, "Nomoi I," 628.

169. In his understanding, humankind is divided into people who should rule and people who should be ruled. Subsequently, people who should rule but are enslaved can fight a just war for the sake of their leadership, and they are authorized to fight people who should be ruled. See Jensen, *Krieg um des Friedens willen*, 26–27; Kleemeier, *Grundfragen einer philosophischen Theorie des Krieges*, 27.

the sake of peace (πόλεμον μὲν εἰρήνης χάριν),[170] which became the pivotal theme in just war tradition.[171] Proceeding mainly from Plato, stoicism incorporates these ideas into its political philosophy, thereby gaining a cosmopolitan perspective combined with outright pacifism.[172]

Cicero then draws on these Greek sources, combining them with *jus fertiale*, the religiously rooted law of war in the ancient Latin world. He not only uses the term *bellum iustum* prominently in his work *De re publica* but also denotes a war unjust and impious (*iniustum atque impium*) if it is not begun under the appropriate circumstances, which are formal announcement (*denuntio*), declaration of war (*indictio*), and the legal, factual cause of war, which is essential self-defense.[173] In another work, *De officiis*, Cicero develops another four criteria. First, he deems physical violence (*vis*) inferior to discussion. War is therefore last resort. Second, the objective of war needs to be the (re-)establishment of a peaceful situation while, third, the ones who "have not been bloodthirsty and barbarous in their warfare"[174] need to be spared after the victory.[175] Finally, he draws a distinction between wars fought for the sake of existence and those fought in order to obtain power.[176]

In a next step, the idea of *bellum iustum* is incorporated into early Christian thought by Augustine, who combines it with the pacifist approach that other church fathers such as Tertullian, Origen, and Lactancius represent.[177] He does so in order to overcome their absolute pacifist approach and to incorporate the possibility of warfare into Christian thinking.[178] Although his teachings target the confinement of violence, they enable Christians to use force within certain boundaries to establish unity

---

170. See Aristotle, "Pol VII, 1333 a," 35.

171. See Jensen, *Krieg um des Friedens willen*, 20.

172. See Forschner, "Krieg und Frieden in der römischen Antike," 214.

173. See Cicero, "De rep III," 23, 34–35; Forschner, "Krieg und Frieden in der römischen Antike," 218. The term *"de repititus rebus"* refers to *jus fertiale* and means things that need to obtain satisfaction.

174. See Cicero, "De off I," 11, 35.

175. See Cicero, "De off I," 11, 34–35.

176. See Forschner, "Krieg und Frieden in der römischen Antike," 221.

177. See Looney, "Augustinus," 226. As I have made clear above, the pacifism of the church fathers is rooted in religious rather than ethical and moral thought and is therefore by no means coextensive with our modern understanding thereof. See 5.1.1. Historical sketch.

178. See May, *Contingent Pacifism*, 87.

and order within this world.[179] There is no single work written by Augustine that consistently develops his theological ideas with regard to war and peace. Rather, his view on that topic is spread throughout his entire body of writings. Augustine presupposes that comprehensive peace cannot be established on earth but will eventually occur in heaven and is therefore primarily eschatological.[180] Throughout the course of life on earth, every human being falls short of living in peace with God because of human sinfulness, namely pride (*superbia*). Augustine then maps this basic assumption onto the relationship between body and soul, as well as to social life.[181] To prevent perpetual war, God appoints monarchs to govern humanity.[182] Although the Bishop of Hippo assumes that war can be just, his intention is to confine it.[183] Therefore, he marks off boundaries for the legitimate use of force, and the one and only authority to go to war (*legitima potestas*) in the first place is the monarch.[184] With regard to just reasons (*causa iusta*), he accepts only one punishment for wrongdoing, which is a reaction to the transgression of the existing order (*ordo*).[185] Moreover, war is always a last resort (*ultima ratio*), and its single intention is to establish peace.[186] While the aforementioned criteria belong to *jus ad bellum*, Augustine also considers some guidelines for the conduct of war (*jus in bello*). Although he does not use the term explicitly, Augustine assumes that war needs to be fought proportionally and especially in line with necessity.[187] Despite the absence of the explicit mention of discrimination between combatants and noncombatants, this principle can be inferred.[188]

In the Middle Ages, Thomas Aquinas incorporated Augustine's ideas into his works, mainly in his *Summa Theologiae II-II q 40*, and

---

179. See Looney, "Augustinus," 226.

180. Augustine, "civ XIX," 5.

181. See Looney, "Augustinus," 227–28.

182. See Looney, "Augustinus," 229.

183. Augustine, "civ XIX," 7.

184. See Looney, "Augustinus," 230, with reference to Augustine, "Contra Faustum, XXI," 75.

185. See Looney, "Augustinus," 231–32; Weissenberg, *Die Friedenslehre des Augustinus*, 146–48. In order to understand this argument, one needs to bear in mind that the way of salvation, as Augustine assumes, is attached to the *ordo*. Thus, an individual can only find salvation if they live in harmony with the God-given *ordo*. See Weissenberg *Die Friedenslehre des Augustinus*, 62.

186. See Looney, "Augustinus," 232.

187. Augustine, "Epistula 198," 6.

188. See Looney, "Augustinus," 234.

The Ethical Framing

amalgamated it with Aristotelian thinking.[189] In *q 40*, Aquinas principally states that war is always sin,[190] since peace (*pax*) is an effect of God's grace (*effectus caritatis*) and war interferes with it.[191] Based on that assumption, he then asks whether there are justified reasons to go to war nonetheless because both the New Testament and Augustine expect people to fight in war.[192] Henceforth, Aquinas lays out three main criteria for just war: the authority of the ruler (*auctoritas principis*), just reason (*causa iusta*), and right intention (*recta intentio*).[193] With respect to *auctoritas principis*, he argues that only the person in charge of the political body (*res publica*) has the right to wage war.[194] Regarding *causa iusta*, Aquinas notes that the attacking enemy bears the blame for committed wrongdoing and therefore can be fought.[195] Concerning *recta intentio*, he states that the right intention is to promote what is good and to prevent what is evil.[196] All of these criteria are related to *jus ad bellum*, because this was Aquinas's main concern. Still, he also considers some aspects of *jus in bello*, such as discrimination and proportionality.[197]

Aquinas's teachings are then referenced by scholars who wrote during the period of Late Spanish Scholasticism.[198] For the sake of this contribution, I will confine my description here to one representative author, namely Francisco de Vitoria, who was the founder of the School of Salamanca and whose teaching had a great influence on the development of international law.[199] The Dominican thinker makes headway in the development of *bellum iustum* as a concept. Teaching and writing during the transition from the Middle Ages to modernity, de Vitoria adapts the Thomistic approach to his own time, thereby laying the groundwork

---

189. See Fuchs, "Thomas von Aquin," 240. One major work, reviewing the teachings of Aquinas with respect to just war is Beestermöller, *Thomas von Aquin und der gerechte Krieg*.

190. Aquinas, "STh II-II q 40 a 1 arg 1."

191. See Fuchs, "Thomas von Aquin," 240.

192. Aquinas, "STh II-II q 40 a 1 s.c."; Looney, "Augustinus," 242.

193. See Aquinas, "STh II-II q 40 a 1 co."

194. Aquinas, "STh II-II q 40 a 1 co."

195. Aquinas, "STh II-II q 40 a 1 co."

196. Aquinas, "STh II-II q 40 a 1 co."

197. See Gašparević, "Die Lehre vom gerechten Krieg und die Risiken des 21. Jahrhunderts," 60.

198. See Stüben, "Die Kriegsethik der Spanischen Spätscholastik," 55–56; Bunge and Gillner, "Die Lehre vom gerechten Krieg," 252.

199. See Bunge and Gillner, "Die Lehre vom gerechten Krieg," 253–56.

for a new international law.[200] He follows Aquinas's teachings by stating that peace is the overall objective (*intentio recta*)[201] and establishes two conditions for going to war. First, war needs to be initiated by a public person, namely the ruler (*legitima potestas*),[202] who is closely connected to the political body (*res publica*) since his power is derived thereof.[203] Second, war is only permissible in the case of defense against an aggression (*causa iusta*).[204] Referring to the latter, he considers three reasons: revenge, recovery, and retribution.[205] Moreover, de Vitoria adds that one ruler can assist another ruler in the conduct of war if the second ruler has been wronged and[206] precludes that war can still be just from the perspective of both belligerent parties.[207] Regarding the ruler's subjects, de Vitoria states that they are not allowed to fight in an unjust war even if they had been forced.[208] He then concedes with issues concerning *jus in bello*. Eventually, he answers the question of whether people are allowed to kill in war positively but simultaneously limits the killing to the necessary amount,[209] ruling out slaughter of people not involved in the fighting, for instance, children.[210] Such practices are only authorized if there is no other way to win a war, as in the bombardment of a city.[211] By the same token, he rules out pillage and looting[212] as well as the enslavement of prisoners of war.[213] From this argumentation, it can be inferred that de Vitoria upholds the criteria of "distinction" and "proportionality" regarding *jus in bello*, though they are not mentioned directly.[214]

200. See Jensen, *Krieg um des Friedens willen*, 142, 225.
201. See de Vitoria, "De iure belli: q4, conclusiones."
202. de Vitoria, "De bello, q40 a 1,3," 80.
203. de Vitoria, "De bello, q40 a 1,3," 80.
204. de Vitoria, "De bello, q40 a 1,3," 80.
205. de Vitoria, "De bello, q40 a 1,3," 80.
206. de Vitoria, "De bello, q40, a 1,5," 82.
207. de Vitoria, "De bello, q40, a 1,7," 84; de Vitoria, "De iure belli, q3, 4 dubium," 576–577.
208. de Vitoria, "De bello, q40, a 1,8," 84; de Vitoria, "De iure belli, q3, 3 dubium," 570–77.
209. de Vitoria, "De bello, q40, a 1,9," 86.
210. de Vitoria, "De bello, q40, a 1,11," 88.
211. See de Vitoria, "De bello, q40, a 1,11," 88.
212. See de Vitoria, "De bello, q40, a 1,12," 88–90.
213. See de Vitoria, "De bello, q40, a 1,18," 94.
214. He debated this in "De iure belli, q 4" and drew the conclusion that the primary objective is to keep peace. Only if this fails—for just reasons—must the war be

The Ethical Framing

In this context, the theology of Martin Luther also needs to be mentioned because his figures of the two regimes, or kingdoms, have been crucial for developing just war theory in its contemporary form. In his writing *Secular Authority: To What Extent it Should Be Obeyed* (*Von weltlicher Obrigkeit, wie weit man ihr Gehorsam schuldig sei*, 1523), the German reformer draws a distinction between the religious and the political spheres by referring to them as kingdoms. I do not interpret the term "the two kingdoms" to refer to two completely separate spheres. By using the term "regime," it is rather my intention to hint at the understanding that both dimensions are under God's reign, so a strict differentiation, such as the term "kingdom" insinuates, is not what Luther had in mind.[215] By drawing this distinction, Luther holds that Christians and non-Christians need different frameworks for maintaining peace: While he expects Christians to behave peacefully, insofar as they are Christians, he deems the political dimension to be in need of political enforcement in order to forestall a state of chaos and belligerence.[216] Within this rationale, the spiritual dimension is concerned with matters of belief, (Christian) religious observance, and the inner human, while the political dimension deals with matters of daily concerns: the life and limb.[217] Generally, and to the extent that matters of daily life are concerned, God has installed the political authorities to govern the political dimension, and Christians also need to follow their ruling, insofar as they are still sinners.[218] For that matter, the political authorities might, for instance, oblige their citizens to fight because they mandate the use of force. This

---

fought in a decent manner, so peace and safety emerge. Furthermore, de Vitoria added that the victory needs to be turned to good account. See de Vitoria, "De iure belli, q4 Conclusiones," 602–5.

215. Also, Bonhoeffer draws on Luther and this distinction. For a further discussion of that matter, see 5.3.3.1 On Bonhoeffer's Account of War and Peace.

216. See Zeyher-Quattlender, *Du sollst nicht töten (lassen)?* 126–27. Zeyher-Quattlender also demonstrates that the understanding of what it means to be a Christian was very high for Luther: Only people who in fact do love their neighbors are true Christians, which entails not resorting to violence. These people, however, are not the selfsame people who call themselves Christians, or members of the church, thereby differentiating between the visible and the invisible church. Accordingly, Luther deems only very few people to have such character. See Zeyher-Quattlender, *Du sollst nicht töten (lassen)?* 127; von Scheliha, *Protestantische Ethik des Politischen*, 27.

217. See Zeyher-Quattlender, *Du sollst nicht töten (lassen)?* 135; von Scheliha, *Protestantische Ethik des Politischen*, 26–27.

218. See Zeyher-Quattlender *Du sollst nicht töten (lassen)?* 129. Christians do not need these rulings because they love their neighbors and enemies already and from within. See also von Scheliha, *Protestantische Ethik des Politischen*, 28.

fundamental structure of sin is also the groundwork for an interpretation of the world that is in need of regulatory regimes that keep the sinfulness of every human, be they Christian or not, at bay. Insofar as Christians are sinful and just at the same time (*simul iustus et peccator*), they lack the capability to act peacefully. This also paves the way for disputable theological interpretations, such as orders of creation.[219]

Another main figure in the development of just war tradition is Hugo Grotius, who addresses the ethics of war and peace mainly in his book *De Iure belli ac pacis, libri tres*. This work was published in 1625 and can be seen as an attempt to limit the scope of violence in the course of the Thirty Years' War.[220] Grotius mainly draws on Late Spanish Scholasticism and relates these ideas to his own time. He proposes that war is essentially gruesome and can only be conducted for the sake of peace.[221] Proceeding from this argument, he derives the specific criteria of just war tradition but, in contrast to the aforementioned thinkers, he develops the idea that war can be just from the perspective of both belligerent sides (*bellum iustum ex utraque parte*)—though the "just" in this case refers to legal not moral reason. On the other hand, Grotius still refers to classical *bellum iustum*, when he considers the moral legitimacy of war.[222] In any case, with Grotius's idea of *bellum iustum ex utraque parte*, a concentration on *jus in bello* ensues, resulting in the development of international humanitarian law.

After the Thirty Years' War, some thinkers still adhered to *bellum iustum*, such as Samuel von Pufendorf, Christian Wolff, and Emer De Vattel, while others focused on developing ideas like international jurisdiction or perpetual peace, for instance, Immanuel Kant in his book *Toward Perpetual Peace* (*Zum ewigen* Frieden, 1795).[223] However, in the

---

219. There are a quite a few modern theological interpretations of this kind, such as the ideas brought forward by Holl and, following him, the theory of autonomy (*Eigengesetzlichkeit*) by Hermann. In a similar vein, also the opponents of such a theory who maintain that there is correspondence from mundane to Christian perspectives, such as Schleiermacher or Barth, would be worthy of discussion in that regard. However, since these discussions would divert too far from the subject in question, I cannot cover them here but only hint at their existence. I am thankful to Notger Slenczka for hinting to that matter, which discloses the connection from peace ethical positions to an overall interpretation of the world.

220. See Jensen, *Krieg um des Friedens willen*, 211, FN 855.

221. Grotius, "De jure belli ac pacis, I, 1. Caput, I"; Jensen, *Krieg um des Friedens willen*, 214.

222. See Jensen, *Krieg um des Friedens willen*, 211–25.

223. I will discuss this work below. See 5.3.1 Preliminaries.

The Ethical Framing

subsequent period, legal positivism succeeded natural law, and just war thinking was sidelined. International law became subject to the sovereignty of individual states and therefore the primary idea to restrict war through an overall principle was no longer convincing. This is at least true for mainland Europe. At the same time, thinkers such as the Scot James Mackintosh continued to engage with the idea of *bellum iustum*.

At the beginning of the twentieth century, political and juristic conditions changed fundamentally. The Hague Conventions of 1899 and 1907 brought the idea of a perpetual peace within reach—a hope bitterly disappointed by World War I. In the interwar period, politico-legal institutions, such as the League of Nations (1920) and agreements such as the Anglo–American Kellogg-Briand Pact (Pact of Paris, 1928) picked up the idea of banning war again by conceptually drawing on *bellum iustum*, though without referring to it explicitly.[224] These attempts failed with the outbreak of World War II, whereupon the UN, with its concept of collective security, was founded. The extent to which *bellum iustum* is part of the legal structure of the UN is still a matter of debate[225] and cannot be examined here, as it is outside the scope of this book. Yet, this development provides the background for the reconsideration of just war thinking in the twentieth century, which was discussed in the US in the context of the Vietnam War[226] and with respect to the question of how to handle nuclear weapons.[227] It is not until this time period after World War II, that the modern distinction between *jus in bello* and *jus ad bellum* was spelled out explicitly and found its way into modern ethics and law.[228]

To conclude, this historical sketch illustrates that the primary objective of the concept of *bellum iustum* for most of its history has been to confine the outbreak and conduct of war. According to a large part of the Western intellectual tradition, the purpose of war lies not in war itself but in establishing peace. This also means that this idea might very well be reconstructed as a tradition favoring pacifism, at least in its contingent version, as I will do below. But first, I want to illustrate the current debates in just war thinking.

224. See Jensen, *Krieg um des Friedens willen*, 268–69.
225. See Jensen, *Krieg um des Friedens willen*, 227–71.
226. See Haspel, "Die Renaissance der Lehre vom gerechten Krieg in der anglo-amerikanischen Debatte," 316.
227. See Lienemann, "Die Revision der Lehre vom gerechten Krieg angesichts der Erfahrungen der Weltkriege und der Atombewaffnung," 302.
228. See Rudolf, *Zur Legitimität militärischer Gewalt*, 33.

5.2.2 Contemporary Just War Tradition

A number of thinkers discuss just war tradition with the attempt to adapt the historical roots to contemporary thought. The Arab–Israeli Six-Day War in 1967 and the American Vietnam War with its devastating impacts have contributed especially strongly to the tradition's renewal.[229] Today, the tradition is generally divided into *jus ad bellum* and *jus in bello*. Those two categories are usually subdivided again into several criteria that echo the traditional thinking, with the major goal being to confine violence. Considerable controversies mark the development of these concepts. For instance, there is an ongoing debate about the importance of establishing a *jus post bellum* resembling *jus ad bello* and *jus in bellum*.[230] Similarly, the general framework referring to multilateralism or unilateralism is in dispute. While the former seeks to establish just war tradition as part of the legal and moral concepts within the political body of the UN, the latter aims to legitimize national politics and sovereignty.[231] Furthermore, alternative ethical approaches exist, which intersect more or less with just war tradition, for instance, the idea of contingent pacifism.[232] Besides the aforementioned debates, one major disagreement revolves around the status of combatants and civilians. The major source for this dispute has been Michael Walzer's main work *Just and Unjust Wars* (1977), which itself is rooted within an ongoing discussion to which mostly Christian thinkers have contributed. I will first elaborate on this revival of just war tradition in the 1960s and 70s and subsequently discuss Michael Walzer's account. I will then cover later developments and illustrate how these ideas have been and are subject to a major scholarly debate, which has brought forward two major strands, which are *traditional just war theory*, following the approach of Walzer, and *revisionist just war theory*, contesting his assumptions. Both strands mainly differ in the emphasis they put on the law, on the one hand, and morality, on the other hand. Along these lines, the addressee also differs: While classical just war approaches address a certain collective such as the nation state, revisionist

---

229. See Haspel, "Die Renaissance der Lehre vom gerechten Krieg in der anglo-amerikanischen Debatte," 316.

230. The first one to consider this idea in detail was Orend. See Orend, "Justice After War."

231. See Haspel, "Die Renaissance der Lehre vom gerechten Krieg in der anglo-amerikanischen Debatte," 321–22.

232. I will refer below to two important works, that both represent a combination thereof: Rodin's *War and Self-defense* and May's *Contingent Pacifism*.

concepts focus on the individual. Both concepts, however, have a great impact on the scholarly debate, especially within the Anglo–American world, so other perspectives such as (contingent) pacifist notions are easily sidelined.[233]

5.2.2.1 The Revival of the Just War Tradition

CHRISTIAN REFERENCES TO JUST WAR BEFORE THE VIETNAM WAR

The Methodist theologian Paul Ramsey is one of the main protagonists who transferred the ideas of just war tradition into modern (political) thinking. In his book *War and the Christian Conscience* (1961), he developed an approach that combines the tradition of *bellum iustum*—closely connected to the teachings of Augustine—with the twentieth century's contemporary weapons technology, namely nuclear weapons. To do so, he asks how war and Christian conscience might be reconciled, drawing the conclusion that war might be justified only in cases where counterforce is needed.[234] In doing so, he does not rule out that both belligerent parties can wage war justly, and neither does he deem the use of nuclear weapons impermissible per se, even though he limits their deployment to reasons of deterrence.[235]

Some years later, in 1969, the Presbyterian ethicist Ralph Potter argued in favor of a renewal of just war thinking in the light of the Vietnam War.[236] He was deeply concerned about the war and proposed finding criteria for evaluating war and violence. A major problem he identifies, drawing on Rolan Baiton, is that within Christian thought, the emphasis is put either on an outright pacifism or on an attitude of crusade. Against both reasonings, Potter argues that

> The vindication of justice requires that self-sacrifice takes the form of contending with evil men for the preservation of their intended victims. In different circumstances, self-sacrificing

---

233. I delineate the different perspectives and their importance above. See 1.4.2 The Ethics of War and Peace.

234. See Ramsey, *War and the Christian Conscience*, 306.

235. See Ramsey, *Limits of Nuclear War*; Holmes, *On War and Morality*, 165–66; Haspel, "Die Renaissance der Lehre vom gerechten Krieg in der anglo-amerikanischen Debatte," 1.

236. See Potter, *War and Moral Discourse*, 7.

love of neighbor may find expression in strikingly different modes of conduct.²³⁷

The tradition of just war might therefore be an appropriate solution by giving categories of assessing violence in its different forms, be it within war, police, or revolution.²³⁸

Additionally, the theologian James Turner Johnson addressed just war tradition from a historical point of view in 1975 and again in a systematic manner in his book *Can Modern War be Just?* (1986).²³⁹ He also deems just war tradition to be an appropriate approach to deal with upcoming questions of war and violence—be they with regard to nuclear or conventional weapons technology—because the rationale behind the tradition of *bellum iustum* is to confine violence, but at the same time "force may be all that remains to protect and preserve values."²⁴⁰ Within this frame, he reaches the conclusion that nuclear weapons especially pose a severe problem because they are inherently disproportional and indiscriminatory in nature, at least from a *jus in bello* perspective. Changing the viewpoint toward *jus ad bellum*, however, hints toward an effective tactics of deterrence that is able to prevent warfare.²⁴¹ For that reason, Johnson deems nuclear weapons a "lesser evil not only politically and militarily, but also morally."²⁴² Therefore, the way in which a certain weapon is used seems decisive: If it is deployed in a way justified by *bellum iustum*, such as deterrence, Johnson does not perceive it as problematic.

Another main strand of this debate took place in the wake of the Second Vatican Council and the statement *Gaudium et Spes*. The Council did not refer to *bellum iustum* tradition explicitly, rather its ideas were insinuated when the total destruction of cities or areas without discrimination was condemned or the relation between justice and peace was reinforced.²⁴³ Similar to the aforementioned positions, the Second Vatican Council deems the deterrence by weapons and the arms race resulting

---

237. Potter, *War and Moral Discourse*, 53.

238. See Potter, *War and Moral Discourse*, 50.

239. See Johnson, *Can Modern War Be Just?*; Johnson, *Ideology, Reason, and the Limitation of War*.

240. Johnson, *Can Modern War Be Just?* viii.

241. See Johnson, *Can Modern War Be Just?* 103.

242. Johnson, *Can Modern War Be Just?* 104.

243. See Paul VI, "*Gaudium et spes*," 77, 79.

from it problematic but does not reject it entirely.[244] The theological background of these statements can be seen where the sinful nature of humanity is behind the rationale underlying the institution of war. In the Vatican's own wording:

> Insofar as men are sinful, the threat of war hangs over them, and hang over them it will until the return of Christ. But insofar as men vanquish sin by a union of love, they will vanquish violence as well.[245]

Related to this account, the role of nuclear threat and its connection to *bellum iustum* was discussed within the Catholic church as well.

All of these proposals attempt to reintegrate just war tradition into contemporary thinking by drawing on the theory affirmatively while applying it on their contemporaneous situation, which is mainly the question of nuclear warfare. The broad thrust of the different approaches seems similar: All of them deem violence problematic but necessary as long as the sinful nature of humankind is involved, "so long the eschaton is not yet here."[246] Therefore, the aim of just war tradition in practice is not to do away with violence once and for all but rather to confine violence to the necessary amount. What is interesting, however, is that all of the accounts prior to the Vietnam War stem from trained theologians. Other attempts to make use of just war tradition, for example, by Robert W. Tucker within the field of political science, do not refer to it in the same normative way. Tucker solely focuses on the political discourse concerning this topic.[247]

Michael Walzer

With the US entering the Vietnam War, the tide turned and just war tradition attracted attention within the field of philosophy as well. Here, Michael Walzer's *Just and Unjust Wars* can be seen as the cornerstone: It has been deemed "extraordinarily influential."[248]

---

244. See Paul VI, "*Gaudium et spes*," 80.
245. Paul VI, "*Gaudium et spes*," 78.
246. Johnson, *Can Modern War Be Just?* 104.
247. See Haspel, "Die Renaissance der Lehre vom gerechten Krieg in der anglo-amerikanischen Debatte," 316–17.
248. Lazar, "War."

An Ethical Evaluation of Lethal Functions in Autoregulative Weapons Systems

The main reason for Walzer to contemplate the ethics of war was the US intervention in Vietnam. His whole approach is casuistic in order to "recapture the just war for political and moral theory."[249] For that reason, he exemplifies his claims with contemporary as well as historical case studies.[250] His major aim is to limit violence and wars.[251] One of his basic assumptions is that the theory of aggression between states would be best described as a parallel to domestic violence. He calls this approach "legalist paradigm" and combines it with a multilateral idea, thereby presupposing a society of independent states who preserve the rights of their members. In this view, every act or threat of force to another member of the international society poses an aggression that would be judged as criminal and could be answered with military force.[252] Accordingly, the use of force by sovereign states against one another would be impermissible, just as a violent crime in domestic law. The only two reasons Walzer acknowledges for the legitimate use of force are self-defense and law enforcement. In any case, only the reaction to aggression can justify war.[253]

He rejects so-called (political) realism from the outset because within this concept, every form of violence in war would be legitimate, as war "is a world apart."[254] Against this, he underscores that war is still embedded within the social world, hence he describes war as "a moral world [. . .] in the midst of hell."[255] This means that he recognizes war to be an extraordinary and atrocious occurrence where moral rules apply nonetheless. These moral rules, however, must not be confused with the morality that prevails in everyday life.

Furthermore, and most importantly, he draws a sharp distinction between the act of aggression— referring to *jus ad bellum*—and the conduct of war itself—*jus in bello*.[256] This also entails that both categories, meaning *jus ad bellum* and *jus in bello*, need to be discussed separately. Walzer argues that, though the reasons for going to war might not be justified from a moral perspective, both belligerent sides benefit from *jus*

---

249. Walzer, *Just and Unjust Wars*, xxvi.
250. Walzer, *Just and Unjust Wars* xxiii-xxviii.
251. See Walzer, *Just and Unjust Wars* 24, 122.
252. See Walzer, *Just and Unjust Wars* 21, 61–62.
253. See Walzer, *Just and Unjust Wars* 62. This entails that the aggression has already been initiated already or is "only minutes away."
254. Walzer, *Just and Unjust Wars* 3.
255. Walzer, *Just and Unjust Wars* 3, 37.
256. See Walzer, *Just and Unjust Wars* 21.

in bello because it is not in the realm of the single soldier to decide on the reasons in favor of or against waging war. The combatant's duty is to fight, and their main ethical concern is how to do so justly.[257] Thus, *jus in bello* is the morally pertinent principle with regard to the soldier fighting, while *jus ad bellum* is decided on by an authority.

Walzer's approach, then, is contested by several thinkers that revise his version of just war, which I will elaborate on in greater detail below.[258] As for Walzer, he clarifies that his account is practical in the sense that he does not simply treat the issue of just war from a theoretical point of view—a standpoint he accuses his opponents of adopting. On the contrary, in addition to referring exclusively to the moral theory regarding that topic, he draws in great part on historical events, wartime journalism, and poetry and novels with the aim of understanding war not only from an abstract perspective but also as "historical or practical."[259] He then elaborates on three points that also concisely sum up the thrust of his account. First, war takes place in extraordinary circumstances, which are very different from civic circumstances: They are extremely coercive, because lives are at risk and the single soldier is part of a chain of command that is not easy to oppose. Second, war is a collective endeavor, which means that fighting in war cannot simply be reduced to self-defense and thereby compared to civic life scenarios. This entails that the single soldier might not easily—or at all—be able to evaluate their deeds from a moral point of view, especially when the coercive structure is taken into account. Finally, he argues that war takes place in a very uncertain scenario, which also means that "regular" moral training and ideas that apply in civic circumstances cannot simply be transferred to a war scene. For these reasons, he infers that "soldiers on both sides have exactly the same rights and obligations."[260] This is important because if only one side is granted the concession to fight in a just war with all its (legal) benefits while the other side is, accordingly, fighting an unjust war, these others are not protected by the same standard. This raises the major question of which party is fighting on the just side. Surely, both belligerent parties believe so and ascribe themselves that status, while denying the others the same rights and respect they demand to be treated with. Thus, Walzer emphasizes the enormous difference between what he calls civic

---

257. See Walzer, *Just and Unjust Wars* 127–37.
258. See 5.2.2.2 Revisionist Just War Thinking.
259. Walzer, *Just and Unjust Wars*, 337.
260. Walzer, *Just and Unjust Wars* 345.

and wartime reasoning, so rules applying to everyday life under peaceful circumstances do not simultaneously pertain to wartime situations. This also means that literature theorizing about war and peace cannot answer the questions asked on the battlefield. These assumptions, however, may also be problematic because this makes it nearly impossible to consider the reason for and the fighting in war from a nonwar perspective, hence this argument is at least under suspicion of being circular.

With regard to a theory of nonviolence, he argues that though to do away with war at all is a well-known and desirable "dream,"[261] it is very unlikely to happen. From his perspective, nonviolent means of conflict management either rest upon assumptions that cannot easily be guaranteed or lack the capacity to resist violent means, so, eventually, nonviolent resistance would be tantamount to suicide.[262]

5.2.2.2 Revisionist Just War Thinking

Jeff McMahan is one of the thinkers attempting to call into question traditional just war thinking as presented by Walzer. McMahan uses analytic philosophy within a deontological framework[263] and argues that *jus ad bellum* and *jus in bello* need to correlate more strongly, meaning that the moral status of the combatant in war, namely whether they fight justly or unjustly, hinges on the moral status of the war: "This means that we must stop reassuring soldiers that they act permissibly when they fight in an unjust war, provided that they conduct themselves honorably on the battlefield by fighting in accordance with the rules of engagement."[264] Therefore, he distinguishes not simply between just and unjust combatants, referring to the way they fight according to *jus in bello*, but between innocence and noninnocence. In his terms, the regular combatant is called material noninnocent because they are able to use force against other people, while a material innocent person would have no such means. Yet, a material innocent person does not need to be morally innocent; they might well be morally noninnocent. By this term, McMahan refers to people who have a stake in an actual war, be it as political leader or propagandist. They simply do not use violent means

---

261. Walzer, *Just and Unjust Wars*, 329.
262. See Walzer, *Just and Unjust Wars*, 330–34.
263. See Meireis, "Jeff McMahan," 329.
264. McMahan, *Killing in War*, 95.

in order to promote war. A morally innocent person, in contrast, would not contribute to an (unjust) war, at least not in this moral sense. According to McMahan, there are therefore four different types of people with regard to war. First, the morally and materially innocent, who are people who neither use force nor support war with ideological or technical means. Second, the morally and materially noninnocent, meaning people who enforce violent means both materially and ideologically. Third, the morally noninnocent but materially innocent, who support war with ideological or technological means only but who are not part of the actual fighting, such as a scientist developing new weapons. Finally, the morally innocent but materially noninnocent, meaning people who use violence but are somewhat reluctant to use physical force, such as "a pure-hearted but simple-minded conscript."[265] In the light of this classification, it becomes clear that, for McMahan, the moral status of the person is more important than the material status, so people posing a moral threat because they promote war with any means whatsoever are liable to attack, while the capability of inflicting harm physically is not sufficient to constitute a legitimate target.[266] This also means that McMahan assesses the role of the civilian at variance with traditional just war thinking: Since not every civilian is innocent by definition, they also bear responsibility for aggression. To the extent that the individual civilian is responsible for their own contribution to war, they are also morally responsible and become liable for attack as a result.[267] However, it is important to note that McMahan draws no legal consequences from his moral argument. Civilians can be assessed in that way, but they are nevertheless under legal protection by necessity of pragmatic considerations.[268] The main thrust of this argument is that both combatants and supporters of any war have to ask themselves whether the war they facilitate fulfills the criteria necessary to be called a just war. Combatants are seen as fully autonomous and therefore responsible for their deeds, entailing that they need to make sure that the war they fight is not an unjust one. If they nevertheless fight in an unjust war, they are not only fighting for unjust reasons but are also never capable of fighting in a just manner.[269]

---

265. See McMahan, "Innocence, Self-Defense and Killing in War," 200.
266. See McMahan, "Innocence, Self-Defense and Killing in War."
267. See McMahan, *Killing in War*, 221–31.
268. See McMahan, *Killing in War*, 234–35.
269. See McMahan, *Killing in War*, 1–7, 15–32.

McMahan's objective is to limit violence and war by sharing the responsibility for its undertaking: "Unjust wars can occur only if enough people are willing to fight them."[270] If everyone who joins the conduct of war scrutinizes the (official) assertions pertaining to the fighting, fewer wars would be fought because people would not go into battle in the first place. Consequently, McMahan draws the conclusion that conscientious refusals need to be granted to soldiers not only generally but also particularly with regard to one specific war. With such kinds of selective conscientious refusal, a soldier could follow their conscience depending on the situation and without refusing all kinds of belligerent endeavors.[271] This main argument is grounded in the assumption that the rationale of normal life and warfare might not be so different at all, but rather that the situations arising in war occur in daily life so rarely that war seems to have a distinct morality. This is important because it makes it possible to transfer common moral ideas to the conduct of war, which would be unfeasible if warfare and daily life constituted two distinct areas.[272] Accordingly, what is valid under regular circumstances pertains also to warfare. This means that while killing an innocent person is wrong in daily life, it is also forbidden in war. Yet, since unjust warriors are not entitled to kill anybody, they themselves become legitimate targets, while targeting innocent people, including just soldiers, cannot be justified.[273]

Another contribution within this paradigm is brought forward by Cécile Fabre, who discusses just war from a cosmopolitan point of view, which she defines as follows:

> Cosmopolitanism is the view that human beings are the fundamental and primary *loci* for moral concern and respect and have equal moral worth. It is individualist, egalitarian, and universal, and insists that political borders are arbitrary from a moral point of view, and more precisely ought not to have a bearing on individuals' prospects for a flourishing life.[274]

---

270. McMahan, *Killing in War*, 5.

271. See McMahan, *Killing in War*, 95–103. McMahan is not the first to demand such a privilege, of course. Famously, Rawls advocates for selective conscientious refusal. See Rawls, *Theory of Justice*, 331–35. This is also an important claim of contingent pacifism. See, for example, May, *Contingent Pacifism*, 233–49.

272. See McMahan, *Killing in War*, 36.

273. See McMahan, "Innocence, Self-Defense and Killing in War."

274. Fabre, *Cosmopolitan War*, 16.

The Ethical Framing

Most importantly, this is a radical individual account: The most decisive part is played by the singular person, therefore most of the cosmopolitan theories favor pacifism.[275] Fabre, however, elaborates on just war thinking in its revisionist version, contesting the traditional account on several grounds. Just as McMahan, she holds that

> Some combatants are liable to being killed—those who [. . .] fight for an unjust cause—and that some non-combatants are also liable to being killed—those who in fact do take part, in relevant ways [. . .] in an unjust war.[276]

To her mind, what legal norms and personal or political choices need to guarantee is that each individual human has the opportunity to lead a "minimal decent life,"[277] whose content she describes with reference to the capabilities approach provided by Amartya Sen and Martha Nussbaum.[278] Within this debate, she adopts a sufficientist/sufficientarian standpoint, meaning that people who are well off and have more than enough need to help those who are destitute.[279] To the extent that legal norms are concerned, the question of whether or not somebody is entitled to fight for their own rights arises. This entails that somebody's interest needs to be taken seriously, so the achievement of this interest is not impaired by others.[280] Generally, however, she holds that the individual is the bearer of (legal) rights as well as the addressee of duties to others and that the individual has no general moral right to prefer the comrade over the stranger. These individual rights, then, are not confined by national borders but rather underlie all human norms.[281] From that point of view, it becomes clear that her main emphasis is not placed on giving somebody a certain status in accordance with their affiliation to one specific group but rather is put primarily on the particular individual.[282] This, in turn, raises the question of why a group of people such as a nation

---

275. See Fabre, *Cosmopolitan War*, 3.
276. Fabre, *Cosmopolitan War*, 6.
277. Fabre, *Cosmopolitan War*, 17.
278. See, for example, Nussbaum, *Creating Capabilities*; Sen, *Idea of Justice*.
279. See Fabre, *Cosmopolitan War*, 20. There is a bundle of open questions pertaining to this approach, for example, where the threshold would be, or if help is even demanded if the person bears the blame for their own poorness. Fabre does not take a clear-cut stance regarding those issues, but rather points to several ongoing debates.
280. See Fabre, *Cosmopolitan War*, 23.
281. See Fabre, *Cosmopolitan War*, 31.
282. See Fabre, *Cosmopolitan War*, 49.

could justifiably defend themselves. In Fabre's view, this kind of collective self-defense, though possible, is not unconditioned: The respective state needs to guarantee that justice rules and that its human rights are guaranteed. If this is the case, the idea of private self-defense can be transferred to collective self-defense. And if these people are organized as a state, they can mandate their leaders to do so.[283] This also means that *jus ad bellum* and *jus in bello* are tightly interwoven, with a certain preference for *jus ad bellum*: A certain war can only be fought justly if the conditions for waging war in the first place are met. She consequently demands "contributory responsibility"[284] instead of the attribution of responsibility solely by the status combatant/noncombatant or the membership to a certain (political) group. Accordingly, she infers that "the life of a civilian who does contribute [to a wrongful lethal threat] should count for less than the life of an innocent civilian."[285] From that point of view also emerges the problem that unintended side effects constitute issues even more severe than in traditional just war thinking because it is not clear on which grounds nonresponsible people could be exposed to such risk. In other words, if wars are basically about human rights, one cannot simply risk the lives of nonresponsible people in favor of other nonresponsible people, at least not according to their status, because both share equal rights.[286]

In any case, to defend one's own rights to live a minimal decent life can be seen as a right. Therefore, it is legitimate to wage war, especially in self-defense. Moreover, it is legitimate to wage a war defending the basic human rights of others, which contrasts with traditional just war thinking. While in the latter, a state's sovereignty is crucial, it is sidelined within cosmopolitanism: A sovereign state is not entitled to wage war or even defend itself per se, but only if they grant their people a minimal decent life. If their minimal human rights are threatened, these people, irrespective of whether they are organized as a state of not, are entitled to defend themselves, while others are authorized to help.

David Rodin develops yet another approach within the discussion of just war when casting doubt on the question of whether national self-defense is an essential right. His argumentation is twofold: First, he reformulates the theory of personal self-defense, and in a second step

---

283. See Fabre, *Cosmopolitan War*, 53.
284. Fabre, *Cosmopolitan War*, 287.
285. Fabre, *Cosmopolitan War*, 287.
286. See Fabre, *Cosmopolitan War*, 287.

he contests that this thought can be transferred to national self-defense. With respect to the former, he doubts whether the generally accepted theory of self-defense—which is that an aggressor, by putting the life of the other at risk, themselves forfeits their right to live, while the other obtains the right to kill without losing their own right to live—withstands scrutiny. Rodin remedies this notion with the consideration of *fault*. To his mind, the gist of a situation of personal self-defense is best described as a relation between victim and aggressor in terms of fault. The victim, with respect to the specific violent situation, is innocent, while the aggression is the aggressor's fault. This asymmetry leads to a situation where the general prohibition against using violence against others is overridden and the victim cannot wrong the aggressor by using force against them. This is important, as otherwise the aggressor could provoke the victim until they resort to violence and afterward purport that they reacted in self-defense, while the opposite is true—or at least some blame would remain on the provoker as well. Furthermore, even the police and the legal system sometimes act violently. In this case, however, the violence is usually inflicted justly, and the addressee of the violence has no right to act in self-defense. Accordingly, the right to kill another person depends on their relation to one another and the amount to which the aggression is the aggressor's fault. Hence, it becomes clear that an innocent threat, meaning a person or an object that does not threaten others voluntarily, is also not a legitimate target per se:

> Self-defense is grounded in the existence of a level of normative responsibility on the part of the aggressor for the threat he poses on the defender. Where this is not present, as in the case of physical compulsion, involuntary intoxication, or unavoidable mistake, self-defense is impermissible.[287]

Even if impermissible, killing out of self-defense might be excused, though. This is possible if the addressee of violence made a reasonable mistake when assuming that somebody else acted on malicious grounds.[288]

Regarding the issue of national self-defense, Rodin deems the supposed parallel between personal self-defense and national self-defense neither self-evident nor persuasive. He therefore reconstructs two different ways to transfer personal to national self-defense: first, the idea that national self-defense is simply the collective form of private

---

287. Rodin, *War and Self-Defense*, 97.
288. See Rodin, *War and Self-Defense*, 70–99.

self-defense, an account Rodin refers to as *reductive strategy*—ascribing it to McMahan;[289] and second, the notion that national self-defense is analogous to personal rights, which Rodin calls *analogical strategy*, associated with Walzer's contribution.[290] Both approaches, however, fail. One major problem Rodin describes is grounded in what he calls the "myth of discrete communities,"[291] meaning the imagination that nations exist as discrete entities, each of them grounded in sovereignty. Yet, this imagination is mistaken because "human communities do not coincide with the boundaries of states."[292] Consequently, the right to self-defense cannot simply be transferred to states; it hinges on communities. Communities, however, cannot easily be constructed in a clear-cut way by identity or individuation, as can be seen with reference to a conflict within a certain community. Therefore this argument is incorrect.[293]

Consequently, he deduces that war and the assessment of its morality are twofold: On the one hand, states appear to be (collective) moral agents conducting war, and on the other hand, individuals can also be described as moral agents waging war. This binary form, however, needs binary assessment for both diverging modes to strike a balance, while the classical theory solely focuses on state actors. By assessing the role of the individual soldier, he emphasizes their own responsibility with respect to their engagement in the collective endeavor of war and draws the (revisionist) conclusion that "soldiers fighting an unjust war have no permission to kill, and there is no 'moral equality' between soldiers."[294] According to Rodin, killing can only be justified within the framework of law enforcement or punishment, therefore he argues in favor of "something like a minimal universal state."[295] "Such a body might, for instance, take action to prevent the invasion of one state by another and could use force to punish those responsible for aggression."[296] He sketches his ideas, drawing on Kant, only in a simplistic manner. What is important here, however, is that while he sees two possible conclusions, namely either pacifism or law enforcement, he advocates for the latter, thereby merging

---

289. See Rodin, "Myth of National Self-Defense," 80–81.
290. See Rodin, *War and Self-Defense*, 6, 104–10, 127–32.
291. Rodin, *War and Self-Defense*, 158.
292. Rodin, *War and Self-Defense*, 158.
293. See Rodin, *War and Self-Defense*, 141–62.
294. Rodin, *War and Self-Defense*, 173.
295. Rodin, *War and Self-Defense*, 163.
296. Rodin, *War and Self-Defense*, 180.

the concept of individual and collective self-defense by shifting the focus from the nation to the individual.

In another contribution, Rodin links the ongoing change of thought within peace ethics to the emerging importance of human rights.[297] To the extent that human rights become important as an ethical and moral argument, the focus shifts from the collective to individuals, so the whole discussion of the realignment of just war is, at least to some degree, entangled with the debate on communitarianism and individualism. Within this debate, Rodin's stance deduces the value of political institutions from their contribution to the individual's rights and develops a position that is neither just war nor pacifism, as it rejects the paradigmatic role of self-defense, on the one hand, but considers lethal force against genocidal aggression as justified on the other hand—an approach Rodin calls "justified interdiction theory."[298]

Helen Frowe has reacted to Rodin's proposal by advocating for what she calls "reductive individualism,"[299] meaning that it is possible and useful to transfer the idea of personal self-defense to national self-defense. She does so on the grounds of proportionality: To the extent that the aggressor is a threat—be it voluntarily or not—the victim is entitled to use lethal force in order to defend themselves. Moreover, self-defense is not restricted to genocidal violence alone but can also take place in reaction to political aggression.[300] She focuses on the role of civilians as well and claims that civilians can be liable targets to the extent that they enforce their own country's unjust wars, for example, "taxpayers, munitions workers, scientists, and anyone supplying their country's armed forces with either military or welfare goods, including food."[301] This means that Frowe draws a very sharp line between just and unjust harm, while rejecting the distinction between combatant and civilian. Accordingly, she emphasizes the potential of unmanned aerial vehicles (UAVs) to reduce the harm on the party using this technology to protect their own soldiers. Particularly from a reductive individualist standpoint, this technology has the potential to protect just combatants.[302]

---

297. See Rodin, "Myth of National Self-Defense," 89.
298. See Rodin, "Myth of National Self-Defense," 89.
299. Frowe, *Defensive Killing*, 13.
300. See Frowe, *Defensive Killing*, 13.
301. Frowe, *Defensive Killing*, 17.
302. See Frowe, *Ethics of War and Peace*, 223–24.

To sum up, the whole idea of revising just war tradition is to take into account the moral independence of every person. This amounts in all its versions to a certain kind of individualization, since the issue is not so much about the status of a certain person—meaning combatant or noncombatant—but about the personal contribution to a particular war. This is in line with everyday morality, where people are socially imagined to be individually liable according to their deeds. While McMahan discusses this correlation in detailed manner regarding the single combatant and noncombatant, Fabre's contribution provides a theoretical basis for revisionist just war thinking by merging just war tradition with cosmopolitan morality. This is a solid approach because the individualism that underlies revisionist just war thinking matches the universalism connected to cosmopolitanism: The inferred individual human rights outrank a group's sovereignty and are therefore worthy of defense, if necessary, by force. The cogency of this approach rests on the idea that it is possible to very subtly assign responsibly to a certain threat. Especially important is the argument that the person responsible for a threat, be they combatant or noncombatant, should also bear the blame. The same thrust is present in Frowe's account. Only Rodin's proposal deviates to some degree because he rather attempts to reconcile political and individual approaches with his idea of a minimal universal state, which amounts to a theory that would embrace just policing rather than just war.

There are, however, at least three problems that accompany these revisions of just war tradition. First, the question of how it is possible to differentiate between just and unjust threats in practice and who should make this decision. This is a problem that arises particularly when Fabre chooses to determine responsibility very delicately: Since individual human rights are by definition individual, they are to some degree also subjective, or at least culturally preconditioned, and therefore a threat to individual rights is easier to feign than a treat to sovereignty—a constellation that would make this approach more vulnerable to exploitation than the traditional approach. Alternatively, this might lead to a conclusion tantamount to a certain kind of contingent pacifism, as Larry May suggests.[303] Second, there are clearly no two universal moralities, one underlying ordinary life and one pertaining to warfare. Yet, there are different imaginations and legal codes with regard to warfare and

---

303. See 5.3.3 On Larry May's Concept of Contingent Pacifism.

ordinary life. This might also make it possible to apply different rules to both ordinary life and warfare. Finally, the notion of personal moral innocence and noninnocence seems too easy. As Henry Shue puts it, "Discussion goes off the track if the term 'innocent' is taken to be the opposite of 'guilty', rather than the opposite of engaged in harming, and especially if it is taken to refer to some subjective guiltiness."[304] This is especially what McMahan's proposal amounts to, but it seems questionable if moral noninnocence is the best available category, as it seems very easy to abuse by justifying essentially unjustified use of force. Yet, this discussion might resemble the question of humanity's sinful nature, which was a premise in the traditional Christian version of *bellum iustum*.[305] It then corresponds with the link between (personal) sin, which might be reconstructed as noninnocence or guilt in philosophical terms, and punishment, which might be reestablished as the permission to inflict violence upon somebody.

5.2.2.3 *Just War Thinking Disputed*

In the light of the revision of just war thinking and theories of nonviolence, Walzer and other traditional just war scholars expound their assumptions. I have already demonstrated how Walzer defends his own approach[306] and will now turn to several other thinkers who follow his notion.

Yitzhak Benbaji and Daniel Statman are among the ethicists following Walzer's trail. In their book *War by Agreement* (2019), they draw on contractarianism and spell out the meaning of this approach for the ongoing debate in just war tradition. With their proposal, the philosophers attempt to account for a "realistic pessimism,"[307] which entails that global peace is threatened by permanent insecurity due to the lack of "any central authority."[308] "Accordingly, we assume that strong armies—viz., armies whose soldiers are obedient and as such easier to activate—make

---

304. Shue, "War," 360.

305. Augustine, for instance, argues that way. See 5.2.1 *Bellum iustum*: History of Ideas. Also, the Second Vatican Council suggests this idea. See 5.2.2.1 The Revival of the Just War Tradition.

306. See 5.2.2.1 The Revival of the Just War Tradition.

307. Benbaji and Statman, *War by Agreement*, 6.

308. Benbaji and Statman, *War by Agreement*, 6.

the world more secure rather than less so."[309] Moreover, wars are part of our socially organized world and will not be overcome, therefore it is very important to establish effective moral rules by which these wars can be fought.[310] Their main assumption is that if the legal system concerning war is "good enough,"[311] existing law outperforms individual morality, which means that the legal norm is binding even if the single person has moral restraints.[312] This means that from a contractarian point of view, the international legal framework is seen as distinctive for an individual, who waives their preconceptual rights if they are bound to such a legal system. Put differently, to the extent that the individual plays a social role, they also follow social rules, thereby losing, to some degree, their natural given rights. By this argument, the authors take the socially created world with its mutual agreements and rules very seriously, in contrast to stating that people exist individually and apart from each other in a preconceptual sphere.[313] With respect to *jus ad bellum* under the ruling of the Geneva Conventions, for example, states lose their right to aggressively attack other states because the right to use force against another state is confined to defensive warfare only. Regarding *jus in bello*, however, states can—to the extent that their social contract is morally fair—enlist soldiers, who follow the rules of their government without making sure if they are fighting a just war, as long as the immunity of civilians is guaranteed. The soldiers fighting bear the same rights and obligations on each side according to the Geneva Conventions.[314] Benbaji and Statman hold that this is the fairest way to organize an undertaking such as war because, that way, a fair agreement can be maintained at its best.[315] Only in the case that the states should ward off the mutual contract can this agreement be overwritten, so the aggressor can be deterred effectively

---

309. Benbaji and Statman, *War by Agreement*, 6.

310. See Benbaji and Statman, *War by Agreement*, 193, 200.

311. Benbaji and Statman, *War by Agreement*, 192.

312 It is, however, not so clear, what "good enough" is supposed to mean. In another instance, the authors argue that law-enforcing agents such as the police need to make sure that the court order they carry out is in agreement with justice. Benbaji and Statman, *War by Agreement*, 57–58. But the authors do not elaborate on the circumstances under which justice is served, when exactly the rules of war are "good enough," and why the existing rules pertaining to the legal just war paradigm are the morally best solution.

313. See Benbaji and Statman, *War by Agreement*, 37.

314. See Benbaji and Statman, *War by Agreement*, 182–83.

315. See Benbaji and Statman, *War by Agreement*, 186.

The Ethical Framing

in order to prevent even more harm without threatening civilian immunity.[316] Taken together, this means that since war is a social undertaking and social rules apply to warfare, even the soldiers play their social role in attending war. In doing so, they waive some of their natural rights but need to uphold the rules by which they fight. In this view, *jus ad bellum* is distinct from *jus in bello* to a high degree: While independent states decide to attack or not to attack—or respectively to defend or not to defend themselves—adhering to *jus ad bellum*, soldiers decide how they fight in war, thereby obeying *jus in bello*. This is important because, otherwise, the social war agreement in itself would be threatened and, accordingly, no rules at all would apply.

Another attempt to make a case for Walzer's assumptions has been made by Henry Shue, who initially highlights that there is no such thing as "killing as such,"[317] meaning that killing somebody always takes place in a certain context, which is why murder, homicide, and assassinations do not fall into the same juridical category. This entails that an action that is usually morally unacceptable might, under certain circumstances, be a moral exception. Further, this means that even if no one is entitled to hurt or even kill another person, there might be individual exceptions if they are able to explain why an exemption should be granted.[318] From this general guideline, Shue contemplates the morality of war. He holds that *jus ad bellum* and *jus in bello* need to be discussed separately[319] but that they nevertheless need to be seen together, since they unfold their full potential to confine war only when they are in accordance. This is simply for the reason that if the war is started for a just cause, meaning *jus ad bellum* is taken into account, the soldiers are entitled to fight. And if they fight, they need to do so justly, which means applying *jus in bello*. This also holds true the other way around: The war in itself can only be justified to the extent that the soldiers fight justly. Soldiers might, however, be mistaken when they attend an only allegedly just war. Indeed, there does not seem to be any reason to engage in hostilities somebody does not believe to be necessary. This is the main reason for Shue to call for the same treatment of all soldiers.[320] Shue then, together with Janina Dill, criticizes both Walzer and McMahan for their idea that soldiers forfeit

---

316. See Benbaji and Statman, *War by Agreement*, 188.
317. Shue, "War," 353.
318. See Shue, "War," 361.
319. See Shue, "War," 355.
320. See Shue, "War," 362.

some of their individual rights when fighting in war, either symmetrical, as Walzer states, or asymmetrical, as McMahan argues. In doing so, both McMahan and Walzer connect individual moral rights with their loss in warfare, meaning that they advocate for "moral individualization."[321] This is problematic as, first, war is a collective endeavor undertaken either by states or nonstate actors: Nobody wages war on their own terms. Second, since neither side of the conflict can be sure about their own justification or the justification of the other side, it would be myopic to grant individual rights to single soldiers according to their private conduct. This is simply unfeasible. Therefore, Dill and Shue draw a very sharp distinction between private conduct of life under regular circumstances and the collective undertaking of war because, generally, the collective undertaking causes more harm than the individual could cause. Therefore, the individual soldier needs to suffer more harm than they would due to their private deeds.[322] For that reason, Dill and Shue propose to assess military necessity in line with legality rather than individual morality, a procedure they refer to as the St. Petersburg Assumption.[323] Within this framework, the infliction of harm is legitimate only to the extent that it is necessary to weaken the hostile forces, so necessity is confined by sufficiency. This also means that harm must not be used to achieve a political goal but only as a means to achieve military superiority. This is important because, otherwise, this criterion would not confine war but the exact opposite. Within this rationale, a distinction between combatants and noncombatants would be maintained for legal reasons but also because combatants form an integral part of war's infrastructure. Therefore, the military's necessity of fighting combatants is higher than the necessity of targeting noncombatants.[324] What is relevant in this proposal is the fact that Dill and Shue follow Walzer in separating ordinary life from warfare, even if they do not follow his individualistic assumptions. While Walzer regards the single soldier as the bearer of individual rights who loses these rights when becoming a combatant,[325] Dill and Shue emphasize the

---

321. Dill and Shue, "Limiting the Killing in War," 448.

322. See Dill and Shue, "Limiting the Killing in War," 448–54.

323. It is called after the St. Petersburg Declaration of 1868, the first international law treaty that banned specific weapons because they were thought to inflict too much harm on the combatants. It was also the paradigm of many international law treaties to follow. See Dill and Shue, "Limiting the Killing in War," 457.

324. See Dill and Shue, "Limiting the Killing in War," 454–57.

325. See Walzer, *Just and Unjust Wars*, 138.

collective character of warfare to the extent that the moral status of the single combatant is no longer relevant.

In summary, traditional thinkers follow Walzer in certain assumptions while rejecting others. One major difference between Walzer and his colleagues is the question of the moral agency of the individual soldier. Walzer emphasizes their status: Because they are soldiers, they gain certain rights and duties, but they also forfeit some of them. In other words, because they are soldiers, they gain the right to kill other combatants and the privilege to be treated as noncombatants in certain circumstances—for instance, if *hors de combat*—while they concurrently lose their right to live if, and only if, they pose a threat to others, being a combatant and thereby a legitimate target. This condition, however, comes by status and individually because it is part of being an individual combatant. The whole discussion regarding traditional just war thinking, therefore, revolves around the implementation of certain rights for groups of people, which are combatants and noncombatants. In that respect, Statman and Benbaji, on the one hand, propose thinking of combatants as being under moral rules within the realm of a social endeavor called warfare. To be clear, all socially organized undertakings are under the ruling of certain moral norms, and war is just one of them with a certain ruling. Shue and Dill, on the other hand, highlight the collective structure of warfare, where the individual soldiers lose their individual (moral) status because they are an essential part of a certain collective. Both approaches, however, make a strong case for the separation of ordinary life circumstances, where civic rules and morality apply, and warfare, where different rules apply: While the individual is liable for their deeds in ordinary life, this does not hold true for warfare. This is because of its ingrained collective character, so humans either lose their individual status per se, or different socially accepted moral norms apply, which are collective in essence.

Ultimately, it is important to note that these approaches consider themselves realistic in comparison to revisionist just war thinking, which is considered to be too theoretical. They dissociate themselves from another kind of realism, though, which is the idea that war wipes out every form of social and moral convention. For traditional just war thinking, the exact opposite is true: Social norms do apply to war, but they do so in a collective and not in an individualistic manner.

5.2.3 Just War Thinking and Autoregulation in Weapons Systems

Taken together, when discussing the status of the individual combatant, the primary issue at stake is an anthropological one, namely the question of whether humans are morally responsible only individually or collectively as well. In that regard, the subject of autoregulative functions in weapons systems is connected to this debate on at least two different levels. First and foremost, it is connected to the question of the status of combatants. Within traditional just war thinking, the deployment of such technologies could be embraced if the technological problem of how to differentiate between combatant and noncombatant could be solved, as well as the problem of proportionality. If the device could be programmed to attack only combatants and if it could do so in proportion to the degree that these combatants pose a (lethal) threat to other human beings, their use might be seen as possible. Statman, for instance, argues in favor of such devices because their moral impact on warfare might be superior to that of humans, since they might meet the *jus in bello* conditions more precisely and because they do not act on account of their emotion, so "new technologies overall mark significant moral progress in the history of warfare."[326] With regard to revisionist thinking, such devices could be argued for by pointing out that just combatants need to be protected by all means. Since an autoregulative weapons systems keeps supposed just combatants out of danger as they do not attend the battlefield, this might make a strong case for their use—an argument Bradley Strawser puts forward regarding unmanned technology that could easily be transferred to autoregulation in weapons systems.[327] The technological requirement would be that the device was able to differentiate between just and unjust targets, or, in order to suffice for traditional just war thinking, between combatants and noncombatants. This development, however, is still out of sight. Therefore, at least at this stage, autoregulative devices cannot be employed safely from a just war point of view. If authors such as Statman argue in favor of autoregulation in weapons technology, they do so by anticipating a technological development.

There is, however, at least one insightful contribution from a (traditional) just war point of view written by the philosopher Alex Leveringhaus. In his book *Ethics and Autonomous Weapons* (2015), Leveringhaus offers detailed insight into the ethical debate revolving around

---
326. Statman, "Drones and Robots," 472.
327. See Strawser, "Moral Predators."

The Ethical Framing

autoregulation in weapons systems.[328] After clarifying some preliminaries, such as defining in general what a weapon is and in particular what "autonomy" in this context means,[329] he refers to the ethical argument brought forward by Ronald C. Arkin, namely that this new kind of technology would spare lives because it is not influenced by human factors as sleep deprivation, fear, or feelings of revenge.[330] Leveringhaus objects to this by pointing out that the same could be true for the programmer, meaning that they could be tired or fearful themselves. He then discusses the argument of a responsibility gap, stated first by Robert Sparrow.[331] Sparrow holds that autoregulation in weaponry would lead to responsibility gaps because in the aftermath of armed conflict, no single person could be blamed for possible crimes or malfunctions. This is due to there being too many people involved in the process of developing, programming, and deploying a weaponized robot, so there is no specific person who could be held liable. Leveringhaus opposes this argument by observing that the operator could indeed be held liable for the operations the machine carries out as a consequence of its programming because it is their task to foresee possible incidents. This then leads Leveringhaus to the issue of risk, which he concludes to be more important than the discussion of responsibility. In his opinion, it may be riskier to deploy autoregulative devices in violent scenarios than it is to deploy human soldiers. Yet, he emphasizes that this outcome is highly dependent on technological information and progression. To resolve this issue, philosophical or ethical treatment is not the preferred approach.[332]

Leveringhaus then proceeds to the argument of human agency, which he brings forward. Most importantly, he claims that a human, in contrast to a machine, has "the ability to do otherwise,"[333] which means that a human can decide not to shoot for various reasons. The main human characteristic Leveringhaus zeroes in on in that respect is that a human can show mercy for the target, who may be a legitimate target

---

328. I will address this contribution and the argumentations brought forward here in greater detail below when elaborating on the ethical discourse revolving around autoregulation in weapons technology. See 6.2 Revisiting the Ethical Discourse on Autoregulation in Weapons Systems.

329. See Leveringhaus, *Ethics and Autonomous Weapons*, 31–58.

330. See Leveringhaus, *Ethics and Autonomous Weapons*, 59–68.

331. See Sparrow, "Killer Robots."

332. See Leveringhaus, *Ethics and Autonomous Weapons*, 69–87.

333. Leveringhaus, *Ethics and Autonomous Weapons*, 92.

An Ethical Evaluation of Lethal Functions in Autoregulative Weapons Systems

according to IHL but nevertheless does not necessarily mean to be a threat. He writes,

> Unless re-programmed, the machine *will* engage the targeted person upon detection. Killing a person, however, is a truly existential choice that each soldier needs to justify before his own conscience. Sometimes it can be desirable not to pull the trigger, even if this means that an otherwise legitimate target survives. Mercy and pity may, in certain circumstances, be the right guide to action.[334]

This means that the perspective of humans within a complex situation such as war is much more aware of the particular circumstances, and that humans can therefore (re-)act much more freely, while the machine will follow its coded paths without making exceptions. Leveringhaus illustrates this point with a child who takes up a gun and by doing so becomes a legitimate target. The same child then puts the weapon on the ground and runs away. A machine would shoot on all accounts, while a human soldier would perhaps wait and see what the child did with the gun and only shoot if the gun was aimed at him or her.[335]

In the end of the book, the author concludes that it might be too risky to deploy machines instead of humans in war and that human agency is so important that it cannot be abandoned on the battlefield. However, he also draws the conclusion that it is hardly possible to endorse or restrict autoregulative weapons categorically, since the case is more complicated than that. In his opinion, endorsement or condemnation of these weapons is dependent on how the technology will improve and if it can meet the standards the proponents anticipate. In terms of juridical regulations, though, Leveringhaus argues that these weapons might already be forbidden by IHL, since they cannot sufficiently distinguish between legitimate and illegitimate targets. For that matter, there might also be no need for a preemptive ban.[336]

In a subsequent contribution, Leveringhaus develops his account further by opposing the view that autoregulative weapons systems are morally repugnant, thereby arguing against António Guterres, Secretary-General of the UN. According to Leveringhaus, even though the use of autoregulation in weapons technology might be morally problematic,

---

334. Leveringhaus, *Ethics and Autonomous Weapons*, 92.
335. See Leveringhaus, *Ethics and Autonomous Weapons*, 89–94.
336. See Leveringhaus, *Ethics and Autonomous Weapons*, 112–23.

it is still not repugnant. This is because such labeling is not sufficiently rationalized in an ethical way, as repulsion refers mainly to personal attitudes, while ethical thinking revolves around rationalization and reasonable argumentation.[337] Within the course of his article, Leveringhaus mentions three further arguments against the deployment of autoregulative functions in weapons systems in addition to his previous ones. First, he notes the possibility that the use of autoregulation in weapons systems might reinforce an existing trend toward covert operations such as the ones undertaken by the US in their so-called war on terror. The reason is that these technologies are nearly impossible to detect, so "an AWS in a stealth mode, without the need to further communicate with a human operator, could enter enemy territory undetected and destroy a particular target [. . .]."[338] In that regard, the question of whether such covert operations are to be reinforced by means of new weapons technology is decisive. Second, Leveringhaus addresses the problem that an autoregulative system cannot be stopped even if the circumstances change. This might be especially problematic if, for instance, a peace treaty or truce is agreed. In such a case, the weapon could not be stopped, since it is its very characteristic to operate without any communication whatsoever. In a final argument, Leveringhaus discusses the problem of unintended and unforeseen side effects. Leveringhaus here mentions that precisely because this piece of technology is expected to be more accurate, it is very likely to be deployed in a high-risk scenario "where accidents and misapplications of force are bound to happen."[339] So, ultimately, the harm inflicted might rise.[340]

All of the three arguments pertain to very different levels of ethical reasoning. The first and last can only be evaluated within a certain peace ethical frame, and depending on that frame, endorsement or rejection of such technology could be sought. The second argument has a stronger technological impact, referring to the differentiation between judgment and reckoning proposed by Brian Cantwell Smith, as introduced above.[341] By the same token, the inherent risk of inflicting more harm by using weapons technology that promises safer deployment can be connected to the risk of a malfunction or unintended side effects. Moreover,

337. See Leveringhaus, "Morally Repugnant Weaponry?" 475.
338. Leveringhaus, "Morally Repugnant Weaponry?" 476.
339. Leveringhaus, "Morally Repugnant Weaponry?" 476.
340. See Leveringhaus, "Morally Repugnant Weaponry?" 476.
341. See 3.3 Reckoning and Judgment.

An Ethical Evaluation of Lethal Functions in Autoregulative Weapons Systems

since proponents of autoregulation in weapons technology refer to the minimization of risk by reducing human failure, risk seems to be an important idea within these discussions and needs further examination.[342]

Taken together, Leveringhaus's approach is of great interest here because he constructs his overall ethical argumentation explicitly within just war thinking. This is exceptional, as the majority of authors does not place their ethical account within a fully-fledged ethical framework but rather refer to issues of technology.[343] To do so, he mainly refers to Walzer but references this with the works of revisionist thinkers. He does not, however, spell out in detail the degree to which a revisionist just war approach might differ from a traditional just war approach with regard to autoregulative weapons systems. He does emphasize, though, that primarily *jus in bello* considerations—namely the criterion of distinction, proportionality of means, and military necessity—are the focus of the current debate and therefore constitute a suitable frame to discuss these technologies.[344] His focus on *jus in bello* in terms of Walzer is coherent with regard to just war thinking in both its variants because the use of a certain weapons technology within war would need to be evaluated along these lines. It is nevertheless questionable whether Leveringhaus's approach spells out the point of revisionist just war theory sufficiently here. This is because the main objective of revisionist just war theory is to probe whether the categories of legitimate and illegitimate targets can be applied categorically to combatants and noncombatants. Leveringhaus, however, does not address these differentiations but seems to refer to traditional just war thinking in that regard. Particularly with respect to autoregulative weapons systems, however, these differences might be important because, following the logic of *jus in bello*, it is to date impossible for a machine to differentiate between combatants and noncombatants. Yet, the differentiation between legitimate and illegitimate targets within

---

342. I will elaborate on that thought in greater detail below. See 6.4 Redistributing Risk.

343. For instance, Sparrow's argument of the responsibility gap works very well without reference toward just war thinking. See Sparrow, "Killer Robots." This is even more true for the argument of human dignity, meaning that the person targeted from an autoregulative device loses their dignity because they are reduced to be a mere data point. See Rosert and Sauer, "Prohibiting Autonomous Weapons." Such accounts rather refer to just war thinking implicitly when taking into account human rights or IHL. See also Asaro, "On Banning Autonomous Weapons Systems."

344. See Leveringhaus, *Ethics and Autonomous Weapons*, 15.

revisionist just war thinking is even harder to provide, so this viewpoint can be expected to oppose the use of such technology even more strongly.

5.3 CONTINGENT PACIFISM

In contrast to an absolute pacifist approach and to an approach that solely draws on just war tradition, contingent pacifism incorporates the possibility of waging war within a pacifist frame. This entails that the focus of this ethical theory rests on peace but grants certain exemptions in the use of force. It is therefore located somewhere between an absolute pacifist and a just war approach in its current traditional interpretation. The most important difference between just war tradition and contingent pacifism, however, is the issue of what exactly is at stake: While resorting to violence might not be legitimized in contingent pacifism, just war tradition makes the case that engaging in war might be justified under certain circumstances and that violence can therefore be legitimized.[345] Consequently, the underlying rationale differs within the two approaches, which is the idea that peace is key and can be achieved by peaceful means only, in the first case, and that violence can be justified for the sake of achieving peace, in the second case.

There are a variety of diverging approaches within contingent pacifism, of which Andrew Fiala draws out five categories. First, approaches that demand pacifism from certain social or cultural groups, for instance, religious institutions. Second, a pacifism that assesses the costs and benefits of a certain war and concludes that a war under these certain circumstances is unwise to fight: Combining pragmatism and pacifism into a *pragmatist pacifistic approach*, for instance, would be categorized here.[346] Third, there are suggestions that attempt to blend just war thinking and absolute pacifism together. Some thinkers do so on philosophical grounds, such as the proposal made by Larry May, while others resort to religious grounds, such as the suggestions offered by the Christian churches called *just peace thinking*. Fourth, versions that can be called *political pacifism*, which are approaches that do not promote war for political reasons such as monetary intentions or other strategic aims. Finally, there is a form of pacifism that might be called *liberal-democratic* or *liberal pacifism*, which according to Robert Holmes proposes that

---

345. For the discussion regarding just war thinking, see 5.2 Just War Tradition.
346. See also Müller, "Pragmatischer Pazifismus."

contemporary warfare is at variance with liberal morality. This is because of its hierarchical structure: Only in absence of such a hierarchical framing might warfare might be possible for liberal-democratic reasons.[347]

In the following section, it is not my aim to provide a comprehensive overview of the plentiful theories in the realm of contingent pacifism but rather to focus on ideas that help to understand the gist of contingent pacifism and bring its specific feature to the fore. The approach that has been taken within Christian peace ethics, which is just peace thinking, will play a particularly major part here, since this idea is in line with other developments in politics, law, and philosophy and can therefore offer a valuable contribution into this ongoing debate that focuses on the establishment of peace and points to the moral costs of war.[348] My main selection criterion for choosing to depict a certain approach is whether the theory in question enables the assessment of autoregulation in weapons technology from a contingent pacifist point of view, so I eventually gain an overview of the current (and partly historic) approaches facilitating the ethical assessment of the subject. This entails the question of whether adding a third category of *jus post bellum* to *jus in bello* and *jus ad bellum* might help to bring together the discussions of just war thinking, from which this category is taken, with the gist of contingent pacifism. I will argue that this is the case.[349]

This section is structured as follows: First, I will outline the framework that makes for a new development in peace ethics and show that it can be grasped in terms such as "contingent pacifism," "revisionist just war approaches," and "just peace theory." Although these approaches do not seem to share a common terminology at first glance, they are very similar with regard to their means and objectives (5.3.1). Subsequently, I will elaborate on the philosophical theory of Larry May because his approach is a coherent contemporary example of how contingent pacifism can be reconsidered under modern circumstances, thereby putting the emphasis on *jus post bellum* (5.3.2). His theory also marks the link between the revision of just war tradition and contingent pacifism because May reconsiders the revision of just war within an explicit pacifist frame, thereby making the inherent intent to confine warfare within this approach even more apparent. In the next step, I will depict the Christian

---

347. See Fiala, "Pacifism."

348. See 5.3.1 Preliminaries.

349. See 5.3.3.3.2 Peace Memorandum of the Council of the Protestant Church in Germany.

approach of just peace thinking in greater detail, thereby referring to the theology of Bonhoeffer, who can be regarded as a main character and pioneer in developing the Protestant version of just peace theory (5.3.3.1), as well as Roman Catholic approaches toward just peace (5.3.3.2). Both strands of discussion then influence each other and lead to seminal texts: in the German Roman Catholic case, a pastoral letter written in 2000 (5.3.3.3.1) and, in the case of the Protestant church in Germany, a memorandum adopted in 2007 (5.3.3.3.2). These texts are still discussed today (5.3.3.3.3). Finally, I will draw some first conclusions for the development and deployment of autoregulation in weapons technology along this line of thinking.

5.3.1 Preliminaries: Just Peace as a Contingent Pacifist Approach Within Contemporary Thought

Contingent pacifism, revisionist just war approaches, and just peace theory share an interest in confining the use of force to a minimal amount. All of these theories have a certain suspicion toward engagement in war and violence for several reasons. For instance, mainly from a contingent pacifist point of view, war is deemed an undertaking too morally risky for the individual to carry out, be it a soldier or a civilian.[350] The aim of the following paragraph is to contour the circumstances under which these ideas could develop and the political and philosophical backdrop against which they have been established.

The theoretical foundation for this development toward peace harks back to Kant's seminal work *Toward Perpetual Peace*, in which the philosopher outlines his idea of a perpetual political peace. Among Kant's assumptions is the thought that peace is rooted in the nature of humanity,[351] as well as the idea that both morals and politics belong together for the sake of humanity, concluding that "all politics must bend its knee before right."[352] Kant's undertaking to establish political and juridical means and bodies that facilitate peace is coherent only against this backdrop. To put it differently, the principles Kant provides are only worthy of consideration if humanity is able to achieve peace and if this

---

350. See May, *Contingent Pacifism*, 44. For the revisionist just war theory, see McMahan "Innocence, Self-Defense and Killing in War."
351. See Kant, *AA*, 8:344.
352. Kant, *AA*, 8:380.

moral prerogative can be established politically. Among these guidelines are six preliminary articles, admonishing nation-state actors to negotiate (peace) treaties that facilitate new wars, to exercise dominion over other countries, to maintain standing armies in course of time, to connect national debts with external affairs, to interfere violently with another state's affairs, and to fight wars in a manner that forestalls the establishment of "mutual trust"[353] in the aftermath of this conflict.[354] Furthermore, Kant delineates what he considers to be preconceptions for the establishment of perpetual political peace, such as a republican civil constitution, a federation of free states able to establish international law, and the limitation of each person's rights to "conditions of universal *hospitality*."[355] Hartwig von Schubert maps Kant's account onto different levels of the rule of law. There is, first, civil right, regulating the relationship between the individual and the (nation) state. Second, there is international law, concerning how different (nation) states are interconnected and how they are bound together within the international community. Third, there is cosmopolitan law, referring to the relationship between the individual and the international community.[356] In that regard, different possible configurations are addressed, and it is ensured that each individual is secured either within a certain (nation) state or within the international community. Inside this configuration, the different (nation) states join a shared rule of law, thereby narrowing one another's power to wage war. This basic thought then found its way into the League of Nations, which was founded in 1920 and replaced by the UN in 1946. It is still tangible in the system of collective security inscribed into the UN Charter in Article 2, which reads in paragraphs 3 and 4:

> 3. All Members shall settle their international disputes by peaceful means in such a manner that international peace and security, and justice, are not endangered. 4. All Members shall refrain in their international relations from the threat or use of force against the territorial integrity or political independence of any state, or in any other manner inconsistent with the Purposes of the United Nations.[357]

---

353. Kant, *AA*, 8:346.
354. See Kant, *AA*, 8:343–47.
355. Kant, *AA*, 8:357. Emphasis original.
356. See von Schubert, "Das Reich Gottes," 88.
357. UN Charter, Art. 2, 3–4.

The Ethical Framing

Ideas such as just peace refer intensely to this already embodied system and propose building on these established forms of collective security.

By the same token, Walter Benjamin's *Toward the Critique of Violence* (*Zur Kritik der Gewalt*, 1921) is of great interest. In this essay, Benjamin scrutinizes the relationship between law and justice and the role violence plays. He writes, "The task of a critique of violence can be summarized as that of expounding its relation to law and justice."[358] At the outset, Benjamin elaborates on the role of violence in natural and positive law, thereby suggesting that even though both paradigms share the belief that "just ends can be attained by justified means, justified means used for just ends,"[359] they differ in respect to their direction. While positive law seeks to "guarantee" that the end is just by establishing just means, natural law pursues the attempt to "justify" the means by justification of the end.[360] Both systems of thought would collapse, however, in the moment the nexus between ends and means would be proven to fail—an attempt the author seeks to make in this essay.

Yet, before drawing this conclusion, Benjamin addresses both argumentations in turn, thereby probing the degree to which either of them could assess the use of force. He therefore rules out natural law right at the outset because within this frame, it is not possible to decide over violent means at all—crucial here is only the end they are used for.[361] Of ostensibly more cogency seems, for Benjamin, the positive law frame because the assessment of violent means seems possible. This overall frame needs to be kept in mind when interpreting the subsequent passage that elaborates on the difference between a law-making and a law-preserving function of violence.[362] The law-making function comes to the fore when "violence is a means to the end of the state,"[363] meaning when violence is used in order to secure legal ends such as the "subordination of citizens to laws."[364] From this, a law-preserving function can be differentiated, which for Benjamin is mainly embodied in conscription. Without delving deeper into the details of this intricate text, it suffices to say that Benjamin's account has been interpreted in very different ways. Axel

---

358. Benjamin, "Critique of Violence," 236.
359. Benjamin, "Critique of Violence," 237.
360. See Benjamin, "Critique of Violence," 237.
361. See Honneth, "Zur Kritik der Gewalt," 199.
362. See Honneth, "Zur Kritik der Gewalt," 200.
363. Benjamin, "Critique of Violence," 241.
364. Benjamin, "Critique of Violence," 241.

Honneth, for example, concludes that both functions of violence serve the purpose of demonstrating that positive law cannot assess the use of violence,[365] while Benjamin's overall objective is to criticize the law as a whole.[366] Wolfgang Huber, on the other hand, emphasizes that violence can be seen as a source of (positive) law because law depends on violence for its enforcement. These processes, however, are then contested by an eschatologically interpreted justice.[367] In doing so, Huber—and also just peace theory as established in the peace memorandum of the Protestant church in Germany—maintain that the sole account of positive law is not sufficient for the establishment of an international legal frame but that ethical critique should rather constitute and accompany these efforts.[368]

Overall, the results indicate that law, justice, and violence are not in simple relationship. Rather, in order to assess the phenomenon of violence, which might be incorporated into law and legal frameworks, ethical perspectives can help to review these. Indicated within this debate, however, is the shift from war paradigm to law paradigm, meaning the idea that the legitimization of law ought to precede the legitimization of violence. Within this frame, violence can only be used as a last resort and for the sake of law, which in turn is tied to human rights as a key legal concept.[369] As Torsten Meireis puts it, "The concept of law-abiding force implies not only to criticize violence permanently, but also to criticize the law."[370] He concludes that what is needed here is therefore not only a

---

365. See Honneth, "Zur Kritik der Gewalt," 202.

366. See Honneth, "Zur Kritik der Gewalt," 209. Honneth writes, "Der Impuls, von dem Benjamins Abhandlung angetrieben wird, ist eine Kritik des Rechts im Ganzen; denn jede Einrichtung der Gesellschaft, die nach Maßgabe des Zweck-Mittel-Schemas erfolgt, muss nach seiner Überzeugung alle menschlichen Angelegenheiten auf den einen Gesichtspunkt des Ausgleichs individueller Interessen reduzieren."

367. See Huber, *Gerechtigkeit und Recht*, 176–78. It must be added that Huber argues also that these processes are confined by the human rights tradition.

368. See Meireis, "Der gerechte Friede und die Ambivalenz rechtswahrender Gewalt," 157.

369. See Huber, "Rechtsethik," 182–83, 154–55. This emphasis on the law, however, might not be as clear as it seems at first glance. This is because law is not a solid formation but comes in different traditions dependent on the cultural and legal background. Therefore, the hint that (international) legal regulation might set aside its importance lacks clearance. See Jäger, "Frieden durch Recht," 4–5.

370. See Meireis, "Der gerechte Frieden und die Ambivalenz rechtswahrender Gewalt," 158. My translation. Meireis writes, "Vielmehr impliziert die Konzeption rechtswahrender Gewalt nicht nur eine permanente Kritik der Gewalt, sondern auch des jeweiligen Rechts. Dass dabei nicht nur an einer Kriteriologie des gerechten Friedens, sondern auch eines gerechten Rechts in Anschlag gebracht werden muss, ist ohne

criteriology of just peace but also of "just law."[371] In that regard, violence can never be justified directly, which is because law is oriented toward recognizing the individual, a process directly opposed to violence. Consequently, the use of force places the agent in a dilemma: "For the sake of the law one resorts to a means that is contrary to law."[372] It is the concept of legal pacifism that elaborates on this question in more detail.[373] When rephrased in terms of theology, however, this precarious structure involves the reflection of guilt: Since the use of violence in itself can never be justified, the agent using it incurs guilt on themselves, which is at variance with justifying violent means.[374] Theologically spoken and referring to Bonhoeffer, this process of incurring guilt is indissolubly connected to the willingness to become guilty[375] (*Bereitschaft zur Schuldübernahme*), which in turn is oriented on Jesus' vicarious representative action (*Stellvertretung*) where the sinless incurs guilt. As can be seen, Bonhoeffer and his thought form the foundation for German Protestant theological thinking with regard to war and peace, which is why I will elaborate on Bonhoeffer and his thought in greater detail below.[376]

Moreover, since the purpose of such law—resting on human rights—is to secure human life, no attempt to harm or destroy such life violently can ever be justified: Somebody will become guilty if violence is used. Such behavior can only be excused legally and not morally when striving to provide a qualified legal rule. Otherwise, guilt would be void. This thought draws on the aforementioned interpretation of Benjamin[377] and is linked to the idea that an ethics of war becomes obsolete, since within a

---

Zweifel eine anspruchsvolle Verschärfung der normativen Herausforderungen."

371. See Meireis, "Der gerechte Frieden und die Ambivalenz rechtswahrender Gewalt," 158. My translation.

372. Huber, "Legitimes Recht und legitime Rechtsgewalt in theologischer Perspektive," 225. My translation. Huber writes, "Diese Legitimität bleibt stets dilemmatisch: Um des Rechts willen wird zu einem Mittel gegriffen, das im Widerspruch zum Recht steht."

373. See Brücher, "Rechtspazifismus."

374. See Huber, "Legitimes Recht und legitime Rechtsgewalt in theologischer Perspektive," 236.

375. I take the terms from the translation of the Dietrich Bonhoeffer edition. Although I decided on this translation of the term, it might also be translated as "the acceptance of incurring guilt."

376. See 5.3.3.1 On Bonhoeffer's Account of War and Peace.

377. As indicated above, however, the interpretation of Huber and Reuter might not be consistent with Benjamin's writing and the interpretation put on this text within current philosophical thought.

legal frame, the criteria to justify the use of force must be consistent with several factors. First, there is the law itself, but it must also be coherent for every use of force, be it by police forces, the military, in civil resistance to a genocidal tyrannic regime, or in immediate self-defense. This is why, from this perspective, it makes far more sense to reconstruct the single criteria for the use of force within an ethics of law-sustaining force than to refer to an explicit ethics of war.[378] Such an approach ultimately amounts to a political concept such as the responsibility to protect (R2P).

The changes intentional politics has undergone in recent decades, described as the advent of so-called *new wars*, forms the backdrop against which the development of the R2P has been made possible. While warfare in the Cold War era typically occurred between (nation) states whose wars were fought between the armies of states, new wars stand out due to a growing asymmetry between the belligerent parties as well as a privatization and autonomization of conflicts. Consequently, combatants are becoming more and more detached from nation-state actors, as can be seen in terrorism, for example. In fact, only 15 percent of the wars fought since the end of World War II and until Russia's attack on Ukraine in February 2022 have been fought between different nation states.[379] These new circumstances resemble those of the Thirty Years' War rather than the situation in the twentieth century, and new approaches are therefore needed to react to this shift.[380] Moreover, the painful experiences of genocides and mass killings around the turn of the millennium connected to names such as Rwanda, Srebrenica, Bosnia, Croatia, or Liberia showed that the legal groundwork would not match the situation on-site: "The internal community was ill-prepared to respond effectively to this

---

378. The English translation for the German terms, such as *rechtswahrende* und *rechtserhaltende Gewalt* are not readily at hand, especially because the translation of Benjamin uses different terminology than the translation of the peace memorandum. To complicate matters further, there has been an inherent critique of the terminology by Reuter himself. See Reuter, "Kampfdrohnen als Mittel rechtswahrender militärischer Gewalt," 39. With regard to the different concepts of Benjamin and the Protestant church of Germany, this diverging terminology might also be used to express differences. When I refer to Benjamin's concept, I therefore use the term the translation of his work indicates, which is "law preserving function," while, for the matter of the protestant perspective, I accept the shift proposed by Reuter, who coined a term that can be translated as "law-sustaining force," thereby repudiating the term "law-abiding force," which is the term the peace memorandum uses. I elaborate on the difference below. See 5.3.3.2.2 Peace Memorandum of the Council of the Protestant Church in Germany, n1055.

379. See Schreiber, "Innerstaatliche Kriege seit 1954."

380. See Münkler, *Die neuen Kriege*.

tide of human misery and was often divided."[381] Facing this calamitous situation, a question arose: Can—and should—the international community interfere in a state's sovereignty in order to protect its citizens? This issue finally led to the establishment of the R2P.[382] This concept was mentioned initially in 2001 and was formally adopted by the UN World Summit in 2005, but remains contested and has not been integrated into the juridical instruments of international law.[383] The basic idea, as declared in the official document of the UN, is that first "each individual state has the responsibility to protect its populations from genocide, war crimes, ethnic cleansing and crimes against humanity."[384] If the respective state fails to execute this task, the international community has the right to interfere, a scenario the UN describes as follows:

> The international community, through the United Nations, also has the responsibility to use appropriate diplomatic, humanitarian and other peaceful means, in accordance with Chapters VI and VIII of the Charter, to help protect populations from genocide, war crimes, ethnic cleansing and crimes against humanity. In this context, we are prepared to take collective action, in a timely and decisive manner, through the Security Council, in accordance with the Charter, including Chapter VII, on a case-by-case basis and in cooperation with relevant regional organizations as appropriate, should peaceful means be inadequate and national authorities manifestly fail to protect their populations from genocide, war crimes, ethnic cleansing and crimes against humanity.[385]

Subsequently, in 2008, UN Secretary-General Ban Ki-moon inferred three pillars of R2P. He emphasized, first, that "governments unanimously affirmed the primary and continuing legal obligations of states to protect their populations—whether citizens or not—from genocide, war crimes, ethnic cleansing, and crimes against humanity, and from their incitement."[386] Second, he highlighted the need to prevent atrocities in a coordinated international effort without the necessity of a

---

381. Bellamy and Dunne, "R2P in Theory and Practice," 5.
382. See Bellamy and Dunne, "R2P in Theory and Practice," 5–6.
383. See Chesterman, "Responsibility to Protect and Humanitarian Intervention," 815–819.
384. UN, A/RES/60/1, §138.
385. UN, A/RES/60/1, §138.
386. Ki-moon, "Responsible Sovereignty."

unanimous vote of the Security Council. If these national and preventive measures fail, however, a third pillar would be a "timely and decisive"[387] response resorting to all means the UN is legally capable of within the respective circumstances.[388]

Following Alex J. Bellamy and Tim Dunne in their evaluation, this implies four main aspects. First, narrowness and universality, meaning that R2P pertains solely to cases of genocide, war crimes, ethnic cleansing, and crimes against humanity, while the protection of a state's population against these crimes is the prime directive of any state at all times. Second, the state guarantees this protection not only to its formal citizens but to its entire population. Third, R2P is consistent with the already established international law and based on the principles of the UN Charter. Finally, the main emphasis of the whole project is not to enable a forceful intervention but to prevent this means from being applied by collecting relevant data, being aware of situations of concern, recommending preventive measures through the Security Council, and resorting to UN bodies in order to enhance the possibility of prevention.[389]

Despite this well-thought-out and politically influential theory, the question of whether R2P is an "established international norm"[390] is highly contested. Melissa Labonte summarizes the two opposing viewpoints in her consideration:

> While R2P sceptics operate on the largely unfounded fear that acting on the norm will usher in a new era of interventionism, R2P adherents operate largely on an equally unfounded optimism that the norm will come to regulate state behavior and in doing so, realize its life-saving promise.[391]

For that matter, Bellamy and Dunne propose thinking of R2P as a regime rather than a norm, thereby relocating it from a merely academic discussion to a rather practical context within the bodies of the UN, integrated into the larger question of how to protect human lives.[392] However, this interpretation might be too positive, following Simon Chesterman,

---

387. Ki-moon, "Responsible Sovereignty."
388. See Ki-moon, "Responsible Sovereignty."
389. See Bellamy and Dunne, "R2P in Theory and Practice," 8–9.
390. See Bellamy and Dunne, "R2P in Theory and Practice," 11.
391. Labonte, "R2P's Status as a Norm," 146; similarly, Janik, *International Law and the Use of Force*, 158.
392. See Bellamy and Dunne, "R2P in Theory and Practice," 10–11.

The Ethical Framing

who succeeds in proving that R2P has been embraced only rhetorically, so the impression is made that international norms and behavior have changed as well.[393] He finally draws the conclusion that "the true significance of R2P may not be the creation of new rights or obligations to do 'the right thing'; rather, it is in making it harder to do the wrong thing or do nothing at all."[394]

It is neither my aim to settle this dispute here nor to scrutinize the current debates revolving around R2P in political thinking in any detail. Rather, I want to scrutinize the way in which this development pertains to current discussions relating to contingent pacifist ideas. Three major and interconnected points are important for my contribution here. They concern the crucial step from a perceptive where the sovereignty of the nation state is the basic principle of organizing international relationships to a view where shared values and laws form the foundation for collective efforts. This is, first, part of the aforementioned shift from war paradigm to law paradigm because within a war paradigm, the nation state is seen as the central authority to decide whether to wage war against another nation state. Second, and in tandem with the aforementioned system of collective security, R2P gives a substantial impulse leading away from this nation state rationale, moving toward a global and cosmopolitan principle where shared and universal ideas and rights form the foundation for the global community, even if this might only make "it harder to do the wrong thing or do nothing at all."[395] The executive body that enforces these rights on an international scale would then, third, no longer be the military but the police, since the international community is no longer seen as opposed to each other, but as an internal political body. The police would serve the needs of such an organization better than an army. Therefore, contemporary thought with regard to the police is of interest for my consideration as well.

Police and military form two separate bodies that share the ability to use force legitimately because both are executive bodies of a certain state. They differ, however, in their aims and methods. The objective of the military is to fight an outside enemy while relying on soldiers who are usually seen as legitimate targets within a violent situation. The police, on the other hand, operate within a certain state with the aim of hunting

---

393. See Chesterman, "Responsibility to Protect and Humanitarian Intervention," 820.

394. Chesterman, "Responsibility to Protect and Humanitarian Intervention," 820.

395. Chesterman, "Responsibility to Protect and Humanitarian Intervention," 820.

and catching criminals. Police officers, however, can never be legitimate targets. The only legitimate target within a violent police scenario is the criminal, who still should not be targeted lethally but is to be incapacitated, ideally with nonlethal means only.[396] Yet, the advent of terrorism and new wars has led to an expansion of military activities, in which police and military interact more and more.[397] This is also connected to the idea of a system of collective security, as there is no reasonable need for different armies to fight each other. Rather, what is needed is a political body legitimized to command an internal army, which in turn is understood as police force because it serves the interest of the entire international community.

Against this backdrop, the German political scholar Ines-Jacqueline Werkner proposed substituting the idea of a military intervention, such as R2P, against a just policing framework, because police operations seem more in line with pacifist ideas than military actions. The just policing model harks back to dialogues between Mennonites and Roman Catholics at the turn of the last millennium and has its source in longing for peace, on the one hand, and in the need to ensure security and peace, sometimes forcefully, on the other hand. Therefore, it aims to apply the criteria of just war tradition to police actions, thereby forming the concept of just policing.[398] In order for such a system to work, Werkner lists three preconditions: first, a well-operating political community commanding its police; second, an overall consensus about what public welfare refers to; and third, the shared interest of the respective community in sustaining this public welfare on behalf of the law. She adds that even though these preconditions might, in most cases, happen to exist in the individual nation state, it is not entirely clear whether they can easily be transferred to an international context, such as the UN. Yet, it might be built on the already established framework with regard to R2P, depicting international politics as "global domestic policy"[399] (*Weltinnenpolitik*). Understood that way, Just policing could be framed in a tripartite way, which would consist of, first, an expression of such global domestic politics; second, means to intervene in breaches of the world peace, thereby

---

396. See Werkner, "Just Policing," 15.
397. See Werkner, "Just Policing," 84.
398. See Werkner, "Just Policing," 6–7.
399. See Werkner, "Just Policing," 86.

The Ethical Framing

virtually superseding the concept of R2P; and, third, means of prevention in cases where international peace is at risk.[400]

There are, however, a bundle of inquiries with regard to just policing, which I will exemplify with a remark given by Nina Leonhard concerning a sociological perspective and revolving around the very dichotomous separation of military and police. Leonhard emphasizes that the concept of police and military is historically contingent and not self-evident. Therefore, the police must be seen as legitimate and benevolent in any case, as can be exemplified easily with respect to the police in Nazi Germany or the violence against African Americans in the US.[401] Vice versa, the military does not always resort to its destroying potential either, as UN peacekeeper missions have shown. Therefore, it might be more helpful to extrapolate who uses violence, to which objective, and where, thereby clarifying where which form of violence is transferred to the other.[402]

The concept of just policing is of interest for my contribution because it is another attempt to intertwine the implications of just war with pacifist thought under current political circumstances. Again, the objective is to confine violence within a legal frame, thereby moving away from a concept of state sovereignty to a framework that endorses a domestic understanding of the global community. As should be clear by now, the problems such an undertaking faces are mainly within the realm of a shared groundwork for international cooperation. To define shared objectives and to determine the joint measures that should be taken in order to achieve this objective is anything but a given, all the more so if the exact understanding of the terms in question—police or military—is histrionically and culturally contingent. These severe hindrances, however, are not mentioned to sideline this concept, but rather to show what difficulties pacifist-oriented thinking has to address.

As for the development in Germany, the antinuclear movement and, within the Christian debate, the development of the *Heidelberger Thesen* in 1959 are worthy of a mention in this context because they paved the way toward today's perception of just peace thinking and have gained importance in the current discourse revolving around Russia's attack on Ukraine.

---

400. See Werkner, "Just Policing," 70–71.

401. Dorlin exemplifies this point with the violence the police inflicted on Rodney King in 1991. See Dorlin: *Selbstverteidigung*, 12–18.

402. See Leonhard, "Just Policing," 78–80.

An Ethical Evaluation of Lethal Functions in Autoregulative Weapons Systems

The *Heidelberger Thesen* can be seen to form the interim theoretical and theological foundation for discussing peace ethics in times of nuclear deterrence. They are structured along two contradictory statements, recurring to the phenomenon of physical complementary—that renouncing the use of nuclear force is imminent—while simultaneously advocating for keeping them available for the sake of maintaining world peace.[403] Such a paradoxical statement was needed in order to strike a balance between the respective contradictory and highly disputed standpoints that were advocated for within the Protestant church, and the concept of complementary was seen to pose a possible figure to express that contradictory thought, at least on a societal level. To be fair, keeping nuclear force available is not identical to deploying them. Nevertheless, the contradictory statement arguing in favor of complementarity can hardly be interpreted other than as being an interim, which puts the individual in an impossible situation because they cannot renounce and make use of (nuclear) force simultaneously.[404] Accordingly, Ulrich Körtner's proposal to recollect these ideas in the light of Russia's attack on Ukraine seems rather surprising.[405] In that regard, Renke Brahm also argues that the situation since 1959 has changed immensely and that a phrasing that was mainly meant to mediate between two contradictory positions within the church can hardly be the seen to legitimize nuclear force. Developing contracts with the objective of abolishing nuclear weapons are therefore of great importance politically, while it is theologically imminent to demythologize the *Heidelberger Thesen*, putting the emphasis on civic means of conflict management.[406]

Politically, the debates on nuclear weapons technology are closely connected with the Easter Marches (*Ostermärsche*) that originated in the 60s as a protest against war, and nuclear weapons technology as a violent means in particular. The protests were sparked due to the NATO double-track decision (*NATO-Doppelbeschluss*) that involved the installation of nuclear intermediate-range ballistic missiles on European ground in order to strike a new balance with the Soviet Union.[407] Among the participants and supporters of the movement, the Christian churches, especially the Protestant church, played an important role within the

---

403. See Huber and Reuter, *Friedensethik*, 170–72.
404. See Huber and Reuter, *Friedensethik*, 170–71.
405. See Körtner, "Flug in die Irre."
406. See Brahms, "Heidelberger Thesen."
407. See Wiechmann, *Sicherheit neu denken*, 16.

The Ethical Framing

movement from the beginning and in forming several peace initiatives in the course of time, such as *Aktion Sühnezeichen*, or *Aktionsgemeinschaft für den Frieden*.[408] Especially in 1989, however, the participants became more and more public, also due to the political significance of the NATO double-track decision, so the movement gained even more momentum in German civic society.

In that regard, the peace prayers and the peaceful revolution in the GDR also need to be mentioned. Under the roof of the church, especially the *Nikolaikirche* in Leipzig, dissidents and opponents could raise their voices, thereby playing an eminent role in processes that led to the German reunification.[409]

All of these occurrences—meaning the *Heidelberger Thesen*, the civic anti-nuclear movement, and the peaceful revolution—were important theoretical and political steps that paved the way for just peace thinking: the *Heidelberger Thesen* in being a bygone interim because the situation today no longer resembles the situation in 1959; the anti-nuclear movement because it can be seen as a major civic movement expressing the wish for peace on a broad societal level; and the peaceful revolution because it was "the first successful democratic revolution in German history"[410] in which the churches played an important role, at least for several months, due to their being somewhat independent from the Socialist Union Party regime in Germany.[411]

In essence, even though the terms "contingent pacifism," "revisionist just war thinking," "just peace theory," or "just policing" seem to differ in meaning and content, all of these concepts aim for a similar objective, which is a legally founded peaceful international frame. Moreover, they propose to achieve this objective by peaceful means and by proving that (current) weapons technology and means are not suitable for that matter. Having this in mind, it is now my intention to introduce several proposals within this contingent pacifist frame, showing the ways in which different authors with diverse backgrounds, be they philosophical or theological in nature, attempt to address the question of violence and peace and make propositions to implement a more peaceful frame. In doing so, I will put a special focus on the question of how violence is

---

408. See Wiechmann, *Sicherheit neu denken*, 22.

409. See Wallmann, *Kirchengeschichte Deutschlands seit der Reformation*, 312–13; Maser, *Die Kirchen in der DDR*, 145–48.

410. Maser, *Die Kirchen in der DDR*, 145. My translation.

411. See Maser, *Die Kirchen in der DDR*, 145, 148–49. My translation.

integrated into this frame, to what end and under which circumstances it might be used, and if there are certain technologies that are ruled out from the outset.

5.3.2 On Larry May's Concept of Contingent Pacifism

One proposal to combine absolute pacifism and just war tradition has been brought forward by Larry May, building on the ideas presented by John Rawls in his *A Theory of Justice* (1971). Rawls writes,

> The conduct and aims of states in waging war, especially large and powerful ones, are in some circumstances so likely to be unjust that one is forced to conclude that in the foreseeable future one must abjure military service altogether. So understood a form of contingent pacifism may be a perfectly reasonable position: the possibility of a just war is conceded but not under present circumstances.[412]

He draws the conclusion that "what is needed, then, is not a general pacifism but a discriminating conscientious refusal to engage in war in certain circumstances."[413]

In this section, the term "contingent pacifism" appears for the first time. May then uses this term to describe the notion he has in mind, couched in the following phrase:

> Contingent pacifism [...] is the doctrine that armed conflict and war is in principle justifiable but that it is unjustified now and into the foreseeable future, and in the past it is highly unlikely that wars have been just wars either.[414]

For that reason, May follows the gist of absolute pacifism, namely the "presumption against going off to war and against using violence,"[415] but not because of an overarching moral principle that would forbid every participation in armed conflict. Rather, he argues that there is a significant risk to participating in actions that serve unjust military actions[416] and that people killed for ostensibly just reasons might actually turn out

---

412. Rawls, *Theory of Justice*, 335. Rawls refers here to Christian thought on nuclear weapons.
413. Rawls, *Theory of Justice*, 335.
414. May, *Contingent Pacifism*, 44–45.
415. May, *Contingent Pacifism*, 44.
416. See May, *Contingent Pacifism*, 44.

to be innocent and therefore unjustified victims.[417] In contrast to classical just war thinking, May applies the act of illegitimate killing not only to civilians or incidental damage, but expands its focus to soldiers who are noncombatants or simply unjust victims, such as a soldier who does not pose an actual threat or an innocent soldier, thereby following McMahan's proposal to revise just war thinking.[418]

Moreover, the soldier fighting might not be able to tell if they are indeed fighting in a just war, either because they simply believe that they are fighting for the right reasons, or because their state has deceived them.[419] On those grounds, the author illustrates how his understanding of necessity and proportionality differs from its classical understanding in just war tradition. Necessity, for example, is often considered within the frame of military necessity only, thereby neglecting the individual soldier as a human being.[420] In May's view, necessity considerations need to reflect the moral status of a soldier as well. He maintains that "soldiers have certain rights that cannot be forfeited and that as a result the killing of soldiers in war is highly problematic morally."[421] He therefore attributes what he calls a "minimal moral status" to soldiers. Accordingly, every person, and therefore every soldier, has "the right not to be killed unnecessarily."[422] This is because the soldier cannot say for sure if they are actually fighting a just war. Thus, by keeping unnecessary harm away from soldiers, they retain their human dignity.[423] Consequently, unjust combatants are protected from unnecessary harm as well, for instance, by retreating soldiers who do not pose an actual threat.[424]

May then asks what makes a person a legitimate target according to his understanding of contingent pacifism. In fact, most soldiers do not fire their weapons and, for that reason, he doubts whether they do really pose a threat to others. What he does concede, however, is that they are complicit in war and therefore pose a threat to other soldiers. But complicity does not naturally include the liability to be killed, what

---

417. See May, *Contingent Pacifism*, 81.
418. See May, *Contingent Pacifism*, 81.
419. See May, *Contingent Pacifism*, 82–83, 103.
420. See also Lazar, "Necessity in Self-Defense and War."
421. May, *Contingent Pacifism*, 87.
422. May, *Contingent Pacifism*, 97.
423. See May, *Contingent Pacifism*, 87. With this thought, May refers Walzer's basic thought that the soldiers of all belligerent parties share the same moral status.
424. See May, *Contingent Pacifism*, 101–2.

he exemplifies with respect to the (humanitarian) aid worker who does indeed contribute to war but is not a legitimate target.[425] He therefore distinguishes two kinds of complicity:

> The primary sense of complicity is that a person is morally or legally responsible for having done acts intending to aid others who are perpetrators of wrongdoing. The secondary sense of complicity is that a person does acts that causally contribute to the perpetration of wrongdoing, but providing such contribution is not the primary aim for which the aid is being provided.[426]

While in the first case, a person intends to do harm, in the second case, the person seeks to help without malicious motives. The intention of a person is therefore decisive in contributing to an actual combat scenario: Since it is not the intention of an aid worker to harm others, they are not liable to be killed. Moreover, proportionality is a major factor: As long as it is sufficient to incapacitate a threat nonlethally, this should be prioritized.[427]

He then broadens this basic moral scope with two political proposals that are of interest. First, with respect to the international legal framework, he holds that the idea of IHL and the original idea of the UN is more in line with contingent pacifism than with just war thinking because the sovereignty of the individual state is confined to a certain degree by these political bodies. What is important here is the fact that he emphasizes the role of a *jus post bellum*, which needs to be installed. As guiding principles for such a theory, May sets out six normative principles, which are "rebuilding, retribution, reconciliation, restitution, and reparation, as well as proportionality."[428] The main intent is to think war from a perspective of peace and therefore also to have in mind that the way war is fought contributes to a lasting peace afterward, not to mention that war can only be considered in the first place if it is thought to be absolutely necessary.[429] In his final part, he turns to the idea of a *selective conscientious refusal*. The idea is based on his overall frame: Although in theory there might be wars that can be fought justly, this is very unlikely

---

425. See May, *Contingent Pacifism*, 123–28.
426. May, *Contingent Pacifism*, 131.
427. See May, *Contingent Pacifism*, 132.
428. May, *After War Ends*, 1.
429. See May, *Contingent Pacifism*, 135–94.

The Ethical Framing

to happen. Therefore, he demands the right to refuse to fight a specific war but not to be excluded from military service in general.[430]

This contribution from May is interesting on several grounds. First, because he rethinks the discussion regarding the revision of just war within a pacifist framework without rejecting the conduct of war in general. This makes room for the question of what conditions need to be fulfilled in order to use armed force and if there are weapons that can be deployed in line with this idea more easily than others. Second, recurring to revisionist just war thinking, he emphasizes the human rights of soldiers, who are living beings no matter which side they fight on. This is crucial because soldiers risk their lives but cannot be sure if they are doing so justly, thereby also risking harm to people who might turn out not to be a legitimate target. Therefore, a soldier should always have the right to refuse a specific military service for reasons of conscience. Third, and most importantly, his main argument against the conduct of current warfare is the moral risk that comes with modern war. Here, he refers to the risk of killing somebody, such as a soldier, who is classically thought to be a legitimate target but who is nevertheless not liable to be killed within the frame of contingent pacifism because they do not pose an actual threat or could also be incapacitated nonlethally.

With respect to autoregulative weapons systems, this contribution offers two main links. First, the degree to which an autoregulative device could help to contribute to sustaining peace in the long run is questionable. As can be seen with the deployment of UAVs in Pakistan, civilian populations are deeply afflicted by the invisible and perpetual threat: "Those living under drones have to face the constant worry that a deadly strike may be fired at any moment, and the knowledge that they are powerless to protect themselves."[431] It is very questionable if the deployment of autoregulative weapons systems will be able to remedy this situation or make it even worse.[432] The other link is the decision of how a technological system could cope with a situation as intricate as war successfully: If May is considered to be right and only the people complicit in war by posing an actual threat to others pose legitimate targets, it is very unclear how an autoregulative device could make this decision on technological grounds. This is because insight into the overall situation

---

430. See May, *Contingent Pacifism*, 233–49.

431. Stanford Law School, "Living Under Drones," vii.

432. I will elaborate on this thought in greater detail below. See 6.4.4 Concluding Remarks: Interpreting Risks.

of a particular war and an evaluation of each person's contribution to this specific combat would be crucial. On a related note, the overall idea of a selective conscientious refusal does not make sense regarding autoregulative devices. A weapon might be programmed not to engage targets for moral reasons, and in some instances, it might then cause less harm than a human charged with the same task. When assessing an overall conflict, however, a technological device that refuses to fight in a particular war simply does not make sense, as fighting is its very task. Such a device would, in case of need, merely be replaced by another device that did not have the same restrictions. Therefore, the whole idea of a selective conscientious refusal with the aim of confining violence is rendered preposterous.

5.3.3 Just Peace Theory as a Christian Approach

As argued above, the main purpose of the concept of *bellum iustum* is to confine violence,[433] so contingent pacifism might draw on the concept of *bellum iustum* as well, at least within a certain interpretative frame.[434]

---

433. See 5.2.1 *Bellum iustum*: History of Ideas.

434. At this point, the question of the degree to which violence is also a religious problem needs to be addressed at least briefly, since just peace thinking approaches violence from a Christian point of view. In that regard, Jäger and Werkner argue that violence as well as peace is an inherent part of Scripture and that, therefore, violent and nonviolent Christian movements can equally refer to the Bible. (See Jäger, "Gewalt in der Bibel und in kirchlichen Traditionen," 3–4; Werkner, "Diskurse um militärische Gewalt," 120–21.) Jäger resolves this discussion, known since the 1970s, with the remark that violence is usually rooted in political interest and not in religious beliefs. (See Jäger, "Gewalt in der Bibel und in kirchlichen Traditionen," 3–4.) Against this assumption, Stümke objects that the current debate revolving around the contribution of Assmann and his assumption that biblical monotheism of truth (*Monotheismus der Wahrheit*) is indissolubly linked to a language of violence that can very easily lead to violent behavior (see Assmann, *Totale Religion*, 125). Assmann, however, does not regard Scripture to be of one piece but recognizes different layers and ideas that each relate to violence in very different ways. In his strict monotheistic form, however, violence is at least part of the religious rhetoric. With regard to another strand of this argumentation, Khan emphasizes the religious roots of the modern nation state and concludes in his reflections on sacred violence, "We deceive ourselves if we think that Western political practices operate in a secular world untouched by faith and the experience of the sacred. The sovereign is a kind of god, and the end of this war, just as in previous wars, is the destruction of the enemy's god. That god exists as long as believers engage in the sacrificial practices that are its historical presence. The sovereign dies when citizens are no longer willing to take up the presence in their own bodies" (Kahn, *Sacred Violence*, 176). Following Assmann and Kahn, it might not be possible to draw a sharp line between religious and political violence and therefore religion might always be regarded as having both potentials at

The Ethical Framing

Against such a pacifist interpretation of *bellum iustum*, the current peace thinking within Christian thought needs to be understood. Following this intention, the ecumenical churches have adopted and adapted its political ethics in recent decades to present circumstances within a pacifist frame. During the early twentieth century, pacifist ideas gained popularity and became increasingly connected to international Christian initiatives in the period after World War I, which is the reason why the formation of an international ecumenical movement became closely linked to pacifist ideas. Theologically, this commitment to peace rests to a large degree on the concept of the kingdom of God, which entails that present social and political circumstances are directly connected to God's heavenly kingdom and rule. To put it differently, by participating in the spreading of Christian values in society, Christians take part in building God's kingdom on earth.[435] Following this rationale, the participants of the first Conference on Life and Work held in Stockholm 1925 rejected war as a means for achieving solutions to international conflicts as contradictory to Christ's teaching, as well as to the conduct of the Christian churches. At the same time, the conference declared that each nation has the sovereignty to defend itself, but it left open how these two principles

---

the same time: peace and violence. The nonviolent and pacifist approaches among just peace theory intend to realize the peaceful potential. In that regard, Meireis argues that violence is, theologically speaking, overcome by the deeds of God and is therefore part of human agency that needs to be overcome as well. (See Meireis, "Liebe und Gewalt," 36.) This concept, consequently, needs to address violence because it is part of humanity's nature. For that reason, Scripture also refers to violence, but with the intention of showing its deviancy. (See Meireis, "Liebe und Gewalt," 36–37.)

435. This thought is mainly connected to the English-speaking community and deeply ingrained into Methodist theology as well. See Klaiber and Marquardt, *Gelebte Gnade*, 240. However, within the context presented here this thought needs to be criticized against the backdrop of the distinction Bonhoeffer draws between the ultimate and the penultimate. While Bonhoeffer defines the ultimate to be "the justification of the sinner by God alone," the penultimate refers to "all that precedes the ultimate." *DBW* VI, 151. Both dimensions belong together because the "ultimate empowers the penultimate," 152. In that regard, Bonhoeffer also holds that preparing the way for Christ might be a troubling thought because Christ's coming needs to be expected the other way around: It is Christ who prepares the way, not the Christian. It is only because of that that Christianity can also take part in that process,159–160. Against this backdrop, Bonhoeffer's critique becomes clear: In talking about the participation in God's kingdom on earth, the ultimate and penultimate are at risk of becoming mixed up.

When I quote Bonhoeffer, I refer to the *Dietrich Bonhoeffer Works* edition (*DBW*). For the sake of simplicity, I quote the original German page number, because the English edition cites this page number as well. If helpful, I also quote the German original in footnotes without referring to the German edition specifically, because page number and volume match the German edition.

would be brought into concordance with each other. At the subsequent conference in 1937, the focus of the discussion shifted to the creation of a necessary legal framework capable of realizing peaceful solutions to international conflicts.[436] Yet, the surge of national socialist ideologies in Europe cast a shadow over these endeavors, which is reflected in the German context by the development of two opposing movements within the Protestant church. One of them became known as the *German Christians*, which rejected pacifism, while the secondary movement, known as the *Confessing Church*, emphasized the importance of pacifism. Within the latter movement, Bonhoeffer's thinking stands out. As mentioned above, his thinking and reasoning has influenced contemporary peace thought deeply within both pacifist strands—absolute and contingent pacifism. Within absolute pacifism, Hauerwas recurs to Bonhoeffer's theology on the one hand, while Huber and Reuter refer to his thought within a contingent pacifist approach on the other hand. Therefore, I will illustrate his pacifist account in the following section before I turn to the more recent developments in just peace thinking.

5.3.3.1 On Bonhoeffer's Account of War and Peace

For the sake of this contribution, it is not my intent to elaborate on the pacifist thought of Bonhoeffer comprehensively—for that matter, I point to Julian Zeyher-Quattlender's work on this specific topic.[437] It is rather my intent to give an overview of the scholarly discussions Bonhoeffer's peace ethics have provoked, as well as to provide some insight into the theological reasoning of Bonhoeffer himself, while drawing on and interpreting three of his contributions in varying intensity, namely a lecture Bonhoeffer gave in 1932 in Ciernohorské Kúpele, called *On the Theological Foundation of the Work of the World Alliance*; another lecture he gave in 1932 in Fanø, referred to as *The Church and Peoples of the World*; and his *Ethics*.

First, and with respect to the ongoing scholarly debates, especially in Anglo–American theological thought, Bonhoeffer's account regarding peace ethics plays an important role.[438] Several questions are discussed,

---

436. See Huber, "Frieden V," 631–34.

437. See Zeyher-Quattlender, *Du sollst nicht töten (lassen)?*

438. See Zeyher-Quattlender, *Du sollst nicht töten (lassen)?* 254. Some authors, such as the Bonhoeffer researcher Clifford J. Green, even perceive the key to Bonhoeffer's entire writings within his pacifist stance.

such as the issue of whether Bonhoeffer's thought changed over time and the specific character of his pacifist thought.[439] It is beyond the scope of my contribution to discuss these questions in detail. What is of concern here is the debate of how to interpret Bonhoeffer's pacifist thought, which is why I will confine myself to this particular strand of the discussion. The major issue in that regard is whether Bonhoeffer must be seen as an absolute pacifist, or whether Bonhoeffer's theory represents a contingent variant of pacifism. As can be seen above, Hauerwas takes the stance that Bonhoeffer's thought is in line with the perspective of John Howard Yoder and therefore interprets his writings to be absolute pacifist in nature.[440] This perspective has been opposed strongly, mainly because it seems impossible to strike a balance between an absolute pacifist point of view and Bonhoeffer's partaking in an attempt to assassinate Hitler.[441] Therefore, the effort to bring Bonhoeffer's thought in line with Lutheran theology, as undertaken by Michael DeJonge, is much more persuasive. DeJonge's main thought is that Bonhoeffer's theology can only be interpreted coherently if the Lutheran theology underlying Bonhoeffer's thought is taken seriously. This approach is mainly formed by the Lutheran idea of the two regimes:[442]

> While there is no doubt that reality is one in the one person of Christ, who is the singular revelation of God's unified being and acting in the world, it remains the case that God's preserving work ought not be confused with God's redeeming work. And while there is no doubt that the Christian lives in the one world as a unified person before God, it remains the case that the Christian proclamation of the gospel is not to be confused with the Christian's work for political justice. These should not be confused any more than they should be separated. The proper relationship of theology to ethics/politics is signaled by the controverted phrase "the two kingdoms."[443]

The way Bonhoeffer harks back to Luther is not strictly oriented on the Lutheran tradition, though. He rather is "a creative, dynamic

---

439. See Zeyher-Quattlender, *Du sollst nicht töten (lassen)?* 262.

440. I discuss this in my remarks on Hauerwas's theory. See 5.1.3.1 Conceptions Bound to Institutions.

441. See Zeyher-Quattlender, *Du sollst nicht töten (lassen)?* 259–60.

442. For my use of these terms and the depiction of Luther's theology in that regard, see 5.2.1 *Bellum iustum*: History of Ideas.

443. DeJonge, *Bonhoeffer's Reception of Luther*, 259.

participant in the Lutheran theological tradition."[444] My own reconstruction of Bonhoeffer's thought relates to this Lutheran line of interpretation, seeking to find a middle ground between an outright pacifist notion and the possibility of asking if there are certain circumstances that might enable the use of force.

For that matter, it seems most important to note that Bonhoeffer was both a pacifist and a member of the resistance against Hitler's rule simultaneously. This ostensibly paradoxical notion is due to the historical circumstances under which Bonhoeffer lived during the Nazi period, which need to be considered when interpreting his writings.[445] Thus, it can be shown that even though Bonhoeffer's thinking evolves over the time and with respect to the historical situation, there are certain elements that recur persistently. For that matter, Bonhoeffer's pacifist ideal is closely connected to his interpretation of ecclesiology and, following the Lutheran strand of interpretation, his account of Luther's concept of the two regimes. DeJonge elaborates on this intricate question in great detail, thereby making the point that the idea of preserving the world through a political or legal order is already deeply inherent in Luther's conceptualization. While God preserves the world by means of politics and law, he directs it toward redemption through faith and salvation. Bonhoeffer then builds on that thought in order to distinguish between church and state rather functionally. In that regard, the church needs to be a witness to God's deeds, while the state's task is to preserve the order of lives. For that matter, however, both entities need to cooperate because both need the respective other's function.[446] This basic thought is deeply ingrained into Bonhoeffer's theology and recurs in his work over time.

In one such historical situation, Bonhoeffer expresses his ideas regarding war and peace in a lecture held at a conference of the World Alliance for International Friendship Through the Churches in 1932, one year before Hitler's rise to power in Germany. Here, his focus on ecclesiology and Luther's teaching of the two regimes already becomes very clear: As far as the Christian church as a whole is concerned, its

---

444. DeJonge, *Bonhoeffer's Reception of Luther*, 263; Zeyher-Quattlender, *Du sollst nicht töten (lassen)?* 264.

445. See Reuter, "Vom christlichen Pazifismus zum aktiven Widerstand," 15–16. It also makes clear that pacifism is not coextensive with nonviolence, but refers to the participation in war only, thereby excluding forms of violence that are not in the same way problematic, such as police force or simple boxing for sport.

446. See DeJonge, *Bonhoeffer's Reception of Luther*, 98–99, 108–9.

preaching stems from, but is not confined to, secular borders—a belief expressed in the formation of international bodies such as the World Alliance of Churches. This is possible because "it is not a holy, sacred district of the world that belongs to Christ but rather the entire world."[447] The church's teaching and preaching, then, is authorized by the presence of Christ on earth (*aus der Vollmacht des Christus praesens*) and therefore speaks to the current situation, meaning that its teaching and preaching is related to specific circumstances. This entails that the word of the church must not be an abstract and ahistorical truth but a ruling that speaks to the here and now concretely. With regard to war, this means that the church does not forbid war under any circumstances, but rather that it condemns and prohibits specific wars.[448] In order to give such concrete rulings, the church needs to gain sufficient knowledge of the subject in question. This, in turn, does not preclude that a certain ruling turns out to be wrong, which is why the church itself is in constant need of forgiveness of sins. Based on this account, Bonhoeffer identifies two sources to state a specific ruling. He calls the first one biblical law (*biblisches Gesetz*), entailing texts such as the Sermon on the Mount, while he refers to the second one as order of creation (*Schöpfungsordnung*). Both codices, however, cannot be applied verbatim but have to be adapted to each situation in question. In the first case, this means that the church needs to interpret biblical law in correspondence with the current circumstances, while in the second case, it entails that the church cannot simply state a universally applicable, divinely sanctioned order of creation. Doing so would merely uphold the status quo without sufficiently taking the world's sinfulness into account. It is therefore important to strike a balance between God's universal promises and commands and an ever-changing positive law that relies on specific conditions—a possibility Bonhoeffer recognizes in what he calls orders of preservation (*Erhaltungsordnung*).[449] The main feature of this order is that its authority does not rest on an already established creation, which then would turn out to be orders of creation, but pertains to Christ himself and God's eschatological new creation. An order of preservation therefore obtains its authority from a transcendent reality amenable to ever-changing circumstances.[450]

---

447. *DBW* XI, 331.
448. See *DBW* XI, 333.
449. See *DBW* XI, 337.
450. See *DBW* XI, 337–38.

An Ethical Evaluation of Lethal Functions in Autoregulative Weapons Systems

With regard to the World Alliance of Churches, which argues in favor of an international peace regime, Bonhoeffer criticizes the kingdom of God rationale among Anglo–American theologians because this idea turns (international) peace into an absolute goal. Yet, in Bonhoeffer's thought, international peace is not an essential element of God's kingdom but rather part of God's order of preservation of this world. Bonhoeffer writes,

> International peace is not a reality of the gospel, not a piece of the kingdom of God, but rather a commandment of the wrathful God, an order of preservation of the world toward Christ. International peace is therefore also not an absolutely ideal condition but rather an order that is aimed at something else and that is not valuable in and of itself.[451]

Such a peace has boundaries, which are truth and justice, so lies and injustice pose a serious threat to peace.[452] In other words, waging struggle as a means of sustaining peace might be a viable solution. Bonhoeffer therefore differentiates between war (*Krieg*) and struggle (*Kampf*): While war annihilates body and mind, it can never be an appropriate means to maintain the rule of law. For Bonhoeffer, contemporary war[453] is of this character. Therefore, it is God's command to object to this particular war and to take a pacifist stance. This, however, does not hold true for struggle, which is a way to preserve peace to the extent that it is oriented toward the future of Christ and his new creation.[454]

The distinction Bonhoeffer makes between order of creation and orders of preservation is crucial because it enables theology to deliberate on political and societal issues with reference to specific circumstances and without insisting strongly and exclusively on unalterable, God-given commands. On the grounds of this distinction, Bonhoeffer neither argues for absolute pacifism in accordance with the Sermon on the Mount nor does he justify the application of violence for its own sake. He rather accepts it as a possibility within the scope of an order of preservation.[455] In short, he does not rule out every form of violence per

---

451. *DBW* XI, 339.

452. See *DBW* XI, 340.

453. Bonhoeffer here seems to refer to all kinds of contemporary wars because such kinds of war seem able destroy both belligerent parties. He then even refers to the "next war" that "must be *condemned* by the church." *DBW* XI, 341. Emphasis original

454. See *DBW* XI, 340.

455. See *DBW* XI, 126–27.

se but rather confines it to a limited amount with the ultimate goal of reconciliation and peace.[456]

Bonhoeffer then put forward a stronger argument for pacifism two years later in 1934, when he spoke again at the conference of the World Alliance for International Friendship Through the Churches in Fanø, Denmark. At that time, however, historical circumstances had changed significantly, and Bonhoeffer now deemed political means for achieving peaceful solutions to have become superfluous, as he recognized the events leading to Hitler's rise of power as a sign that war was imminent.[457] His explanation now stressed Christological thought even more: As Christ came into the world, and continues to be in this world, peace is imperative. "Peace on earth" Bonhoeffer states, "is not a problem, but a commandment given at Christ's coming."[458] Only for those Christological roots does the church have the right to exist and mirror Christ's example:

> There shall be peace because of the Church of Christ, for the sake of which the world exists. And this Church of Christ lives at one and the same time in all peoples, yet beyond all boundaries, whether national, political, social, or racial. [...] All these ties, which are part of our world, are valid ties, not indifferent; but in the presence of Christ they are not ultimate bonds.[459]

Here, Bonhoeffer contrasts a Christological unity tying different people who are separated by cultural and national borders together: Since Christ overcomes these divisions, there is no justification for their separation by means of war. This entails that peace cannot be established merely via a political or economic system or through military means because in doing so "peace is confused with safety."[460] For Bonhoeffer, *Sicherheit* (safety/security) is the opposite of peace because demanding *Sicherheit* creates mistrust "and this mistrust in turn brings forth war."[461]

---

456. See Reuter, "Vom christlichen Pazifismus zum aktiven Widerstand," 21–22.
457. See Huber, *Dietrich Bonhoeffer*, 143–44.
458. *DBW* XIII, 302.
459. *DBW* XIII, 303.
460. *DBW* XIII, 303.
461. *DBW* XIII, 303–4. Confusingly, the English translation uses three different words to translate the German term *Sicherheit*, which are safety, security, and guarantees. The differences that seem to be addressed in the English version do not exist in the German text, so disparate implications cannot be inferred easily.

Peace, on the other hand, means to trust in God, who reigns over the world. Therefore, "battles are won, not with weapons, but with God."[462]

What becomes clear from this is that Bonhoeffer believes peace to be a primary—but not absolute—goal of Christians and the church, since the individual Christian is part of a system that overcomes worldly principles with a unifying rationale. Following that argument, a Christian would hurt Christ himself when using force against other individuals.[463] I do not interpret this statement to argue for an absolute version of pacifism, though. As becomes clear when comparing his speech with the earlier lecture and later statements, following Wolfgang Huber, I argue that what Bonhoeffer has in mind is rather a kind of contingent pacifism.[464]

The underlying pacifist rationale is, accordingly, still present when Bonhoeffer chooses to join the resistance movement against Nazi rule in Germany. His reflections on that topic, expounded in his *Ethics*,[465] cannot be separated from the historical situation, which is marked by a rising nationalism threatening the church. Concretely, the Bonhoeffer's *Ethics* is situated in 1942, shortly after Bonhoeffer visited, in conjunction with the member of the ecclesiastical council Johannes Schönfeld, the Bishop of Chichester in order to discuss the possibility of peace in the aftermath of Hitler's death. That situates Bonhoeffer's *Ethics* right at the time when he made the decision to collaborate in assassinating Hitler and the Nazi authorities, thereby acting against the fourth and fifth commandments of the Decalogue.[466] Consequently, his writings should be seen as part of an ethics of resistance (*Ethik des Widerstands*[467]) in addition to his pacifist

---

462. *DBW* XIII, 304.

463. See *DBW* XIII, 300.

464. Huber portrays Bonhoeffer's thinking that way, thereby integrating different steps of Bonhoeffer's thinking with the attempt to reconstruct an overall coherent picture. See Huber, *Dietrich Bonhoeffer*, 150, 155–56.

465. The *Ethics* was not completed by Bonhoeffer himself and its several passages were compiled by scholars posthumously. Here, the text I mainly refer to, *A Theological Position Paper on State and Church*, occupies an even more special place because it has been published only in the appendix of some editions. It is, however, in line with the thought Bonhoeffer expounds in the paragraphs published in his *Ethics* and I will therefore refer to it as part of the *Ethics*. The difference, however, can be seen in the quoting, as the *Theological Position Paper on State and Church* has been published in the sixteenth volume of the *DBW*, while his *Ethics* have been released in the sixth volume.

466. See Slenczka, "Die unvermeidbare Schuld," 103.

467. Reuter, "Vom christlichen Pazifismus zum aktiven Widerstand," 28. In a similar way, Huber refers to "theology of resistance" (*Theologie des Widerstands*). See Huber, *Dietrich Bonhoeffer*, 172–77.

stance, a rationale that is already inherent in Bonhoeffer's earlier contributions.[468] From now on, and in contrast to an earlier, stronger focus on pacifism, Bonhoeffer's view shifts to a progressing political stance.[469] His resistance to Nazism rests on the thought that any given political government (*Obrigkeit*) is generally instated by God and represents God to the earth. He writes, "Government is the power set in the vicarious representative action of God on earth."[470] Since individual Christians are part of worldly structures, they also need to accept their subordinate role within the political government, a thought resembling the Lutheran differentiation between the spiritual and the secular regimes. According to Bonhoeffer, the authority of any specific government, therefore, does not depend on the way it emerged but on its mere reality or "existing" (*Sein*). Since this existing is a given, it is neither inherently good nor bad: "Like everything that exists, government is also in a certain sense beyond good and evil—i.e., it has not only an office but also a historical being."[471] Any given political government has a divinely sanctioned mission, whether or not it is aware of that, which is to exercise worldly jurisdiction and to implement the rule of sword and law on behalf of Christ.[472] By that, Bonhoeffer does not mean to imply that any given political order is invested with divine authority. Rather, he focuses on the tasks a government is supposed to fulfill toward its citizens and society in general.[473] In doing so, the government itself, as well as the realms of work, marriage, and church are mandated by God to operate quite autonomously. This also entails that both Christians and non-Christians are situated in the realm of mundane principles, which in turn are an expression of its divine root.[474] This entails that only the government is entitled to make political decisions without the church or other entities interfering.[475] To fulfill its task, the government has to punish wicked deeds and command the good and godly by exerting legal power and educating for the good. How good and bad are determined, however, must be in line with Christ's

---

468. Especially clear in *The Church and the Jewish Question* (1933). See *DBW* XII, 349–58.

469. See Reuter, "Vom christlichen Pazifismus zum aktiven Widerstand," 29.

470. *DBW* XVI, 507.

471. *DBW* XVI, 518.

472. See *DBW* XVI, 519.

473. See Huber, *Dietrich Bonhoeffer*, 176.

474. See *DBW* VI, 31–32.

475. See Friederike Barth, "Widerstehende Gewalt," 276.

dominion, which is then made apparent by the church, on the one hand. On the other hand, this characterization must also be assigned to non-Christians by the commandants of the second table of the Decalogue in accordance with worldly law.[476] As a consequence thereof, ordinary people, including Christians, are bound to follow the government's ruling unconditionally, at least until the ruling of the government is in direct opposition to Christ's ruling:

> The duty of Christians to obey binds them up to the point where the government forces them into direct violation of the divine commandment, thus until government overtly acts contrary to its divine task and thereby forfeits its divine claim.[477]

This quote is insightful, as it not only marks the boundaries of the individual's obedience but also unveils the fundamental reason for this, which is the forfeiture of the entitlement to rule. In other words, at the point at which a certain government urges its citizens to act against Christ's commands, it is no longer authorized by God unconditionally. Yet, this does not entail that the government forfeits its authority entirely; it only loses its claim with regard to this particular instance.[478] Such an idea entails that one single misruling does not relieve the government of its duty. Consequently, the Christian embarks on a risky venture if they shoulder responsibility in order to counteract the government, since such a case is not easy to identify. Bonhoeffer states, "The refusal to obey within a specific historical political decision of the government, as well as the decision itself, can only be a venture of one's own responsibility."[479]

What can be seen in comparison to Bonhoeffer's earlier thought is the idea that Christology underlies all theological thinking even more. The same applies to Bonhoeffer's ecclesiology, as his political thought is rooted in his account of Christ. In doing so, his objective is to overcome the thinking in two realms (*Denken in zwei Räumen*), which is the idea that mundane and Christian realms need to be kept apart categorially: Within the realm of the church, spiritual leaders have all authority, while the political government is authorized to rule within the political

---

476. See *DBW* XVI, 519–20.

477. *DBW* XVI, 521–22.

478 The rationale behind this argumentation is that if the church were in opposition to the government entirely, this would result in an apocalyptic situation where the government was in total antagonism to Christ. See *DBW* XVI, 522.

479. *DBW* XVI, 523.

The Ethical Framing

domain, without both of these spheres intersecting. Bonhoeffer, however, holds that Christ reigns over both of them, and they gain their respective authority only from him. Therefore, both need to be evaluated with regard to Christ's teaching and dominion.[480] Undeniably, there is a certain tension when making this differentiation between politics and spirituality while at the same time underlining their affiliation. Yet, as DeJonge argues, "this is less a contradiction than a tension, and one that arises out of the two-kingdoms framework Bonhoeffer adopts."[481] Accordingly, to resist the government due to minor or major misconduct is not an issue that can be justified easily. Additionally, only the individual, after having considered the issue carefully and concluded that resistance is needed, can carry out such an undertaking. Yet, in doing so, they do not stay innocent, but shoulder responsibility for their deeds by incurring guilt on themselves. Here, the concepts of freedom and responsibility form the foundation for such an extraordinary necessity. Bonhoeffer writes, "The extraordinary necessity appeals to the freedom of those who act responsible."[482] What Bonhoeffer has in mind is a form of responsibility constituted within a historical situation affecting the relationship between free people subordinated under the authority of Christ. To put it differently, certain individuals always reach the decision to shoulder responsibility within specific historical and social circumstances, while these concrete circumstances are nevertheless seen as being under the dominion of Christ. This process is what Bonhoeffer zeroes in on when talking about vicarious responsible actions (*Stellvertretung*). These are actions enabled by the giver of the mandate and aiming at the individual who then acts in relation to somebody else.[483] This, as should be clear by now, does not constitute a theoretical and everlasting principle thought to exculpate the individual in their deeds but aims, on the contrary, at the individual's free responsibility to resist, which necessarily entails that they incur guilt.[484] This is possible because Christ did so himself: "Because Jesus took the guilt of all human beings upon himself, everyone who acts responsibly becomes guilty." And further, "Because of Jesus Christ, the essence of responsible action intrinsically involves the sinless,

---

480. See *DBW* VI, 40–51.
481. DeJonge, *Bonhoeffer's Reception of Luther*, 116.
482. *DBW* VI, 274.
483. See *DBW* VI, 258–61.
484. See Friederike Barth, "Widerstehende Gewalt," 285.

those who act out of selfless love, becoming guilty."[485] By acting in a vicarious responsible way, humans might nevertheless exculpate themselves or be exculpated by other humans. In relation to God, however, they "hope only for grace."[486] By the same token, the individual acts as an individual. In other words, if somebody chooses to resist a certain government (violently), they do so privately without transferring their individual decision to others.[487]

Having scrutinized the peace ethical account of Bonhoeffer, another thought within this body of work is of interest with regard to ever more automated technology, especially when considering the impact of a rule-based system such as an algorithm: In acting responsibly, Bonhoeffer marks a difference between obedience on the one hand and freedom, on the other hand. While obedience is a stance that follows some ruling blindly, freedom means to act in accordance with an overall understanding of the situation. Responsibility, however, is built on both: "In responsibility both obedience and freedom become real."[488] This is because obedience alone would make the individual a slave, while pure freedom makes for arbitrariness. Only when freedom and obedience intertwine do they result in responsible agency.

In summary, my reconstruction of Bonhoeffer's account emphasizes his pacifist notion but suggests a contingent pacifist interpretation rather than an absolute pacifist reading. This means that even though Bonhoeffer rejects violence as an appropriate means, he does not rule out every possibility of using force. This entails that Bonhoeffer endorses pacifist ways of engaging (political) questions, which can be seen very clearly in the lectures he gave at the conferences of the World Alliance for International Friendship Through the Churches. However, he also makes clear that the use of force might, under certain circumstances, be a possible

---

485. *DBW* VI, 276. See also Huber, *Dietrich Bonhoeffer*, 204. This is, however, a theological problem, as Reuter has shown. Bonhoeffer identifies Christ and the Christian with regard to their ability to assume foreign guilt. While this is plausible for theological reasons concerning Christ, for he is thought to be without sin, it cannot be true for the Christian in the same way. For that matter, Christ burdens foreign sin and guilt, while humans must deal with their own sinfulness, so eventually this thought might contradict the idea that Christ dies once and for all. This is coherent in Bonhoeffer's specific situation but can hardly be transferred to be an ontological principle. See Reuter, "Vom christlichen Pazifismus zum aktiven Widerstand," 40–41.

486. *DBW* VI, 283.

487. See Reuter, "Vom christlichen Pazifismus zum aktiven Widerstand," 27.

488. *DBW* VI, 288.

The Ethical Framing

way of (re-)action. This becomes clear as early as 1932 and gains even more weight in his later work. Bonhoeffer does not simply deem violent means to be the "Jey.,"[489] though. He rather speaks of violence tentatively and with respect to *ultima ratio*. Only in the case of extraordinary necessity (*außergewöhnliche Notwendigkeit*) and as a last resort is a human entitled to use violence. If they do so, however, they will find themselves outside the realm of the law:

> In such a situation, one must completely let go of any law, knowing that one must decide as a free venture. This must also include the acknowledgment that here the law is being broken, violated; that the commandment is broken out of dire necessity, thereby affirming the legitimacy of the law in the very act of violating it. In thus giving up the appeal to any law, indeed only so, is there finally a surrender of one's decision and action to the divine guidance of history.[490]

What is important here is that in the case of an extraordinary necessity, humans might break the law. Still, the law is valid and what the person does is wrong from a legal and political point of view. They can do so only because they see themselves in the hands of God and will eventually be judged by him.[491] In this case, violent means might be possible, but they cannot be justified in themselves, rather the individual bears the blame, since they act clearly outside legal boundaries but according to their conscience. There is, however, a major problem connected to this idea, at least within a socioethical framing: Bonhoeffer addresses an individual acting according to their conscience, while the socioethical framing requires a collective, political framework. For Bonhoeffer, this approach is consistent, since he ponders the decision to resist in a situation where his own government is failing.[492] Taken seriously, this means that the individual soldier can only fight within a certain war if they act according to their conscience, which would make the case for a selective conscientious

---

489. Howard and Paret, *Carl von Clausewitz: On War*, 87.

490. *DBW* VI, 274.

491. Obviously, Bonhoeffer draws on Schmitt's idea and his account of sovereignty: "Sovereign is he who decides on the exception." Schmitt, *Political Theology*, 5. In doing so, he contrasts the political thinking of Schmitt with his theological idea that God ultimately decides. Put differently, not the sovereign but the responsible individual bound to Christ decides over the necessary exemption.

492. See Reuter, "Vom christlichen Pazifismus zum aktiven Widerstand," 37.

An Ethical Evaluation of Lethal Functions in Autoregulative Weapons Systems

refusal, on the one hand,[493] and point toward an interpretation that comes close to revisionist just war thinking, on the other hand. This is because only the individual, by being an individual and taking a private decision, can freely shoulder responsibility. It is therefore not clear how a certain government of any state could act in place of the private person. Rather, each person attending a certain war needs to come to their decision individually as far as their conscience is concerned.

Yet, in order to establish his theory, Bonhoeffer seems to borrow the criterion of last resort from just war thinking, which has a strong political and therefore collective tradition.[494] With respect to Bonhoeffer's writings, however, it is the free and responsible individual who suffers the consequences if they use force. They will eventually be judged by God alone, so the ability for a vicarious responsible action hinges on the freedom and responsibility of the respective agent. This focus on freedom and its described nexus to obedience within the individual is important with respect to the issue of the extent to which a machine might be able to make moral decisions. Although there are various approaches, Russel and Norvig, for instance, define AI with respect to a rational approach. They write, "A *rational agent* is one that acts so as to achieve the best outcome or, when there is uncertainty, the best expected outcome."[495] According to this definition, an artificial agent is by definition rational and consequentialist. Bonhoeffer, however, writes, "The ultima ratio lies beyond the laws of reason; it is irrational action."[496] This means that in the case of violence, what is needed is responsible yet irrational behavior because the individual needs to act in direct opposition to rational law.

---

493. See also Huber, *Dietrich Bonhoeffer*, 154.

494. The question remains as to what degree this thought can be transferred to the individual in the first place and might then be retransferred into a collective frame. This entails that in cases of extraordinary need, such as the severe abuse of human rights, violent means might be last resort in order to come to the victim's aid. Doing so would then require for the specific collective to be held responsible for their intervention by an internationally accepted political body and to be judged by internationally accepted law, which leads to the question of whether or not a specific collective agent might act outside the realm of the law to be even more severe within this political context. Even though this intricate problem cannot be addressed adequately in this book, it points to the ethical debate among traditional and revisionist just war thinkers, because either the individual is the main responsible agent within a certain war and bears the moral onus, or there is a political entity legitimized to decide over these questions on their behalf. This political entity would then be held responsible, while the single actor is per se exculpated.

495. Russel and Norvig, *Artificial Intelligence*, 4. Emphasis original.

496. *DBW* VI, 273.

There might be, however, rational laws concerning war and violence, so it might be possible to apply distinct rules. The question of when to act against these rules for moral reasons though, cannot be made by a machine, as machines simply lack the (ir-)rationality underlying this concept. This becomes even clearer when ideas such as freedom and responsibility are taken into account. Since an artificial system cannot be autonomous or free, as shown above: They simply lack this necessary quality to make a responsible decision. This already entails that machines cannot shoulder responsibility for theoretical reasons because they do not have the necessary preconditions to act responsibly. Machines also cannot bear responsibility for practical reasons because it would simply be nonsense for them to stand trial. I will draw on these ideas below when connecting the discussion of responsibility with the idea of incurring guilt with regard to autoregulation in weapons systems.[497]

5.3.3.2 Questioning Just War Thinking Within Roman Catholic Peace Thought

During and due to the period of World War II, both major churches within Germany found different ways to adjust their thinking of war and peace. Within the Roman Catholic church, this shift is closely connected to the papal encyclicals revolving around this topic. Already within World War II, Pope Pius XII emphasizes the task of the church to promote peace and to support the end of the ongoing war. By the same token, there are several other Roman Catholic thinkers who cast doubt on the question of whether just war thinking is able to assess the historical situation of World War II adequately, such as Bishop Michael von Faulhaber, the moral theologian Joseph Mausbach, and Archbishop Conrad Gröber.[498] Contrary to that point of view, many German moral theologians tend to adhere to just war thinking and advocate for conscription.[499] The pope also argues in favor of just war tradition in 1956 once more, thereby questioning the ability of the Roman Catholic citizen to refuse military service when being ordered to by a legitimate authority. A definite change within this thinking comes to the fore in the 1960s when Pope John XXII

---

497. See 6.6.1 The acceptance of guilt in responsible action.

498. Schockenhoff scrutinizes the viewpoint of these theologians. See Schockenhoff, *Kein Ende der Gewalt?* 300–313.

499. See Schockenhoff, *Kein Ende der Gewalt?* 319.

declares in his encyclicals that a universal commonwealth of all needs to be the focus of the church's social teaching. These roots form a backdrop for turning away from just war tradition, as war is no longer thought to be an appropriate means to achieve peace.[500] This more pacifist notion is then ingrained into the Second Vatican Council, where the nexus between peace, justice, and commonwealth is emphasized for the sake of peace through legal means. The rising threat of nuclear destruction plays an especially important role in the effort to promote a shift toward just peace thinking.[501]

In contrast to Protestant peace thought, however, Roman Catholic theology does not refer to the body of works by one theologian, while contemporary Protestant peace ethics is rooted in the theology of Bonhoeffer because theologians such as Huber and Reuter refer to his works in order to develop their own thinking. For the sake of brevity and clarity, I will therefore forgo the depiction of these processes within Roman Catholic thinking in detail, but instead refer paradigmatically to the theology of Eberhard Schockenhoff within the contemporary discourse on just peace thought below, with special regard to his assessment of autoregulation in weapons technology.[502]

5.3.3.3 Just Peace Theory

What has been said so far shows that the experience of World War II has been decisive for the developments within Christian peace thought. These developments brought forth just peace theory, an idea that has been formally adopted not only by the German branch of the Roman Catholic church and by the Protestant church in Germany but also by the World Council of Churches. In the *Statement on the Way of Just Peace* (2013) they write,

> Together, we believe that the Church is called to unity. Therefore we acknowledge that churches are to be just and peaceful communities reconciled with other churches.[503]

---

500. See Huber, "Frieden V," 639–40.

501. See Huber, "Frieden V," 639–40; Schockenhoff, *Kein Ende der Gewalt?* 340.

502. See 5.3.4 Contingent Pacifism and Autoregulation in Weapons Systems. Schockenhoff describes the Roman Catholic pathway toward pacifist thinking in great detail and can be consulted if specific aspects are of interest. See Schockenhoff *Kein Ende der Gewalt?*

503. World Council of Churches, "Statement on the Way of Just Peace," 2.

The Ethical Framing

And further:

> For peace among the nations, churches must work together to strengthen international human rights and humanitarian law, promote multilateral negotiations to resolve conflicts, hold governments responsible for ensuring treaty protections, help eliminate all weapons of mass destruction and press for reallocation of unnecessary military budgets to civilian needs.[504]

The basic phrasing for that change, namely "just peace," has been brought forward within the institutional framework of the World Council of Churches, which was held on the soil of the former GDR in 1989 when participating churches within the GDR held an assembly within the so-called *conciliar process for peace, justice and the integrity of creation*. With regard to the devastating effects of contemporary weapons technology such as atomic bombs, the authors involved ask whether it is useful to resort to war under these circumstances. They declare,

> Having through necessity overcome the institution of war, the doctrine of a just war intended by the Churches to humanize war is likewise becoming invalid. That is why we need to develop a doctrine of just peace now, grounded in theology and oriented by virtue of its openness toward universal human values.[505]

Here, the main intention of current just peace thinking comes to the fore: The gist of just peace is the idea that, given the development of weapons technology, a justification of war and violence is no longer possible considering the circumstances. Such justification can be seen in just war tradition, though. In contrast to just war, the declaration puts the main emphasis on the connection between peace and justice. In doing so, just peace couches a development that emphasizes the seriousness of the historical changes undergone in the last century and is also in line with political developments of that time, as could be shown above.[506] I therefore will zero in on that theory in the remainder of this section in greater detail, introducing the main approach of this theory within both Roman Catholic and Protestant Churches in Germany and the discussions that followed, especially with regard to autoregulation in weapons systems. The seminal texts for developing Christian approaches to this particular understanding of war and peace are the pastoral letter of the

---

504. World Council of Churches, "Statement on the Way of Just Peace," 3.
505. German Bishops, "Just Peace," 1.
506. See 5.3.1 Preliminaries.

An Ethical Evaluation of Lethal Functions in Autoregulative Weapons Systems

Roman Catholic German bishops of 2000, and the Protestant peace memorandum of 2007. Both approaches have been disputed strongly within the respective communities.

This entails several disclaimers: For the sake of my contribution, I will not refer to the discussions revolving around nuclear weaponry within Christian churches in the second half of the twentieth century. Churches conducted intense and contentious debates on this specific topic beginning in the 1950s and continuing ever since.[507] Even though a consideration thereof might be insightful, I need to confine myself to the remark that these discussions lead to the understanding that world peace is necessary given the atrocities nuclear weaponry brings in its wake.[508] Moreover, I cannot illustrate in any detail the processes within the churches that led to adopting just peace and which was accompanied by several official statements.[509] Instead, I put the emphasis on more recent developments that keep these discussions in mind, even if I do not highlight them. Furthermore, I cannot present in detail the abundance of discussions and contributions that followed the introduction of just peace within the churches. I will confine myself solely to depicting the debates that took place concerning autoregulation in weapons technology. I will refer to them in an inferior way only to the degree that adjacent topics such as cyberwar and drones are concerned.

5.3.3.3.1 Pastoral letter by the German bishops (2000): The Roman Catholic position

In 2000, the German bishops of the Roman Catholic church wrote a pastoral letter that directly referred to the conciliar process for peace, justice, and the integrity of creation. They state that after twenty years and a changed political situation, it is time to review the ethical position of the Catholic church toward peace and war. This entails, on the one hand, noticing the (violent) situation of the world while, on the other hand, providing a direction for further thinking and political development. This direction is caught in the term "just peace" because, as the bishops make clear, it is not enough to establish a situation where war is simply absent, rather justice needs to be installed, thereby referring

---

507. I refer to this development briefly in 5.3.1 Preliminaries.
508. See Huber and Reuter, *Friedensethik*, 134–35.
509. See Huber, "Von der gemeinsamen Sicherheit zum gerechten Frieden."

The Ethical Framing

to Galtung's notion of positive peace. The document is structured along three areas of interest: first, the traditional Christian sources and their approach to peace; second, the political dimension of peace and the use of force; and, third, the contribution of the church.

At the outset of the document, the bishops collect the biblical data on the topic, which entails pacifist notions such as paradisical and everlasting peace but also humanity's striving for violence.[510] Moreover, the bishops reconstruct biblical and traditional views regarding peace and violence very thoroughly.[511] They then conclude that messianic peace must not be confused with worldly peace: While messianic peace will establish itself and violence will no longer play a part in this, it might still be necessary to establish worldly peace with violent means. They write,

> The world order that we share with humanity today soberly assumes a human propensity for violence. It premises that violence can fly in the face of good sense and break out between individuals and whole nations. That is why mechanisms were developed to prevent violence and check its spread in order to maintain peace. Such mechanisms are reasonable and appropriate. By contrast, the peace of the Messianic people of God presupposes the miracle that man has implicit trust in God and his fellow man and is in a position to renounce the use of violence.[512]

Against this backdrop, the bishops turn to the political dimensions of just peace in our contemporary world. In the beginning, they repudiate a point of view that seeks to establish the kingdom of God on earth by political means. For that matter, church and politics need to be kept apart. Yet, both entities—meaning church and politics—cannot be separated completely because the church influences the people's view of society and therefore shapes social and political thought.

Having thus set the course, the bishops turn to seven dimensions of just peace within a political perspective. First, they focus on the socioethical perspective of just peace, entailing human dignity, which is bestowed upon humans because they are God's counterpart and made in his image.[513] For that reason, all humans share the same entitlement to live a humane life free from violence and injustice. This also means to pave the way for international public welfare, as well as justice and solidarity

---

510. See German Bishops, "Just Peace," 11–22.
511. See German Bishops, "Just Peace," 23–50.
512. German Bishops, "Just Peace," 56.
513. See German Bishops, "Just Peace," 58.

on a global scale.[514] The bishops, second, demand the prioritization of civic measures to solve conflict and, third, emphasize the role of human rights, which are the legal expression of human dignity. In doing so, they also highlight that democratic structures depend on peace and therefore the rule of law, so democracy and peace are closely knit together. If human rights ought to be protected, this must be done on a global scale, which also means the "orientation toward a global commonwealth"[515] and the "protection of the world's natural resources."[516] In order to reach such an objective, however, the pastoral letter turns, fourth, to global cooperation, which entails that different countries treat each other with confidence, but also that international political bodies such as the UN or the EU play an important role in this interdependent global order.[517] Subsequently, the authors emphasize that, fifth, conflict aftercare is an important means of preventing further conflicts and that it is therefore necessary for preventing violence as well.[518] Sixth, the bishops turn to the role of civic society in peace processes, such as journalists reporting from combat zones, before they finally focus on "the significance and limitation of military means."[519] In doing so, they underscore the benefit of political, international means to address arms control, such as the Treaty on the Non-Proliferation of Nuclear Weapons. They discern that the role of armies and soldiers within violent scenarios has changed since 1989, though, and then elaborate on armed intervention by asking, "Are there any situations in which the use of counter-violence is justified?"[520] They argue that there might be such situations, but at the same time, they set boundaries for the use of force which are a last resort and aiming toward striving for peace. Furthermore, they underline the importance of proportional and minimal use of force and the application of *jus in bello*, mainly entailing the protection of civilians. Moreover, the pastoral letter makes clear that the intervening parties need to take care in the aftermath of an armed conflict, entailing the contribution to an operating infrastructure and laying the foundation for sustaining peace.

514. See German Bishops, "Just Peace," 61–65.
515. German Bishops, "Just Peace," 92.
516. German Bishops, "Just Peace," 96.
517. See German Bishops, "Just Peace," 100–107.
518. See German Bishops, "Just Peace," 108–21.
519. German Bishops, "Just Peace," 129.
520. German Bishops, "Just Peace," 150.

The Ethical Framing

In a last step, the authors of the pastoral letter elaborate on the contribution of the church toward peace. They write,

> The Church works as a sacrament of peace by overcoming all barriers of race, nationality, ethnicity and society that separate people from one another and turn them all too often into enemies. As part of the Church we find ourselves in a place in which the peace made possible by Christ can develop and grow to encompass all dimensions of reality.[521]

This quote condenses the meaning of the following paragraph concisely, and I will unravel some of its implications by following the course of the pastoral letter. Apparently, in the bishop's view, two different dimensions intersect within the church—or more precisely within the sacrament—thereby transcending the borders between people. While different people are separated by worldly categories, they are bound together within the realm of the church because they are incorporated into a community, which ought to overcome the barriers between them. This is only possible if the church does not resort to the same measures as the world, though, thereby making a difference and striving for the promised just peace. More concretely, the church will fulfill this task if it enables people to reconcile and advocates for justice regionally as well as globally.[522] The pastoral letter detects test cases for such an undertaking in interreligious and ecumenical relations and likewise in the way foreigners and woman are treated.[523] Culturally, this means educating a spirit of nonviolence within the different institutions of the church.[524] Such undertakings, however, are always confined by the humble knowledge that peace in the biblical sense might never be achieved within this world, but "ultimately [. . .] will only succeed with God."[525]

In summary, the pastoral letter makes the shift from just war tradition to just peace thinking by arguing that just peace as a worldly category is deeply affected by transcendent biblical ideas that, even though they might never be realized entirely, inspire the deeds of believers and therefore exercise influence on this world. There are, however, some limitations to this contribution, which I see foremost in its inherent

---

521. German Bishops, "Just Peace," 162.
522. See German Bishops, "Just Peace," 162–83.
523. See German Bishops, "A Just Peace," 184–96.
524. See German Bishops, "Just Peace," 197–203.
525. German Bishops, "Just Peace," 208.

ecclesiastical tone, a fact that is not astonishing given the character of the document. The problem, however, is that politics, ethics, and ecclesiology are so closely knit together that different levels of consideration seem to be mixed up. The third and last part in particular remains too closely within the borders of the church, even though the authors argue that the church might influence the political thought of the people. In my opinion, the document does not unlock the potential of the idea of just peace by confining it that strictly to the church and its institutions. Moreover, the question of where the line between Messianic and worldly peace can be drawn is not settled, so it is ultimately not clear if the approach is meant to be realistic or utopian in character. Finally, the use of force is not sufficiently taken into account. Although the bishops elaborate in the second part on the use of force and attempt to confine it to a minimal amount by referring vaguely to some categories in the tradition of *bellum iustum,* they do not recur explicitly to a definite theory that might serve as an indicator of when the use of force might indeed be necessary. These and other inefficiencies led to a wide and controversial debate on the concept of just peace within the Roman Catholic church[526] but also to a positive reception and further development of these ideas, the peace memorandum of the Protestant church in Germany being one of them.

5.3.3.3.2 Peace memorandum of the Council of the Protestant Church in Germany

In 2007, the Council of the Protestant Church in Germany submitted a peace memorandum with the intention of making a shift from just war thinking to just peace theory, similar to the Roman Catholic approach brought forward in 2000. Documents such as the peace memorandum are not primarily academic in character but rather of normative ethico-political nature, which means that they recourse to scholarly debates but also aim to be a contribution to public debate on fundamental and societal issues.[527] They therefore seek to take a well-informed standpoint within a plural world.[528] With respect to the peace memorandum, this means that this document primarily aims to call Christians, but also all

---

526. See, for example, Justenhoven and Schumacher, *Gerechter Friede.*
527. See EKD, *Das rechte Wort zur rechten Zeit,* 7.
528. See EKD, *Das rechte Wort zur rechten Zeit,* 46–48.

humans, to engage in peace rather than violence. This momentum finds its expression in the concluding words:

> The Church of Jesus Christ is called to bear witness to peace and work for reconciliation in places governed by mistrust, violence and suppression; these are an inalienable responsibility of all Christians.[529]

Having this in mind, I will now reconstruct the main ideas of the peace-memorandum with a special focus on the individual principles of just peace theory, as well as elaborating on the concept of law-sustaining force.

Primarily, the bishop at that time, Wolfgang Huber, states in his foreword the importance of peace for Christian ethics and the need to revise the peace concept of the Protestant church in Germany due to the current situation. Subsequently, in the first section, the peace memorandum addresses several threats to peace, such as socioeconomic issues or the international political shift to unilateralism that impairs the work of international bodies such as the UN. Here, for instance, the reaction of the US in response to the 9/11 attacks is mentioned with concern.[530] In the following section, the potential of a Christian contribution to peace is elaborated on. Such concepts are based on biblical Scripture and involve individual approaches, such as peace education and respect for the individual's conscience.[531] This individual perspective is then expanded with concepts such as reconciliation and just peace. With reference to God's overarching and forgiving love, the peace memorandum therefore addresses the need to reconcile, especially in the aftermath of a violent conflict. Processes like these do not only include spiritual aspects, such as the forgiveness of sins, but also the work of political bodies, such as courts and truth-finding institutions.[532] The concept of just peace also exceeds the individual's perspective and approaches society.

Elaborating on the implications of the just peace approach in detail, the authors of the memorandum initially emphasize the connection between peace and justice, which is rooted in biblical texts such as the Psalms and Isaiah.[533] Bearing in mind the biblical tradition, the authors argue in favor of peace founded in four dimensions, which are the

529. EKD, "Live from God's Peace," 197.
530. See EKD, "Live from God's Peace," 8–35, esp. 35.
531. See EKD, "Live from God's Peace," 36–66.
532. See EKD, "Live from God's Peace," 67–72.
533. See EKD, "Live from God's Peace," 74.

An Ethical Evaluation of Lethal Functions in Autoregulative Weapons Systems

rejection of the use violence, the promotion of freedom and cultural diversity, and the alleviation of want.[534] With these principles, the peace memorandum integrates Galtung's perspective of positive peace, which proposes widening the concept of peace as mere absence of war significantly. Thus, peace is qualified through justice. In detail, this primarily entails avoiding the use of force but also qualifying human life with dignity in the three aforementioned aspects. With regard to freedom, the authors write,

> Peace with freedom means the chance to live our lives together protected from violence and oppression, the chance for people to exploit their own potential and skills to make decisions for the good of their communities.[535]

This also entails counterbalancing the state's monopoly and avoiding a situation where representatives of a certain state can force their will upon its citizens. Second, this means avoiding poverty, as a widening gap between poor and rich as well as the decrease of natural resources is very likely to engender violent scenarios. Third, and with respect to cultural differences, the promotion of cultural diversity in a globalized world is key when people with different cultural backgrounds want to live together peacefully.[536] Generally, however, all of these aspects are processes of more or less freedom, poverty, or diversity, meaning that they must be seen as a varying scale within a possible continuum that is not simply present or absent.

In order to establish such processes, however, a legal-normative framework is needed not only within a certain state but also internationally. Within such an international framework, the aforementioned principles can be transferred to the international sphere, meaning that the avoidance of violence and the protection of the further principles are generally implemented in international law. On the one hand, such a law entails international political bodies, such as the UN, as well as the foundation for peaceful principles. One main principle here is the system of collective security. In such a system, the states agree not to go to war against each other, thereby ruling out international conflict.[537] On the other hand, individual human rights serve to protect the single individual

---

534. EKD, "Live from God's Peace," 80.
535. EKD, "Live from God's Peace," 82.
536. See EKD, "Live from God's Peace," 82–84.
537. See EKD, "Live from God's Peace," 87.

from the use of force and to secure their life in dignity. Even though such rights are given universally to every person, the authors of the peace memorandum argue that the nation state is the legal place where such rights are granted. Furthermore, nonpolitical actors, such as companies, also need to take these laws and principles into consideration and act according to them.[538] With respect to poverty alleviation, the authors of the peace memorandum argue in favor of transnational social justice, which means a fair distribution of chances for development within different social contexts. This entails the establishment of a societal infrastructure involving, for instance, health care and social security as well as the practice of good governance, aiming to counterbalance injustices.[539] Finally, the peace memorandum makes the case for cultural diversity instead of unification.[540]

Within the context of establishing just peace through law, there might be a need to use violence in order to sustain law enforcement.[541] The theory of law-sustaining force, established as a result of this insight, serves to replace the criteria of just war thinking without limiting the scope of this tradition to war. It does, however, recur to the principles of *bellum iustum* in order to confine law-sustaining violence. The authors of the peace memorandum address the problem that just war thinking developed within a natural law context, which presupposed that it is possible to identify one illegitimate aggressor who ought to be punished. Yet, this basic thought already lost its approval of a shared common good in the time of the Reformation and therefore can no longer serve as the framework to reconstruct the thrust of just war tradition. Within the aforementioned bodies of the UN and the system of collective security, it is no longer reasonable to refer to a theory where the possibility of one nation waging war against another nation is justly presupposed. Instead, the current legal framework allows the use of force in two possible scenarios only: first, an authorization of the UN Security Council and, second, self-defense until the Security Council reaches a decision. Even

---

538. See EKD, "Live from God's Peace," 89–90.
539. See EKD, "Live from God's Peace," 91–95.
540. See EKD, "Live from God's Peace," 96–97.

541. The peace memorandum calls this principle law-abiding force. In this contribution, however, I follow Reuter in his proposal to instead use the term "law-sustaining force." This term intends to be more open to the idea that law is not wrapped up in the thought of a positive given right but merely refers to a very basic law that finds its expression in human rights. See Reuter, "Kampfdrohnen als Mittel rechtswahrender militärischer Gewalt?" 39.

though this new context is no longer in line with just war thought, the criteria of *bellum iustum* serve as a marker of whether the use of force might be legitimate. Therefore, the classical criteria of *jus ad bellum* and *jus in bello* are reconstructed. These are, first, "permissible causes," such as severe violent attacks against human rights; second, "authorization" entailing the privilege to represent the rights of the concerned party legitimately; and, third, "right intention," referring to the "defense against a present, evident attack"[542] but only insofar as this aims at the creation or preservation of peace. Fourth, violence needs to be an "ultimate resort"[543] in cases where all other means have failed. "Ultimate" in this context, however, does not necessarily need to be understood as referring to the last in time, but can also indicate that among all of the possible measures, violence is the only reasonable way to manage a severe situation.[544] The fifth principle, "proportionality of consequences,"[545] means that the harm following in the wake of a violent scenario must not lead to even greater harm—not only with respect to violence but also with regard to socioeconomic and cultural aspects. Sixth, "proportionality of means"[546] means that the party using violence needs to strike a balance between the chance of success and the limitation of harm. Seventh and finally, the "principle of discrimination"[547] serves to draw a line between people and institutions that should never be (legitimate) targets, such as civilians and hospitals. Ultimately, the peace-memorandum ascertains that these seven criteria need to be met in order to use force in the first place as well as in the conduct of warfare. This, however, does not mean that the use of violence is simply justified. Instead, the incurring of guilt that is indissolubly linked with every recourse to violence is paramount: "In any situation where the responsibility for our own or others' lives forces us to take actions that will themselves endanger or destroy life, not even the most careful assessment of consequences will free us from the risk of incurring guilt."[548]

Law-sustaining force, however, has limitations given by the political order. Within a system of collective security under the umbrella of

542. EKD, "Live from God's Peace," 102.
543. EKD, "Live from God's Peace," 102.
544. See EKD, "Live from God's Peace," 102.
545. EKD, "Live from God's Peace," 102.
546. EKD, "Live from God's Peace," 102.
547. EKD, "Live from God's Peace," 102.
548. EKD, "Live from God's Peace," 103.

the UN, the UN Security Council is the only political body entitled to authorize the use of force. There are, however, ongoing controversies revolving around the right to self-protection, such as the concept of R2P or (armed) peace missions. With regard to self-defense, the authors of the peace memorandum claim that it must not be interpreted too widely, which means that the addressee of an attack only has the right to strike preemptively in the case of an imminent attack. Particular weapons as a means of self-defense, however, such as atomic or chemical bombs, are ruled out from the outset. With respect to R2P, the peace memorandum allows the use of armed force only in cases where "present and grave acts of injustice, which prevent a political order from fulfilling its minimum function of keeping the peace altogether"[549] are carried out. The only institution to authorize such an undertaking is the international community itself, namely the UN.[550] Regarding international peace missions, the peace memorandum makes the case for strictly limiting such operations in time and to their objective in order to confine the outburst of (further) violence within a certain region.[551] The four objectives mentioned in this context, which are "safeguarding a ceasefire that has already been negotiated, ensuring that a peace agreement is reached, demobilizing armed forces, and creating a safe space for self-supporting civilian political, economic and cultural reconstruction"[552] are very close to what Rodin has called *jus ad terminationem belli*, which refers to the circumstances under which a certain violent scenario might end. This, however, can be distinguished from *jus post bellum*, which refers to the moral principles that accompany the transition from war to peace.[553]

In the remainder of the peace memorandum, the authors outline the political tasks to be addressed within a globalized world. They argue in favor of strengthening international and universal political bodies, discuss Europe's responsibility for peace, demand the reduction of arms, recognize the urge to expand civilian conflict management and discuss the need to realize human security and human development. The last

549. EKD, "Live from God's Peace," 112.

550. Being aware of the factual problems of a deadlock in UN Security Council, the memorandum also mentions the possibility of intervening without such authorization. In such cases, however, the situation needs to be evaluated very carefully, as this might also entail undermining the political power of the international political bodies. See EKD, "Live from God's Peace," 114.

551. See EKD, "Live from God's Peace," 117–23.

552. EKD, "Live from God's Peace," 119.

553. See Rodin, "Two Emerging Issues of Jus Post Bellum," 54.

point in particular, which is the connection to secure human life as well as facilitate its development, is in line with the thrust of just peace outlined in the memorandum.[554]

In order to summarize the gist of the peace memorandum and to draw some conclusions, I quote one focal passage as an example. The memorandum emphasizes,

> In the context of contemporary international law, military force may be authorized only as a kind of international police action under the rules of the UN Charter.[555]

This quote is insightful for several reasons. Primarily, it indicates a tripartite shift. First, it moves away from just war tradition to just peace thinking, thereby prioritizing peace not only as an end but also as a means to achieve peace. Second, this shift expresses the change of the overall paradigm, from war paradigm to law paradigm, as war is neither seen as standing outside juridical regulations nor simply as an area regulated by law. It is rather ruled out by the given political and juridical framework. Third, two formerly distinct spheres—the military and the police—come to intermingle within this demand, a transformation I mentioned above. Here, it suffices to say that the peace memorandum is highly aware of and approves these processes.[556]

Furthermore, what can be inferred from the quote is the idea that in the aftermath of a conflict, the opposing parties will have to reconcile. This, however, opens the frame of the peace memorandum to the questions addressed by *jus post bellum*: "Jus post bellum normally concerns how to move to a situation of stability after war."[557] The peace memorandum does not mention this term because it is a part of just war thinking the memorandum wishes to overcome. Yet, the idea of *jus post bellum* and the peace memorandum share common ground.[558] This is because, within a frame where armies no longer fight each other but police forces are authorized by the international community, it is clear that the focus of the undertaking rests on the outcome, meaning the need to establish

---

554. See EKD, "Live from God's Peace," 184–93.

555. EKD, "Live from God's Peace," 104.

556. I refer to this development above. See 5.3.1 Preliminaries.

557. May, *After War Ends*, 6.

558. Since the peace memorandum reconstructs the principles of *bellum iustum* within the theory of law-sustaining force, thereby going without a differentiation between *jus ad bellum* and *jus in bello*, the omission of *jus post bellum* is consistent.

a sustaining peace in the aftermath of a conflict. This includes processes such as reconciliation, rebuilding, and restitution.[559]

With respect to current weapons technology, though, the peace memorandum is clearly not up to date. Neither hypersonic weapons, quantum technologies, neurological military inventions, nor autoregulation in weapons are mentioned, which is obviously because, in 2007, such technologies could not have been foreseen. Yet, this omission gives rise to the question of whether, from the just peace viewpoint, such technologies could be deployed and, if this question is answered in the affirmative, in which scenarios.

Among others, questions such as these have been the reason why the just peace approach has been discussed within the Christian churches in Germany intensely. From 2018 to 2020, Ines-Jacqueline Werkner and Sarah Jäger edited twenty-four volumes discussing the ideas and methods of the memorandum within the framework of a consulting process.[560] In addition, several other volumes and monographs have been published that resort to just peace theory with the aim of probing this concept or updating it. One aspect of these discussions is that it has not been confined to the Protestant church alone; theologians, philosophers, sociologists, and so on from various standpoints and confessions have contributed to this process. Finally, the memorandum of the Protestant church in Germany, *Freiheit digital*, concerning digitization needs to be mentioned because it also addresses warfare under the umbrella of digitization. In this context, autoregulative functions in weapons systems are also assessed, thereby mainly hinting toward human participation in autoregulative technology.[561] As already mentioned, it is beyond the scope of my contribution to depict the discussions within these books in detail. I rather confine myself in the remainder of this chapter to outlining the contributions that relate to contingent pacifism in general and just peace theory in particular.

5.3.4 Contingent Pacifism and Autoregulation in Weapons Systems

Contingent pacifism, and just peace theory in particular, refer to weapons technology within a pacifist framework, which means that peace is

---

559. See May, *After War Ends*, 6.
560. See Stümke, "Gerechter Friede in der Debatte," 315–16.
561. See 5.3.4 Contingent pacifism and autoregulative weapons systems; EKD, *Freiheit digital*, 133–36.

the overall objective. At the same time, just peace is open to the possibility that the use of force might sometimes pose the lesser evil, so the use of weapons, such as autoregulative weapons systems, cannot be ruled out from the beginning. Therefore, several contributions have been made that assess the use of this kind of weaponry. The most important and extensive among them is an ethical assessment prepared by Bernhard Koch and Bernhard Rinke for the technology assessment report of the German *Bundestag* (*Technikfolgenabschätzungsbericht*).[562] The physicist Jürgen Altmann published articles on that topic and within the frame of just peace thinking too, as well as the Protestant theologian Hartwig von Schubert and the Roman Catholic theologian Eberhard Schockenhoff. Moreover, the memorandum of the Protestant church in Germany revolving around digitization also points to the issues surrounding autoregulation in weapons technology. In addition, the Protestant theologian Hans-Richard Reuter has referred to drones, and his thought might be transferred to autoregulation in weapons systems, while Torsten Meireis has written an article concerning cyberwar. I will depict all of these approaches here in order to provide an overview of the positions held.

The philosopher Bernhard Koch, who is deputy director of the Institute for Theology and Peace (*Institut für Theologie und Frieden, ithf*) operated by the Catholic Military Chaplaincy (*Katholische Militärseelsorge*) also discusses the development and deployment of autoregulative weapons systems from an ethical perspective. Even though Koch does not refer to contingent pacifism or just peace theory verbatim but to just war thinking, I interpret his writing as contributing to just peace thought. This is because the way I interpret just peace theory to be the legitimate successor of *bellum iustum* is in line with Koch's account of just war.[563] I therefore present his account here.

---

562. Even though neither author is a trained theologian, I discuss their approach here, as they have contributed to ongoing discussions on autoregulative weapons systems from a Catholic perspective. This especially applies to Bernhard Koch, since he is part of a Catholic research institution. In this same context, Rinke has also published several contributions, so it seems reasonable to discuss their approach within this chapter.

563. This does not mean that every account of just war amounts to just peace. In Koch's writing, however, the pacifist notion becomes very clear, especially when hinting toward the still underrepresented viewpoint of *jus post bellum*. Autoregulation in weapons technology is, then, discussed under the umbrella and in the terminology of just war rather than referring to just peace thinking in order to remain compatible— especially in the Anglo–American world where just war thinking seems to be without any alternative because this is the main discourse. See Koch and Rinke, *Ethische Fragestellungen im Kontext autonomer Waffensysteme*, 29–30.

The Ethical Framing

In their literature assessment, Koch and Rinke discuss autoregulation in weapons systems with respect to just war thinking, which means that they address these technologies within the criteriology of just war for pragmatic reasons.[564] They note that the discussion mainly rests on *jus in bello*, while *jus ad bellum* and especially *jus post bellum* are only rarely taken into account. Regarding the literature addressing *jus ad bellum*, the authors perceive the fear that warfare might become less risky and therefore the probability of fighting a war might rise. This is because since there are fewer or even no lives at stake, it might be easier to justify the decision to go to war in the first place.[565] This, in turn, would lead to a violation of *jus ad bellum*. At variance with this position, Leveringhaus argues that there is no empirical evidence for this phenomenon and therefore this argumentation does not seem imperative. In that regard, the issues of humanitarian intervention and R2P need to be discussed—though these matters do not necessarily pertain to autoregulation in weapons systems.[566] What becomes clear in this debate is that the majority of discussions take place within *jus in bello*, which is closely linked to IHL, so ethical and legal discussion overlap in this regard.[567] Especially the principles of distinction, proportionality, and precautions of attack play a major role. With respect to all of these principles, however, the majority of the literature is skeptical about whether autoregulative devices would be able to meet the standards of IHL.[568] Within the frame of just war, Koch and Rinke address the issue of responsibility as well, which is closely connected to the aforementioned discussions, as the main question is who holds responsibility if an autoregulative device violates *jus in bello*. Since this topic will be addressed in greater detail below, it suffices to say that one major strand of the ethical argumentation revolves around the question of responsibility. The positions range from the argument that the occurrence of a responsibility gap leads to the prohibition against deploying autoregulation in weapons systems; to the position that there are no such gaps, since the situational reactivity of the system is explicitly desired; to the position that these gaps pose

---

564. See Koch and Rinke, *Ethische Fragestellungen*, 29–30.
565. See Koch and Rinke, *Ethische Fragestellungen*, 50.
566. See Koch and Rinke, *Ethische Fragestellungen*, 57.
567. See Koch and Rinke, *Ethische Fragestellungen*, 67.
568. See Koch and Rinke, *Ethische Fragestellungen*, 88, 94, 96. See also 6.1 Legal Framework.

no problem for the deployment of autoregulation in weapons at all.⁵⁶⁹ In addition to these arguments connected to just war thinking, Koch and Rinke also address the questions of human dignity, the issue of whether there is an obligation to act nonlethally, the importance of human agency, and the danger of misuse. Here, the authors find that the ethical literature addressing the role of human dignity in the context of autoregulative killing leads to a problem.⁵⁷⁰ The dignity argument works as follows: When being killed by a machine that has neither conscience nor consciousness, the dignity of the targeted person (and in some cases the person operating the system) is violated. This argument is brought forward in several variations, whereas the respective concept of dignity might differ, so the main discussions in that regard do not question whether or not human dignity is violated but what human dignity is.⁵⁷¹ In a second step, the authors depict the position of Robin Geiß, who argues that the scenarios for deploying autoregulation in weapons systems need to be narrowed down in advance with a certain preference to operate nonlethally.⁵⁷² Subsequently, Koch and Rinke turn to human agency, which they reconstruct to be twofold. On the one hand, there is the argument brought forward by Leveringhaus as depicted above, which is that the machine—in contrast to human agency—lacks the possibility of making a meaningful choice. In addition to this, the virtue ethical position of Shannon Valor, who argues that the deployment of autoregulation in weapons systems would lead to a loss of virtue for the agents, is taken into account. This is because soldiers understand themselves to develop certain virtues that are necessary within warfare. Those would be lost if lethal operations were undertaken by machines.⁵⁷³ Finally, Koch and Rinke discuss the dangers of misuse, which is a danger not only inherent in autoregulation in weapons systems. Here, the focus changes. The topics addressed so far pertain to the intended use of these weapons. Interestingly, this topic only plays a minor role in the current discussions, maybe because the dangers of misuse do not explicitly refer to autoregulation in weapons technology or because this topic has been addressed in great

---

569. See Koch and Rinke, *Ethische Fragestellungen*, 101–5. The first position is mainly connected to Sparrow's account, while the second is the position Leveringshaus holds. The latter position is discussed by Vincent C. Müller.

570. See Koch and Rinke, *Ethische Fragestellungen*, 107.

571. See Koch and Rinke, *Ethische Fragestellungen*, 108.

572. See Koch and Rinke, *Ethische Fragestellungen*, 127.

573. See Koch and Rinke, *Ethische Fragestellungen*, 132.

The Ethical Framing

detail with respect to drones.[574] After having introduced the main discussions and position within the ongoing debate, the authors turn to their own position. Before doing so, they discuss whether a consequentialist approach can be convincing with regard to autoregulation in weapons systems. Even if this approach is widespread, the authors argue that the exact consequences cannot be foreseen easily when assessing the use of new (weapons) technology, so virtual consequentialist approaches turn out to be nonconsequentialist approaches in effect.[575] This is the major reason why Koch and Rinke assess their subject within a nonconsequentialist approach. In doing so, they address the single criteria of just war tradition as ethically binding within IHL. Regarding *jus in bello*, the authors argue that the principle of refraining from war is ingrained in IHL. Similar to the use of drones, however, autoregulation in weapons systems might facilitate a use below the level of outright conflict, thereby running counter to the intent of IHL. Regarding *jus in bello*, the authors address the problem that in order to meet the standards of IHL, the device would need to make a distinction between combatant and noncombatant, and it would need to assess whether the harm inflicted is proportional to the intended outcome. Both assessments, however, are processes of judgment, where a certain context needs to be taken into account—a requirement a technological device cannot meet for the time being.[576] In a third step and regarding the principle of prevention, Koch and Rinke address the expectation of sparing the lives of combatants. From a traditional perspective, however, the principle of prevention refers to the need to secure the lives of noncombatants. To put it bluntly, if the circumstances enable the loss of combatants to fall to zero, this would necessitate that the loss of lives of noncombatants would also fall by the same amount, which seems impossible to ensure.[577] Since this dimension of *jus post bellum* is not sufficiently addressed within the current debate, the authors confine themselves to remarking that from a peace ethical perspective, the advent of autoregulation can be expected to impede rather than promote sustaining peace.[578]

---

574. See Koch and Rinke, *Ethische Fragestellungen*, 134.

575. See Koch and Rinke, *Ethische Fragestellungen*, 145.

576. See Koch and Rinke, *Ethische Fragestellungen*, 151–53. See also 3.3 Reckoning and Judgment.

577. See Koch and Rinke, *Ethische Fragestellungen*, 154–55.

578. See Koch and Rinke, *Ethische Fragestellungen*, 155–56.

Subsequently, Koch and Rinke turn their focus to the issue of responsibility. They argue that machines lack moral responsibility, since they lack consciousness.[579] Here, the authors rely more strongly on the strand of revisionist just war thought, arguing that resorting to war cannot easily be legitimized collectively but needs individual legitimacy, meaning that only the entity able to use violence (for self-defense or the defense of others) shoulders the burden of deciding whether or not the use of (lethal) violence is legitimate. As mentioned above, this exceeds the capabilities of the machine.[580] Finally, and with regard to dignity, Koch and Rinke argue that the concept of human dignity is closely connected to the concept of recognition: In order to recognize the dignity of another person, a person is needed. In that regard, the authors of the report principally agree with the assumption that human dignity is violated if a person is killed by a machine. This argument is in line with another argumentation brought forward by Koch, where he holds that heavily automated technology might alienate us from ourselves. This is due to us understanding ourselves in the mirror of these technologies and, in turn, our anthropological understanding becoming "machinized."[581]

Ultimately, Koch and Rinke draw the tentative conclusion that the bulk of the arguments indicate an international ban against the development and deployment of autoregulation in weapons systems. Such an ethical assessment, however, does not necessarily entail imminent political and juridical action.

The depicted report is illuminating because it gives a broad overview of the current ethical discussion and its legal—and to some degree also political—implications. Koch and Rinke show plausibly that the ethical discussion is closely connected to the legal one and why this is the case. In their assessment, they remain within the scope of just war thinking, and when widening their view by discussing several connected questions, such as responsibility or human dignity, they usually tie these discussions back to just war tradition for pragmatic reasons. What is important for my own account, however, is the way they treat this tradition, and two remarks stand out here. First, there is the hint that *jus post*

---

579. See Koch and Rinke, *Ethische Fragestellungen*, 156–60.

580. See Koch and Rinke, *Ethische Fragestellungen*, 160–65; 3.3 Reckoning and Judgment.

581. See Koch, "Maschinen, die uns von uns selbst entfremden." My translation of Coeckelbergh's account might be interpreted to refer to a similar procedure, even though Coeckelbergh is not critical toward that development in the same way.

bellum is not sufficiently taken into account within the ongoing debate. Yet, the authors themselves do not add something new to this debate but rather point to this gap. Second, within the discussion of whether or not an autoregulated device can be legitimately used for killing, the authors leave the ground of traditional just war thinking and therefore IHL. They instead turn to the revisionist just war approach with its individual account. This is important because both points indicate that Koch and Rinke do not mainly argue within the realm of just war tradition but rather take into account contingent pacifist thought.

Another contribution has been brought forward by Hartwig von Schubert, embedding autoregulation in weapons into a bigger peace ethical picture. In his monograph *Down with the War* (*Nieder mit dem Krieg*, 2021), he elaborates on three main theses, which are first, that violence is highly ambivalent in character; second, that violence therefore needs to be confined politically, thereby overcoming violence at all; and, third, that Christian belief is the right place to discuss and promote peaceful processes.[582] His position therefore aims at balancing out the theological idea of the kingdom of God, the philosophical concept of peace, and the legal notion of an international law of peace (*Friedensvölkerrecht*).[583] With respect to the kingdom of God, he interprets the absolute pacifist account of the Sermon on the Mount in tandem with Romans 12 and highlights the relation of the individual Christian to God in this context. Only within this context was it possible that the Christian churches accepted the law of the ancient Roman state. In doing so, however, Christians are morally bound to the rule of God and will influence the political system from the bottom up.[584] Von Schubert then goes on to connect this idea to the doctrine of the two regimes and finds that the political authorities are entitled and expected to impose juridically sanctioned violence, while Christian communities are clearly not. Here, the pacifist ethos is expected to rule and might urge the authorities to act in the same way, but it cannot impose this pacifist notion on the political authorities.[585] In a second step, von Schubert discusses the coresponsibility of every free citizen, including the Christian, for the political rule, an aspect

---

582. See von Schubert, *Nieder mit dem Krieg*, 25.

583. See von Schubert, "Das Reich Gottes," 60. Von Schubert discusses the notion of Romans 13 and its relation toward modern politics in greater detail in *Nieder mit dem Krieg*, 166–85.

584. See von Schubert, "Das Reich Gottes," 66.

585. See von Schubert, "Das Reich Gottes," 68–69.

that includes a global human rights perspective threatened by the use of violence. Such a perspective results in reflecting the inherent pacifism and modifying it to a realistic—meaning legal—pacifist perspective.[586] This is because the Christian bears political responsibility in the sense that they engage in civic discussions not by introducing a certain, Christian point of view but diverse perspectives under the roof of Christianity. This facilitates complexity and guards against religious fanaticism.[587] Finally, von Schubert elaborates on the idea of preserving peace through the rule of justice. This is closely linked to Kant's philosophy of justice and proceeds on the assumption that the same rights need to be granted to each member of a certain community in two directions: first, with regard to the single individual (human rights) and, second, with respect to the rule of law of a certain community. The latter entails that the political authorities are entitled to secure the individual's rights—even by force, in case of need. If the political authorities would not be entitled to do so, no guarantee could be given and society would recede to a state of nature.[588] This results in Kant's notion of perpetual peace, as depicted above,[589] which forms the foundation for international discussions.[590]

When assessing the meaning of new weapons technology, von Schubert identifies the risk that the fascination for modern technologies might lead to an interchange of ends and means, as the technological possibility (means) seems irresistible, while the objective disappears from view.[591] With respect to the technological potential, he admonishes not to be deceived by the anthropomorphized language and argues in support of debunking the myth of artificial intelligence.[592] In concrete terms, he deems AI in weapons systems to be a "useful idiot"[593] (*nützlicher Idiot*) for the time being, thereby referring to its potential benefit as an expert system, while warning against its overestimation.

---

586. See von Schubert, "Das Reich Gottes," 74–75.

587. See von Schubert, "Das Reich Gottes," 78.

588. See von Schubert, "Das Reich Gottes," 83.

589. See 5.3.1 Preliminaries.

590. See von Schubert, "Das Reich Gottes," 89.

591. See von Schubert, Ethische Herausforderungen digitalen Wandels in bewaffneten Konflikten, 7. Unfortunately, von Schubert does not spell out in detail what this entails.

592. See von Schubert, "Jenseits von Eden."

593. von Schubert, "Jenseits von Eden." My translation.

The Ethical Framing

The theologian Eberhard Schockenhoff also developed a peace ethical account in his book *Kein Ende der Gewalt? Friedensethik für eine globalisierte Welt* (2018). In this book, Schockenhoff not only traces peace ethical and just war thinking throughout history and reconstructs the biblical foundation but also explicates the concept of just peace systematically and addresses the problem of autoregulation in weapons technology. I will not reconstruct his historical account here because this is beyond the scope of my contribution, but I will concentrate on his systematic account, as well as his assessment of autoregulative weapons technology.

Schockenhoff commences his systematic approach with peace and its dimensions and draws the conclusion that relating peace and justice to each other also means extending the notion of negative peace and qualifying peace through justice. Referring to Huber and Reuter, Schockenhoff emphasizes that the idea of a messianic peace overcoming all suffering and pain has the objective of orientating humans' deeds in this world, where it might only be possible to achieve fragmentary notion of this overarching peace.[594] In a second step, Schockenhoff turns to the anthropological premises that underlie the idea of a natural inclination toward violence, on the one hand, and the capability of humans to live and act peacefully, on the other hand.[595] Even though this predicament cannot be solved, Schockenhoff argues that it might be useful to ask which circumstances facilitate peaceful solutions—a path the idea of just peace follows.[596] The underlying anthropological principle for doing so is the concept of original sin, which, as he understands it, does not simply entail that humans forfeit all of their capability to do good but rather refers to the inclination toward the bad within humans, which nevertheless does not consume humans totally: There is not total depravity but only a certain tendency that humans can resist if they want to.[597] Following this through, Schockenhoff establishes the idea that there are certain virtues that might stand against the inclination toward the bad, which are, for example, tolerance, the renunciation of the use

---

594. See Schockenhoff, *Kein Ende der Gewalt?* 515.

595. This turn is worthy of note because, as Bernhard Koch rightly notes, authors scrutinizing the role of peace do not usually factor in the anthropological basis on which their account rests. Yet, this is an important question because a pacifist account will only make sense if an author deems humans able to act peacefully. See Koch, "Die kirchliche Friedensdebatte."

596. See Schockenhoff, *Kein Ende der Gewalt?* 517–18.

597. See Schockenhoff, *Kein Ende der Gewalt?* 548–49.

of violence, the willingness for dialogue and compromise, bravery, and moral courage instead of obedience, determination, and patience, as well as willingness for reconciliation.[598] Alongside these virtues, Schockenhoff determines four pillars of just peace, which form the foundation for establishing it. These are, first, the protection from human rights violations and extreme poverty; second, promotion of democracy and the rule of law; third, economic cooperation and just trade relations; and, finally, the strengthening of the international community and their political bodies.[599] Among the contemporary challenges peace ethics faces, he also mentions new weapons technology such as autoregulation. He addresses this topic within the framework of targeted killing, finding it closely connected to the use of drones, and perceives mainly two ethical problems, which are responsibility and the problem that the international community does not want to ban this technology in advance. With respect to responsibility, he sees the major problem in the tendency to reduce or even extinguish human agency. But since human agency is the prerequisite to assign responsibility, Schockenhoff deems this technology morally illicit not only in the form of autoregulation but also in cases where decisions are prestructured in a way that makes it virtually impossible for humans to do otherwise. Besides this mere technological argument, Schockenhoff also indicates that drones in particular threaten the civic population in an extraordinary way.[600] With respect to international humanitarian law, Schockenhoff deplores the unwillingness of some states to ban autoregulation in weapons systems from the outset. This is also because he does not deem the prevailing law to hinder countries that have developed this kind to technology to deploy it, even though it does not technologically meet the demands of international humanitarian law, such as discrimination or proportionality.

Schockenhoff's account is of interest here because he elaborates on just peace against a Roman Catholic theological backdrop and with respect to contemporary problems. His results show that this strand of just peace thinking shares the same implications within Protestant and Roman Catholic thought in Germany. This can be seen not only in the substantial commonalities shared but also in quoting Protestant authors of just peace theory, such as Huber and Reuter. My major conclusion

---

598. See Schockenhoff, *Kein Ende der Gewalt?* 556–77.

599. See Schockenhoff, *Kein Ende der Gewalt?* 589. Schockenhoff then elaborates on the respective pillars in greater detail, 589–665.

600. See Schockenhoff, *Kein Ende der Gewalt?* 720–25.

here is therefore that just peace theory is not the achievement of either Roman Catholic or Protestant thought but develops in between as a virtually ecumenical thought. Accordingly, the claims Schockenhoff makes, especially when referring to the pillars of just peace theory, are reminiscent of the ideas brought forward in the peace memorandum of the Protestant church in Germany.

Taken together, Schockenhoff's main objective is to reconstruct just war thinking aiming to confine violence, commencing his systematic thinking with peace as the groundwork for this pacifist approach. In doing so, the author does not address the remodeling of the single criteria of *bellum iustum* within the law-sustaining theory explicitly but rather refers to this concept rarely and without explaining its details. Irritating, however, is the unconnected array of peaceful virtues and pillars of just peace. This theoretical gap indicates that the individual's striving for peace in its anthropological grounding does not easily correlate with the political and societal dimension of peace. With respect to autoregulation, I do agree with Schockenhoff that autoregulation in weapons systems as well as drones are an important challenge of the present day. However, his description of autoregulation in weapons technology, which revolves solely around the use of a single flying vehicle, underestimates the impact and range of repercussions these technologies bring in their wake because they are not simply the expansion of drone technology and they are not merely confined to a single device. Autoregulation rather constitutes a qualitative step from controlled to uncontrolled technology that can be applied to every device. Moreover, the most important impact of autoregulation in weapons technology might not be achieved with respect to the single device, but rather within swarms or systems of systems, where this qualitative step might seem indispensable and a rather natural development. For those reasons, his approach seems rather naive.

In addition, Reuter engages in the ethical discussion revolving around combat drones and refers within this contribution to the ongoing automatization of weapons technology, meaning autoregulation. Although mainly referring to uncrewed drones, Reuter's thought applies here: He puts this development into a broader peace ethical perspective of ever more developing technology, asking whether moral progress comes with (weapons) technology, and in doing so makes arguments that can be applied to autoregulation in weapons technology mutatis mutandis. He first opposes to the idea that technological progress necessary entails ethical improvement, a theory Herfried Münkler advocates for. Yet, the practice of extralegal killing that seems to come with drones (even though it does not come with them naturally), the ongoing problems with posttraumatic stress disorder also affecting drone pilots, and the increasing expansion of warfare toward civilian territory disapproves that idea. Reuter then assesses the conduct of war by deploying combat drones against the normative frame of just peace thinking and draws three main conclusions. First, and with respect to discrimination, he maintains that due to asymmetrical warfare the differentiation between people involved in warfare and those not involved is hard to make. Especially if targeted people are to be arrested rather than killed, this option seems to be ruled out principally with a combat drone. Second, and regarding proportionality, an accurate identification of people seems hard to make due to the distance. Finally, concerning the distribution of risk, combat drones pose a major problem. This is because soldiers are allowed to kill in war, as they are supposed to be a mutual threat to one another's lives. Yet, such a threat no longer exists with the use of drones—at least for the side deploying them. In contrast and taking into account the inherent asymmetry behind such a scenario, police action is ruled out as well because the purported criminal cannot be targeted nonlethally. For Reuter, these problems speak against the deployment of combat drones. Even more interesting for my contribution is that, for Reuter, combat drones are one step toward ever more automated warfare, a development he deems troubling from an ethical point of view. This is because moral responsibility can hardly be assigned, and to define meaningful human control, it needs to be made clear what human means in this context.[601]

By the same token, the 2021 memorandum of the Protestant church regarding digitization also addresses autoregulation in weapons systems. The whole memorandum is structured along the Ten Commandments and discusses weapons technology within the sixth commandment, "Thou shalt not kill." (Exod 20:13, KJV). The authors of the memorandum refer mainly to the problems with regard to responsibility, holding that even though legal responsibility might be assigned, the problem of moral responsibility is not addressed sufficiently. In other words, even if

---

601. See Reuter, "Kampfdrohnen als Mittel rechtswahrender Gewalt?" This last thought is particularly remarkable because the current discourse seems to focus rather on defining the terms "meaningful" and "control." See, for example, Roff and Moyes, "Meaningful Human Control, Artificial Intelligence and Autonomous Weapons."

humans might be ostensibly omitted, the machines are still programmed by humans, so responsibility might fall back upon them. Moreover, given the acceleration of technology, it is not clear what meaningful human control can mean in this context.[602]

Moreover, among the twenty-four volumes published at the *Forschungsstätte der Evangelischen Studiengemeinschaft* (FEST), two volumes stand out regarding autoregulative functions in weapons technology. First, there is a volume discussing the ramifications of uncrewed warfare, and second, another dealing with cyberwar. The volume on uncrewed warfare refers to remotely controlled as well as autoregulative weapons systems. Here, I will highlight one discussion that seems insightful for the debate on autoregulative devices in general, which is the definition of autoregulation in weapons systems. Werkner here refers to a classification of technology brought forward by the philosopher Michael Funk, who recognizes six evolving steps of technological development ranging from premodern tools, to hypermodern automated systems, to postulated autonomous systems.[603] The problem with such a classification is, first, that "autonomous" technology is only postulated here, which also means that "autonomy" in this context does not refer to the kind of technology developed today but rather to a device that "realizes its own end and is therefore no longer an instrument of a human,"[604] a problem Funk identifies. If an "autonomous" weapons system is defined that way in order to assess it ethically, it is unclear whether this technology will exist eventually, for it is not certain if any algorithm will achieve the necessary requirements at some point. This is also the reason why Altman, in his contribution, defines "autonomy" differently and with regard to the target cycle, harking back to the definition of the US DOD. This definition does not focus on the algorithmic equipment but rather the device's programming to select and engage targets without human interaction. According to this second definition, autoregulative devices already exist and are no longer postulated.[605] Consequently, the way an author defines autoregulation—or autonomy, for that matter—reveals a lot about how

602. See EKD, *Freiheit digital*, 133–36.

603. See Werkner, "Unbemannte Waffen," 5, referring to Funk, "Drohnen und sogenannte 'autonom-intelligente' Technik im Kriegseinsatz," 168–69.

604. Funk, "Drohnen und sogenannte 'autonom-intelligente' Technik im Kriegseinsatz," 170. My translation.

605. See Altmann, "Autonome Waffensysteme," 112–13. In that regard, I also differentiate between purported and anticipated "autonomous" technology, as Funk defines, and my account of autoregulation, which is in line with the definition Altmann brings forward.

they perceive the need for political regulation. Accordingly, Werkner contents herself with listing several arguments for and against the development of autoregulation in weapons technology without giving any hint of whether she approves of this development or not, while Altman concludes that an immediate regulation, or better a preemptive ban of this technology is necessary.[606]

From the second volume mentioned, I will sample out the contribution of Torsten Meireis, as his insights into cyberwar are of interest for my contribution. Meireis questions the narrative of a cyberwar. This is because when reconstructing matters of cybersecurity within a narrative of war, a war paradigm is conjured, which in turn is at variance with the contingent pacifist notion of just peace theory that prioritizes means of peace over means of war. Moreover, when couching matters of cybersecurity in terms of war, this also enables one to make cyberwar a "self-fulfilling prophecy."[607] Therefore, Meireis concludes that the same pacifist rules that are established for the use of force on the mundane battlefield also apply when cyberspace is concerned. This reconfiguration is not sought to belittle the severe damage a cyberattack might bring about, but to confine and regulate violent means and retaliation also within cyberspace.[608] What is important here is that the underlying, socially shared presumptions have an enormous impact on how these things are perceived and regulated. If a certain scenario is perceived as a violent assault, then the appropriate answer could also use violent means for matters of self-defense. However, if, the same occurrence is perceived to be a nonviolent threat, the answer to this is more likely to be nonviolent, or at least nonlethal. This shifts the focus from the phenomenon in question to the framing in which it is embedded.

---

606. Within this volume, Bernhard Koch has also contributed an article where he assesses the ethical implications of autoregulative functions in weapons technology. For his stance toward the issue in question, see above.

607. Meireis, "Gerechter Frieden und Cybersicherheit," 116. My translation.

608. See Meireis, "Gerechter Frieden und Cybersicherheit."

The Ethical Framing

EXCURSUS: APPROACHES AMONG JEWISH TRADITIONS[609]

Discussions revolving around political conceptions of war and peace are a relatively new phenomenon within Jewish traditions.[610] This is because for the majority of their history, Jewish traditions have not been bound to a specific nation state, so war and peace have barely been considered in a political way but have become rather spiritualized concepts.[611] This characteristic is eminent when pondering peace as well as war and violence. The urge to develop a contemporary approach has only become inevitable with the rise of the nation state Israel. Since then, an ethics of fighting and especially military ethics (מוסר/אתיקה צבי) based on Jewish traditions and the present situation has been developed and is still developing.[612] It is not my objective to delve deeper into these approaches—such a discussion would go beyond the scope of this book. It is rather my aim to depict approaches within Jewish thought that elaborate on autoregulation in weapons technology from a religious point of view. This also entails that I will not address any political, juridical, or philosophical conceptualizations regarding autoregulation in weapons systems, such as the notions the Institute for National Security Studies at Tel Aviv has brought forward,[613] the philosophical approach given by Daniel Statman,[614] or the ideas brought by jurists Eliav Lieblich and Eyal Benvenisti.[615] Yet, in order to frame the religious discussions, I will briefly introduce how the ideas of peace and war are conceptualized from a Jewish religious perspective in order to outline the background of the discussions.

---

609. As I have made clear in the introduction to this chapter, Jewish approaches toward war and peace exceed the classification I have chosen in linking morality and warfare. I therefore present my reference to these approaches as an excursus. Yet, this does not mean that they do not offer valuable insights for the discussion.

610. Jewish traditions abound. They are far from having one specific approach that depicts one perspective within the Jewish world. I will therefore not operate with the term "Judaism," which suggests that there might be such a single attitude, but use the term "Jewish traditions" instead, which implies a multitude of approaches.

611. See, especially, Ravitzky, *AL DAÀT Ha-MaQom*, 21 (Hebrew).

612. See, for example, Kasher, *Military Ethics* (Hebrew).

613. Here, Antebi has made several contributions. See Antebi, "Who Will Stop the Robots?"

614. See Statman, "Drones and Robots"; Statman, Drohnen, "Roboter und die Moral des Krieges."

615. See Lieblich and Benvenisti, "Obligation to Exercise Discretion in Warfare"; Lieblich, "Autonomous Weapons Systems and the Obligation to Exercise Discretion."

An Ethical Evaluation of Lethal Functions in Autoregulative Weapons Systems

This excursus will first introduce, briefly and paradigmatically, some Jewish conceptions regarding peace and war (1), then proceed by introducing three different argumentations assessing autoregulation in weapons technology in greater detail (2), and finally draw a conclusion for my own argument (3).

1. Conceptualizing War and Peace Within *Halacha*

Jewish traditions address current ethical problems in the context of *halacha*. Halacha refers to the body of religious law, which has developed over the course of time. According to Lawrence H. Schiffman's historical examination, "For the rabbis, halacha denotes the life of Torah, encompassing all areas of human life, including civil, criminal, political, religious, moral, ritual, and familial issues."[616] Torah here does not refer solely to the first five books of the Tanakh, but rather to the broader traditions of the Jewish law-making process expressed in the Talmud, referred to as the oral Torah. This also means that halacha is the main approach to matters of socioethical nature mainly within Orthodox Jewish tradition. Benjamin Brown mentions three areas addressed within halachic discourse in the modern age: "(1) matters of technological change, including the use of new technologies in the performance of Jewish rituals; (2) new sorts of jobs and activities among Jews, including the broadened realms of interaction with non-Jews; and (3) new currents of thought among modern Jews."[617] This entails that halacha develops with the issues that need to be resolved and depends on the topics members of the Jewish community address and the halachic responses they develop. Consequently, halacha seems to be the area within Jewish traditions where autoregulation in weapons technology would be discussed from a religious viewpoint.[618]

The following suggestions can be mapped onto three different approaches, as proposed by Suzanne Last Stone. All of them deal with the halachic lacuna toward war and peace in a different way. According to

616. Schiffman, "Art.: Halacha, A," 2.
617. Brown, "Art: Halacha E," 20.
618. My assumption is anything but self-evident. As will be shown below, there is a large discussion within Jewish tradition if halachic ruling can be applied to modern warfare in particular and contemporary questions in general. This is also due to the contested nature of halacha—political, religious or juridical See Last Stone, "The Jewish Law of War," 346, 348. However, since my interest is to look for religious patterns that might facilitate the ethical assessment of modern weapons technology, I assume that such a transfer is possible and useful.

The Ethical Framing

Last Stone, Jewish thought addresses war either following a diasporic pattern that "turns not to war as a halakhic category but rather to already well-developed categories within the halakha to analyze killings: self-defense and aggression or pursuit."[619] This means that the gap in halachic thought is filled with similar conceptions rooted in Jewish traditions. Or, within a collectivist approach where the few halachic sources are applied directly to modern thinking, thereby referring not strictly to halachic ruling but also using aggadic narratives, biblical ruling, or commentaries for that matter. Finally, there are cosmopolitan concepts that reject halachic sources altogether and instead refer to international law and contractions. In my opinion, the first kind of thinking within the diasporic pattern can be seen when the Jewish Scholar Shlomo Zuckier develops his concept of self-defense. The second, collectivist approach is mirrored in the ideas of Elliot N. Dorff, while the third strand is clearly that of Michael Walzer. All of these approaches will therefore be addressed briefly below. As for the approaches toward autoregulation in weapons technology, they seem to stand between a diasporic and a collectivist concept. While Nadav Berman is rather taking a collectivist approach by building his argumentation on biblical narratives, Nevins addresses the issue within a collectivist frame by applying halachic ruling to current situations.[620] This again hints at the diversity of Jewish traditions and the way they can or cannot be transferred to issues of our present.

Even if considering war and peace politically is a rather new phenomenon within Jewish thought, it does not mean that the conceptions are unknown in any way to Jewish traditions: Peace in particular has been pondered metaphysically and spiritually.

Peace as a Hebrew term has a wide variety of meanings, referring rather to the concept of positive peace. Aviezer Ravitzky writes,

> The Hebrew term "peace" (שלום) is derived from the linguistic root שלם and is found in Israeli literature in the term "wholeness" (שלמות) in its different aspects. Its meaning is therefore not confined to a political context of non-war and hatred, or to a social situation of non-argument and dispute. It is rather translated differently in different areas: blessed physical conditions, ethical norms and values, also cosmic principles and godly

---

619. Last Stone, "Jewish Law of War," 344.

620. The cosmopolitan approach has not been addressed here because it is not different from the international political discussion. For Berman and Nevins, see Excursus 2 Assessments of autoregulation in weapons technology within Jewish traditions.

characteristic. Moreover, the conversations lasting generations and specifically devoted to political peace—to stop fighting between nations and countries—rise in many cases up to utopic heights, distanced from the historical reality: The Peace longed for exceeds history and touches/overcomes the boundaries of the end of the days.[621]

In his study, Ravitzky demonstrates that the main sources in Jewish traditions ponder peace within a broad sphere—among them feeling safe and calm—as well as the absence of war, yet, "Not every peace is better than every war."[622] In that context, Ravitzky hints at the tremendous gap between the violent nature of humans as narrated in the stories of their genealogy and the picture of world peace the prophets draw. The important question is therefore whether such a concept is suitable for political and ethical engagement. On the one hand, the utopic character of peace has strong ethical potential because it gives substantial motivation and comfort. On the other hand, the objective might be too idealistic, so small achievements might lose meaning.[623] Ravitzky leaves this question open: "The answer to these questions is not graved into the halachic sources and thought, it is not set in stone (אינה חרותה על הלוחות)."[624] The degree to which the depicted concept of peace could influence actual politics and behavior is therefore an open discussion.

By the same token, Alick Isaacs proposes, in a rather mystical approach, distinguishing between two different concepts of peace found within Jewish traditions: first, "to resolve situations of conflict" and, second, "the ultimate world peace that the prophets spoke of."[625] The second, messianic dimension in particular might hinder concrete political solutions due to its utopic character. For the sake of political solutions, it might, therefore, be better to differentiate both conceptions, giving way to a political process of peace. This does not mean abandoning the concept of prophetic peace completely, though, but rather finding places where such a concept might be practiced.[626]

Ethical reflections of war, similarly, have to cope with the lacuna within Jewish traditions toward that topic. In 2006, Michael Walzer wrote,

621. Ravitzky, *AL DAÀT Ha-MaQom*, 13. My translation.
622. Ravitzky, *AL DAÀT Ha-MaQom*, 19. My translation.
623. See Ravitzky, *AL DAÀT Ha-MaQom*, 32–33.
624. Ravitzky, *AL DAÀT Ha-MaQom*, 33. My translation.
625. Isaacs, "Concept of Peace in Judaism," 3.
626. See Isaacs, "Concept of Peace in Judaism," 42.

The Ethical Framing

> There is no Jewish theory of war and peace, and until modern times, there were no theories produced by individual Jews. Discussions of war and peace indeed find a place, though a very limited one, within the Jewish tradition. [...] Jewish writers argued almost entirely among themselves, in the peculiar circumstances of exile, without reference to any existing international society with its practices and codes.[627]

And in 2012, Elliot N. Dorff, professor of Law, confirmed Walzer's findings:

> The only times before 1948 when Jews ruled themselves and made their own decisions as a nation as to when to go to war and how to wage it were between c. 1250 B.C.E. and 586 B.C.E. (the conquest of Canaan and the First Temple period) and between 165 B.C.E. and 63 B.C.E. (the Maccabean period). Jewish sources on war are therefore either very old or only theoretical, without a base in the actual experience of deciding to go to war and the strategies to use.[628]

Both authors agree on the general condition of traditional Jewish thought regarding war and peace and hint at the rather theoretical character of this account, as indicated above. Yet, they draw very different conclusions: Walzer argues that this theoretical lack cannot keep up with the current philosophical debate and therefore that Jewish traditions would do best if they filled this lacuna, for the time being, with the well-developed, Christian just war tradition.[629] Dorff, however, argues that Jewish conceptualizations follow their own rationale, and he therefore develops a methodology on those grounds[630] based on the position that God, as well as human nature, is described ambivalently in Scripture and tradition. God is the "Lord of Armies" (יהוה צבאות) as well as the "Lord of Peace" (יהוה שלום);[631] human nature consists of an inclination to do good, meaning to serve the other (יצר הטוב), and an inclination to do bad, meaning self-interest (יצר הרע). And, according to Ecclesiastes 3:8, there

---

627. Walzer, "Commanded and Permitted Wars," 149.

628. Dorff, "War and Peace," 643. Polish comes to the same conclusion. See Polish, "Just War in Jewish Thought," 1.

629. See Walzer, "Ethics of War in the Jewish Tradition."

630. This debate is part of a larger discussion revolving around the general issue of whether an ethics of war can and should be built on Jewish principles at all. Questions like this also pertain to the issue that Israel is a modern nation state that does not regard itself as being religious in nature, while at the same time halachic ruling plays an important role in daily (and political) life. See Last Stone, "Jewish Law of War," 343.

631. See Dorff, "War and Peace," 644–46.

is a time for both war and peace.⁶³² While waging war is problematic per se,⁶³³ "the Jewish tradition is not pacifistic,"⁶³⁴ a statement that is echoed by other Jewish scholars, too.⁶³⁵ Self-defense in particular is deemed to be justified along the lines of Jewish traditions, a tenet phrased by the sages in the term "whoever comes to kill you, kill him first" (הבא להורגך השכם להורגו). This, however, is only legitimate if the intent of the other is indeed to do such harm.⁶³⁶

Turning to the Jewish traditions regarding war and peace in particular, the seminal text is found in Deuteronomy 20, which is the Kings' Law. Within this text, the command is given that before attacking a certain city, peace should be offered, a case where the surrendered people would serve as forced laborers. In the case of a military strike, however, spoils of war would be taken and the non-Jews living in Israel would have to be killed. Yet, when besieging a city, trees need to be spared (בל תשחית).⁶³⁷ These commands have been analyzed by the sages within Midrash and Talmud, where a differentiation between commanded (מלחמות מצות), permitted (מלחמות רשות), and preemptive war (מלחמת חובה) is made.⁶³⁸ Since all of them require bygone cultic regulations,

---

632. See Dorff, "War and Peace," 646–48. During his explanations, Dorff also points to the different interpretations of Genesis 3 within Christian and Jewish traditions. While Christian sources have interpreted this biblical text as original sin, corrupting human nature entirely, Jewish traditions perceive this text with far less skepticism, arguing that in this initial moment, God gave humans the ability to decide between good and evil, thereby laying the groundwork for following rules in the first place. This is because, without knowing what is good or bad, humans would not be able to follow God's commandments.

633. See Dorff, "War and Peace," 651.

634. Dorff, "War and Peace," 651.

635. The same statement is made by Berman, for instance. See above and Berman, "Jewish Law, Techno-Ethics and Autonomous Weapons Systems," 93. Such a premises can be claimed for Walzer. See, Walzer, "Ethics of War in the Jewish Tradition"; Walzer, "Commanded and Permitted Wars." Here, as well as in Berman's account, this demarcation seems to come rather from an absolute pacifist conception.

636. See Dorff, "War and Peace," 651–56.

637. An assumption that has found its way into contemporary Jewish environmental ethics as well. This is because halachic interpretations of this passage have focused on the prohibition against cutting down fruit trees, thereby leaving aside the war context, so this passage ultimately became an ecological ethical principle—which is not uncontested, of course. See Yoreh, *Waste Not*, 45, 230–31.

638. There is a scholarly dispute about whether Jewish traditions in fact recognize three kinds of wars and what they are. In contrast to Dorff, Walzer and Ravitzky hold that there are in fact only two kinds of wars known to the tradition, which are commanded and permitted wars. Missing within their theories, however, is a third category

The Ethical Framing

Dorff draws the conclusion that "the only type of war allowed was a war not explicitly listed here but presumably assumed—namely a war carried out in self-defense."[639]

Therefore, fighting in self-defense is an important concept. Zuckier has elaborated on that topic in a contribution, distinguishing between defending oneself and defending others. In order to do so, he interprets two passages (סוגיות) from the Talmud. The first passage is about a person digging a tunnel underneath somebody's house. The Talmud rules that the house's owner may defend themselves if it is uncertain whether the person digging the tunnel has malicious intent. bSanhedrin 72b reads:

אם ברור לך הדבר כשמש שיש לו שלום עמך אל תהרגהו ואם לאו הרגהו.

> If it is clear to you as daylight (literally: as the sun) that he comes in peace, don't kill him. If not, kill him.[640]

Zuckier interprets this *sugia* to show that only in cases where it is very clear that the person digging means no threat would it be illegitimate to kill them. However, since this might hardly be the case in such a scenario, where the dark atmosphere of the tunnel is in sharp contrast to the reference to the sun, this indicates that this is a clear case where self-defense would be legitimate.[641]

In another *sugia* found in bSanhedrin 73a, the sages discuss a scene where a pursuer (רודף) tries to harm another person by killing or raping them. In such a case, the sages state that killing the pursuer would be legitimate.[642] Zuckier, however, draws a distinction between the two cases, where the first refers to one person's right to self-defense, which can be

---

of prohibited wars, a concept Walzer demands and Ravitzky proves to already exist—at least roughly. See Walzer, "Commanded and Permitted Wars"; Ravitzky, "Prohibited Wars." Neither of them, however, recognizes what Dorff calls "preemptive war." This disagreement is rooted in different tradition within Jewish traditional literature. While the Misha and some passages within the Talmud refer to the three aforementioned versions of war, Maimonides and Nahmanides only elaborate on permitted and commanded warfare. See Firestone, *Holy War in Judaism*, 134.

639. Dorff, "War and Peace," 657.

640. My translation. bSanhedrin 72a also knows the ruling vice versa but interprets this ruling to apply only when the father of the house owner is digging a tunnel. See also Zuckier, "Halachic-Philosophical Account of Self-Defense," 36.

641. See Zuckier, "Halachic-Philosophical Account of Self-Defense," 36.

642. See Zuckier, "Halachic-Philosophical Account of Self-Defense," 28. The reasons the sages mention are also interesting. On the one hand, by killing the pursuer, the pursuer themselves would be rescued from committing a sin, while, on the other hand, the person pursued would clearly be rescued from the pursuer.

seen in line with the aforementioned principle "whoever comes to kill you, kill him first" (הבא להורגך השכם להורגו), and the second to the defense of a third party. While both cases seem reasonable and can be justified on the grounds of Jewish traditions, they differ in their limitations. Especially in the second case of the pursuer, the rules applied for killing in order to come to the aid of a third party are stricter. Zuckier writes, "If an observer lacks sufficient evidence to properly understand the situation, how could he possibly invoke justice to kill a possible attacker?"[643] In the case of the tunneller, however, where somebody's own life is at stake, the Torah gives a more lenient ruling, including cases of uncertainty.[644] Similarly, Maimonides allows the tunneller to be killed, while the pursuer must only be injured, if this is sufficient to stop them.[645] Yet, this does not mean that an innocent bystander can be killed in order to save somebody's life, which is made clear with the hint at the Talmudic story where two persons are traveling in the desert, and only one of them has a jug of water. In this case, the person owning the jug of water does not need to share the water with the other person, which would mean putting their own life in danger. It would not be legitimate, however, to kill the other person in order to prevent them from taking the jug of water.[646] From this, Zuckier draws the following conclusion:

> The case of *rodef* [pursuer] teaches the principle of intervention against a clear attacker which may be carried out by anyone, as it is based on justice and the attacker's forfeiting his life, and it has higher standards and therefore often enjoys narrower application. The case of *ba ba-mahteret* [the tunneller] teaches the principle of self-preservation in the face of an attack, where the person partial to the situation may invoke a Divinely granted right and kill his (possible) attacker.[647]

Applying Zuckier's concept to autoregulation in weapons technology means that these systems are clearly under the ruling of the pursuer,

---

643. Zuckier, "Halachic-Philosophical Account of Self-Defense," 37.

644. See Zuckier, "Halachic-Philosophical Account of Self-Defense," 38.

645. See Zuckier, "Halachic-Philosophical Account of Self-Defense," 38–39. Yet, whether the attacker can defend themselves against the attacked is ruled the other way around: This might only be legitimate in the case of the tunneller, given the unclear circumstances, while in the case of the pursuer the situation is clearer due to the third party involved.

646. See Zuckier, "Halachic-Philosophical Account of Self-Defense," 46–48.

647. Zuckier, "Halachic-Philosophical Account of Self-Defense," 50–51.

because they have no life to lose. This then makes the restrictions for their killing very strict, as well as the rationale to harm but not to kill. Yet, this is only possible in situations that are clear. Otherwise the third party, meaning the weapons systems, cannot kill at all.

Having this in mind, deploying autoregulation in weaponry is only legitimate for reasons of self-defense, since self-defense is the only legitimate reason to wage war in the first place. Yet, if these kinds of systems are deployed, the rules are stricter than the rules deployed if a human's life is threatened directly. In such a case, analogous to the tunneller, the person might defend themselves, while in the case of a third party involved, analogous to the pursuer, the system needs to "understand" the situation first before it attacks the purported attacker. But since technological systems lack this kind of understanding (so far),[648] it would be illegitimate to deploy them.

2. Assessments of Autoregulation in Weapons Technology Within Jewish Traditions

Autoregulation in weapons systems is addressed within ethical-halachic thought only to a minor degree. I could identify three instances, which I will introduce in this section: first, a thorough assessment the Jewish philosopher Nadav Berman prepared in an article; second, a contribution written by Rabbi David Nevins, who addresses autoregulative weaponry in the broader context of automatization; finally, the Rabbi Michael Abraham, who gives a response to this topic when asked.

Berman undertook the work of writing an ethical-halachic contribution on the topic of autoregulation in weapons technology. Even though his observation does not constitute a halachic ruling per se, his aim is to contribute to the scholarly debate that might enable an halachic ruling.[649] He observes that there are no ethical assessments of this kind of technology from a halachic point of view so far but deems this topic worthy of investigation.[650] Berman states right at the beginning of his article that his approach is not pacifist in nature, but rather violent means are

---

648. See 3.3 Reckoning and Judgment.

649. See Berman, "Jewish Law, Techno-Ethics and Autonomous Weapons Systems," 97.

650. See Berman, "Jewish Law, Techno-Ethics and Autonomous Weapons Systems," 92.

permitted if "*practices* of this power" are under "moral critique,"⁶⁵¹ which is also why the public has a say in the development and deployment of new weapons technology such as autoregulation. His halachic approach is then not confined to members of the Jewish community but rather includes non-Jewish perceptions as long as they are in line with "humane ethics," meaning "a plain human sense of morality, which is significant in Jewish law," which, in turn, "is relevant to AWS too."⁶⁵² He therefore draws the conclusion that the concerns against autoregulation in weapons technology might not only be rooted in biblical thinking but also that biblical and religious traditions might offer ethical principles facilitating an assessment of this kind of weaponry. One of these principles is the teaching of *Imago Dei* from which a prohibition of unnecessary killing can be derived. Combined with the halachic idea of self-defense (אם בא להורגך השכם להרגו),⁶⁵³ which assumes that there needs to be a direct threat to the life of a person. This is already a strong hint suggesting that there needs to be a human involved in the act of killing another living being.⁶⁵⁴

In order to examine the topic more thoroughly, Berman briefly classifies techno-ethical and ethical approaches to war and peace from a halachic stance, thereby locating autoregulation in weapons systems at the nexus of these two topics. Regarding techno-ethics, Berman finds that issues of technical nature are tackled by Jewish authors in a way that adapts traditional approaches to contemporary cases, thereby not separating sharply between law and ethics. Addressing imminent questions such as autoregulation in weaponry, however, is no simple undertaking due to the omission of a systematic approach to war ethics within the Bible. This is also due to the issues that are dealt with in this field of research focusing on different topics, such as the individual soldier, who needs to stick to halachic rules while serving in the army. On a related note, Walzer's (re-)framing of the just war approach might not cover autoregulation because of the technology's inherently strong asymmetry.⁶⁵⁵

---

651. Berman, "Jewish Law, Techno-Ethics and Autonomous Weapons Systems," 93. Berman seems to have an absolute pacifist concept in mind here.

652. Berman, "Jewish Law, Techno-Ethics and Autonomous Weapons Systems," 95.

653. For more details, see Excursus 1 Conceptualizing War and Peace Within *Halacha*.

654. Which is also why Jewish ritual slaughter insists that a human slaughters the animal. See Berman, "Jewish Law, Techno-Ethics and Autonomous Weapons Systems," 97.

655. See Berman, "Jewish Law, Techno-Ethics and Autonomous Weapons Systems," 102; referring to Benvenisti, "Law of Asymmetric Warfare."

The Ethical Framing

Most importantly, however, Berman puts an emphasis on humans or, to be precise, the agency of the combatant targeting another being. He writes,

> It is less the morally legitimized military *act*, than the ethical legitimacy of its technological *production*. Put differently, it is not what makes somebody a justified target for military attack, or the question of the proportionality of military force, but the moral agency of the combatant (which is robotic in the case of AWS). What we are interested in here is thus *whether an artificial agent, a sophisticated AI-operated lethal machine, ought to be considered a worthy moral agent.*[656]

Berman then develops three ethical principles underlying his account, which are in line with this emphasis on humans. Berman mentions, first, the relational character of ethics, which in his view remains attached to humans and contrasts with individualistic western approaches that concentrate only on a detached individual. Similarly, such an approach is pragmatic in the sense that it overcomes dualistic ideas due to a "holistic body-mind dependence" that it is metaphysical in the sense that "the 'is' does not exhaust the 'ought.'"[657] Second, harking back to Genesis 1, Berman opposes the premise that technology is neutral. Criticizing the term "moral machines," he objects that "if humans are fallible, and by no means *inherently* good, it is surprising that the works of humans are considered 'moral' per se."[658] Finally, Berman radically opposes transhumanist ideas and is also skeptical against posthumanism. Since his approach revolves around humans, he deems posthumanist

---

656. Berman, "Jewish Law, Techno-Ethics and Autonomous Weapons Systems," 102–103. Emphasis original.

657. Berman, "Jewish Law, Techno-Ethics and Autonomous Weapons Systems," 105. This approach, however, contrasts with relational-critical posthumanist approaches that aim to overcome the focus on humans and consequently propose widening this relational attitude to nonhumans such as animals or artifacts. See, for example, Haraway, "Cyborg Manifesto"; Latour, *Pandora's Hope*. I discuss this stance below and with respect to responsibility. See 6.5.2 Responsibility Without Agency?

658. Berman, "Jewish Law, Techno-Ethics and Autonomous Weapons Systems," 106. Emphasis original. The tradition Berman quotes in the context of his argumentation, referring to Hans Jonas, Erich Fromm, Jaques Ellul and others, is skeptical regarding the general nature of technology. This is also manifest when Berman refers to Genesis 1. Doing so places technology dogmatically in the field of creation. But since humans are fallen creatures, their manifestations can hardly be good in nature. Accordingly, other attempts to conceptualize technology ethically might be more preferable. See, for example, Schwarke, "Technik und Theologie."

concepts aiming to overthrow anthropocentrism problematic, while he rules out altogether transhumanist ideas that aim to overcome humans by technological means. Especially against the latter, Berman points to the prohibition of idolatry, which he sees instantiated when transhumanists embrace technology.[659]

Proceeding on these assumptions, Berman turns to the ethics of autoregulation in weapons systems, encapsulating the proponent's arguments in Bradley Strawser's principle of unnecessary risk. Strawser holds that by deploying machines instead of human soldiers, damage could be avoided, and therefore "creating and using AWS is not only legitimate but, in fact mandatory."[660] Against this, Berman turns to the problem of accountability, the uncertainty of whether other parties will care (morally) in the same way, and the inherent danger that civilians will ultimately be targeted in order to spare soldiers' lives.[661] Berman then objects to the idea that morality can be formalized algorithmically, because "ethics is by its nature fallible, dialogical, and inter-human."[662] The argument for an artificial moral agency is rather an anthropological misunderstanding. In order to develop moral agency, artificial entities need a body, and "robots have no *body*." Yet, "it is by the body that we come to understand what 'good' and 'evil' are."[663] What Berman refers to here is not the robotic material of the entity, which incorporated algorithmic systems surely have, but the wholesale experience of being "vulnerable and punishable."[664] From this more general and rather philosophical discussion, Berman subsequently turns to the specific ethical-halachic perspectives he perceives by referring to the American pragmatist Mark Johnson's concept of moral imagination. In this concept, Johnson argues that moral reasoning does not mainly follow rational thinking but rather adopts an imaginary structure based on prototypes and metaphors and framed in narratives. This framing then makes all the difference to how

---

659. See Berman, "Jewish Law, Techno-Ethics and Autonomous Weapons Systems," 107–10.

660. Berman, "Jewish Law, Techno-Ethics and Autonomous Weapons Systems," 111.

661. This point is not entirely clear. It seems to be a critique of revisionist just war thinking, where the line between combatants and noncombatants is blurred, and the main principle is to save the (just) soldier's life. That this connection between revisionist just war thinking and autoregulation in weapons technology can be drawn has also been discussed by Meireis. See Meireis, "Die Revisionist Just War Theory," 336.

662. Berman, "Jewish Law, Techno-Ethics and Autonomous Weapons Systems," 113.

663. Berman, "Jewish Law, Techno-Ethics and Autonomous Weapons Systems," 114.

664. Berman, "Jewish Law, Techno-Ethics and Autonomous Weapons Systems," 114.

The Ethical Framing

a certain moral act is carried out and evaluated. Johnson writes, "Moral understanding is in large measure imaginatively structured. The primary forms of moral imagination are concepts with prototype structure, semantic frames, conceptual metaphors, and narratives."[665] Further, imaginary morality is emphatic in the sense that we put ourselves in somebody else's shoes, which in turn does not mean that moral thinking becomes "a private, personal, or utterly subjective activity. Rather, it is the chief activity by which we are able to inhabit a more or less common world—a world of shared gestures, actions, perceptions, experiences, meanings, symbols, and narratives."[666] This entails that moral thinking is no longer structured unambiguously but rather characterized by "multivalence and open-endedness."[667] Narratives do take this open form and may, in addition "help to figure out profound ethical implications that would otherwise be latent."[668]

Against this backdrop, the biblical narratives Berman calls "the sword devours" might facilitate an ethical analysis of autoregulation in weapons systems. Two stories illustrate the problem: first, the story of killing the priests of Nob (1 Sam 22) and, second, the murder of Uriah (2 Sam 11). In the former story, King Saul feels betrayed by the priests of Nob, who have kept the whereabouts of David from him, and consequently sentences them to death. His guard, however, refuses to obey this order for reasons of conscience, so Saul needs to find another person, Doeg the Edomite, who kills the priests. In the latter story, King David orders Uriah the Hittite to fight in the hope that he will be killed, so he can marry his wife Bathsheba. When David is informed that Uriah died on the battlefield, he sends a messenger to Joab, his commander of army, to tell him, "Do not let this thing displease you, for the sword devours one as well as another" (2 Sam 11:25). While the first story makes a strong case for a conscientious refusal, the second one addresses the problem of responsibility. This entails, first, that an autoregulative weapons system would not refuse for reasons of conscience, since it has none and would do whatever it is told to do. Regarding halachic reason,

---

665. Johnson, *Moral Imagination*, 198. I depict Johnson's theory here, as it is a very sophisticated way of moral thinking that cannot (easily) be formalized. This entails a strong argument against the moral possibilities of machines, since they only reckon but do not judge. See Smith, *Reckoning and Judgment*.

666. Johnson, *Moral Imagination*, 201.

667. Johnson, *Moral Imagination*, 204.

668. Berman, "Jewish Law, Techno-Ethics and Autonomous Weapons Systems," 115–16.

however, the possibility of objecting against a command for reasons of conscience is crucial, therefore it cannot be done away with. Second, this means that by describing the sword as an autonomous agent devouring "one as well as another," David diverts the attention from his own responsibility. Berman concludes that, "Remoteness from the battlefield does not excuse one from responsibility for the chain of events that one has set in motion."[669]

Finally, Berman assesses the use of autoregulation in weapons technology against the backdrop of Israel: With respect to the military procedures and responsibility, he proposes that, "*At least two soldiers* (or commanders)"[670] should be engaged if an offensive UAV is deployed. Underlining the importance of "national collective democratic decision-making over possible sectorial considerations,"[671] Berman conceives the dangers that accountability might no longer be traced effectively, that autoregulation might not stay within the military context but will be deployed also by the police, and that the privatization of the defense industry in Israel might eventually jeopardize the role of Israel's model of a "people's army."[672] Finally, Berman highlights that anthropomorphizing technology, for instance, by giving it "names, rights, sympathy, and intrinsic value,"[673] is a case of idolatry and therefore problematic from a halachic perceptive. This, however, is very likely to happen when autoregulating technology.

Taken together, developing and deploying autoregulation in weapons technology is problematic from this halachic perspective. In order to come to this conclusion, Berman considers philosophical as well as theological reasoning, thereby intertwining ethics of war and peace as well as ethics of technology: The focus within the former rests on the Jewish concept of self-defense, while the focal point of the latter is humans. The decisive argument rests on the biblical stories and their inherent ethical potential, though, because these narratives uncover the danger of following a given command blindly and blurring responsibility. Both

669. Berman, "Jewish Law, Techno-Ethics and Autonomous Weapons Systems," 118.

670. Berman, "Jewish Law, Techno-Ethics and Autonomous Weapons Systems," 119. Emphasis original.

671. Berman, "Jewish Law, Techno-Ethics and Autonomous Weapons Systems," 120.

672. What Berman refers to is that every member of the Israeli nation state is expected to take part in the army and to risk their lives, while at the same time the army promises security. Berman, "Jewish Law, Techno-Ethics and Autonomous Weapons Systems," 121.

673. Berman, "Jewish Law, Techno-Ethics and Autonomous Weapons Systems," 122.

The Ethical Framing

principles, meaning conscious objection and responsibility, are deeply human in nature and cannot be outsourced to machines. This is even more the case if ethics is not about rules and principles but about imaginations woven into metaphors and narratives.

In 2019, Rabbi David Nevins gave answers to questions regarding AI and autoregulation in machines. These discussions revolved mainly around the issue of whether an uncontrolled system can observe Jewish law, who is responsible if it doesn't, and whether halachic principles should be implemented into machines.[674] In responding to these questions, Nevins develops a halachic perspective on advanced technology in general and addresses the issue of autoregulation in weapons systems in particular.

Regarding the issue of advanced technology and especially the purported agency of such devices, the rabbi introduces two principles from the sages (חז"ל). Both rest on the concept of legal agency or representation (שליחות), which must not be confused with the philosophical concept of agency. What is meant here is whether an agent (שליח) can legally and from a halachic viewpoint be regarded as the legal representative of the principal, or sender (שולח). For that matter, Nevins first cites the statement "that 'a person's agent is [legally considered to be] like him' (ששלוחו של אדם כמותו),"[675] which is a widely accepted ruling in traditional literature, even though the ruling has some intricate specifications depending on whether or not the depicted agent is a Jew,[676] whether or not the agent in question is employed,[677] and whether or not a specific incident is ritual in nature. Yet, the Talmud also describes circumstances

---

674. The responses have been approved by the Committee on Jewish Law and Standards, which is part of the Rabbinic Assembly of Conservative Jewish Tradition. Its task is to address questions from its members, thereby making halachic policy. For more information, see The Rabbinical Assembly, "Committee of Jewish Law and Standards." The responses have been authorized also by the other members of the respective counsel, who are Rabbis Pamela Barmash, Elliot Dorff, Baruch Frydman Kohl, Susan Grossman, Judith Hauptman, Joshua Heller, Jeremy Kalmanofsky, Steve Kane, Jan Kaufman, Gail Labovitz, Amy Levin, Daniel Nevins, Micah Peltz, Robert Scheinberg, Deborah Silver, Ariel Stofenmacher, Iscah Waldman, and Ellen Wolintz Fields.

675. Nevins, "Halakhic Responses to Artificial Intelligence and Autonomous Machines," 10.

676. See Nevins, "Halakhic Responses to Artificial Intelligence and Autonomous Machines," 10–11.

677. See Nevins, "Halakhic Responses to Artificial Intelligence and Autonomous Machines," 11–12.

An Ethical Evaluation of Lethal Functions in Autoregulative Weapons Systems

where nonhuman agents such as monkeys are used. Nevins therefore quotes from b.Eruvin 31b:

דתניא: נתנו לפיל והוליכו, לקוף והוליכו—אין זה עירוב. ואם אמר לאחר לקבלו הימנו—הרי זה עירוב. -ודילמא לא ממטי ליה?—אמר רב חסדא: בעומד ורואהו.—ודילמא לא מקבל ליה מיניה? אמר רב יחיאל: חזקה שליח עושה שליחותו.

> For it is taught in a *beraita*: If they gave it [i.e., an item to establish an extension of the Sabbath boundary] to an elephant, and it carried it, [or] to a monkey and it carried it—this is not a [valid] *eiruv*.[678] But if he said to another [person] to receive it from him [i.e., the animal], then it is a [valid] *eiruv*. But what if it [the animal] does not deliver it? Rav Ḥisd says, the case is when the [principal] stands and watches. And what if [the human receiving agent] refuses to accept it from him [the animal]? Rav YeḤiel says, it is established that an agent completes his appointed task.[679]

Leaving beside the halachic discussion of the *eiruv*, the case is interesting because the monkey and the elephant are—under certain circumstances—used as carriers. Accordingly, Nevins writes,

> We may infer that if a ritually obligated individual both initiates and completes an action, then a non-obligated agent, and even a non-human agent, might be permitted to carry out an intermediate segment of the task.[680]

Referring to a second principle from the sages, Nevin cites "the rule 'there is no agency for transgression' (אין שליח לדבר עבירה)," which means that an agent who is sent out to something against the law bears the responsibility for doing so themselves, even though the principal also "remains morally culpable."[681] In this context, the sages also discuss the possibility of inanimate objects, such as a courtyard, counting as agents, but oppose this view. Nevins writes, "*Obligation is an essential qualification*

---

678. An Eiruv is a ritual boarder that defines anything within it as private, thereby allowing the individuals to carry certain objects, such as books or keys on Shabbat.

679. Nevins, "Halakhic Responses to Artificial Intelligence and Autonomous Machines," 12.

680. Nevins, "Halakhic Responses to Artificial Intelligence and Autonomous Machines," 12. Emphasis original.

681. Nevins, "Halakhic Responses to Artificial Intelligence and Autonomous Machines," 13.

The Ethical Framing

for agency, and an inanimate object cannot become an agent."[682] Here, Nevins quotes another *sugia*, which deals with the owner of livestock who allows them to pastor in a land owned by somebody else:

ושלח את בעירו. מכאן אמרו מסר צאנו לבנו לשלוחו ולעבדו פטור, לחרש שוטה וקטן חייב.

> *He sends his livestock.* From here they said, if he handed his sheep to his son, to his agent, to his servant/slave, then he [i.e., the owner] is exempt, but [if he handed his sheep] to a person who is deaf-mute, mentally ill or a minor, then he [i.e., the owner] is liable.[683]

Here, the sages decide that an agent needs to have the "the capacity for independent judgment"[684] in order to be held responsible. If they lack this capacity, the responsibility rests with the principal. This ruling is especially important for the discussion of autoregulative machines, since they do not have the same kind of agency humans have. Moreover, they cannot be punished. Nevins therefore draws the conclusion that machines are neither obligated nor have free will, thus responsibility for their operations needs to stay, at least to a certain extent, with humans. To discuss this matter further, Nevins recurs to traditional literature and other rabbinical thoughts, referring mainly to autoregulative driving, and advocates for a limited liability of the users—at least in cases where a problem could have been foreseen. Yet, in cases of freak accidents and other unforeseen incidents, the users must not be held responsible.[685] Concerning responsibility, Nevins refers to Rabbi Aharon Lichtenstein and Hans Jonas, pointing out that the more technology advances, the more the risk increases that responsibility for a certain act can no longer be assigned to a responsible agent.[686] Subsequently, the author discusses the possible agency of androids, a topic that is not unfamiliar to Jewish

---

682. Nevins, "Halakhic Responses to Artificial Intelligence and Autonomous Machines," 15. Emphasis original.

683. Nevins, "Halakhic Responses to Artificial Intelligence and Autonomous Machines," 15. Emphasis original.

684. Nevins, "Halakhic Responses to Artificial Intelligence and Autonomous Machines," 15.

685. See Nevins, "Halakhic Responses to Artificial Intelligence and Autonomous Machines," 17–21. In this context, Nevins turns to other related issues that are not in the direct focus of my question here, such as the trolley problem.

686. See Nevins, "Halakhic Responses to Artificial Intelligence and Autonomous Machines," 27–29.

reasoning because of the Golem tradition. Nevins finds that even though the Golem did resemble a human, this "did not secure equal status. A *golem* was not born, it lacked speech and creative capacity, and therefore it could be useful, but it could not sanctify God."[687] Therefore, it cannot have the same status as humans.

Having cleared the halachic ground, Nevins then draws his conclusions, thereby directly addressing autoregulation in weapons technology, where he argues against the deployment of such technology when targeting humans. His main concern is, in line with the argumentation presented above, a possible responsibility gap. Most interesting, however, is that Nevins in his final judgment turns away from the responsibility argument and introduces the argument that nonlethal means must be used if possible, referring to the story of David sparing the life of King Saul (1 Sam 24:26). According to Maimonides, even if being attacked, the "defender who kills an attacker when non-lethal options are available is liable for the death."[688]

Nevins's responses are insightful because he does not discuss autoregulation in weapons technology separately but integrates the topic into a broader halachic discussion of technology. This is important because the question of whether an autoregulative entity can have agency to a certain degree or not is also important for the question of how responsibility can be attributed. Jewish traditions offer an interesting perspective, as the questions of whether animated and unanimated nonhuman entities can be considered to be agents of some sort has been asked over and over through the course of time. The discussions show that responsibility is the core these discussions revolve around. Moreover, even if Nevins touches on this topic only briefly and without explaining any deeper halachic meaning, the necessity of using violence nonlethally is also a concern that has to be considered.

Rabbi Michael Abraham approaches the topic from another perspective. In 2018, he was asked by a questioner whether rabbinical authorities are aware of the new developments within military technology that might lead to the deployment of autoregulation in weapons technology (within the Israeli army) and how he assesses this issue. When answering, Abraham unambiguously approved of this development

---

687. Nevins, "Halakhic Responses to Artificial Intelligence and Autonomous Machines," 34.

688. Nevins, "Halakhic Responses to Artificial Intelligence and Autonomous Machines," 41.

within autoregulative weaponry, arguing that it will save the lives of "our soldiers" (חיילנו) and that "the chance of an error by him [the robot] is much smaller than the chance of an error by the human."[689]

He also argues that it is not self-evident that the lives of the innocent (חפים) need to be spared while the soldiers' lives can be jeopardized, as this needs to be assessed with respect to the overall situation. Furthermore, he holds that the responsibility for the machine must stay with the programmer and the commander.[690] In another contribution on the same topic, Abraham argues that from an ethical standpoint, there does not seem to be a difference between a human's and a machine's decision: Both could fail, and both have advantages and disadvantages. Ultimately, however, the autonomous machine might mean an improvement in weapons technology.[691] Unfortunately, he does not give any halachic or traditional explanation for his opinion.

5.4 CONCLUSION

My reconstruction of peace ethics shows several insights and problems that accompany the respective approaches. In this section, I will summarize my findings and draw conclusions thereof. The main objective is to gain an overview of the cogency of the approaches presented and, at the same time, point to the questions that need to be addressed when assessing autoregulative functions in weapons systems ethically. For that reason, I will first address the results I obtain from discussing the ethical conceptions in general, each in turn, before I turn to specific conclusions I draw for autoregulation in weapons systems here.

First, and with respect to the concepts scrutinized within absolute pacifist thought, those ideas share the rationale that peaceful, nonviolent means should be preferred individually and politically, meaning primarily that this paradigm takes the idea of a peaceful world community seriously. This entails that absolute pacifist authors consider questions of war and peace methodically from a pacifist perspective. Referring to Holmes, this entails that war is always morally wrong and that the meaning, idea, and implications of peace are scrutinized rather than the concept of war. Consequently, peace is the paramount perspective, so this

---

689. Abraham, "Q & A" (Hebrew). My translation.
690. See Abraham, "Q & A." My translation.
691. See Abraham, "On Fear of Technology" (Hebrew).

paradigm addresses questions of peace, such as: What does peace mean? What does it entail? Under which circumstances can peace flourish? As Fox demonstrates, it is possible and useful to assess questions of violence within such a pacifist frame. However, giving preference to peace means scrutinizing first and foremost what enables peace, and only within this scope can the question of circumstances that might necessitate the use of force be considered—and negated. This concurrently entails that absolute pacifism is reluctant to accept the ongoing technological shift in military technology. Fox, Holmes, and the Protestant Church of Baden explicitly refer to this ongoing process and deem it problematic. In other words, none of these technologies is expected to make the world a better place from a pacifist stance, including autoregulation in weapons technology.

Another important thought revolves around the imaginaries and narratives, meaning that implicitly, and in the case of Butler also explicitly, the authors assume that the social sphere and its mechanism is built upon well-established social practices and imaginaries, which can be either peaceful or violent. Moreover, these imaginaries can be transformed. This is either done with reference to educating individuals in nonviolent means or practicing (self-)awareness, which in turn emanates into society. This notion is important because the shift from a war paradigm to a peace paradigm can only make sense if this is true and the underlying social imaginaries can be transformed. Combining this thought with the ongoing technological shift means that the question of the sense in which imaginaries and narratives about (weaponized) technologies shape the way we perceive war and its means arises. If such technologies are depicted in a way that suggests that war can be fought more securely and with fewer lives claimed than traditional warfare, the deployment of such technology seems only reasonable. If, however, such technologies are described in a way that creates a climate of fear, such as in the Terminator motif, a preemptive ban seems much more consistent. Here, a closer look to the (reasonably expectable) possibilities might serve to critically evaluate such narratives.

Some problems, however, have also materialized. One major problem within the approaches scrutinized is the tremendous gap between the large-scale political and institutional level of pacifism and the individual, small-scale dimension—an issue all of the analyzed approaches share. The authors succeed in demonstrating that the individual should live in peace with themselves and their surroundings and then make a more or less strong attempt to transfer this thought to the political sphere, but ultimately fail to explain how these two different approaches interact. Holmes even negates the benefit of a collective approach entirely.[692] To put it differently, it might be feasible to achieve inner peace and peace with the neighbor, but this does not naturally entail that peace is achievable to the same degree and by the same means as peace on a political and societal scale. This pertains to the question of how ethics relates to individuals and society alike. The point is that ethical questions can be addressed from both perspectives: the individual's standpoint and a societal angle, which usually also entails the question of juridical scale.[693] Yet, both perspectives cannot be separated from each other, meaning that social structures form the foundation for the individual's decision and deeds, while the individual's standpoint and actions likewise shape societal structures. In modern societies in particular, the awareness of the determining character of the societal frame rises, so addressing individual behavior in matters of societal scale might not be sufficient.[694] This rather general insight also pertains to the question of ethics discussed here. It might not be sufficient to request that individuals live peacefully with one another or to educate them in matters of peace. To the degree that juridical questions and issues of international concern are addressed, social and political dimensions need to be considered as well.[695] To some degree, the notions of Butler and Hauerwas might alleviate this problem for different reasons. In the case of Butler, the way Butler introduces social imaginaries seems to indicate that individuals have a share in the imaginaries of a society and vice versa. But as I demonstrated above, the link between both perspectives is rather loose and needs further conceptualization.[696] In the case of Hauerwas, this is because his account aims noticeably at a medium-scale approach focusing on the church. Here, however, it is not sufficiently clear how the church relates to the

---

692. See 5.1.3.2 Noninstitutional Conceptions.

693. See Reuter, "Grundlagen und Methoden der Ethik," 18–19. Reuter illustrates this point with reference to abortion, describing that, in that case, the pregnant person is addressed on an individual scale, while society needs to deal with this issue by finding juridical procedures pertaining to all members of society.

694. See Meireis, *Ethik des Sozialen*, 268.

695. I am aware that this remark does not answer the question of how the individual and societal spheres interrelate to any sufficient extent. But, since this piece of work revolves around the matter of autoregulation in weapons technology, this brief comment at least addresses the tremendous problems absolute pacifist accounts need to face.

696. See 5.1.3.2 Noninstitutional Conceptions.

An Ethical Evaluation of Lethal Functions in Autoregulative Weapons Systems

political realm when asking questions of international relevance, such as arms control. This is because the answer for such modern political questions exceeds not only individuals but also particular communities and therefore cannot be answered simply by following the example of Christ. This pertains also to the international debate on autoregulation in weapons systems, since individuals do not discuss issues of international concern legitimately. It is unclear whether the possibility of addressing the development and deployment of new weapons technology at all from an individual standpoint exists.

Alongside this conceptual issue, the problem of how to define peace stands out. Fox and Hauerwas in particular, but to a minor degree and with respect to (non-)violence also Butler, share the thought that positive peace is hard to define because its final state is difficult to delineate. Even though this might be true, it becomes precarious when an already established or desirable objective is to be defined: Here, it seems necessary to come to at least a rough conceptualization of what peace entails.

These objections suggest that absolute pacifist theories offer a cogent perspective, such as addressing matters of peace within a pacifist frame, which means to commence the conceptualization with peace and to put the focus on peaceful means. By the same token, the narratives that shape our common worlds of life might be decisive, so the question of whether these narratives are peaceful or violent in nature might not simply be a peripheral issue. However, simply rejecting the use of force under all circumstances, entailing every kind of weapons technology, seems neither convincing in a violent scenario[697] nor suitable for an ethical assessment of new weapons technology.

Second, and concerning just war thinking, this paradigm might offer an alternative, as it aims to confine violence by finding criteria of when and how to conduct war and asking to what extent war can contribute to peace. The cogency of the approach rests on the idea that in order to achieve peace, violent means need to be confined and deployed in a way that enables peaceful outcomes. All of the proposals introduced share this objective but do so on different terms. The most important and fundamental difference relates to the issue of whether war is "a world apart."[698] While traditional just war thinking underscores the separation

---

697. I follow the insight of just war thinking that nonviolent resistance might in some cases mean suicide rather than resistance. See 5.2.2.1 The Revival of the Just War Tradition.

698. Walzer, *Just and Unjust Wars*, 3.

of ordinary, civic moral circumstances and reasoning, revisionist just war tradition does not support such a division. This also makes for different results: If war and ordinary life are thought of as consistent with each other, this means that ordinary situations and morality can be applied to warfare, hence the individual is liable for their deeds and needs to be treated as such. This entails that soldiers cannot simply be targeted legitimately via their status but are only legitimate targets to the extent that they as individuals have supported this specific unjust war, be it by engaging in it with a weapon or inciting others to do so. Moreover, revisionist thinkers highlight that soldiers fight for several reasons, including deception by their government or haven enlisted in times of peace. The same is expected to hold true for civilians, depending on their involvement in acts of war and violence, when producing and broadcasting propaganda, developing and disseminating weaponry, or declaring war. Accordingly, the demarcation between just and unjust targets shift to individual contributions and personal responsibility is reiterated. On the opposite side, if warfare and ordinary life are seen as different in essence, they are governed by different moral codes: Since the single soldier becomes part of a collective, they lose some of their individual rights and duties. This entails them becoming legitimate targets via their status within a certain socially constructed and morally governed collective and being entitled to kill other soldiers according to the same rationale. Accordingly, *jus ad bellum* and *jus in bello* need to be treated separately in line with traditional just war thinking, since *jus ad bellum* is still under the ruling of ordinary life circumstances, which means that politicians decide whether to resort to war, and they do so by following civic rules and morality. The conduct of war, on the other hand, takes place in quite a different social context, which is warfare, and soldiers who did not get the chance to decide over it still have to fight within this context. The only thing left for them is to do so morally, which means following *jus in bello*.

Furthermore, this basic difference between traditional and revisionist approaches also leads to a divergent assessment of the individual and their responsibility. Seth Lazar and Laura Valentini have suggested that the difference can be described as political, on the one hand, and individual, on the other hand.[699] While political approaches, such as traditional approaches toward just war, underscore the importance of institutions

---

699. See Lazar and Valentini, "Proxy Battles in Just War Theory."

as compared with individuals, individual approaches put the emphasis on the single person. In doing so, however, they might not utterly be at variance with each other. Lazar and Valentini write,

> Political just war theorists might develop the most plausible account of the institutional norms governing war; non-political just war theorists might develop the most plausible account of our interpersonal moral duties; but their proposals would not strictly compete, because each presupposes an approach to the site of normative theorizing about war that the others reject.[700]

What is meant is that the differences about the status of combatants and noncombatants mainly occur because different presuppositions are made. Therefore, in order to cope with the apparent differences, it is useful to tackle the issues behind these disputes. Against this backdrop, the major conflict is an anthropological one, namely the question of whether humans are to be seen mainly as morally independent entities, having moral rights and duties and being completely responsible for their deeds, or if humans are mainly socially inclined and therefore moral norms are institutionalized politically within a certain community, so systems and communities share responsibility. This issue gives rise to the same question absolute pacifist approaches bring to the fore, namely how the individual relates to society and if issues of individual relevance can be transferred offhandedly to questions of societal concern. Again, this is not the place to tackle this question; I rather hint at this imbalance within just war approaches.

Besides, Lazar and Fabre brought to attention the difference between traditionalists and revisionists concerning self-defense.[701] While traditional just war thinking considers self-defense to be a legitimate reason to resort to war per se, Rodin contests that view—and most of the revisionist thinkers adopt his stance.[702] Rodin's critique that national self-defense cannot simply be deduced from personal self-defense, neither by analogy nor by reduction, presupposes that nations do not coincide with communities and that they do not naturally share the same identity markers. A nation, therefore, is not entangled with another nation in the same way as people are entangled with one another. Consequently, another institution would need to decide whether or not to resort to war. Moreover,

---

700. Lazar and Valentini, "Proxy Battles in Just War Theory."
701. See Fabre and Lazar, *Morality of Defensive War*, 3.
702. See 5.2.2.2 Revisionist Just War Thinking.

concerning the extent to which Rodin stresses the value of individual human rights, private persons play the most decisive role and the previously illuminated opposition between political structures and individuals emerges.

A major problem within this paradigm, however, is the tacit assumption that war constitutes an integral part of the social sphere. Traditional just war approaches in particular take the occurrence of war and violence for granted and for that reason refuse nonviolent means.[703] While I agree with Walzer that nonviolent resistance might not be appropriate in every situation and hinges essentially on the previously established immunity of noncombatants, I doubt that violent means enable peaceful outcomes. Here, the insight of pacifist approaches that peace can only be achieved peacefully seems rather convincing. To put it bluntly, to delineate criteria for fighting war justly is nowhere near to making warfare just—or even promoting justice and peace. With respect to autoregulation in weapons technology, a just war paradigm leads first to the question of whether these weapons can meet the criteria of *jus in bello*, such as discrimination and proportionality. Depending on this estimation, such weaponry will either be favored or refused. Yet, the question of what the deployment of such weaponry entails for achieving peace is not considered, just like the implications of deploying such weaponry for a certain society. Against this backdrop, it is therefore reasonable to strike a balance between the pacifist and just war approaches, considering the respective advantages.

Third, contingent Pacificist theories provide such a perspective. Being located between utter condemnation and justification of violence, a contingent pacifist viewpoint primarily changes the focus from questions of security and war to peace while at the same time considering the use of force under certain circumstances to be the lesser evil. Moreover, it raises the question of which basic assumptions accompany violent means. Therefore, a contingent pacifist point of view commences with questions of peace and, in a second step, assesses violent means from that perspective.

Historically reviewing the idea of *bellum iustum*[704] demonstrates that the intention of just war has been to confine violence, and it has therefore been adopted to the respective situations. In our current time, this means that just war tradition merges into concepts that seek to secure peace

---

703. See Walzer, *Just and Unjust Wars*, 329–34; 5.2.2.1 The Revival of the Just War Tradition.

704. See 3.2.1 *Bellum iustum*: History of Ideas.

politically, such as the system of collective security institutionalized in the political bodies of the UN. This also entails that peace is secured by means of law rather than by means of war. Taking into account the aims of confining violence and establishing and securing peace, the assumption that war and violent means can ever be justified—as the term "just war" suggests—is questioned. Therefore, reestablishing the ideas of *bellum iustum* in terms of the contingent pacifist idea of just peace, which includes a concept of law-sustaining force, seems to grasp the development within philosophy and political thinking correctly.[705]

With respect to autoregulation in weapons technology, this means that the question just war thinking asks, namely whether and to what degree this kind of weapons technology can be used within the frame of just war thinking by applying the single criteria of *jus in bello* as codified in IHL, changes. The center of focus is now the question of whether this kind of weapons technology can be expected to promote the establishment of sustaining peace and to what extent. Within a contingent pacifist framework, the emphasis is put on establishing just legal structures that in turn might enable sustaining peace. In that respect, issues such as whether or not these weapons will make it more difficult to reconcile in the aftermath of an armed conflict come to the fore. If expressed in terms of *bellum iustum*, the center of attention becomes *jus post bellum*, a dimension poorly addressed within the ongoing debate.[706] I will elaborate on this topic below in greater detail.[707] Here, it suffices to say that reconciliation in the aftermath of an armed conflict might be easier to achieve if autoregulation in weapons systems caused lesser harm, as the proponents argue. Yet, it might make reconciliation more difficult if these weapons engendered more harm, be it in terms of gaps in or diffusion of responsibility,[708] the lack of human agency,[709] the violation of human dignity,[710] or the risk inherent in such technologies.[711] Issues such

---

705. See also 5.3.1 Preliminaries.

706. See Koch and Rinke, *Ethische Fragestellungen*, 38.

707. See 6.3 Finding Just Peace after Violence.

708. With respect to responsibility gaps, see Sparrow, "Killer Robots." This must not be confused with the idea of responsibility diffusion. See also 6.5 Gaps or Diffusion of Responsibility.

709. See Leveringhaus, *Ethics and Autonomous Weapons*, 89–118.

710. See Asaro, "On Banning Autonomous Weapon Systems."

711. See, with respect to drones, Reuter, "Kampfdrohnen als Mittel rechtswahrender militärischer Gewalt?"; 6.4 Redistributing Risk.

as the possibility of reconciling in the aftermath of an armed conflict need to be addressed when assessing the deployment of autoregulation within a contingent pacifist frame. This is even more plausible when the reframing of traditional just war theory in terms of its revision and the overlap with the concept of just policing is considered.

Another advantage of contingent pacifism, and especially just peace thinking, is the way peace is defined and conceptualized. This concept gains its cogency from an eschatological account, meaning that the objective pursued is a kind of wholesale peace described in Scripture and utopian in nature. This utopic objective makes apparent a multidimensional peace process where peace and justice interrelate and peace is understood to be a process of ever more justice, while justice is based on peaceful structures.[712] In giving such a processual definition, peace is not defined in a strict sense but rather delineated, so it is open to a final state, as absolute pacifism demands. At the same time at least a rough account is given, so more explicit objectives, such as the rejection of violence, the promotion of freedom and cultural diversity, and the alleviation of want can be derived.[713]

Since the Christian churches developed their account of just peace interrelatedly, the teaching of the Protestant and Roman Catholic sources are very similar in nature. In their reorientation, both Christian churches, as well as the World Council of Churches, move away from just war thinking and focus on just peace theory. Alexander Merkl traces this development with regard to the Roman Catholic church within the papal encyclicals and with a special focus on the encyclical *Fratelli tutti* from 2020, where Pope Francis demands, "Never again war!"[714] According to Merkl, this encyclical is in line with Pope Francis's other contributions, as well as with popes prior to him who paved the way to turn away from just war thinking toward a peace-through-law account.[715] Moreover, the shift

---

712. See Reuter, "Was ist gerechter Friede? Die Sicht der christlichen Ethik," 15.

713. See EKD, "Live from God's Peace," 80.

714. Pope Francis, "*Fratelli tutti*," 258.

715. Here, the author refers to Justenhoven, whose work needs to be mentioned when discussing Roman Catholic peace thought. Justenhoven especially emphasizes this turn toward legal regulations. See Justenhoven, "Friede durch Recht." Ultimately, Merkl draws the conclusion that *Fratelli tutti*, in line with other papal contributions, does indicate an even more radical shift within Roman Catholic peace thought, but its realignment is still expected. See Merkl, "Das 'trügerische Gespenst des Krieges.'"

to just peace thinking is also an ecumenical one endorsed by the World Council of Churches.[716]

However, the aforementioned theoretical lack within absolute pacifism and just war—meaning the question of how individual and societal approaches interrelate—becomes apparent also with respect to contingent pacifism, especially if their overlap with other, similar approaches such as revisionist just war thinking is taken into account.[717] May, for instance, follows McMahan in his assumptions, thereby adopting the emphasis on individuals, which in turn leaves open the question of how the relation between individual and community is balanced out.[718] If this is taken into account, the differentiation between legitimate and illegitimate targets becomes much more serious individually—and morally riskier. It is beyond the scope of this book to elaborate on that topic in detail. Yet, I hint at the necessity of striking a balance between both approaches, as ethical problems cannot be solved by individuals only, simply because the individual is bound to a societal and legal frame.[719] Therefore, juridical and ethical questions need to find a middle ground.[720] This pertains especially to the question of how legalist paradigms, such as classical just war thinking, and moral ideas, such as revisionist just war approaches, might strike a balance. The peace memorandum of the Protestant church in Germany argues in that regard that "ethics can no more replace law than law replace ethics. Even international law cannot replace peace ethics; rather, any peace ethics must always be brought to bear on international law."[721] Accordingly, such a close relatedness of law and ethics might be a possible solution for redressing the imbalance between either collective law or individual morality. This issue pertains to my question because the shift to the individual has implications for discussing autoregulation in weapons systems. The compliance of autoregulative functions in weapons systems with the ruling of IHL, such as discrimination and proportionality, is already highly contested. Yet, if these norms become even more individualized, it seems likewise ambitious to solve the problem technologically.[722]

716. See Justenhoven, "Concept of Just War," 67.

717. See 5.3.1. Preliminaries.

718. See 5.3.2 On Larry May's Concept of Contingent Pacifism.

719. See Meireis, *Ethik des Sozialen*, 268; Reuter, "Grundlagen und Methoden der Ethik," 18–19.

720. See EKD, "Live from God's Peace," 85.

721. EKD, "Live from God's Peace," 85.

722. See 3.3 Reckoning and Judgment.

A related problem becomes apparent in Bonhoeffer's thinking, when Bonhoeffer builds his concept on the individual's inclination or need for peace and interrelatedness, but at the same time seems to take the idea of resistance from last resort within (collective) just war thinking. Yet, this individual decision to resist is then necessarily applied in a political way, since to resist against a certain political government violently is per se political rather than individual. Bonhoeffer expresses this in the theological term "guilt," respective of the individual's willingness to become guilty (*Schuldübernahme*) when resorting to violence. I interpret Bonhoeffer to refer with this term to the same phenomenon May describes as moral risk.[723] Yet, the theological term exceeds the philosophical concept of risk and gains a transcendental perspective with two main implications. First—and this is important to underscore in this context—there is an individual who can incur guilt, who burdens their conscience when resorting to violence. Second, a way to deal with this heavy burden is offered without simply and carelessly appeasing the conscience, as the excuse for such an undertaking is granted by God alone and is therefore precarious from a solely immanent perspective.[724] An open question, however, is to what degree political processes and responsibility can be rephrased in terms of personal guilt.

Linked to this issue is the question of which relation law and violence bear, or more precisely to what extent resisting violence can be located outside the realm of the law. In that regard, just peace thinking emphasizes the nexus between peace and law: Only to the extent that just juridical structures evolve can peace as a process be facilitated. Yet, there might not be a genuine contradiction here because if law and justice form the foundation for a certain political order, there is no need to resist against such an order. Only if the law does not meet the standard of justice might (violent) resistance become a means to react to that distortion. This is again in line with just peace thinking. To stand outside the realm of the law in resistance therefore refers to a positive law that is not just in nature. Yet again, the question of whether this thought can be transferred to a political collective arises, as the theory of law-abiding force necessarily assumes.[725]

---

723. See 5.3.2 On Larry May's Concept of Contingent Pacifism.

724. See 5.3.3.1 On Bonhoeffer's Account of War and Peace.

725. In that context, Bonhoeffer draws a differentiation between safety/security, on the one hand, and peace on the other hand. In his view, the quest for safety/security carries mistrust in its wake, which finally engenders war. Even though Bonhoeffer does not

An Ethical Evaluation of Lethal Functions in Autoregulative Weapons Systems

One final remark is necessary, though, due to the political developments regarding the Russian attack on Ukraine in February 2022, which lead to intense discussion within peace ethics, especially within just peace theory. It seems clear to me that the attack does not question just peace thinking in general, but rather the criteria of just peace, including a nation's ability of defend itself and its citizens.[726] The recent debates rather provide insight into the compromise just peace thinking provides when resorting to both absolute pacifism and just war theory, as both interpretations become apparent in the recent discussions.[727] I will not comment on that debate here, but rather emphasize that the reality of war does not change the long-standing and normative objective of striving for just peace, even though it might entail the need to reconsider the political and international framework,[728] an issue that did not only became apparent on February 24, 2022.

Fourth, the excursus toward halachic approaches also discussed here points to a variety of implications regarding autoregulation in weapons technology. Chief among them is the subject of responsibility, which has been brought into consideration by Berman and Nevins. Both authors highlight the possibility that this kind of weaponry will cause problems when responsibility is to be assigned. Berman illustrates the issue with the story of David, who denies his responsibility for the death for Uriah through his saying of the sword devouring. In a similar way, Berman underscores the lack of consciousness and conscience within machines, which entails that they would not refuse for reasons of conscience to follow an order given.

Moreover, and with respect to the idea of self-defense, the rule to harm somebody nonviolently if possible is to be considered. This is even more important since violence does not pose any threat to a technological device. Only in cases where the overall situation makes it crystal clear that the attacker is in fact the attacker and therefore can be targeted (lethally) would an autoregulative device be allowed to target this person. If so, it still preferably needs to do this without lethal force. The main

---

elaborate on this idea in detail, this thought seems central for the question of whether just war thinking within a security political framework can meet the demands of peace. If Bonhoeffer is right, then the striving for peace in terms of security is precarious from the beginning. I cannot follow this thread here, unfortunately, but only point to this.

726. See Reuter, "Der internationale Rechtsfrieden zwischen Realismus und Idealismus," 153.

727. As can be seen in the debates within "Zeitzeichen" in March, April, and May 2022. I also depict these debates briefly above. See 5.3.1 Preliminaries.

728. See Daase et al., "Frieden am Ende?"

problem here, however, is the technological issue that machines, however well developed, lack the capability to assess and judge a situation, so the inherent risk of an unintended outcome is likely to happen. Here, I especially disagree with the assessment of Michael Abraham because I deem his standpoint to be too optimistic in that regard.

Generally, however, my brief discussion of Jewish-halachic contributions served to show that the difference between contingent pacifism, such as in just peace theory and the Jewish approaches discussed here, might not be too sharp. Both suggestions emphasize the meaning of peace and that, first and foremost, peaceful solutions are to be favored. Resorting to violence is only possible at all in cases where peaceful approaches are not successful. This does not mean that both approaches share the very same reasoning and ideas: The long tradition of just war thinking in particular has deeply shaped just peace thinking, while Jewish approaches are not bound to this kind of tradition. Moreover, since Jewish (and Christian) approaches abound, this surely does not count for all contributions. However, the main goal to put peace first can be inferred from both approaches, especially when the utopic character of peace thinking within Jewish literature is considered. This is even more important when taking into account the fact that that ideas such as *peace through law* can be traced through a long-rooted history within Jewish traditions. The open question of whether the eschatological and utopic character of such an account might help or hinder actual political solutions is a question worthy of discussion among religions and might, in my opinion, facilitate and motivate peaceful approaches.

Ultimately, the results discussed indicate that the so-far underrepresented perspective of contingent pacifism qualifies for assessing autoregulation in weapons systems technology for several reasons. First, it opens up a new perspective within the ongoing debate, which so far focuses mainly on just war thinking[729] if the devices are considered at all within a peace ethical frame.[730] Moreover, contingent pacifism grasps the intent of philosophical approaches such as revisionist just war theory, political concepts such as R2P, and theological ideas such as just peace

---

729. See, explicitly, Leveringhaus, *Ethics and Autonomous Weapons* and Horowitz, "The Ethics and Morality of Robotic Warfare," as well as implicitly in Statman "Drones and Robots," or with respect to IHL in Scharre, *Army of None*, 251–70.

730. Especially the consideration of responsibility is not explicitly linked to a violent scenario and can therefore be reconstructed within a technological ethical framework alone.

theory and also the ethical-halachic approach, which is to confine violence, thereby shifting the viewpoint toward peace and casting doubt on the classical approaches to war and security.[731] If this is correct, the idea of just peace, even if rooted in a Christian and therefore particular background, might be transferred to other philosophical or political contexts, as well as it is surely influenced thereby. In other words, Just peace theory is the Christian reaction to and rephrasing of political and philosophical insights over the recent decades and, in doing so, it might inform these concepts as well. With that said, I proceed with the assumption that theology is public in nature, adopting the stance of critical public theology. This paradigm holds that the church and its theology are in a mutual relationship to the public sphere and that theological concepts serve the purpose of reflecting and accompanying public discussions critically.[732] Therefore, contingent pacifism—or more explicitly just peace theory—is a perspective worthy of investigation with respect to autoregulation in weapons systems. This is because it enables a different viewpoint, which primarily means that the essential ethical question is whether and to what degree autoregulative weapons systems can contribute to peace. This overall perspective keeps an eye on the objective of contingent pacifism, which is to overcome violent theaters and move to situations of peace.

My account will therefore focus in the following on some key ethical points that have come to the fore, such as risk and responsibility, and address these issues from a contingent pacifist stance.

---

731. This does not mean that these pacifist-oriented paradigms gain more weight than paradigms that refer to traditional just war tradition, as Reuter illustrates with respect to both realism—instantiated with the theory of the political scientist Carlo Masala—and idealism. See Reuter, "Der internationale Rechtsfrieden." The major strand of security policy seems particularly to retain the classical approach. Yet, the discussed concepts challenge the classical view and can therefore change the way political reality is perceived and might, in the long run, change the given social practices.

732. See Meireis, "Berliner Realismus"; Meireis, "Evangelische Orientierung im öffentlichen Raum."

6

Violence Without Guilt

Transferring the Decision Between Life and Death to Machines

THE ETHICAL IMPLICATIONS OF autoregulation in weapons systems have been discussed now for over ten years. Ronald C. Arkin proposed his ideas on that topic as early as 2009. From then, the discourse emerged mainly politically and juridically but also ethically. This chapter serves to bring together the findings of the theological, technological, and philosophical insights regarding autoregulative weaponry gained in the preceding chapters. This means that I will not consider just some isolated technological device but take the human–machine collaboration in its projected context (i.e., the solution of conflict) into account from a peace ethical perspective. This is because the technological device always and necessarily depends on humans and their forms of life, be it in terms of data or with respect to the objective of a certain joint action. Therefore, the terminological stress of the subject in question is put on the *system* in autoregulative weapons systems. Or, even more precisely, the issue it comes down to is the (lethal) autoregulative function within a weaponized human–machine system. This is because the system is not devoid of humans: This is clear when the human part(s) of the collaboration still work together with the system in real time, as proposed in FCAS, while this collaboration is rather concealed in a system where the weapon ostensibly operates on its own, as in Super aEgis II. It is nevertheless still humans who provide the necessary data to train the algorithm, and it is humans who determine the objective, which is, in the case of weapons systems, to kill. Therefore, humans are still in place even in such cases, though not in real time.

As for peace ethics, my reconstruction of the ongoing peace ethical discourse has shown that perspectives of contingent pacifism—or, in terms of just war reasoning, stances that approach autoregulative functions in weapons systems from a *jus post bellum*—are currently underrepresented. This constitutes not only some sort of academic lacuna but also an eminent political and moral problem. The theological just peace perspective I am following here starts from the assumption that it is necessary to first prioritize nonviolent means of conflict resolution and, in the case of an unavoidable use of force, to focus on the establishment of a just and sustaining peace, which has consequences for the way force is applied. The main question is, then, whether this specific technology might even prevent nonviolent conflict resolution by encouraging the use of force or impeding peace processes in the aftermath of a violent conflict. If this is the case, and my study indicates that it is, deploying autoregulative functions in weapons systems is better refrained from. This, however, must not mean that every form of autoregulation is inherently problematic. I rather suggest that the decisive feature might be human control: If humans are in control of the overall system, there might be clear-cut situations where deploying an autoregulative function is feasible. The following chapter will address these issues in greater detail.

Yet, before presenting my own approach, I will briefly introduce the main features of the legal discussion (6.1) and summarize the ethical arguments made so far within the ongoing debate (6.2). My own argument then consists of three major points, which I discuss from a contingent pacifist stance. In terms of just war thinking, this means to relate questions of *jus in bello* to those of *jus post bellum* and even *jus ad bellum*, arguing that the deployment of autoregulative weapons (*jus in bello*) might be at odds with the general prohibition of warfare as stated in the UN Charter (*jus ad bellum*) and with the question of peace building (*jus post bellum*) (6.3). I will first argue that the risk an autoregulative weapons system promises to mitigate is made at the expense of inflicting harm, especially to civilians (6.4). I will then turn to the crucial question of responsibility, thereby mainly discussing whether and to what degree gaps in responsibility occur, arguing that legal responsibility needs to be addressed in terms of diffusion, while morally a gap might indeed occur if no control of the system is maintained (6.5). The implications of this problem become even more severe if put in theological terms. Along the lines of Bonhoeffer's ethics, I will argue that autoregulative functions might serve as a means to eschew responsibility and are therefore deeply troubling for theological ethical reasons, as they might even serve to let violent, warlike aggression appear as a morally unproblematic and feasible option (6.6).

6.1 LEGAL FRAMEWORK

Next to political and ethical considerations, it is mainly legal considerations that form the foundation for the current scholarly debate on autoregulated functions in weaponry. This is because, with regard to autoregulative functions, legal problems stand out in particular, since one of the major questions concerns the extent to which such a device could meet the demands of existing law[1] and who, in the case of failure, would be held accountable. The question here reads, "If a machine's actions amount to war crimes or other breaches of a norm of international law, who can be held responsible, and according to which regime?"[2] For that matter, the political debate revolves mainly around the establishment of a new arms control regime. Within this debate, the focus is primarily on military uses; other kinds of uses such as deployment by the police are disregarded.[3] Since it is not the aim of this ethical scrutiny to explicitly discuss the legal implications in detail, I will only outline the most important legal problems currently discussed. I nevertheless mention this discourse here because ethics and morality are closely connected to law,[4] a connection particularly obvious in the ethical assumptions encapsulated in IHL.[5]

---

1. See Geiß, "Autonome Waffensysteme," 44.
2. Geiß and Lahmann, "Autonomous Weapons Systems," 375.
3. The reason for this might be that the political debate currently takes place within the UN and therefore domestic issues are subordinated. However, violent uses of autoregulated functions are not taken into account within academic literature either, which is problematic all in itself and not just from a just peace perspective, as lethal autoregulative weaponry is drifting into police work as well.
4. See Huber, *Gerechtigkeit und Recht*, 127.
5. IHL is a collection of different rules concerning armed conflict and mainly addressing issues of *jus in bello*. Its codification originates in the nineteenth century and the insight that modern means of warfare need legal containment. The most important legal collections are the Geneva Conventions and their Additional Protocols, as well as the Hague Conventions. See ICRC, "What Is International Humanitarian Law?"

Such assumptions are, for instance, the discrimination and proportionality principle. Since IHL is informed by just war reasoning, the juridical debate is connected to the ethical reasoning and vice versa, which implies that the ethical just war foundations of IHL may be challenged from a just peace perspective. That said, my objective here is to describe the discussion of autoregulative functions within weapons systems in the existing IHL framework.

The legal debate hinges on the question of to what extent autoregulative functions in weaponry appear to be a completely new phenomenon, which might turn out to be a game changer in the history of conflict and is therefore likely to alter the way force will be applied. If this is the case, existing laws such as IHL might not apply, at least not in their present form, because the law proceeds on the assumption that humans make decisions.[6] In this case, Article 36 of the Additional Protocols of the Geneva Conventions and the Martens Clause determine the decisive normative foundation. If, on the other hand, autoregulation is not inherently different from previous stages of automation and the existing legal framework is flexible enough to incorporate these new technologies, IHL applies.[7]

In order to show which legal norms are central to the current discourse limited to warfare, I will focus in the following on the legal framework of IHL, namely the Additional Protocols of the Geneva Conventions and the Martens Clause, as recorded in the preamble of the Hague Convention (II) with respect to the laws and customs of war on land. I will introduce each of them in turn, thereby illustrating their meaning and importance for the ongoing debate, before I turn to the question of accountability and draw a conclusion.

With respect to Additional Protocol I of the Geneva Conventions, three basic principles seem important,[8] which are the principles of distinction, proportionality, and precautions in attack. These precepts constitute a pivotal nexus between ethics and law because they are rooted in the tradition of just war reasoning. To date, it is an open question whether an autoregulative weapons system could (ever) comply with these principles. Perhaps even more importantly, this predominantly

---

6. See Geiß and Lahmann, "Autonomous Weapons Systems," 378–83, 399. With reference to Asaro, "On Banning Autonomous Weapons Systems."

7. See Reeves and Wallace, "Modern Weapons and the Law of Armed Conflict"; Marauhn, "Meaningful Human Control."

8. See Geiß, "Autonome Waffensysteme."

seems to be a technological question,[9] which is why I will point to some technological deliberations and limitations in the following.

First, the principle of distinction according to Protocol I, Article 51(2) reads,

> The civilian population as such, as well as individual civilians, shall not be the object of attack. Acts or threats of violence the primary purpose of which is to spread terror among the civilian population are prohibited.[10]

Here, IHL states that a civilian never represents a legitimate target, so the central question is whether an autoregulative device can distinguish between combatants and civilians. From a technological perspective, this is highly doubtful,[11] all the more so if dynamic scenarios that constitute modern warfare, such as asymmetry, denationalization, and the automatization of war[12] are taken into account. Especially in complex war zones, such as an urban area, the agent would need to decide according to the overall situation who is a combatant and who is a civilian. In such a situation, it would not suffice to notice who was holding a gun or wearing a special uniform because even a civilian might carry weapons on their person for reasons of self-defense, while a soldier might wear civilian clothes.[13] Under such circumstances, the system would need to assess the context of a situation, comprehend gestures and mimics, and infer from that whether the person in question represents a legitimate target. Of course, human soldiers face these kinds of problems too—and on top of that feel anger, fear, or bias and have to defend themselves. Nevertheless, there is no reason why machines should follow the same normative rules as humans, who unquestionably need to defend themselves. For that reason, it would make sense to apply IHL to an even higher moral standard when advanced technology is involved.[14] This, in turn, casts doubt on the overall appliance of customary law with regard to heavily automated technology, so it is not only questionable if an autoregulative device could comply with the principle of distinction in an actual war scenario but also if IHL principles would apply at all.

9. See Geiß and Lahmann, "Autonomous Weapons Systems," 395.
10. Protocol I additional to the Geneva Conventions, 52(2).
11. See Scharre, *Army of None*, 252–53.
12. See Münkler, *Die Neuen Kriege*, 10–11.
13. See Scharre, *Army of None*, 253–55.
14. See Geiß, "Autonome Waffensysteme," 46–47.

The second main standard is proportionality, stated in Protocol I, Article 51(5)(b) and Article 57(2)(iii):

> Among others, the following types of attacks are to be considered as indiscriminate: an attack which may be expected to cause incidental loss of civilian life, injury to civilians, damage to civilian objects, or a combination thereof, which would be excessive in relation to the concrete and direct military advantage anticipated.[15]
>
> With respect to attacks, the following precautions shall be taken: those who plan or decide upon an attack shall: refrain from deciding to launch any attack which may be expected to cause incidental loss of civilian life, injury to civilians, damage to civilian objects, or a combination thereof, which would be excessive in relation to the concrete and direct military advantage anticipated.[16]

The main idea of this principle is that the damage a weapon can entail as a side effect has to be proportional to its military benefits. To ponder such kinds of decisions assumes the character of a "judgment call"[17] rather than a decision based on clear evidence that could be computed. Since it is a highly complex decision, a machine might apparently help to determine the main parameters in order to make a rational decision. The issue, however, is that the overall context, based on values, needs to be considered and judged. The actual military benefit is usually not evaluated separately with respect to the single operative decision but has to be seen on a larger, tactical, and strategic level. This kind of assessment might be especially hard for a machine to make.[18]

Finally, the IHL states that precautions in attack have to be assured, according to Protocol I, Article 57(1):

> In the conduct of military operations, constant care shall be taken to spare the civilian population, civilians and civilian objects.[19]

That norm again emphasizes the necessity of sparing the lives and property of civilians, while it puts the focus on prior stages such as the planning of an attack and the development of a certain device. This entails

15. Protocol I additional to the Geneva conventions, 51(5)(b).
16. Protocol I additional to the Geneva conventions, 57(2)(iii).
17. Scharre, *Army of None*, 255.
18. See Geiß and Lahmann, "Autonomous Weapons Systems," 396–97.
19. Protocol I additional to the Geneva conventions, 57(1).

that the development of weaponry is already part of warfare and that it needs to be ensured that it will not harm civilians intentionally and by design[20]—an issue that is in itself troubling from a just peace perspective and shows why the *si vis pacem para bellum* principle of just war theory needs to be overcome in favor of a rationale of *si vis pacem para pacem*. This also entails securing that considerations made in the planning stage still apply in the moment they are performed.[21] This point raises the question of the extent to which an operator always has to stay in or on the loop in order to make sure that the weapon will not do something harmful in real time, especially if civilians are involved.[22]

In summary, all of the previously mentioned articles stress the importance of sparing the lives and property of civilians, so the primary issue with regard to autoregulative functions is whether a certain device would be able to, first, distinguish between civilians and combatants and, second, assess not only the whole operational context but also tactical and strategic implications. While some authors hold that an autoregulative weapon might even outperform a human in these situations,[23] others maintain the contrary.[24] The considerations presented so far in this book strongly point to the second conclusion.

In addition to the aforementioned principles of IHL, Article 36 of Additional Protocol I of the Geneva Conventions establishes a frame to review new technologies in weaponry.[25] It is supposed to oblige the contracting members to ensure that every newly developed technology is in line with the existing law. It reads as follows:

> In the study, development, acquisition or adoption of a new weapon, means or method of warfare, a High Contracting Party is under an obligation to determine whether its employment would, in some or all circumstances, be prohibited by this Protocol or by any other rule of international law applicable to the High Contracting Party.[26]

20. See Geiß and Lahmann, "Autonomous Weapons Systems," 395.
21. See Geiß and Lahmann, "Autonomous Weapons Systems," 397.
22. See Geiß, "Autonome Waffensysteme," 49–50.
23. See Arkin, "Governing Lethal Behavior"; Müller, "Autonomous Killer Robots Are Probably Good News."
24. See, for example, Sharkey, "Staying in the Loop."
25. Whether this article can be applied, though, hinges on the question of whether autoregulation in weaponry can indeed be seen to be a new phenomenon.
26. Protocol I additional to the Geneva Conventions, 36.

The contracting states do so by means of a weapons review.[27] This process, however, is not formalized, so the concrete means and measures of the protocol vary from state to state. In addition, only few states realize them at all, which means that the procedure faces fundamental problems in practice.[28] Furthermore, there are at least two issues regarding autoregulation. First, the complex technology needs to be understood and evaluated, which requires that the legal experts understand how the machine operates, on the one hand, and that the legal norms are implemented into the technology, on the other hand, so a translation process is necessary in both ways.[29] Second, a self-learning and -adapting system changes constantly, which means that, strictly speaking, new technology is involved every time a device "learns" something new, in which case a new review protocol would be necessary—which is hard to carry out.[30]

Yet another legal principle is indicated in the Martens Clause, which is a paragraph in the preamble of the Hague Conventions (II) referring to the laws and customs of war on land. It reads as follows:

> Until a more complete code of the laws of war is issued, the High Contracting Parties think it right to declare that in cases not included in the Regulations adopted by them, populations and belligerents remain under the protection and empire of the principles of international law, as they result from the usages established between civilized nations, from the laws of humanity and the requirements of the public conscience.[31]

The Martens Clause, however, would only apply if autoregulation in weapons systems could indeed be seen as a new phenomenon. If so, it might not so easily fall under the scope of the existing jurisdiction but would need to be evaluated according to "laws of humanity" and "requirements of the public conscience."[32] What that precisely means and to

---

27. See Ford, "International Humanitarian Law, Article 36, and Autonomous Weapons Systems," 82.

28. See Boulanin and Verbruggen, *Article 36 Reviews*, 1; Garcia, "Autonomous Weapon Systems and International Law," 105.

29. See Ford, "International Humanitarian Law, Article 36, and Autonomous Weapons Systems," 82; Boulanin and Verbruggen, *Article 36 Reviews*, 33.

30. See Ford, "International Humanitarian Law, Article 36, and Autonomous Weapons Systems," 82.

31. Convention (II) with Respect to the Laws and Customs of War on Land and its Annex, Preamble.

32. Convention (II) with Respect to the Laws and Customs of War on Land and its Annex, Preamble.

what extent it can be applied to various situations is highly contested.[33] Within the debate, however, the Martens Clause serves to indicate that a machine that is able to take lives without human control in real time does withstand "public conscience," though it is not clear whose conscience should be taken into account.[34] In order to establish this point, some polls have been conducted, which indicate that people share a common restraint against the use of autoregulation in weaponry.[35] But since the Martens Clause is vague in general and the conducted polls are not representative, it is hard to derive a general prohibition or permission thereof.

Another issue disputed with respect to law is the question of accountability. This question is huge, since, as Robert Sparrow argues, there might be a responsibility gap that would make the deployment of an autoregulated weapons system "unethical."[36] Even though the question of responsibility is also discussed within the field of ethics,[37] a major legal discussion exists in that regard. Robin Geiß and Henning Lahmann conclude that, at least from a legal point of view, responsibility might not be the central issue at stake. By establishing a regulation regime and necessary procedures, states could be held responsible for the deployment of an autoregulative weapon. The same would be true for individuals deploying such a device, though, as they point out, this might be more intricate to undertake.[38]

Taken together, the main legal factors relevant to the debate are the principles of distinction, proportionality, and precautions in attack founded in IHL. Geiß and Lahmann, however, have recently cast doubt on the issue of whether IHL is the right place to discuss this question because it addresses human beings in their overall human nature, involving human characteristics and responsibilities. From that perspective, it seems inherently wrong to ask whether the design of an autoregulative lethal weapon would be possible in compliance with existing law, simply because any kind of artifact or its design cannot be addressed as a

---

33. See Ticehurst, "Martens Clause and the Laws of Armed Conflict."
34. See Amoroso et al., "Autonomy in Weapons Systems," 33–34.
35. See, for example, Open Roboethics Initiative, "Ethics and Governance of Lethal Autonomous Weapons Systems"; Ipsos, "Global Survey Highlights Continued Opposition to Fully Autonomous Weapons."
36. Sparrow, "Killer Robots."
37. See 6.2 Revisiting the ethical discourse.
38. See Geiß and Lahmann, "Autonomous Weapons Systems," 385–94.

subject by the laws that currently exist. This does not mean that the guiding principles—meaning distinction, proportionality, and precautions of attack—are generally wrong or outdated, though. It rather means that a new balance needs to be struck that mirrors the actual circumstances that come along with the advent of autoregulation in warfare. In that case, a whole new legal framework might be necessary to deploy autoregulation, a framework that might even urge for higher standards than the actual IHL. For that reason, Geiß and Lahmann infer, IHL might not cover autoregulation and therefore human control needs to be exerted.[39] On the other hand, there are researchers who advise against the transfer of the concept of meaningful human control from the field of politics toward the law, which would entail that the legal corpus needs revision and extension. Thilo Marauhn, for instance, argues that the idea of exerting meaningful human control does not contribute something inherently new to the existing regulations, but "the inclusion of this concept runs the risk that it blurs some of the clarity included in the existing rules."[40] This is because even though the term has been an important driver of the political discussion, it turns out to be hard to define.[41] Moreover, the autoregulative system is not free of human influence and can thus rather be seen as the continuation of distancing humans from the actual battlefield.[42] In addition, as long as the technological device does not develop any free will, it cannot do anything intentionally and is therefore bound to human influence in programming.[43] Finally, Marauhn argues, the decisive criterion does not lay within any form of human control, but rather within the consideration of proportionality, which the machine cannot ensure.[44] For that matter, he concludes, "The law should not be changed, and the concept of meaningful human control should not become part of the law,"[45] even if he does admit that the term may play an important role outside the legal sphere.[46]

39. See Geiß and Lahmann, "Autonomous Weapons Systems."
40. Marauhn, "Meaningful Human Control," 217.
41. See Marauhn, "Meaningful Human Control," 212.
42. See Marauhn, "Meaningful Human Control," 214–15.
43. See Marauhn, "Meaningful Human Control," 215–16.
44. See Marauhn, "Meaningful Human Control," 216.
45. Marauhn, "Meaningful Human Control," 217.
46. See Marauhn, "Meaningful Human Control," 217.

Violence Without Guilt

Having sketched the legal framework for these discussions and having shown the problems it entails regarding lethal autoregulative functions in autoregulative weapons, I will now turn to the ethical considerations.

6.2 REVISITING THE ETHICAL DISCOURSE ON AUTOREGULATION IN WEAPONS SYSTEMS

As for the ethical discussion of autoregulation in weapons systems, there are two major viewpoints: While proponents of the technology argue in favor thereof, opponents advise strongly against their use, thereby mirroring the dystopic and utopic polarization of the general debate on digitization and automatization.[47] Arkin is the most influential figure in this debate, arguing for developing and deploying such kinds of weaponry. He not only brought forward the idea that autoregulation in weapons systems might help to make warfare safer, and therefore morally better, but also developed ideas to implement ethical procedures into machines.[48] That way, Arkin argues, harm might be prevented on both sides. Clearly, the physical and psychological health of the soldiers using such a device would benefit because they are simply no longer involved.[49] The lives of civilians might also be spared because the potentially overtired, revengeful, and frightened human is replaced by a system that is not distracted by its emotions and can compute far faster than humans. Moreover, such a device would not need to fear for its own life and shoot for reasons of self-defense.[50] The cogency of Arkin's approach depends on the ability to program moral procedures into machines, though.[51]

By the same token, the ethicist Vincent C. Müller holds that it might be more morally valid to deploy an autoregulative device than a human soldier, and they should therefore be embraced rather than banned. In a paper he wrote in 2016, Müller assesses the potential impact of autoregulative devices on the regulation of IHL, discussing discrimination and proportionality as well as the problem of responsibility. He draws the conclusion that

---

47. See Höhne, "Darf ich vorstellen," 25.
48. As I depicted in great detail in 3.7.2.1 Arkin's Artificial Ethical System.
49. See Galloit, "Lethal Autonomous Weapons Systems," 85.
50. See Arkin, "Governing Lethal Behavior," 29–30.
51. See 3.7 The Implementation of Moral Behavior into Robots.

> 1. Killer robots pose no substantial challenge to humanitarian law; 2. Killer robots pose no substantial issue of responsibility; 3. Given 1 and 2, the crucial issue is whether the overall consequences of killer robots are positive; 4. The overall consequences of killer robots are probably positive; 5. Therefore, we should not ban killer robots.[52]

Given that positive result, he does not regard this kind of technology as a possible threat that needs to be banned from the outset but infers some advice for regulations that might alleviate the possible problems. He proposes to

> 6. Develop binding technical standards that spell out manufacturers' responsibilities; 7. Maintain a clear chain of command and collect data, assuring responsibility for actions and enhancing provability of war crimes; 8. Affirm and defend the humanitarian law "just war" requirements, especially clear differences between war and peace, between combatants and civilians (distinction) and between necessary and unnecessary force (proportionality). These requirements are under threat with current remote-controlled weapons, and this threat will continue with LAWS.[53]

The problem Müller perceives is therefore not so much the technology in itself but rather its immoral and illegal deployment in targeted killings.

Similarly, the philosopher Daniel Statman draws a positive conclusion too, pointing out that the main problem is that drones and autoregulative weapons are used for targeted killing. Yet, Statman argues that this practice is not necessarily connected to the devices, which

> 1. [...] comply better than other tools of war with the requirements of discrimination and proportionality; 2. [..] enable states to reduce the risk to their own soldiers; 3. [..] weaken moral arguments against involvement in wars of humanitarian intervention; 4. [...] make it possible to respond effectively against perceived aggression without the need to engage in a full-scale war; 5. [...] are cheaper in comparison to human-operated tools of war and thus leave more public money available for other causes.[54]

---

52. Müller, "Autonomous Killer Robots Are Probably Good News," 78.
53. Müller, "Autonomous Killer Robots Are Probably Good News," 78–79.
54. Statman, "Drones and Robots," 475.

Statman further holds that the arguments against the deployment of autoregulation in weapons systems—which are deemed to be unfair, disrespectful, riskless, and without virtue—are very weak and not sufficient to ban this technology in advance.

Taken together, the proponents find that the potential positive outcomes might outweigh the possible threats, thereby reducing the overall harm of armed conflict. In doing so, these authors proceed on the assumption that the technology lives up to the standards given by IHL and are able to discriminate better than humans between different targets. The reason for the reluctance against autoregulative devices rests on problematic uses thereof rather than on the devices themselves.

At the other end of this discussion, opponents have voiced serious concerns about autoregulation in weapons systems, and I recognize four main arguments within this debate revolving around responsibility, risk, human agency, and dignity. I will only outline these argumentations briefly here because I address at least three of them in the course of this contribution in greater detail.[55]

Among the first arguments made against autoregulative devices is Sparrow's evaluation, holding that autoregulation in machines will bring a responsibility gap in its wake because nobody could be held liable if the machine made an error. This is because there are so many hands involved in the process of developing and deploying such a device that it might be hard to ascertain whether the person blamed for a certain failure is indeed the person responsible—if there is somebody to blame at all given the autoregulation of the device.[56] Another main problem might be the role of risk. As Paul Kahn argues, warfare becomes more and more riskless for the side deploying the weapons, thereby creating the paradox that the moral legitimation often brought to the fore in just war thinking—which is the reciprocated lethal threat combatants pose to each other[57]—becomes obsolete. In Kahn's words:

> The paradox of riskless warfare arises when the pursuit of asymmetry undermines reciprocity. Without reciprocal imposition of risk, what is the moral basis for injuring the morally innocent?[58]

---

55. I will ponder the topic of risk and responsibility in the course of this chapter.
56. See Sparrow, "Killer Robots." This stance is contested by Leveringhaus. See Leveringhaus, *Ethics and Autonomous Weapons*, 59–88.
57. See Walzer, *Just and Unjust Wars*, 34–37.
58. Kahn, "Paradox of Riskless Warfare," 2.

Furthermore, human agency is an argument closely connected to the political demand for meaningful human control and can pertain to several things. While meaningful human control refers to the collaboration of humans and machines and hints at the inability of the machine to judge a complex situation, Leveringhaus emphasizes that the machine cannot do otherwise while humans can. This ability, however, might be crucial in moral situations in war.[59] Finally, Christof Heyns has brought forward the argument that an autoregulated weapon would strongly oppose human dignity because humans are thereby objectified[60]—an argument that has been further developed by Frank Sauer and Elvira Rosert.[61]

In addition, there are other argumentations I do not turn to and I will not unravel. This pertains to reasons of effectiveness such as higher speed, lower costs, or higher endurance.[62] I do not elaborate on these because the framework of just peace I consider here expresses the general concern that increasing the effectiveness of weapons does not serve to make violence more acceptable. I also do not cover political debates regarding a new arms race[63] but rather hint at the moral problem of such weapons effectively lowering the threshold of violent engagement as they protect their users.

In summary, the ethical discourse regarding the deployment of autoregulative functions in weapons systems includes three major arguments I will recur to here, which are the role of risk, the idea that responsibility might not be addressed and allocated properly, and the crucial role of human agency. I have elaborated already and in great detail on the difference between human and so-called artificial agency, arguing that

59. See Leveringhaus, *Ethics and Autonomous Weapons*, 89–118.

60. See Heyns, "Human Rights Perspective on Autonomous Weapons in Armed Conflict," 153–57.

61. See Rosert and Sauer, "Prohibiting Autonomous Weapons."

62. See Arkin, "Governing lethal behavior," 30. Geiß and Lahmann also mention the argument that more data could be gathered (see Geiß and Lahmann, "Autonomous Weapons Systems," 372–73), while others hint at the advantage that due to the missing communication link, such a system would be harder to track and might operate more precisely because it would not depend on any transfer rate. Consequently, the devices would also continue working even if the transfer were disrupted. See Altmann and Sauer, "Autonomous Weapon Systems and Strategic Stability"; 119; Scharre, *Army of None*, 16. To date, drones that lose their communication link, for instance, abort their mission and fly back to their home base. Yet, since radio and satellite communication might be jammed or distorted, this makes the device prone to disturbances.

63. See Altmann and Sauer, "Autonomous Weapon Systems and Strategic Stability," 128, 131–32.

there is an inherent difference between humans and machines and that the technological device therefore depends on humans in issues of moral concern.[64] In the remainder of this chapter, I will discuss the significance of risk and responsibility within a contingent pacifist frame, arguing from a wider just peace ethical perspective on conflict regulation that includes what is usually framed in terms of *jus ad bellum*, *jus in bello*, and *jus post bellum*. It especially considers nonviolent means of conflict resolution to avoid warlike confrontation, and it scrutinizes such confrontation, if unavoidable, from a perspective that prioritizes peacebuilding. In the Anglo-Saxon debate that is preeminent in peace ethics, such aspects are often considered from a *jus post bellum* perspective to which I turn here to connect to that discourse.

6.3 FINDING JUST PEACE AFTER VIOLENCE: JUS POST BELLUM

According to Larry May, "jus post bellum [...] concerns how to move to a situation of stability after war"[65] and defines the transition along the six normative principles I mentioned above,[66] among them reconciliation. What is made explicitly clear within the concept of *jus post bellum* is the overall objective of moving toward a situation of peace, and that this is anything but a given. This entails that *jus post bellum* mainly refers to the category of right intent within *jus ad bellum*, because it entails the need to "establish and bolster what's needed for a just and lasting peace."[67] It is, however, open to discourse which principles such a further category must entail. While May proposes six principles, Mark Allman and Tobias Winright, in their book *After the Smoke Clears* (2010), refer to four principles, which are just cause, reconciliation, punishment, and restoration. The link with just causes in particular highlights the reference toward *jus ad bellum*, thereby connecting *jus post bellum* toward

---

64. See mainly 4.5 Conclusion.
65. May, *After War Ends*, 6.
66. See 3.3.2 On Larry May's Concept of Contingent Pacifism.
67. See Winright and Hibner, "Costs of *Jus Ante Bellum* and *Jus Post Bellum*," 202. The authors suggest that not only *jus post bellum* but also *jus ante bellum* should be installed. *Jus ante bellum* refers to the undertakings made in order to prevent warfare from happening. While I am convinced that this is a reasonable thought, I do not refer to these discussions here because autoregulation in weapons technology is a means of violence and therefore cannot constitute a feasible way to prevent it.

An Ethical Evaluation of Lethal Functions in Autoregulative Weapons Systems

classical just war thinking. What is important here is that by linking *jus ad bellum* and *jus post bellum* in that way, the question of whether a certain violent undertaking has been made for the right reasons is the most decisive, at least from a perspective that applies the *jus ad bellum* logic. Only in this case might the use of force be exculpated. This also pertains to the question of accountability, which Allman and Winright refer to in their approach: They emphasize the need to assess, in the aftermath, whether the reasons the party claims to have had for fighting are indeed legitimate. If this turns out not to be the case, this party bears the blame.[68] By laying out such factors and principles, proponents of *jus post bellum* provide guidelines that might help to establish peace. Essentially, such a perspective sheds light on the way violence is justified and applied, which means that it might be much easier to come to a situation of peace if the reason for and the conduct of a violent undertaking have not been morally repugnant in the first place. In addition to just case, proportionality might be the most important—and already established—norm running through all of the pillars just war thinking is built on, amounting to the consideration of whether conducting a certain war might result in more harm than refraining from it.[69] If it is possible to show that the deployment of autoregulation in weapons systems is inherently nonproportional because it is overly harmful, morally repugnant, and abhorrent, this might make the case against this technology even in a just war tradition. As Leveringhaus demonstrates, however, this might not hold true, at least not in this cogency.[70] I attempt to show in the remainder of this chapter that autoregulation in weapons systems might nevertheless pose severe problems in that regard because they might impede rather than encourage reconciliation and therefore just peace in the aftermath of an armed conflict. This is because the physical risk shifts from the combatants deploying the device toward the addressee, including harm to civilians, while the moral risk of wronging somebody lethally increases significantly (6.4). In addition, the establishment of just peace might turn out to be inherently problematic if nobody, or not the responsible person, can be held accountable if harm was inflicted (6.5). In my opinion,

---

68. See Allman and Winright, *After the Smoke Clears*, 87–88.

69. See Winright and Hibner, "Costs of *Jus Ante Bellum* and *Jus Post Bellum*," 195.

70. See 5.2.3 Just War Thinking and Autoregulation in Weapons Systems. Despite the fact that Leveringhaus falls short of deeming autoregulative devices repugnant and abhorrent, he does not approve of them, deeming the technology problematic from an ethical stance.

it is plausible to present an argument against autoregulative functions in weapons systems not only from a just peace perspective but also in a just war framing, meaning *jus post bellum* by way of an overlapping consensus.[71] This makes for the question of whether and to what degree an autoregulative device might help or hinder the establishment of peace in the aftermath of a violent undertaking.

6.4 REDISTRIBUTING RISK

"Risk" is a hard term to define because it is not a clear-cut expression; it merely designates different kinds of phenomena within different fields of interest depending on whether risk is discussed within technologies, biological research, or sociology. Yet, all of these different approaches share the notion that the outcome of a certain decision or action is not known in advance. As Sven Ove Hansson states in *SEP*, "When there is a risk, there must be something that is unknown or has an unknown outcome. Therefore, knowledge about risk is knowledge about lack of knowledge."[72] Ulrich Beck introduces in his book *Risk Society* (*Risikogesellschaft*, 1986) a sociological perspective toward the phenomenon of risk, where he develops, among other things, the idea that "existence and distribution of dangers and risks is always mediated argumentatively."[73] Beck shows that the perception of risk is done with the help of scientific means such as "theories, experiments, measurement tools,"[74] which need to be interpreted in order to be become visible in the first place. Therefore, risks are not simply there to be quantified in an objective manner; they are open to discussion and interpretation, which also involves a trade-off between certain kinds of risks, so the social consequences are not coexistent with the scientific data. This is even more reasonable, since there are only few cases where the scientific discourse reaches a common consent.[75] This means first distinguishing risk expressed in numbers, calculations, statistics, or study results, on the one hand, and discussion of risks within a certain (or the international) community, on the other hand, because the former does not necessarily lead to the latter.

---

71. See Rawls, *Theory of Justice*, 340.
72. Hansson, "Risk."
73. Beck, "Risikogesellschaft," 35. My translation.
74. Beck, "Risikogesellschaft," 35. My translation
75. See Beck, "Risikogesellschaft," 42.

An Ethical Evaluation of Lethal Functions in Autoregulative Weapons Systems

This, however, does not mean that the assessment of risk has no importance for technological design and reasoning. It is rather important to conceptualize risk in that regard to reveal the potential benefits and harm of a certain technology.[76] For that matter, the objective of avoiding risk and creating safety share a common ground, so safety factors play an important role in alleviating risk. Since risk is a concept considered relatively seldom within ethical thought, the results within this field of research are, according to Hansson, still limited. He does, however, make three suggestions, which I want to draw on here. First, he argues that it might be helpful to think about risk in terms of "actions of risk-taking and risk-imposing"[77] because in doing so, causation, intention, and the benefits associated become clear. Second, according to moral intuition, each person is expected to have the right not to be exposed to any risk. Yet, for enabling social life this right sometimes might be overridden, thereby leading, third, to a kind of risk exchange: While one person endangers another person with their behavior, for example, when driving a car, it is reasonable that the second person has the same right.[78] This exchange makes the case for attributing risks equally. To Hansson, therefore, risk is a process of interchange between somebody causing it and somebody taking it. This perspective is of importance because it might reveal who is in charge—and who is not. As for the undertaking of warfare, the thought of sharing risks equally is of importance as well because it is exactly this moral intuition that is addressed in the problem of *riskless warfare*.

More generally, the rationale of risk is relevant because the different strands of the ethical discussion can be conceptualized under this umbrella. Regardless of whether the topic is responsibility, the role of agency, or the (im-)possibility of adhering to IHL, the viewpoint can—and usually is—taken from a perspective of risk. As for responsibility, for instance, there is a risk that responsibility cannot be assigned, and it is hard to ascertain that responsibility will be assigned unambiguously.[79] Regarding agency, this pertains to the risk that artificial systems might

---

76. See Doorn and Hansson, "Design for the Value of Safety," 493–94.

77. Hansson, "Risk."

78. See Hansson, "Risk." Hansson adds that in the case of disability or disease, the social system is expected to compensate for such an inequality.

79. This problem might already exist, at least according to Beck's assumption that the complexity of modern systems makes for the eschewal of responsibility. I discuss this problem below and with respect to responsibility. See 6.5.5 Striking a Balance Between Responsibility and Risk.

not be able to function in a proper way because our cultural world and the meaning of life is hard, or even impossible, to compute and express in numbers.[80] Also, with respect to IHL, there is a risk that these systems lack the capacity to play by the existing rules, meaning mainly proportionality and discrimination, thereby jeopardizing the lives of people.[81]

With that said, I now turn to the discourse on autoregulation in weapons technology from the perspective of risk, thereby focusing on three major argumentations. First, proponents of the technology argue that the risk war puts people at is reduced with this kind of technology because it is humans putting other human beings at risk here, be it by making mistakes, or feeling tired, overworked, revengeful, or fearsome.[82] The DOD argues, for instance, in their strategic paper addressing the deployment of AI in the military:

> *Using AI to reduce the risk of civilian casualties and other collateral damage.* We will seek opportunities to use AI to enhance our implementation of the Law of War. AI systems can provide commanders more tools to protect non-combatants via increased situational awareness and enhanced decision support.[83]

Second and in another respect, risk is addressed by Paul Kahn, who identifies the paradox of riskless warfare.[84] Yet, even if both argumentations refer to the same term, they operate on different levels. For the first case, reducing the risk of harm on both sides of the battlefield means pondering who might do more harm: the human being, or the machine? The emphasis here is put on the (physical) safety of the persons taking part in a theater of violence, be they combatant or noncombatant. As for the second case, the concern is far more fundamental and theoretical: If the risk is no longer distributed equally, at least to some extent, warfare becomes immoral, destroying the equilibrium of risk. In that regard, autoregulation in weapons technology contributes to the growing asymmetry in warfare.[85] Both arguments are connected, though, as it is shown

---

80. See 3.3 Reckoning and Judgment.
81. See 6.1 Legal Framework.
82. See Arkin, "Governing Lethal Behavior," 33.
83. US DOD, "Summary of the 2018 Department of Defense Artificial Intelligence Strategy," 16. Emphasis original.
84. See Kahn, "Paradox of Riskless Warfare."
85. See Münkler, *Die Neuen Kriege*.

An Ethical Evaluation of Lethal Functions in Autoregulative Weapons Systems

by the following quote from Arkin, who describes how the deployment of robots will add to the asymmetry of warfare:

> In my view the proposition will not be risk-free, as teams of robots (as organic assets) and soldiers will be working side-by-side in the battlefield, taking advantage of the principle of force multiplication where a single warfighter can now project his presence as equivalent to several soldiers' capabilities in the past. Substantial risk to the soldier's life will remain present, albeit significantly less so on the friendly side in a clearly asymmetrical fashion.[86]

What is important here is that the asymmetry emerges because the side deploying these weapons obviously gains a military advantage, and that Arkin clearly approves of this development. This is even more important because Arkin and the DOD argue that risk will not only be reduced unilaterally but also for civilians, so the question of whose risk will be reduced more and what this entails arises. Both argumentations mentioned—meaning the possible reduction of risk and the paradox of riskless warfare—can thus be assessed apart from each other because the question of the way in which risk is reduced, redistributed, and assessed is rather technological in nature, while the problem of riskless warfare is an ethical and theoretical issue depending on whether reducing risk unilaterally is perceived to be troublesome.

In addition, there is a third argumentation within peace ethics emphasizing that the moral risk of partaking within war increases significantly if the personal involvement is considered rather than the status of combatants and noncombatants. In other words, the risk of harming somebody unjustified increases if the engagement of civilians and the innocence of soldiers is taken in account.[87] The major question with regard to autoregulation in weapons technology is, then, whether an autoregulative system can make this distinction, as well as the issue of whether an operator deploying such a system can foresee what the machine will do and whom it will target. If it cannot be ensured that the system works properly, then somebody else, such as the operator, will have to bear this responsibility, making the moral involvement of the operator riskier. However, such a device might be used to eschew responsibility because the operator can argue that they have handed over the decision to the

---

86. See Arkin, "Governing Lethal Behavior," 13.
87. See May, *Contingent Pacifism*, 131; McMahan, "Innocence, Self-Defense and Killing in War," 200.

machine, so the moral risk seems to rest with the machine. While the latter question will be discussed below in greater detail,[88] I will consider in this chapter whether the moral risk of engaging in a violent theater where autoregulative devices are deployed increases.

Generally, however, the perception going along with the notion of risk can also be expressed in terms of secularization: Klaus Rasborg holds that the gist of these ideas "is linked to the idea that the future is not determined by fate or Providence, but by probabilities. As such, it can be calculated—and managed."[89] Risk, in this societal metaperspective, is the viewpoint reality is perceived in: It is then considered to be a sphere of probabilities that can be dealt with, aiming to make the world a safer place.

For the sake of clarity, I will address the argumentation that the risk is reduced unilaterally or with respect to civilians by referring to the technological risk (6.4.1); the problem that the risk of partaking within warfare might increase in contemporary wars deploying autoregulative devices (6.4.3); and the paradox of riskless warfare as such (6.4.2). Finally, I will make some concluding remarks, wrapping these discussions into the frame of risk interpretation (6.4.4).

6.4.1 Technological Risk

If the proponents of autoregulation in weapons systems are in the right, such devices will reduce the risk of harming civilians and soldiers. That the physical and mental risk for the side deploying this technology decreases is obvious because they no longer partake within the violent undertaking—neither physically nor mentally. Consequently, they are safe from harm. While this argumentation seems plausible unilaterally, the effect on civilians is rather unclear. Arkin claims that the technology is designed to "exceed human levels of capability in the battlefield from an ethical standpoint."[90] This is because Arkin deems the human part problematic, for humans fail, become tired, and so on, while he holds that technology operates without such constraints. Yet, this might not be totally correct: I have already pointed to research that shows the

---

88. See 6.5 Responsibility.
89. Rasborg, *Ulrich Beck*, 14.
90. Arkin, "Governing Lethal Behavior," 120; 3.7.2.1 Arkin's Artificial Ethical System.

constraints of algorithmic systems with respect to algorithmic bias,[91] as well as unintended side effects[92] and problems that might occur when humans and machines work together, namely automation bias and the out-of-the-loop performance problem.[93] All of these effects pose a risk for deploying or working with algorithms and autoregulation, especially in high-risk scenarios where the lives of people are at stake. This is particularly severe if people are targeted in a racist or gender-related way, as this could be proven with respect to civic algorithms.[94] Part of these problems is that algorithms operate more accurately if they are trained on lots of data. Yet, for bellicose scenarios, the relevant data might not be as easy to acquire.[95] This is even more problematic when taking into account the fact that warfare rests on surprises and confusion. On a related note, the more complex a certain theater becomes, the more problematic it might be to rely on an algorithmic solution. This can be exemplified with reference to autoregulative driving, where deploying self-driving cars in clear and neatly arranged situations is unlikely to pose any bigger problems, while driving in complex scenarios with a high degree of unexpectedness, such as inner cities, still faces unresolved questions.[96]

Taking into account all of these unresolved issues, the risk of deploying lethal autoregulative systems might still be in place; it only becomes less visible or is relocated within the machine. To put it bluntly, a human might become tired, but a technological device might also classify certain data incorrectly; a human might be afraid, but a technological device might also operate in an unintended way; a human might want to take revenge, but the system might not always work appropriately either.

According to this rationale, the decisive question is whether the system will cause fewer or more problems—and therefore risk—than humans. As Leveringhaus puts it:

> If autonomous weapons systems do not prove to be riskier means of warfare than alternative methods, including the deployment of soldiers, defenders of autonomous weapons on humanitarian

---

91. See 4.2.4 Algorithmic Bias.
92. See 4.2.5 Black Boxes and Unintended Side Effects.
93. See 4.2.2 The Out-of-the-Loop Performance Problem.
94. See O'Neil, *Weapons of Math Destruction*; Noble, *Algorithms of Oppression*; 4.2.4 Algorithmic bias.
95. See Grünwald and Kehl, *Autonome Waffensysteme*, 57.
96. See Broggi et al., "Intelligent Vehicles," 1191–95; 3.5 Artificial Entities as Moral Agents.

grounds have won the debate. If the use of machine autonomy in weapons remains incredibly risky, the critics have won.[97]

This, however, is hard to tell, because there are no criteria to make a valid estimation here. If, as Arkin assumes, humans are the major problem, a technological answer might be appropriate. If, as Paul Scharre argues, the technological problems are too severe, human control might be key.[98] Accordingly, the ultimate issue seems to be a technological one: If the technology was sophisticated enough—meaning if all technological risks could be alleviated—then there would be a moral imperative to resort to this technology, at least from a just war reasoning. But apart from this perspective, this rationale (and the prospective answer being either yes or no) is flawed from the beginning for two reasons. First, the answer given hinges on anthropology. This means that if humans are considered to be the problem, a possible solution—next to remedying their shortcomings via a technological solution—might be to address the framework and to ask in which way the ethical, cultural, and juridical structures could be changed for the better. Conceptions of nonviolence, such as the proposal given by Judith Butler,[99] or notions of contingent pacifism, such as just peace,[100] can be seen as an attempt to take this approach. Second, the simple juxtaposition of humans and machines might not be appropriate because upcoming research areas, such as techno-anthropology,[101] or established fields, such as science and technology studies, point out that technology and humans are already connected very intimately. Proceeding on this assumption, the either-human-or-machine rationale seems to offer the wrong alternative because technology is by nature linked with humans, as humans are inherently linked with technology.[102] Consequently, the perception that automatizing a certain device for the sake of humanity is an approach without alternative is not convincing.

With respect to the risk posed by such systems, a more plausible viewpoint might therefore be to ask how to mitigate the risk posed by the human–machine collaboration. For that matter, the ethical strength of

97. Leveringhaus, *Ethics and Autonomous Weapons*, 90.
98. See Scharre, *Army of None*, 189–95.
99. See 5.1.3.1 Conceptions Bound to Institutions.
100. See 5.3.3.3 Just Peace Theory.
101. See Puzio, "Zeig mir deine Technik und ich sag dir, wer du bist?"
102. See Coeckelbergh, *Using Words and Things*; 2.1 Connecting Humans and Machines.

An Ethical Evaluation of Lethal Functions in Autoregulative Weapons Systems

Arkin's proposal rests on the idea that a certain ethical framework might be programmed into machines, such as areas or people who are off-limits for reasons of IHL—children, for instance, or graveyards: If a device is programmed that way, it simply will not engage these targets. The cogency of this argument, however, dissolves the moment the machine has no human counterpart to reassure its operations, so it is unclear if an otherwise legitimate target, such as a missile defense system or a military base planted on such a location would be engaged, or targeted, or not, especially if such devices could not assess proportionality of means in a reasonable way. Moreover, failures of the systems would go without notice.[103] This makes the case for a real-time collaboration between humans and machines and means that the positive effect of areas or people the machine is prohibited from engaging might be programmed into the machine, making the human counterpart think twice about whether or not to engage the target. For reasons of safety, therefore, an artificial ethical advisor in combination with a human collaborating with the machine in real time seems most promising in my opinion. This, in turn, leads up to what has been demanded in the political discourse as meaningful human control.[104] Implementing human control in concert with algorithmic assistance, therefore, might make the overall system safer.

Yet, one point needs to be underscored here: Autoregulation in warfare is very likely to make warfare more secure for the side deploying these devices from a physical and maybe even mental point of view. This, however, raises another ethical concern, namely the paradox of riskless warfare.

6.4.2 The Paradox of Riskless Warfare

The paradox of riskless warfare is a phenomenon described in the context of deploying drones, but it is easily transferred toward autoregulation in weapons systems. The general idea is that the risk for the side deploying the device drops to practically zero, while the side targeted bears the whole cost. This has two implications: It increases the asymmetry between the parties fighting, thereby undermining the assertion that a soldier can legitimately defend themselves against a lethal threat because the technological system is under no such condition.

---

103. See Scharre, *Army of None*, 178–79.
104. See 4.4 Meaningful Human Control.

Anders Henriksen and Jens Ringsmose refer to Kahn, who described the paradox as early as 2002, couching the problem in the following terms:

> Drone warfare is seen as problematic because it conflicts with an underlying ethical assumption that war must not be a completely one-sided affair where one side does all of the killing and the other side all of the dying. For warfare to be morally defensible—the assumption is—there must be a minimum of reciprocity and both sides must be exposed to the deadly realities and risks of the battlefield.[105]

The rationale behind the problem is that there needs to be at least some reciprocity in warfare from a just war perspective, as shown above.[106] While Kahn, as well as Hendriksen and Ringsmose following him, presume that both arguments, namely the right to self-defense and the growing asymmetry, coincide, I argue that both argumentations follow different principles: First, the growing asymmetry is a major problem within traditional just war reasoning because the soldiers fighting each other need to have the same status in order to target each other. For another thing, the right to self-defense is a problem discussed within revisionist just war thinking because, here, the right to defend oneself in civic life is transferred to situations of war.[107] Walzer, on the contrary, holds that "war as an activity (the conduct rather than the initiation of the fighting) has no equivalent in a settled civil society."[108] So, consequently, the problem of riskless warfare has two intertwined yet different implications that need to be discussed differently.

With respect the aspect of self-defense, assuming that the weapon needs to and can legitimately defend itself does not make any sense. It can rather be assumed that it defends somebody else, who is not part of the scene, which is the party deploying the system. This perspective in turn changes the categories from asking how a certain war can be fought justly, namely *jus in bello*, toward the question if this party can be defended justly, which is a matter of *jus ad bellum*, so by deploying

---

105. Henriksen and Ringsmose, "Drone Warfare and Morality in Riskless War," 286.

106. See 6.4 Redistributing Risk.

107. See Rodin, *War and Self-Defense*, as described in 5.2.2.2 Revisionist Just War Thinking.

108. Walzer, *Just and Unjust Wars*, 127. To assume that national self-defense is meant here does not make sense because within the conduct of war, the reason for fighting is irrelevant.

an autoregulative device, the whole rationale of legitimate self-defense in war is taken *ad absurdum*. Consequently, we can no longer assume that self-defense is a justification for the use of force here, but rather that somebody else is defended instead. As I depicted with respect to halachic sources, defending oneself is not coexistent with defending others: While in a situation of self-defense, for instance, the halachic rules are less rigorous when it comes to defending a third party, they adhere to stricter rules, such as not targeting somebody lethally, if possible. An assessment and understanding of the situation is required as well.[109] Ultimately, this amounts to an immense problem for ethical justification.

As for the growing asymmetry, this might rather be a problem within traditional just war thinking, where the moral status of all the soldiers is perceived to be alike. Yet, within its revisionist counterpart, there is a strong asymmetry between the parties and the single persons involved all along: While one side is clearly in the right and therefore fighting legitimately, the other side is accordingly in the wrong, their fight being illegitimate per se.[110] The problem with respect to autoregulation therefore occurs only if reciprocity among soldiers is of importance. If it is not, the problem no longer exists: Autoregulation might rather be a way to keep just soldiers safe from harm.[111] Yet, within revisionist just war thinking, another problem arises, which is bound to the idea of innocence and noninnocence. McMahan argues that noninnocent people can legitimately be a target, while innocent people cannot, independent of their status as civilians or not. A system, however, can neither be innocent nor noninnocent, since it only operates on its given parameters, so the categories do not apply at all to the system. This is especially a problem because the system cannot make the distinction of *jus ad bellum*, meaning it cannot assess and know whether the war it is fighting in is worth fighting. Here, the operator bears the cost: They need to assess the situation. Yet, the situation might change, facing the operator with the problem that the autoregulative system cannot be informed. As Leveringhaus puts it, "With no direct control over AWS, it is unclear how AWS can be deactivated once hostilities have been concluded."[112] The same question arises if a certain war turns out to be wrong.

---

109. See Excursus 1 Conceptualizing War and Peace Within *Halacha*.
110. See 5.2.2.2 Revisionist Just War Thinking.
111. See Meireis, "Die Revisionist Just War Theory," 332.
112. Leveringhaus, "Morally Repugnant Weaponry?" 486.

Therefore, within traditional just war thinking as well as within revisionist just war thinking, the problem connected with autoregulation is serious. Yet, there is another point Kahn brings to attention, which is that the more warfare turns into a situation of asymmetrical risk, the more it resembles a police action rather than a war. This is because (traditional) war is assumed to be a situation of mutual risk, while nobody would demand the same to be true with regards to a police officer and a criminal. Since the criminal has wronged somebody, they can legitimately be punished for their wrongdoing, even though this does not normally entail being killed.[113] As Kahn writes:

> While one can demand of the police that they assume risks in order to protect the morally innocent, there is no moral demand upon the police of symmetrical risk: policing is better to the degree that the police can accomplish their ends without risk to themselves.
>
> A perfect technology of justice would achieve a perfect asymmetry: the morally guilty should suffer all the risk and all the injury. This would simultaneously be the ideal technology of policing and the end of warfare.[114]

This also means that the intuition of mutual risk, as described by Hansson,[115] no longer pertains to such a scenario because the situation is asymmetrical in nature all along. In other words, the police offer is not expected to expose themselves to the same risk as the criminal—police officer and criminal simply do not belong to the same moral universe.

Given this finding, there seems to be little room to discuss autoregulation in weapons systems from a just war point of view because war might no longer be the appropriate framework to take into account here. Approaches, such as just policing or just peace, where the use of force is considered in a more comprehensive way, seem to be more applicable. With respect to just peace theory, for instance, the use of force is considered detached from its specific context in war, so the established criteria pertain to different scenarios, be it police action or war.[116] The question then turns out to be detached from asymmetrical risk, while the problem of self-defense persists: An autoregulative device cannot legitimately

---

113. See Kahn, "Imagining Warfare," 205.
114. Kahn, "Paradox of Riskless Warfare," 4.
115. See 6.4 Redistributing Risk.
116. See EKD, "Live from God's Peace," 68.

defend itself, it only comes to somebody else's aid, so again, other rules than the traditional ones might apply.

6.4.3 Moral Risk

With the term "moral risk," I refer to the discussion within contingent pacifism and revisionist just war thinking, revolving around the problem of harming an unjust person, be it civilian or soldier.[117] As May puts it:

> Contingent pacifism begins with the idea that there is a presumption against going off to war and against using violence during war because of the risk that a soldier takes given how difficult it is in any given war to tell whether soldiers will be justified in serving in that war.[118]

The basic idea is that it is only justified to target those people engaging in an unjust war because they facilitate the violent undertaking in one way or another, with or without firepower. Two relevant questions pertain here. First, whether a certain war is just, or respectively, which party is in the right. Only the party who is in the right can target other individuals legitimately, which means that *jus ad bellum* needs to be considered. Second, conducting war, a differentiation is necessary between people who partake intentionally within that unjust war and people who do not, such as soldiers being deceived by their governments, thereby applying *jus in bello*. Now, the risk of partaking within an unjust war is high, given the possibility of deception or misinformation.[119] Moreover, the chance of targeting an unjust person within a just war is also high because the line between just and unjust targets is hard to perceive when it is not linked to the uniform of the soldier or what is known to be a military target. In any case, the soldier fighting within war exposes themselves to the risk of doing something morally wrong.

When considering an autoregulative weapons system in this context, the question of whether such technology will help to mitigate the moral risk imposed on soldiers arises. This might be the case if the weapon could differentiate between just and unjust wars, on the one hand, or

---

117. See May, *Contingent Pacifism*, 81; 5.3.2 On Larry May's Concept of Contingent Pacifism.

118. May, *Contingent Pacifism*, 44.

119. May, *Contingent Pacifism*, 82–83, 103; 5.3.2 On Larry May's Concept of Contingent Pacifism.

Violence Without Guilt

between just and unjust targets, on the other hand. Here, two diverging notions convene. First, such systems are, to date, unable to distinguish between combatants and noncombatants or to secure proportionality.[120] It is presently unclear how the differentiation between just and unjust targets would be possible for the device. Second, the standards for sophisticated technology are higher than the standards for humans: While errors from humans, even if they are lethal, can be exculpated and are expected to happen, machines are expected to work properly. This entails that it needs to be ensured that a system does not fail. For now, it seems impossible to solve this dilemma, so the person deploying, operating, or programming an autoregulative system runs the moral risk of harming persons illegitimately.

Furthermore, it might be argued that this technology saves soldiers from moral harm because they no longer carry the responsibility for killing. Yet, this perception is a severe misunderstanding of the technology, as will be shown below with respect to theological thought.[121]

6.4.4 Concluding Remarks: Interpreting Risks

Given these findings, autoregulation in weapons technology is a complex phenomenon. Even though all of the concepts discussed share an element of uncertainty, they differ significantly in meaning and range. Assessing whether the technology will work properly (technological risk), whether the specific war is an undertaking that justifies killing (moral risk), or whether modern technologies create a paradoxical asymmetry that no longer justifies killing at all are inherently different processes.

Therefore, simply arguing that the risk for the side deploying the technology, or even both sides, is reduced seems flawed because the risk of human failure is merely replaced by technological failure, which again makes somebody responsible because the machine simply does not operate on its own.[122] Ultimately it seems hard to find criteria here: While from an utilitarian point of view, it might be tempting to add up the harm done in human warfare against its technological counterpart,[123] I can hardly imagine any way to calculate such a bill—even more if, as discussed

---

120. See 6.1 Legal Framework.
121. See 6.6 Waging War Without Guilt.
122. See 4.4. Meaningful Human Control.
123. See Charters, "Killing on Instinct."

above, the numbers do not speak for themselves. This is also true given that risk is imagined to be some kind of interchange: The interchange is not simply between imposing and taking risk, but also between different kinds of risk imposing and risk taking because the technological risk imposed changes if it is a risk imposed by a machine, thereby transforming the whole framework and criteria for its assessment.

This also pertains to the discussion of responsibility. To shoulder responsibility for a device that operates in situations of high risk without it having the necessary capabilities for bearing responsibility appears even riskier from a moral point of view. In contrast, the physiological health of the side deploying the device is improved definitively, which seems to be the right course of action in a clearly asymmetrical theater, where one party is the villain while the other is hailed as hero. Furthermore, from a just peace perspective, it may be added that even in police action it might not be always clear who is the perpetrator. Until proven guilty, suspects hold their civil rights, so the use of force is severely restricted. Here, the disagreement between traditional and revisionist just war thinking is crucial because under the condition of revisionist just war thinking, the growing asymmetry seems welcome. Moreover, this also entails that developing autoregulative devices as a preemptive measure within such an asymmetrical scenario might not pose any problems. From the perspective of risk, though, this seems inherently problematic if risk needs to be attributed equally. This would be the case again if the enemy side was equipped with the same technology, so the issue of asymmetry loses its point.

This brief summarizing discussion shows that the interpretative framework is decisive: Whether the technology is framed within traditional just war thinking, revisionist just war thought, or just peace reasoning makes a substantial difference. Yet, at the same time, the technology itself changes the rules of risk assessment and the interpretative framework. In concrete terms, autoregulation in weapons systems does not only entail that (technological) risk is imposed or alleviated; it also changes the structure of violent conflict by intensifying the asymmetry—at least to the point where the opposing party can resort to the same technology. Yet, as could be shown, a scenario of high asymmetry requires another framework than (classical) just war thinking. Here, imagining warfare as a police action seems more appropriate. This, however, is only perceivable within an international political body because to decide whether a certain party or state is in the wrong and therefore needs to face trial or punishment, the issue needs to be assessed by more than only one party.[124] The most important problem, then, is whether a certain (violent) situation is indeed a justification for an international police action. Here, the criteria that apply to just peace thinking pertain again but under an asymmetrical scenario, where the police officers would have every right to be kept safe. Autoregulation in weapons systems might help to mitigate the risk on a physiological level, while, on the other hand, it increases the moral risk—at least as long as the technology cannot meet the demands of distinction and proportionality.

From a perspective of contingent pacifist reasoning, meaning the extent to which such technology can or cannot contribute toward just peace, these problems are crucial because if autoregulation makes the use of force more unfair by making it more asymmetrical, establishing (just) peace in the aftermath seems harder to achieve. This, however, is very likely to happen. As can be already seen with respect to the deployment of drones in Pakistan, these weapons have a disastrous effect on civic society. This is not only because civilians are harmed physically far more often than expected, but also because their daily lives are affected severely. As the Stanford report *Living Under Drones* reveals, "those living under drones have to face the constant worry that a deadly strike may be fired at any moment, and the knowledge that they are powerless to protect themselves."[125] The taxi driver Haroon Quddoos depicts his situation in his words:

> We are always thinking that it is either going to attack our homes or whatever we do. It's going to strike us; it's going to attack us ... No matter what we are doing, that fear is always inculcated in us. Because whether we are driving a car, or we are working on a farm, or we are sitting home playing ... cards—no matter what we are doing, we are always thinking the drone will strike us. So we are scared to do anything, no matter what.[126]

Situations as this are especially problematic for children, who grow up under constant fear.[127] Of course, violence always puts people under threat, and civilians must fear that they are targeted either by accident or

---

124. Given the current political situation, there is simply no institution existing that could do so right now. This, however, does not do away with the demand that such structures be (re-)instantiated for the sake of peace.

125. Stanford Law School, "Living Under Drones," vii.

126. Stanford Law School, "Living Under Drones," 82.

127. See Stanford Law School, "Living Under Drones," 88.

as a side effect. The fear with respect to drones described here is different, though, because it combines the possibility of constant surveillance with lethal capabilities. One way to express and depict the problem is "drone art." Philipp Preußger examines two pieces of this kind of art. Both of them express their intention with the image of an eye, resembling the expression "eye in the sky," which stems from contexts of religion and popular culture.[128] Preußger interprets these imagines to hint at the trend of drones making surveillance possible everywhere and at every time, while at the same time, the person surveilling becomes invisible—a trend resembling Jeremy Bentham's *Panopticon* (1791), as depicted by Foucault in *Discipline and Punish* (1975). Yet, while expressing this fear in the image of the all-seeing eye, Christian iconography is used, showing the ambivalence of drones—located between hopes, such as lesser harm due to better technology, and fears, such as technological risks.[129] This entails that drone technology gives rise to a specific kind of fear, which is that of being seen and targeted. This fear contrasts with the principle established by Hansson that every person has the right not to be exposed to risk, and if so, the risk needs to be attributed somewhat equally—a situation that is clearly no longer the case here. This situation is also unlikely to be alleviated if there is no longer a human controlling the system. This is because in addition to feeling constantly under surveillance and in danger, a failure of the system might have more severe consequences simply because a human would not repeat a mistake over and over again with enormous speed.[130]

Given these problems inherent to the technology, the discussion of risk shows that the problems might be more severe than the unilateral affliction of risk, at least if the party at risk is of no legitimacy to be targeted, such as civilians living their daily lives. In order to make use of drones and autoregulative devices, however, these systems need to sweep an area constantly, thereby necessarily threatening civic society—and therefore imposing risk.

Taking a look at the bigger picture, the intent to make the world a safer place with the help of machines driven by algorithms capable of harming people lethally seems prone to errors because there are several incalculables here, ranging from the misperception of technology operating in a failsafe way to the assumption that the risk for the people taking part in a violent scenario is reduced—it might simply recur in a

128. See Preußger, "'Drone Art' zwischen Anschauung und Vermittlung."
129. See Preußger, "'Drone Art' zwischen Anschauung und Vermittlung."
130. See Scharre, "Autonomous Weapons and Operational Risk," 189–95.

modified way at another point. The danger in quantifying the increase or decrease of risk is in creating the narrative that, first, this is possible at all, and second, that this is no longer open to discussion. Again, this does not mean that the risk assessment of a certain technology is flawed. On the contrary, this is a process of high value. Yet, it needs to be kept in mind that the data produced in this assessment are controversial and open to political and societal consideration. From that point of view, the discussion of risks reveals the quest for safety, which might, at a closer look, turn out to be a flawed narrative: The numbers this belief is based on might not tell the whole, or in the worst case even an erroneous, story because it is always based on presuppositions that might or might not be true. One example thereof is the assumption that the human part of the collaboration is the one making the mistakes and proposing to find a technological solution to fix this issue. This, however, means that the numbers and presuppositions need to be examined critically, on the one hand, and that the ethical and political discourse has an inherent value, on the other hand. This is because this discourse interprets and adapts the quantifications toward our forms of life, while it still maintains a correlation with them. To put it in terms of risk and autoregulative weapons, if the risk is imposed only unilaterally, the scenario becomes more asymmetrical, resembling a police action rather than war. If the risk is reduced on both sides, the change is not overly fundamental. Yet if, as it seems to be the case, the risk becomes not only more asymmetrical but also mainly to innocent people who are targeted due to potentially lethal surveillance technology, there seems to be some kind of fault in the narrative of reduced risk. This is because the risk is clearly transferred from the purportedly innocent soldier to the potentially suspected civilian. This exchange, however, is a major problem because it not only runs counter to the existing rules, such as IHL, and the moral intuition to distribute risk equally but reverses the gist of these ideas into their opposites, thereby challenging the establishment of sustaining just peace from the outset. From the perspective of risk, therefore, autoregulation in weapons technology seems to pose a challenge rather than being beneficial.

6.5 RESPONSIBILITY

Responsibility is one of the key issues in the ethical debate on autoregulation in weapons systems and has been the first argument made

An Ethical Evaluation of Lethal Functions in Autoregulative Weapons Systems

against these machines: Sparrow brought forward that it is not clear who, in effect, will be held responsible given the many hands involved in the process of developing and deploying autoregulative machines and the impossibility of holding a technological device responsible.[131] Leveringhaus, on the other hand, argues that this argument might not be entirely persuasive, since it only pertains to individual and backward-looking responsibility. Yet, if responsibility is approached as a collective endeavor and rather concerned with "supervising, controlling, or caring for someone or something in the future,"[132] the problem might be less severe—if it exists at all. Moreover, whether a target is liable to be attacked is not considered in this approach but might deprive the argument of its normative power. This is because if somebody poses a severe threat to other people's lives, the question of responsibility might be sidelined. In addition, Leveringhaus points toward the developers of the system, who he thinks have a share in responsibility depending on how the system is designed. He finally illustrates that in the overall picture of a war, it is mainly state actors in charge of the violent undertaking, so ultimately the state deploying this kind of weaponry could be held responsible. From that, Leveringhaus concludes that ascribing responsibility for the operation of autoregulative weapons systems is not as severe a problem as perceived.[133] In addition to the ethical treatments of this topic, there are a bundle of approaches that address the issue from a juridical angle, mainly focusing on individual responsibility in the framework of IHL and sometimes on collective state responsibility as well.[134]

As for my own approach, the question of responsibility is closely linked to agency. Along the lines of what has been established so far in the course of my argument, the crucial question is whether responsibility can be assigned without proper agency, and if this question is answered

---

131. See Sparrow, "Killer Robots."
132. Leveringhaus, "Morally Repugnant Weaponry?" 479.
133. See Leveringhaus, "Morally Repugnant Weaponry?"

134. A detailed and thoughtful juridical account is provided by Bo, Brunn, and Boulanin from the Stockholm International Peace Research Institute *sipri*. In their report, the authors address collective state responsibility as well as individual criminal responsibility in relation to IHL, finding that autoregulation in weapons systems poses a challenge toward IHL, especially in terms of responsibility, but there might be ways to mitigate this problem if the involvement of the diverse parties and persons in the decision-making process is determined sufficiently. See Bo et al., "Retaining Responsibility," 11. Further contributions are provided by Chengeta, "Accountability Gap"; Jain, "Autonomous Weapons Systems.."

in the negative, how responsibility should be alternatively ascribed, especially if humans and machines collaborate. This is important for the overall aim of assessing whether this kind of weaponry could contribute to or hinder the establishment of just peace in the aftermath of armed conflict: If it turns out that responsibility cannot be assigned toward somebody if the machine does not operate as intended, this might impede the formation of peace. As Vogelmann shows, this issue is also at the center of the contemporary discourse on responsibility in the context of work. For instance, to the degree that responsibility shifts to be decentralized, it also diffuses, so the nexus between individual agency and responsibility becomes more and more detached.[135]

In the following, I will first provide some introductory remarks on responsibility, and especially the concept of moral responsibility. In doing so, I will also discuss how agency and responsibility are intertwined (6.5.1). This then leads me to discuss whether responsibility and agency could be decoupled in a way critical posthumanism proposes (6.5.2). While I am skeptical toward this decoupling, the idea of regarding responsibility as a networked phenomenon seems convincing, though it necessarily entails a diffusion of responsibility, even if this must not entail that an outright responsibility gap exists. In that context, I will also delineate how responsibility could be conceptualized within a human–machine collaboration without giving up the centrality of humans in that regard (6.5.3). Subsequently, I will introduce the concept of responsible AI (6.5.4) and discuss this concept critically along the lines I have developed so far (6.5.5).

---

135. See Vogelmann, *Im Bann der Verantwortung*, 163. Within the scholarly debate on responsibility, therefore, the reverse question of whether assigning responsibility makes for agency has also been of great importance. Picht argues that in shouldering responsibility, the subject transgresses the self and therefore their very agency. See Picht, "Der Begriff der Verantwortung," 338–39. Similarly, Bayertz understands liability (*Gefärdungshaftung*) along these lines when he explains that even though a person has not intent to do harm, they are made liable for a certain (negative) outcome, so the issue of proper agency is sidelined in that regard. See Bayertz, "Eine Kurze Geschichte der Herkunft der Verantwortung," 29. Another example critically assessing the direct line from agency toward responsibility is found in the work of Günther, who shows that responsibility and recognition (*Anerkennung*) are not only in a very close relation to each other but hinge on rules prior to both of them. These rules are not naturally given but gained in a common discourse "*from* responsible persons through their common reconstruction of their own self-conception *as* responsible persons." Günther, "Anerkannte Verantwortung," 181. My translation, emphasis original. This necessarily entails that the concept of responsibility, as well as recognition and agency, is not fixed but dynamic and open to discourse. See Günther, "Anerkannte Verantwortung," 181.

6.5.1 Moral Responsibility and Agency

"Responsibility" is not an easy term to define and not a simple concept to grasp. Definitions and concepts abound, and what exactly it entails hinges largely on the definition in place.[136] Moreover, responsibility as an ethical concept gained momentum in the second half of the nineteenth century and is accordingly relatively new, which entails that the conceptions underlying the term are due to a shifting understanding of human behavior and agency.[137] However, a general definition is given by Ludger Heidbrink, who delineates responsibility as "the giving assurance (*Einstehen*) of an agent for the consequences of their deeds in relation to a prevailing norm. A is responsible for D in relation to N."[138] Heidbrink points out that this is not coextensive with the classical concept of duty because—in contrast to theories of duty—responsibility focuses on consequences that follow from acting according to a certain norm. This is important because from that perspective, responsibility is not only about applying normative rules but also about foreseeing and deliberating the consequences thereof.[139] Such a differentiation can also be found in the writings of Bonhoeffer, who couches this tension in terms of obedience and freedom: both need to be in place to shoulder responsibility. As Bonhoeffer holds, pure obedience would make the agent a slave, while freedom alone results in arbitrariness, so only their nexus begets responsibility.[140]

As for Heidbrink, he points to the conditions for responsibility, which can be conditional, on the one hand, enabling responsibility to be ascribed, and generative, on the other hand, defining what enables agents to act responsibly. Conditional parameters (*konditionale Bedingungen*) include the freedom of the agent, causality, intentionality, and

---

136. See Heidbrink, "Definition und Voraussetzungen der Verantwortung," 4–5.

137. See, Bayertz, "Eine kurze Geschichte der Herkunft der Verantwortung," 24–25.

138. Heidbrink, "Definition und Voraussetzungen der Verantwortung," 5. My translation.

139. Heidbrink then goes on to shed light on several aspects of responsibility, such as sanity (*Zurechnungsfähigkeit*), jurisdiction (*Zuständigkeit*), legitimacy based on the consequences (*folgenbasierte Legitimität*), a contextualized principle of reflection (*konzeptualisiertes Reflexionsprinzip*), and a principle of structure and control (*Struktur- und Steuerelement*). While all of these aspects are of great importance for the concept of responsibility, the detailed analysis of them is beyond the scope of my contribution.

140. See 5.3.3.1 On Bonhoeffer's account of war and peace.

knowledge,[141] while generative conditions include opportunity, competence, and willingness to shoulder responsibility.[142]

Heidbrink concludes that responsibility entails mainly four features. First, responsibility amounts to more than solely following ethical and juridical norms; it also involves social roles and tasks which are voluntary in character. Second, responsibility is not only oriented toward intentions but also toward the consequence of a certain deed. Third, responsibility is always bound to a certain context and needs to be reflected on within a specific background. Finally, responsibility is not bound to individuals alone but also applies to systems.[143] As far as systems such as responsibility in the political and the social sphere[144] are concerned, systematic insecurity can be reduced by binding the system toward a certain codified behavior—rules that manage issues of responsibility and liability (*Haftung*) in order to address the problem of diffusion of responsibility.[145]

In addition, there is a general difference between forward- and backward-looking responsibility, and the success notions of responsibility ensue is closely connected to the changed understanding of responsibility shifting from backward- to forward-looking notions. While backward-looking responsibility focuses on the classical question of how to assert responsibility in the aftermath of an action, forward-looking responsibility factors in the consequences of a certain action. In that regard, the realization that acting always entails risks and that therefore risk and responsibility are in very close relation to each other is of great importance and can be addressed more plausibly within a forward-looking account.[146]

These general remarks pertain to responsibility in diverse fields. Yet, the way scholars conceptualize responsibility hinges to a large degree

---

141. See Heidbrink, "Definition und Voraussetzungen der Verantwortung," 23–24. This entails that the agents needs to have the chance to do otherwise, that they have (co-)initiated the act effectively, that they planned to do so, notwithstanding that there might be unintended side effects, and that they know what their deeds entail and the ramifications thereof.

142. See Heidbrink, "Definition und Voraussetzungen der Verantwortung," 25–26.

143. See Heidbrink, "Definition und Voraussetzungen der Verantwortung," 27–28.

144. See Heidbrink, "Definition und Voraussetzungen der Verantwortung," 7.

145. See Heidbrink, "Definition und Voraussetzungen der Verantwortung," 24–25. The regulation of systems via their political and societal context follows the rationale of the respective system.

146. See Bayertz, "Eine kurze Geschichte der Herkunft der Verantwortung," 45.

on the respective field they are working in, so judicial concepts differ from social or political ones, while consequentialist approaches can be distinguished from nonconsequentialist approaches.[147] As for my own approach, I will focus on moral responsibility here.[148] Verena Rauen, for instance, elaborates on moral responsibility in a rather classical way, arguing that moral responsibility refers to the relation between one individual (subject of responsibility) and another (object of responsibility), even though this dualistic and close-range perspective can be extended to collectives and systems as well. Generally, for Rauen, responsibility involves four relational elements, which are:

> 1. the entity (*Instanz*) responsible for something (Who is responsible?); 2. the entity (*Instanz*), somebody is responsible to (To whom?); 3. the item, which shouldering responsibility pertains to (For what?); 4. the normative point of reference (in respect of which responsibility?).[149]

By positioning the relation of one individual subject toward another answering a certain demand,[150] the responsible individual is such a relation and needs to be thought of as a free agent. In addition, the respective deed needs to be made with a clear intent, and the responsible subject needs to be in the know about the consequences of their behavior.[151] Vogelmann determines such as position that merges moral agency and responsibility as a subject position (*Subjektposition*) because, since the subject in question is already part of the definition, their agency is necessarily entailed.[152] He also finds that this position in particular is at variance with responsibility in the field of work, for instance, where

---

147. For further approaches and their implications, see Heidbrink et al., *Handbuch Verantwortung*.

148. Rauen distinguishes between moral and ethical responsibility. In her approach, ethical responsibility refers to being responsible toward somebody else in a rather broad sense, while moral responsibility refers to a certain area of application, such as economical ethics. This, however, does not seem to be coextensive with the English definitions because Talbert defines moral responsibility very similarly to what Rauen terms "ethical responsibility," as well as Frankfurt. I will therefore refer to what Rauen calls ethical responsibility as moral responsibility here, for the sake of clarity. For further information, see Rauen, "Ethische Verantwortung"; Talbert, "Moral Responsibility"; Frankfurt, "What Are We Morally Responsible For?"

149. Rauen, "Ethische Verantwortung," 546. My translation.

150. See Bayertz, "Eine kurze Geschichte der Herkunft der Verantwortung," 16.

151. See Bayertz, "Eine kurze Geschichte der Herkunft der Verantwortung," 14.

152. See Vogelmann, *Im Bann der Verantwortung*, 163.

responsibility that needs to be assigned without that agency can be presumed.[153] In any case, from such a subject position, artificial entities such as robots fall short of counting as responsible entities because they are not free, have no intentions of their own, and cannot know what their calculations entail.[154]

This must mean that artificial entities are not part of the responsible relations. Yet, with respect to machines, the difference between moral and causal responsibility is of great importance. Matthew Talbert introduces this concept as follows:

> Young children, for example, can cause outcomes while failing to fulfill the requirements for general moral responsibility, in which case it will not be appropriate to judge them morally responsible for, or to hold them morally responsible for, the outcomes for which they may be causally responsible. And even generally morally responsible agents may explain or defend their behavior in ways that call into question their moral responsibility for outcomes for which they are causally responsible.[155]

This means that even though it is obvious that somebody has caused a certain outcome, they might not always be responsible in the same, clear way. The reference toward children (in the same article, Talbert refers also to nonhuman animals, people with developmental disabilities or dementia) is especially important here because it shows that there are already entities we perceive to affect our worlds of life causally, while they are not responsible for the outcomes of their actions in the same way. In fact, children are perceived to be "agents in the minimal sense"[156] also because they depend on societal structures, such as their family.[157] From this thought, the possibility of asking whether machines might be conceptualized in a way that makes for responsibility without agency seems at least feasible.

When it comes to concepts that explicitly address responsibility with respect to machines, Janina Loh's contribution *Ethics of Robots (Roboterethik*, 2019) stands out. Loh takes an approach that focuses on

---

153. See Vogelmann, *Im Bann der Verantwortung*, 163.

154. Even though an artificial entity might calculate the probability of a consequence, this does not mean that it understands the meaning thereof, while the concept of responsibility seems to anticipate exactly that.

155. Talbert, "Moral Responsibility."

156. Matthews and Mullin, "Philosophy of Childhood."

157. See Matthews and Mullin, "Philosophy of Childhood."

An Ethical Evaluation of Lethal Functions in Autoregulative Weapons Systems

intersubjectivity and asks whether it is possible to transfer typical human competencies such as agency, reasoning, and autonomy to machines. In doing so, Loh does not simply refute the possibility of assigning responsibility within a human–machine collaboration[158] but, on the contrary, attempts to apply responsibility, thereby changing the concept of responsibility considerably by shifting the classical focus from the relata of responsibility toward the relation between them.[159] To do so, Loh first makes out three groups of competencies that form the foundation to hold somebody responsible in the first place, which are the ability to communicate (*Kommunikationsfähigkeit*), agency (*Handlungsfähigkeit*) or autonomy, and judgment (*Urteilskraft*). Loh defines all of these abilities to be on a spectrum: "It is possible to speak of more or less ability to communicate and agency and depending on this of more or less responsibility."[160] A specific focus is accordingly on the subject of responsibility. All of the competencies Loh points out are precarious with respect to artificial entities: I have already made clear the categorial difference between reckoning and judgment,[161] pointed out that the artificial entity in itself cannot be described appropriately as an agent,[162] and clarified that the attempt to implement explainable artificial intelligence does not mean that the algorithm gives an explanation,[163] which casts doubt on whether the artificial entities can in fact be said to communicate. Given this finding, the idea of ascribing responsibility toward machines seems impossible. Yet, Loh deems some robots capable of simulating these competencies at least to some degree. Some minimal kind of ascribing of responsibility seems feasible to Loh, even though humans are better equipped for that, so in the case of a collaboration, humans excel and attract responsibility.[164] In this context, she also introduces Christian Neuhäuser's term *network of responsibility*, which entails that

---

158. See, for example, Wagner, *Künstliche Intelligenzen als moralisch verantwortliche Akteure?* 188.

159. Loh defines the *relata* within the concept of responsibility in a slightly different way than Rauen by splitting up the entity somebody is responsible for—Talbert's second relational element—into two different entities: the direct addressee of responsibility, for instance, the person affected by a crime, and the authority (*Instanz*) to which the subject of responsibility has to answer. See Loh, *Roboterethik*, 128.

160. Loh, *Roboterethik*, 128–29.

161. See 3.3 Reckoning and Judgment.

162. See 4.4 Meaningful Human Control.

163. See 4.2.4 Black Boxes and Unintended Side Effects.

164. See Loh, *Roboterethik*, 145.

in a certain scenario, there is not necessarily only one subject bearing responsibility but there might be different parties involved that might take over responsibility to certain degrees. Loh exemplifies this with a driving scenario, where not only different areas of responsibility—such as legal, moral, and political responsibility with their specific norms—intersect, but also different people or entities are involved and might have a share in the responsibility. This becomes even more intricate if assisted driving is part of the scenario because the assistance system might be a minor responsible entity according to Loh.[165] Even though I am skeptical about whether the assistance system itself might assume responsibility here, the company that provided the technology might at least be considered as a potential bearer of responsibility.

6.5.2 Responsibility Without Agency? The Relational Turn in Critical Posthumanist Thought

This thought of a network where responsibility might overlap and could be shared to some degree seems especially worth pondering with respect to a human–machine collaboration. This is also very close to concepts that shift the focus toward the relation between the different entities, a concept closely connected to critical posthumanist thought.[166] Here, the focus shifts from humans toward the network of relations they are part of. This paradigm might yield the possibility of applying responsibility without ascribing agency because, here, responsibility is not linked to the agent but toward the relation between subject and object. One of the main protagonists in this context is Allan Hanson, who introduced a concept called *extended agency*. In his theory, he turns away from the classic view—the view Rauen mentions as the one where freedom, agency, and responsibility are seen to be closely knit together[167]—toward a view where humans are only one part of a greater chain of entities. He maintains,

---

165. See Loh, *Roboterethik*, 147–48.

166. Critical posthumanism must not be confused with technological posthumanism or transhumanism. While transhumanism aims at transforming humans by means of technology, technological posthumanism stretches their goal even further by intending to overcome the human creature with the help of technology. Critical posthumanism, however, takes a critical approach toward humanist thinking by reviewing anthropocentric and essentialist humanist ideals. See Loh, *Trans- und Posthumanismus*.

167. See 6.5.1 Moral Responsibility and Agency.

> The basic reasoning behind this extension of agency beyond the individual is that if an action can be accomplished only with the collusion of a variety of human and nonhuman participants, then the subject or agency that carries out the action cannot be limited to the human component but must consist of all of them.[168]

These methodological assumptions amount to the idea of *joint responsibility*, where the whole network is taken into account instead of the single individual. Hanson does not conclude that computers or machines of any sort should bear responsibility for their operations. Instead, he even holds that this would be "unwise."[169] The problem with this is not only that computers lack the necessary requirements, but also that "this perspective's focus on nonhuman agents in their own right actually shares the moral individualist tendency to separate them from humans. Extended agency and joint responsibility theory aims to overcome precisely that separation."[170] According to Hanson, these phenomena are not new, but the perception of the individual agent forestalls a joint perspective, while ever more automated technology and the interweaving of human and machine, for instance, in the case of cyborg technology,[171] challenges this view. The most central thought within this approach is therefore that the relations in a human–machine interaction should not be considered as separate entities acting apart from each other, each of them ruler of their own self. Instead, they interact, while the human is the principal bearer of agency to whom responsibility is ascribed.[172]

In another contribution, Loh, in conjunction with Coeckelbergh, draws on Emmanuel Levinas and Bruno Latour, in order to challenge the individual paradigm. They hark back to Levinas, elaborating on the thought that I face the other as a stranger, who addresses me, and asks for response. Coeckelbergh and Loh write,

> Before my active response, there is a kind of "passivity" and "reception," in the sense that the responsibility is received, the response invited. This so to speak "takes over," "turns around," and transforms the entire structure of responsibility into a relation

168. Hanson, "Beyond the Skin Bag," 92; Loh, *Roboterethik*, 193.
169. Hanson, "Beyond the Skin Bag," 94.
170. Hanson, "Beyond the Skin Bag," 92.
171. With cyborg technology, I refer to existing technologies such as cochlear implants, artificial body parts, brain implants, or the like.
172. See Hanson, "Beyond the Skin Bag," 98.

that starts with the other. The other takes a central and "highest" place in the structure.[173]

This means that in encountering the other, I relate to them, and from this encounter, responsibility originates. Responsibility is not a quality of an individual but only comes to bear within the relation of (at least) two entities.[174] However, this might not be the only way to interpret Levinas. The Jewish scholar Hava Tirsoh-Samuelson objects intensely to this kind of interpretation[175] because she emphasizes that, for Levinas, the Other[176] could never be other than human. In her understanding, philosophers who attempt to transfer Levinas's thought to technology deeply misunderstand Levinas's Jewish background. Tirosh-Samuelson writes,

> According to Levinas, God can be accessed only through one's responsibility for the Other, but the Other is decidedly human. The Other cannot be contained; the Other is infinite, only pointing in the direction of the transcendent God who cannot be known but who is revealed in responsibility for the Other. The ethical life thus consists in responding to the moral call of the Other, but, let me reiterate: The Other is decidedly a human being whose embodied human needs obligate the self to respond.[177]

This critique has severe consequences because it means that the relational view might be flawed from the beginning by overlooking the transcendent core of Levinas's idea. This is because the Other is not coextensive with some kind of material—the issue at stake here is rather that the Other opens up the potential to encounter God, so responsibility from this viewpoint needs to gain a transcendent dimension, which it only can if there is some transcendency in the Other. Since artificial

173. Coeckelbergh and Loh, "Transformation of Responsibility in the Age of Automation," 16.

174. See Coeckelbergh and Loh, "Transformation of Responsibility in the Age of Automation."

175. Tirosh-Samuelson refers to the theories established by Gunkel, who also draws on Levinas to challenge the individual paradigm and to contend that nonhumans, including machines, do not necessarily have to be excluded from being ascribed a moral status. See Gunkel, *Robot Rights*. I depicted his view above. See 3.6 Artificial Entities as Moral Patients.

176. I capitalize "the Other" in reference to the writing of Levinas and Tirosh-Samuelson, because these authors do so with respect to the transcendence the Other implies.

177. Tirosh-Samuelson, "Jewish Philosophy and the Critique of AI Technology," 247.

An Ethical Evaluation of Lethal Functions in Autoregulative Weapons Systems

entities cannot have this, it might be difficult to address them as responsible entities.

In a second step, Loh and Coeckelbergh refer to Latour to show that things can be representatives for a certain responsibility.[178] While they do not go as far as ascribing responsibility toward machines, they question the difference between humans and nonhumans.[179]

There are, however, several issues that accompany this approach. First, there is the severe critique Tirsoh-Samuelson brings to attention. This is crucial because Levinas's theory forms the philosophical foundation for addressing nonhumans morally—and ascribing to them some kind of responsibility. But if Coeckelbergh's and Loh's interpretation fails to transfer the main impact of Levinas's work, thereby reducing the transcendent notion that underlies the encounter with the Other in a relation of responsibility, the concept as a whole is cast into doubt. This is because within a networked approach, it is not evident that each entity needs to be addressed in the same way—an assumption that to treat others as Other seems to imply.

Second, what Deborah Johnson describes with respect to the morality of machines[180] can similarly be brought forward against the idea of such a posthumanist assemblage: Machines are not morally responsible in a meaningful way, but this does not simply mean that they play no part in our responsible actions: Recurring to an example used by Hanson,[181] there is a difference whether somebody participates in traffic with a bicycle, a car, or even a tank. Here, it is not the human subject that changes but their network: the technology they are involved with. This, however, does not make the technology itself responsible but rather changes the way responsibility is assigned. This is even more the case if the car is highly automatized, such as in assisted driving, since here, the company

---

178. I elaborate on Latour's ideas in greater detail above. See 2.1 Connecting Humans and Machines.

179. See Coeckelbergh and Loh, "Transformation of Responsibility in the Age of Automation," 16–17.

180. See Johnson, "Computer Systems." For more details, see 3.5 Artificial Entities as Moral Agents.

181. Hanson describes a father admonishing his daughter when she learns to ride a bicycle using the phrase, "Be careful not to run into people or things, don't crash your bike or hurt yourself, and especially don't ride into the street without looking.' (Hanson, "Beyond the Skin Bag," 97). While this is a reasonable suggestion when riding a bike, it becomes more severe if the daughter learns to drive a car. The admonishing might stay nearly the same, but the responsibility that comes with driving a car is weightier than when riding a bike. See Hanson, "Beyond the Skin Bag," 97.

building the technology becomes part of the responsibility network. Third, a major lack in the previously mentioned reconceptualization in a critical posthuman way is that the conceptions stay extremely vague. Loh and Coeckelbergh conclude that further work needs to be done to elaborate on the concept,[182] and Hanson also stays on a highly theoretical level when establishing his theories, so it seems ultimately unclear how this new paradigm could be implemented into real-life scenarios.

In summary, even though the idea of detaching agency and responsibility in a kind of networked and relational perspective seems compelling, the theoretical foundation, as well as the unclear practical ramifications, seem too vague to be seriously taken into account here. This is especially true for theological reasons because, coming back to Tirosh-Samuelson, applying responsibility to machines might cut humans off from their transcendence. Therefore, the difference between encountering a human Other in responsibility and encountering a nonhuman entity cannot be overcome by establishing a framework of responsibility because in the second case there is simply no Other, even though it might seem that way. This limitation, however, does not do away with all of the implications discussed so far, but brings to the fore the still undertheorized anthropological ramifications of networked and interdependent humans and nonhumans. This can again be combined with Latour's approach as I interpret it, the ideas of Coeckelbergh intertwining games of language and technology, and the paradigm joint cognitive systems. All of these approaches share the notion that it is not the individual and single human devoid of all relationships that acts and shoulders responsibility for their deeds. These conceptions rather point to the interrelatedness of humans and nonhumans, while this does not mean that all of them share the same influence and agency within the assemblage. As I pointed out when referring to agency and control, it is humans who establish the goal of the joint venture, and it is humans providing agency when collaborating with machines. Therefore, humans also need to bear responsibility. This, in turn, does not mean that the operator of a system is the only one to address. On the contrary, the network of agents involved needs to be addressed here, so the fear Sparrow expresses, meaning that the involvement of too many hands might lead to a problem when ascribing responsibility, is a reasonable concern.

---

182. See Coeckelbergh and Loh, "Transformation of Responsibility in the Age of Automation," 19.

An Ethical Evaluation of Lethal Functions in Autoregulative Weapons Systems

6.5.3 Gaps or Diffusion of Responsibility?

Sparrow has brought forward the concern that autoregulative weapons systems might pose a threat to responsibility because they necessarily result in a responsibility gap: Since the artificial device itself cannot be held responsible, it is unclear who in effect will bear the blame if the system malfunctions. Sparrow rules out the operator because they cannot know in advance what the algorithm will do, so ultimately nobody might be held accountable.[183] Leveringhaus, in contrast, argues that the operator might very well be the one who bears responsibility because they deployed the autoregulative system, even though they knew that this was a risky course of action. Accordingly, Leveringhaus concludes that risk is a matter or greater importance than responsibility.

According to the approach I have taken so far, the solution Leveringhaus proposes seems to be too simple, especially with respect to the entanglement between humans and machines in a collaboration, where the machine specifies and predetermines a course of action, and humans (re-)act accordingly. The question of the circumstances under which humans can still be said to shoulder responsibility is more complex and cannot be solved simply by pointing to the operator who needs to know how risky the device is. The crucial point might rather be that the more complex the system becomes, the harder it might be to address the operator(s) as responsible because they are integrated into a human–machine framework that might or might not give them the chance to exert control according to time, knowledge, competence, and resources.[184] If these preconditions are not met, it is hardly possible to maintain control and therefore to attribute responsibility to the operator.

This, however, does not mean that I agree with Sparrow, maintaining the position of a responsibility gap. It is rather my objective to widen the view away from the operator(s) of the system and toward the multiple hands and stakeholders in the process of developing and deploying an autoregulative device. This means that, even though there are many agents involved in the production of an autoregulative device, responsibility does not simply vanish: it diffuses.

Diffusion of responsibility is a concept rooted in psychology, referring originally to the issue that bystanders at a certain event, such as a

---

183. See Sparrow, "Killer Robots."

184. See Hollnagel and Woods, *Joint Cognitive Systems*, 75. As described above, see 4.1 Joint Cognitive Systems.

car crash, do not come to the aid of the victims because everyone expects the others to act.[185] Similarly, with respect to automatized technology or issues on a societal scale, the problem has been addressed under the term "the problem of the many hands," which depicts a situation where a lot of people—and companies—are involved in developing, programming, and deploying a technological device, so the responsibility for a certain event might be hard or even impossible to trace and attribute.[186] Consequently, a responsibility gap might indeed occur if diffusion of responsibility has not been addressed. Helen Nissenbaum hinted toward these effects as early as 1996, pointing out that "computing is particularly vulnerable to the obstacles of many hands."[187] This is because, first, companies developing software abound, so the market is already highly fragmented. Second, the systems themselves are composed of individual units, which again are either constructed by individuals or teams. Third, many systems and functions operate in addition to other systems and can be combined with each other, thereby forming a new overall system, so it is hard to tell if the enhanced system is still the same as the original one. Finally, the nexus between hard- and software is often so strong that it might be hard to identify which component led to a failure.[188]

The philosopher Ludger Heidbrink researches the diffusion of responsibility pertaining to issues such as climate change or economic mismanagement, which are phenomena that naturally include more than one agent within complex societal systems. His descriptions and solution can also be paradigmatic for the question of human–machine collaboration because many hands are also involved, so responsibility diffuses.[189] According to Heidbrink, the rise of the concept of responsibility is

185. See Bierhoff and Rohmann, "Diffusion von Verantwortung," 216–17.

186. See, with respect to computers, Nissenbaum, "Accountability in a Computerized Society"; with respect to society, Poel, "Problem of the Many Hands," 50.

187. Nissenbaum, "Accountability in a Computerized Society," 29.

188. See Nissenbaum, "Accountability in a Computerized Society," 29–30. In her seminal article, Nissenbaum also elaborates on bugs in the system, the proneness of humans to use the computer as a scapegoat for their own faults, and the outright denial of accountability even if the artificial device is under one's ownership. All of these concerns pose severe problems. As for my contribution, however, I concentrate on the problem of the many hands because this seems to be the most decisive aspect with respect to responsibility: How a society deals with bugs can be resolved, and whether a certain failure was due to the system or to human operators might be traced. Also, denying responsibility must not entail that somebody cannot be held responsible.

189. I do not refer to Jonas's *Das Prinzip der Verantwortung* here, even though Jonas's description is still worth reading today, for instance, when he elaborates on the

understandable only due to the challenges that accompany processes of differentiation in modern society: Humanity is overwhelmed with moral judgment in complex scenarios with outcomes that can hardly be foreseen but need to be anticipated and conceptualized nevertheless.[190] In this context, the concept of responsibility is not self-evident but rather hinges on preceding normative frameworks without being coextensive to them. Especially in encountering others, responsibility exceeds causal reconstructions and becomes a relational term, evoking ideas such as care and solidarity.[191] As such, responsibility can be easily conceptualized too narrowly, referring only to causation. But it might equally easily become a catch-all term, referring to all kinds of things. Heidbrink's account attempts to conceptualize responsibility in between,[192] while one of the areas he scrutinizes is diffusion of responsibility. The backdrop here is that complex societies may be understood to undergo a process of ever-increasing functional differentiation, thereby delineating the different areas that generate their own logics for ascribing responsibility, while they are nevertheless intertwined on a societal level.[193] This tension is exactly the challenge diffusion of responsibility needs to address. In application to human–machine systems, this has several implications. First, it means that human–machine systems that stem from different contexts do not necessarily address the same challenges, so no one-size-fits-all solution can be given: Contexts of high risk differ from contexts of care, which again are separate from contexts of driving, so questions of technology and machine ethics become concrete only in their respective fields of application. For that matter, autoregulative driving must be seen as different from autoregulative weapons systems and care robots. Second, and

---

tremendous effect of technology for humanity or hints toward the shrinking places for nature within culture. I, however, disagree with his instrumentalist and determinist view: Jonas deems technology a mere tool and continually maintains that technology entails naturally certain societal consequences. Yet, both ideas are too easy. Humans and machines are intertwined more deeply than in an instrumentalist manner, forming instead networked assemblages, thereby co-shaping each other. Moreover, how a society deals with a certain technology is open to discussion and hinges on the cultural background, as well as the technological structure and the design, which are architectures that are built from companies and engineers with a certain intent. These intentions, the responsibility that comes with them, and, most importantly, the opportunity to influence the design and use of a certain technology are veiled when such technological determinism is conjured.

190. See Heidbrink, *Kritik der Verantwortung*, 20.
191. See Heidbrink, *Kritik der Verantwortung*, 24–25.
192. See Heidbrink, *Kritik der Verantwortung*, 26.
193. See Heidbrink, *Kritik der Verantwortung*, 26.

vice versa, this entails that the single human–machine assemblage must not be separated too strictly from other systems. In that regard, issues that pertain to autoregulative weapons systems relate to other domains of heavily automated technology, such as autoregulative driving, as can be seen with respect to the term "meaningful human control," stemming from the political discussions of autoregulative weapons systems, which Filippo Santoni de Sio and Jeroen van den Hoven propose to transfer to other domains of autoregulative technology as well.[194] Finally, this means that an ethical account of responsibility within heavily automatized scenarios of violence needs to locate the issues of joint human and machine ventures pertaining to the ethics of technology within the field of peace ethics. In referring to peace ethics, the concrete ethical background is taken into account, focusing on the objective of the use of force, which is peace. This is crucial because, otherwise, the means of violence would become an end in itself to the ethical assessment. When considering issues of technology ethics, such as human–machine collaboration, the concerns caused by automized technology come to the fore, thereby linking automized use of force to societal matters. In that regard, the question of how to maintain control is closely related to responsibility, and the discussion of maintaining or losing control within violent contexts characterizes an archetype and serves as a catalyst for the discussion of autoregulation in general. This is because notions that stem from this extreme case might enrich the general debate on the ethical significance of autoregulation in other domains to a high degree. Yet again, this does not mean that the outcomes here can be transferred directly; the respective field of applications needs to be considered as well.

As for diffusions of responsibility, Heidbrink combines the expansion of responsibility with theories of risk, showing that the challenge is not to make a decision where the person deciding knows that the outcome is uncertain, but to make decisions that are built on ostensibly certain knowledge. This is because, in fact, the person deciding considers only what they know and disregards of their ignorance.[195] From that, Heidbrink infers five consequences. First, the context of a certain deed is worthy of consideration, including all necessary information and expectations. Second, this means to focus on consequences rather than on reasons and causes, considering that making a decision is a process that builds on

---

194. See Santino de Sio and van den Hoven, "Meaningful Human Control Over Autonomous Systems."

195. See Heidbrink, *Kritik der Verantwortung*, 31.

decisions made in advance and outcomes that cannot be predetermined. This entails that side effects might occur that cannot be foreseen, which is also because there are many hands involved in the process, which are often represented in companies and associations, rather than in individual agents. The third implication Heidbrink elaborates on is the dedifferentiation (*Entdifferenzierung*) of diverse areas of actions, which means that in the process of globalization, national laws, norms, and boundaries become sidelined, while simultaneously no new political body exists that binds the multiple rationales together. This process refers to both place and time because due to globalization and digitization, the world becomes smaller and procedures quicker. As a result, the attribution of actions expands because the single decision transcends the small area of application in time and place: The bigger picture takes the place of the concrete context, a development that is mirrored in the term "sustainability."[196] Finally, all of these phenomena condense in the term "responsibility," which replaces former concepts such as (causal) accountability and norms. It is due to the separation of intention and consequences and articulates all of the previously mentioned diffusion processes.[197]

These observations are not only the reason why the term "responsibility" currently thrives; they also necessarily entail that responsibility comes with diffusion.[198] This, however, makes the concept of responsibility rather blurred and inconsistent, producing at least five tensions, which Heidbrink elaborates on. First, there is the tension between present foundation and temporal extension, emphasizing that it only makes sense to ascribe responsibility if there is a temporal coherence between a certain deed and the outcomes. Second, Heidbrink refers to an imbalance between linear structure and complex application, thereby running counter to rather simpler causation processes. In a third consequence, Heidbrink focuses on the impersonal attribution, which contrasts with the classical personal constitution of responsibility: Therefore, companies and systems need to be structured along the lines of individuals in order to conceptualize them in terms of responsibility in the first place. Similarly, this pertains, fourth, to the general indivisibility of responsibility, which becomes

---

196. Heidbrink refers to ecological sustainability. It is, however, noteworthy that in the area of peace ethics, the term "sustaining peace" experiences a similar boost as a concept adopted by the UN. See UN, "Sustaining Peace."

197. See Heidbrink, *Kritik der Verantwortung*, 32–38.

198. Heidbrink refers to some reverse tendencies as well. For my contribution, however, it suffices to concentrate on the described challenges.

divisible in complex scenarios because it might be necessary to ascribe responsibility only partially to the diverse agents involved. Heidbrink hints, fifth, toward the tension between self-organization and being responsible for oneself, which entails not only what an agent does—which would be the classical understanding—but also what they do not do. Finally, there is an imbalance between voluntariness and coercion. While voluntariness is a self-evident basis for classical and individual responsibility, it is unclear whether a deed can indeed be called voluntary within the context of a system. In summary, responsibility is therefore a highly diffuse and ambivalent concept.[199] This, however, does not mean that the concept of responsibility is of no use. On the contrary, if these effects are taken into account, responsibility might rather serve as a very useful way of addressing complex systems ethically because it shows where the exact problems of a certain system might be. To do so, Heidbrink develops his own account, building on the classical structure insofar as he refers to a subject that is made responsible for an object on behalf of certain normative evaluations either on a subjective, objective, or social level. Furthermore, he adheres to the difference between certain kinds of responsibility, such as legal, moral, or causal responsibility. On those grounds, he then distinguishes between a primary principle of responsibility pertaining to the individuals and a secondary dimension, which involves mainly "groups, collectives, institutions, or cooperations."[200] This secondary form of responsibility is involved in specialized contexts, mainly in processes that expand over a larger time and space, for instance, taking into account the responsibility toward further generations. Most importantly, Heidbrink does not predetermine a one-size-fits-all solution in his approach but rather finds that such secondary concepts of responsibility come in multiple ways depending on the respective context. Such an extension, however, is only legitimate in cases where it serves the explanation and clarification of context better than the primary variant. This rule serves the interest of diffusing responsibility no more than necessary and maintaining as much clarity as possible.[201]

Heidbrink's ideas can be transferred to the discussion of autoregulation in weapons systems. When rereading the approaches taken toward responsibility, Sparrow's responsibility gap approach seems especially shortsighted, as the problem of pinpointing only one person to be held

---

199. See Heidbrink, *Kritik der Verantwortung*, 47–51.
200. Heidbrink, *Kritik der Verantwortung*, 317. My translation.
201. See Heidbrink, *Kritik der Verantwortung*, 317–19.

responsible can be solved by ascribing gradual levels of responsibility to various agents.[202] Similarly, Leveringhaus's account, which proposes to ascribe responsibility either to the nation state or to the operator, seems to be oversimplified.[203] If Heidbrink is right, responsibility might rather be ascribed gradually toward the several involved parties, among them surely the nation state and the operator but also the companies that provided the algorithm and the designers of the system. This entails that in order to ascribe responsibility in a reasonable way, it might be necessary to develop a networked approach for the single system in which the particular allocation of responsibility is assigned. This might also serve as an ethical test for the single device: The system might only be deployed if it is possible to ascribe responsibility in a reasonable way, preventing gaps in moral responsibility. Since the individual technological systems differ inherently and systems such as Super aEgisII and FCAS can hardly be compared to each other because they operate in very different ways, solutions have to be tailored to the case in question. This means that in the case of Super aEgis II, the responsibility for an autoregulative lethal operation needs to rest rather with the company providing the algorithm and the data, as well as with the agent who put the system into action, which might be the nation state. In more complex systems, such as swarms or systems of systems, the human operator(s) might rather be in focus because they are in local and temporal connection to the control system. This solution, however, might still be too easy, at least when it comes to complex systems of systems that mainly draw on AI.

It is exactly these problems Hannah Bleher and Matthias Braun address in the context of medicine ethics and with respect to algorithm-driven clinical support decisions, for instance, for detecting breast cancer. Their example brings the most important points to the fore. When deploying such a device, the algorithm trained on detecting breast cancer recommends a certain course of action and treatment, thereby changing the way responsibility is ascribed, moving away from the treating physician toward the technological device. Bleher and Braun depict three issues with respect to the concept of responsibility, which are causality, morality, and legality. With respect to causality, a problem might occur when it is not clear how the algorithm produced a certain outcome, so the question how to address and distribute causal responsibility might be

---

202. See Sparrow, "Killer Robots."
203. See Leveringhaus, "Morally Repugnant Weaponry?" 478–80.

Violence Without Guilt

hard to resolve. Explainable AI might reduce the problem to some degree because it might be clearer how a certain output has been produced.[204] Even though the algorithm cannot give proper reasons for its conclusion, reconstructing how the conclusion was produced might be sufficient to track causal responsibility. Yet, Bleher and Braun hint at the opaqueness of decisions made by physicians and that, in a clinical context, it might be sufficient that the system produces precise outcomes. While this might be true with regard to causal responsibility, Bleher and Braun show that this could no longer be the case with regard to moral responsibility: In the case of a malfunction, the question of who is in charge for flawed data or a damaged algorithm resulting in inadequate guidance by the system is crucial. This brings a lot of people and parties to the scene, and it might not be clear who holds responsibility and to what degree. This is especially problematic if legal regulations are concerned and harm done needs compensation. If it is not clear who could be the subject of such compensation because responsibility cannot be traced, juridical regulations cannot be effective. For that matter, Bleher and Braun call for controllability of the system, proposing to design the system in a way that enables its control and considers the sociopolitical background. Furthermore, they urge implementing a participatory approach, taking into account clinical and legal standards as well as the stakeholders' interests and claims, thereby incorporating the idea of the relational turn, where it is no longer one subject answering for their behavior but a multidimensional situation. Finally, the authors ask for an effective fault management.

The situation depicted by Bleher and Braun, though taking place in clinical context, reinforces the argumentative weight of Heidbrink's rather general remarks with respect to highly automated systems: Given the opaqueness of AI, it might be difficult to ascribe causal responsibility, while the problem of the many hands involved might blur moral responsibility, resulting in a scenario where legal responsibility cannot be allocated appropriately, so controllability and participatory features come to the fore. To be more precise, this entails that the design of autoregulative functions needs to be constructed in a way that enables procedures of human control in an effective way, providing knowledge, competence, resources, and time.[205] Moreover, the role of the single agents involved in the process is sharpened because maintaining control is the most important issue,

---

204. See Bleher and Braun, "Diffused Responsibility."

205. As the authors of the concept of joint cognitive system propose. See 4.1 Joint cognitive systems.

so responsibility might be ascribed to the operator(s) only to the extent that system ensures controllability. If it fails to do so, the deployment of a certain system cannot be endorsed for ethical reasons. If it is deployed nevertheless, the agent who puts it into use bears the blame because they acted against their better judgment. If, however, the technological part of the system fails, the responsibility needs to be attributed to the companies who fabricated the product, at least as long as it has not been misused. That way, the problem of moral responsibility might be addressed, even if it is no longer one single agent who shoulders responsibility.

This is the case at least as far as ethics of technology is concerned because this consideration pertains to complex technological systems in diverse backgrounds. When it comes to weapons systems, the peace ethical background must be taken into account as well. And with respect to peace ethics, an allocation of responsibility toward single agents involved represents only one side of the coin, since this pertains to questions addressed classically in the frame of *jus in bello*. On the other side, there is the question of whether the reason force is used is legitimate, which means applying categories of *jus ad bellum*. If this is not the case, the deployment of any weapons system whatsoever is irresponsible from the outset, so the question of responsibility is answered very easily and with regard to the context. This raises another issue, which is that an autoregulative weapon cannot assess this overall context. It depends on the person(s) controlling the system and will do as they say, at least as long as there is a person in control.[206] If there is no person in control and the reason for using force is illegitimate, it means that the person deciding over the deployment of an autoregulative device might have a very powerful weapon because it does not judge the overall situation and therefore it would not disagree. Just war theory, of course, be it in its traditional or revisionist version, does not directly refer to responsibility that way. This might also be the case because weapons technology has, until now, seldom raised questions of responsibility with a similar severity, as it is normally assumed that humans are responsible for their deeds. This issue

---

206. Theoretically, and following Arkin's suggestion, there would be the possibility to program weapons not to engage certain targets for ethical reasons, such as graveyards or hospitals. To me, however, it seems rather unclear what tactical and military use a weapon that refuses to shoot for moral reasons can have, especially if war is an opaque theater with quickly changing scenarios. It is also conceivable that ostensibly civic places will be designated that, in fact, serve miliary functions or vice versa. For that reason, it is not very persuasive to consider that opportunity, even though it seems to be exactly that option that might make warfare more humane at first sight.

only becomes central to the extent that the technology becomes detached from humans in real time. That responsibility is indeed crucial for peace ethics as well, especially (contingent) pacifism, can easily be inferred, though, and is due to the emphasis that is put on just and sustaining peace: If peace is the overall aim of every use of force, then it seems imperative to ascribe moral responsibility in a reasonable way, since the belligerent parties might otherwise forestall sustaining peace from the beginning. This is because if a system does not operate in a foreseeable way, thereby killing people, and nobody can be blamed in the aftermath, it is hard to imagine how a peace process might succeed because there is nobody who can be held reliable for such far reaching flaws.

The crucial question is therefore whether human control of the system can be guaranteed to a reasonable degree. Again, this does not necessarily entail that every single function, including lethal functions, might never be automatized. But it means that control in terms of time, knowledge, resources, and competence needs to be in place, meaning that the human part(s) of the collaboration have sufficient time to consider deploying a function autoregulatively; that they know what this entails in the given situation and what the system in fact is suggesting; that they have the resources to make that decision; and that they have the competence to understand what it going on and how this is likely to influence other parts of the system.[207] Then, control is exerted and the demand for responsibility is met.

To conclude, even though responsibility can be attributed to the agents involved in the process, be it in terms of the operator(s), the companies involved, the designers, the programmers, or the nation state deploying the system, the question of how control can be maintained to ascribe responsibility is still open. As has been said with respect to human–machine interaction,[208] this especially pertains to the time given in order to make a lethal decision, or likewise to make the decision about whether the system should engage a certain target lethally and autoregulatively.

6.5.4 Forward-Looking Responsibility

So far, I have addressed responsibility mainly in a backward-looking manner. In contrast to such conceptions, there is also the idea that

---

207. See 4.1 Joint Cognitive Systems.
208. See 4.4 Meaningful Human Control.

responsibility might be conceptualized in a forward-looking way, which is plausible if the focus on the consequences of a certain deed is considered. As Heidbrink puts it, responsibility is a principle of actions aware of contingencies (*kontingenzbewußtes Handlungsprinzip*) and risks. For that matter, the responsible agent cannot stand alone; the system they are embedded in needs to be taken into account as well, which also entails that a further normative and operational framework needs to be considered in addition to responsibility, thereby forming systemic responsibility.[209] In that context, both ideas—namely the insight that responsibility can be oriented toward an uncertain future and that it necessarily takes place within a certain theater and framework—make responsibility a highly risky concept because the situation when using force, such as in war, might change very quickly and in unforeseeable ways. To deploy a lethal device autoregulatively entails that nobody can say for sure how the device will operate in the given situation because it might not be entirely clear how the situation will evolve. This also pertains to the question of how such a device could be informed about a truce or a peace agreement, as Leveringhaus has pointed out.[210] Given that the human part(s) of the collaboration maintain control and decide intentionally to deploy such a device, they will be held responsible if the situation turns out to be different than expected. That way, responsibility and control do not pose a problem for deploying the device, but the risk that accompanies its deployment is very high. This entails that a forward-looking moral account might not be implementable into juridical or even moral concepts. In the scenario of an autoregulative system, it would only be the operator who bears the blame because they know in advance about the risk of their endeavor, and it therefore serves to make the operator(s) realize how risky their work is. While this is surely important, it might not help to deal with the problem of diffusion of responsibility because, then, the issue of responsibility focuses on the human part(s) of the collaboration, who could have known that systems fail or give bad advice. Consequently, the hint at forward-looking responsibility in the context of autoregulative weapons systems points rather to the high risk that accompanies the deployment of autoregulative functions—at least from the operator's perspective.

---

209. See Heidbrink, *Kritik der Verantwortung*, 203.
210. See Leveringhaus, "Morally Repugnant Weaponry?" 486.

6.5.5 Striking a Balance Between Responsibility and Risk

From a more distanced ethical perspective, the diverse angles of responsibility—be it forward- or backward-looking—ought to strike a balance, which means that responsibility and risk always and necessarily need to be addressed in concert. From this perspective, the forward-looking notion brings to attention the fact that deeds are necessarily contingent, and that these contingencies are likely to increase with the deployment of autoregulative functions, thereby making acting riskier. At the same time, humas are not acting devoid of a given structure and framework, especially when cooperating with machines that are designed in a specific way and that operate according to certain algorithms that preselect what options the human part(s) of the collaboration in fact have. This makes it imperative to consider the training of the algorithm, the design of the device, the control of humans, and the overall context. At least these four features need to strike a balance in order to maintain responsibility:[211] a poorly trained and untested algorithm might fail due to unintended side effects[212] or algorithmic bias,[213] for instance; the design of a device might nudge humans to collaborate with the machine in a misperceived or harmful way, for example, if it facilitates anthropomorphization;[214] the lack of time, resources, knowledge, and competence might do away with agency and control of the human part(s) of the collaboration, thereby losing overall agency and control of the system;[215] and an illegitimate use of force will make every resort to weapons irresponsible, no matter which.[216] Consequently, from a peace ethical perspective, the deployment of an autoregulative device needs to meet the demands of safe software, appropriate design, human agency and control, and a justified context.[217] Such a device might only be deployed if these features are met. This also puts the demand for human control into perspective, as simply demanding human control without considering the technological part of the collaboration seems rather shortsighted. Moreover, to have such a fourpartite approach might help to resort to means of autoregulation in

---

211. As described above, see 6.5.3 Gaps or Diffusion of Responsibility?
212. See 4.2.4 Black Boxes and Unintended Side Effects.
213. See 4.2.3 Algorithmic Bias.
214. See 3.6 Artificial Entities as Moral Patients.
215. See 4.4 Meaningful Human Control.
216. See 6.5.3 Gaps or Diffusion of Responsibility?
217. See 6.5.3 Gaps or Diffusion of Responsibility?

certain cases if the overall control of the system is warranted. This entails suggestions such as adaptive or adaptable automation, where the level of automatization within a collaboration might increase or decrease due to the workload of the human part(s) of the collaboration. It is highly reasonable to predetermine features that need the direct control of the human part(s) under all circumstances, while there might be scenarios and circumstances that facilitate an increase in the automatization level, up to the autoregulation of specific functions. As I suggested, this might be feasible along the lines of the clarity of a certain situation, ranging from very clear scenarios within the deep sea, for instance, where human oversight might not be decisive or because people might not even be involved, up to very complex scenarios such as in urban fighting, where the current technology cannot meet the necessary demands.[218] Another assessment marker would be the need for human judgment:[219] Generally, situations that include moral reasoning—for example, killing a person—would be considered to be situations where the automatization of a system's function is inherently problematic. Consequently, such situations should remain under human control. If, however, human agency and control is in place and the overall situation is clear, the human part(s) of the collaboration might indeed decide to deploy a lethal autoregulative device. It would then be within their responsibility to do so. This is feasible especially in situations where the overall workload is high and there are complex situations that need human judgment more than others. It is perceivable that clear (lethal) situations might then be outsourced to the machine, while others remain under human control. This, however, does not do away with the inherent trouble of killing but only applies peace ethical norms of discrimination and proportionality.

With respect to juridical concepts, the issue of responsibility is also addressed by Marta Bo, Laura Brunn, and Vincent Boulanin when discussing autoregulative features in weapons systems from a collective state perceptive in line with an individual criminal account. The hold that

> There is an opportunity for states to (re)elaborate and formalize aspects of the decision-making process in the command-and-control chain where AWS are involved. Having a clear scheme in place that delineates the different roles and responsibilities in the decision-making process involving AWS would arguably

---

218. See 4.4 Meaningful Human Control.
219. See 3.3 Reckoning and Judgment.

make it easier to detect where in the chain a potential breach occurred.[220]

This means that from a legal perceptive, the problem of responsibility might also be accounted for if the concepts are elaborated enough. Open questions pertain to the ability of the system to adhere to focal IHL norms such as discrimination and proportionality as well as the concrete meaning of "human conduct" and "effective command and control."[221] These legal debates and challenges toward responsibility, however, are not identical with the moral dimension: If no control is exerted over the system, then a formalized scheme might indeed help to ascribe responsibility in a legal sense, holding somebody accountable, while the actual moral responsibility is still unaccounted for. This is because the system itself is no agent and therefore not responsible. Yet, if the human part(s) of the collaboration do not fulfil their task of maintaining control, there is simply no (morally responsible) agent who in fact bears this responsibility.

This is connected to another and rather general problem when it comes to responsibility in automated systems, which Nadav Berman has hinted at in his Jewish account: It is the possibility that an autoregulative device and the automatization of lethal force in general might serve the intent of eschewing responsibility.[222] This is a very reasonable and serious concern, as it entails that the purported increase of "humane" warfare by means of automatization, meaning removing humans from the battlefield due to their failings,[223] might come at the cost of responsibility and finally runs counter to the objective. If this is true, the effort of maintaining responsibility is most decisive for ethical reasons. I will consider this issue in more detail below and with respect to Bonhoeffer's idea that shouldering responsibility also requires the willingness to become guilty.

6.6 WAGING WAR WITHOUT GUILT

While the practical philosophical debate about autoregulative functions in weapons systems revolves a great deal around the term "responsibility,"

---

220. Bo et al., "Retaining Responsibility," 56.

221. Bo et al., "Retaining Responsibility," 53.

222. See Excursus 2 Assessments of Autoregulation in Weapons Technology Within Jewish Traditions.

223. See Arkin, "Governing Lethal Behavior," 29–36; as described in 3.7.2.1 Arkin's Artificial Ethical System.

An Ethical Evaluation of Lethal Functions in Autoregulative Weapons Systems

a more theological notion might conceptualize these issues in different terms. With respect to peace ethics, this has already been depicted in the concept of just peace, since this theory is rooted in theological thinking. In the following section, I will combine this peace ethical theological thought with Bonhoeffer's concept of responsibility and the necessity of incurring guilt. In order to make that argument, I will first introduce Bonhoeffer's idea in that regard (6.6.1) and subsequently suggest that warfare without shouldering moral responsibility is an attempt to eschew guilt, thereby getting tangled up in even more guilt (6.6.2). In a final step, I will make the argument that killing with the help of machines might be interpreted to be a case of what Bonhoeffer calls *cheap grace*: an attempt to instrumentalize the Christian doctrine of justification to escape moral responsibility (6.6.3).

6.6.1 The Acceptance of Guilt in Responsible Action

For delving deeper into Bonhoeffer's ideas, I want to draw on the thoughts he develops in his ethical fragments.[224] As already mentioned,[225] for Bonhoeffer, obedience and freedom are dimensions of acting responsibly. While the responsible agent is bound in a vicarious representative action (*Stellvertretung*) and in accordance with reality (*Wirklichkeitsgemäßheit*), they take on guilt (*Schuldübernahme*) in freedom.[226]

With respect to vicarious representative action, Bonhoeffer perceives the agent to be in close relation to the concrete other of the neighbor (*Nächster*), a circumstance he exemplifies with respect to being a

---

224. To refer to and interpret a piece of work that has the character of a fragment is precarious for at least two reasons. First, the text is recorded in two different versions, which sometimes differ. Second, the thoughts are not presented in their final form, so it is unclear which concept the author would have incorporated in a final version thereof. Accordingly, there are still some incongruencies and ill-conceived thoughts. See Slenczka, "Die unvermeidbare Schuld," 23, 38. Having issued that caveat, I nevertheless do so because the ideas Bonhoeffer presents here are of great importance for my question.

225. See 5.3.3.1 On Bonhoeffer's Account of War and Peace. See also Zeyher-Quattlender, *Du sollst nicht töten (lassen)?*

226. See *DBW* VI, 289. Bonhoeffer compiles two lists. The prior list reads, instead of "taking on guilt," "my accountability [*Selbstzurechnung*] for my living and acting," 257. In the prior list Bonhoeffer also associates the binding feature with vicarious representative action and accordance with reality, while he perceives freedom to entail my accountability for living and acting, as well as venture [*Wagnis*]. Within the text, however, Bonhoeffer does not come back to the prior term but refers to taking on guilt only, which is why I structure my rereading along those lines.

father or a teacher: In such cases, it is clear that the responsible agent acts vicariously in place of somebody else. In this close connection, which Bonhoeffer calls vicarious, the relationality of responsibility becomes very clear, for it is always bound to the concrete other I am responsible for. For that matter, Bonhoeffer maintains that

> Vicarious representative action and therefore responsibility is possible only in completely devoting one's life to another person.[227]

In such a relation, the responsible agent becomes selfless, which Bonhoeffer perceives to be coextensive to "truly *live*."[228] For that matter, responsibility refers to a relation between humans, while it cannot pertain to things—this, in turn, would be idolatry.

As for accordance with reality, Bonhoeffer holds that responsibility necessarily takes place within a certain and concrete context. At the same time, reality does hint at "the Real One" (*der Wirkliche*),[229] which is Christ, so acting in reality means simultaneously acting in relation to Christ: This means the realm of concrete responsibility, finding its boundaries in our createdness but remaining at the same time oriented toward Christ because it means acting according to Christ.[230] There is, however, a boundary for shouldering responsibility, which is the individual's conscience. Both concepts, conscience and responsibility, share the orientation toward certain norms. Their major difference lies in the idea that responsibility is situated in relation to a third other, an object, while conscience refers rather to an inner relation. According to Wolfgang Huber, the knowledge of oneself, as the term "*con-science*" indicates, forms the foundation for assuming responsibility.[231]

---

227. *DBW* VI, 258. Surprisingly, the English translation changes the plural *der anderen Menschen* into a singular "to another person." I only hint at that incongruence.

228. *DBW* VI, 258. Emphasis original.

229. *DBW* VI, 261. Emphasis original.

230. See *DBW* VI, 260–61.

231. See Huber, *Ethik*, 108. Huber hints at the roots of the term "conscience" in Greek and Latin, which is συνείδησις (*syneidesis*) and *conscientia*, translating to joint (*con-*) knowledge (*scientia*). Accordingly, Huber holds that knowledge from humans of themselves is meant here. However, it needs to be added that conscience is not an easy idea to grasp, and interpretations abound in philosophical as well as in theological thought. See Giubilini, "Conscience." One theological interpretation is given by Slenczka, who shows that the term "conscience" is closely connected to theological thought and oriented toward the last judgment. Conscience, then, is understood to be "the judging (*wertend*) knowledge of a subject of themselves and their identity, which can

In that regard, Bonhoeffer writes, "A responsibility that would force a person to act against conscience would thereby condemn itself."[232] Here, conscience and responsibility are closely interrelated. Within the context of violence and war, these thoughts are closely linked to Martin Luther's teaching of the two regimes he develops in his writing *Secular Authority: To What Extent it Should be Obeyed* (*Von weltlicher Obrigkeit, wie weit man ihr Gehorsam schuldig sei*, 1523).[233] While generally, the citizen needs to obey the political authorities, the boundary to rule over their citizens is the individual's freedom of religion.[234] Luther writes,

> Since, then, belief or unbelief is a matter of every one's conscience, and since this is no lessening of the secular power, the latter should be content and attend to its own affairs and permit men to believe one thing or another, as they are able and willing, and constrain no one by force. For faith is a free work, to which no one can be forced. Nay, it is a divine work, done in the Spirit, certainly not a matter which outward authority should compel or create.[235]

---

be summarized in the term 'I'" (Slenczka, "Gewissen und Gott," 236, my translation). It is therefore a relation with oneself, which is incorporated into the self as another's look. This other, in Slenczka's view, is not a concrete other human being, but an (imagined) other the I encounters as inescapable (*unentrinnbar*), inaccessible (*unverfügbar*), and involuntarily (*unwillkürlich*), 245.

This self-relation from the perspective of conscience, then, is a negative one because it is a "inner courthouse" (*innerer Gerichtshof*) alienating the self from itself by integration of the other's look, 236. The theological term "conscience" thus hints at the existential experience that humans cannot come to be reassured and calm selves but remain "to be caught in a suffering relation, keeping to oneself," 260. An interesting feature of this account is that Slenczka, though not writing in capital letters, uses terms that indicate a transcendent dimension. I only hint at this, as it might indicate that the other the self encountered within itself can hardly be of artificial nature, as I have attempted to show above (see 6.5.2 Responsibility without agency?). Slenczka goes on to discuss the phenomenon of conscience for conceptions of identity. While these are very intricate thoughts for conceptualizing humans and their identity, it goes beyond the scope of my contribution. This also pertains to the question of whether the traditional terms such as "last judgment" or "conscience" refer to a future and still pending judgment of God, foreshadowed within the individual's inner life, or whether the terms symbolize an inner human relation. I am prone to follow the latter interpretation. This, however, does not have any ramifications for the point I want to make here.

232. *DBW* VI, 276.

233. As for the terms I refer to here and the theological background with regard to Luther, see 5.2.1 *Bellum iustum*: History of Ideas.

234. See Zeyher-Quattlender, *Du sollst nicht töten (lassen)?* 135; von Scheliha, *Protestantische Ethik des Politischen*, 31.

235. Luther, *Works* III, 253–54.

This is also the theological background for conscientious objection:[236] In cases where the orders given contrast with one's conscience, the person addressed must object to them. Luther explains in that regard that a citizen does not need to fight in an unjust war begun by the ruler even if obliged. He therefore points to Acts 5:29, reading, "We ought to obey God rather than men."[237] The peace memorandum incorporates this thought when it hints at the individual responsibility of the single soldier. It reads, "They [i.e., the soldiers] are individually accountable under national and international law for their actions, and [...] the responsibility of officers does not exempt subordinates from any of their individual responsibilities."[238]

With that said, in Bonhoeffer's thought, conscience and responsibility also strike a balance in Christ: Only if the conscience of a person is Christ are they indeed able to act responsibly. In doing so, they are free and obliged concurrently: They are free because they are not bound by any specific law but they are obliged by Christ. As Bonhoeffer puts it:

> Jesus Christ is the lord of conscience. So responsibility is bound by conscience, but conscience is set free by responsibility. It has now become evident that these two statements are saying the same thing: those who act responsibly become guilty without sin; and only those whose conscience is free can bear responsibility.[239]

---

236. I am aware that, in the nineteenth century, there is a contingent historical development leading Christian churches to endorse conscientious objection to partaking in a war has not been subject to any quarrels, and Schleiermacher even appreciates war to be a legitimate means of political self-assertion given the constraint of a "defensive tendency" (von Scheliha, *Protestantische Ethik des Politischen*, 121). Within the twentieth century, however, the understanding that wars are humanmade gains acceptance, and concurrently the idea that God does not want humans to participate in war prevails. Accordingly, Dibelius demands in 1930 that the church must support those who do not want to partake in war for conscientious reasons. Similarly, Brunner argues three years later that contemporary wars cannot be compared to former warfare and need to be opposed for reasons of responsibility. In the 1950s, the Christian churches in Germany paved the way to support conscientious refusal without condemning the soldier's service. See Schrey, "Krieg IV Historisch/Ethisch," 44. Clearly, the Lutheran idea that the political influence stops at a human being's conscience has driven the development of conscientious refusal.

237. See Schrey, "Krieg IV Historisch/Ethisch," 38.

238. EKD, "Live from God's Peace," 65.

239. *DBW* VI, 283.

As Notger Slenczka shows, this feature of Bonhoeffer's ethics contrasts with morals governed only by conviction (*Gesinnungsethik*)[240] but not with responsibility for the foreseeable consequences of one's actions because it places the responsible agent within a concrete situation, whereas the agent is oriented toward the consequences of their behavior.[241] Such a situation cannot be merged into an ethical one-size-fits-all solution. To make this point, Bonhoeffer establishes the notion that humans aspire to have a unified conscience, which means that acting against the conscience amounts to self-condemnation. It might, however, not be sufficient if the conscience is oriented toward "a general law of the good."[242] This is because if the self of the person is built upon an autonomous "I," this "I" binds itself to their very own rules, which must not necessarily be coextensive with acting according to Christ. If the conscience is in accordance with Christ, though, it relates to Christ—and the neighbor. It also goes beyond the "unity of the human existence"[243] because in being found in Christ, the "own ego and its law"[244] is transgressed. In that case, it might even contrast to a given law, just as Christ broke the law of Shabbat out of love for his disciples. Accordingly, "the freed conscience aligns itself with the responsibility, which has been established in Christ, to bear guilt for the sake of the neighbor. Rather, precisely in doing so it will prove its purity."[245] This notion already shows what Bonhoeffer has in mind when referring to freedom and venture (*Wagnis*): A person is primarily bound to their conscience, which might—in some cases—not be in line with a certain given law. In this case, the person oriented toward Christ and their neighbor risks incurring guilt by acting responsibly.[246] This entails that this person is not justified simultaneously, even though they are free to act for Christological reasons: How a certain deed is justified is up to God's judgment, so the responsible agent is left with the hope for grace alone.[247] As Zeyher-Quattlender shows, this means that "acting responsibly does not only not preclude any means principally, but

---

240. Max Weber famously introduces this differentiation. See Weber, *Politik als Beruf*, 56–57.

241. See Slenczka, "Die unvermeidliche Schuld," 109–10.

242. *DBW* VI, 277.

243. *DBW* VI, 278.

244. *DBW* VI, 279.

245. *DBW* VI, 279.

246. See *DBW* VI, 283–84.

247. See *DBW* VI, 274.

also that deliberately transgressing ethical norms one takes for granted, is included into these means."[248] This, however, does not qualify the deed to be morally good, which is why Bonhoeffer expresses this notion in terms of incurring guilt. At the same time, such a view stands against a rationale where the end justifies the means. It rather means that only in cases of extraordinary need is it necessary to transgress the law in order to observe an even greater law.[249] On the other side of that coin, this means that in not acting responsibly, the responsibility eschewed would lead to an even more hopeless guilt.[250]

6.6.2 Eschewing Responsibility and Incurring an Even More Hopeless Guilt

Combining this notion with Bonhoeffer's peace thought means that in an "extraordinary situation of ultimate necessities that are beyond any possible regulation by the law,"[251] the individual human can decide to act against the law and thus kill, for instance. However, if they do so, they are not exculpated but bear the blame for their behavior. In front of God, they can hope for grace, but in relation to other humans, they have to account for what they have done.[252] It is this thought the peace memorandum draws on, when holding that

> In any situation where the responsibility for our own or others' lives forces us to take actions that will themselves endanger or destroy life, not even the most careful assessment of consequences will free us from the risk of incurring guilt.[253]

---

248. Zeyher-Quattlender, *Du sollst nicht töten (lassen)?* 332. My translation.

249. See Zeyher-Quattlender, *Du sollst nicht töten (lassen)?* 332.

250. See *DBW* VI, 276. The English edition translates the German *heillos* with the term "egregious." This, however, is not what the German term indicates, because egregious does not incorporate the impossibility of salvation insinuated with the German term. I therefore decide to use the term "hopeless" in its place.

251. *DBW* VI, 273.

252. See 5.3.3.1 On Bonhoeffer's Account of War and Peace.

253. EKD, "Live from God's Peace," 103. The peace memorandum draws on this thought, but simultaneously exceeds Bonhoeffer's notion, as Bonhoeffer clearly intends no juridically binding solution for such extraordinary cases. The peace memorandum, however, suggests exactly that. For that matter, the peace memorandum—and also the solution I aim for—goes beyond this idea of Bonhoeffer by still harking back to Bonhoeffer's thought.

This means that taking lives, even in war, does not free the agent from becoming guilty. Guilt, however, is a term indissolubly linked to the conscience and, in a Christian perspective, therefore to the idea of a last judgment oriented toward categories such as good and evil.[254]

For Bonhoeffer, incurring guilt is indissolubly linked to acting responsibly: A person that does not want to risk becoming guilty cannot act responsibly. Yet, if they do act responsibly and are thus running the risk of incurring guilt, they do not stand alone but are part of a responsible community originating in Jesus Christ. Most importantly, however, people who attempt to eschew responsibility, not taking the risk of incurring guilt, might lose an even greater good because they incur an "even more hopeless"[255] guilt, so not becoming guilty might in that case be even worse.

Reading these parts of Bonhoeffer's ethics has two major implications for the theological argument I suggest. First, as I have mentioned above,[256] these complex and internal processes cannot be transferred to machines: With regard to incurring guilt and acting responsibly, the technological device falls short of the necessary condition, which is having a conscience. Such devices relate to neither an inner nor an outer other being, such as an internal I or a concrete neighbor. They only simulate doing so.[257] This refutes the claim of being able to implement morals into machines: Simply reconstructing a behavior that appears to be responsible does not make the artifact responsible in itself. This is because responsibility rests on relatedness qua being a responsible agent. This does not mean that humans and nonhumans do not relate to each other in a kind of network because nonhumans, such as machines, form an important part of our forms of life.[258] However, this neither guarantees that humans will in fact act responsibly, which brings me to my second point.

A human eschewing their responsibility loses an even greater good. According to Bonhoeffer, to assume responsibility naturally entails the risk of incurring guilt, which is not an easy process for the individual, so in the end, the will to disclaim responsibility seems natural. In my

---

254. See Slenczka, "Gewissen und Gott," 243.
255. *DBW* VI, 276.
256. See 6.5.5 Striking a Balance Between Responsibility and Risk.
257. See Coeckelbergh, "Moral Appearances, Emotions, Robots and Human Morality."
258. See 2.1 Connecting Humans and Machines; See Latour, *Pandora's Hope*; Coeckelbergh, *Using Words and Things*; Haraway, "Cyborg Manifesto."

opinion, the idea of transferring moral decisions toward machines complies with exactly that wish: Then, an autoregulative weapons systems is a means to duck responsibility because they are ostensibly more humane. This is feasible in two ways. First, it might be possible to see the machine to be responsible in itself, so the people involved in the human–machine network are discharged. Second, the people in collaboration with the machine might lose control of the system, so the overall system is devoid of agency and responsibility. Both cases would lead to an actual and outright shrinking in moral responsibility: The moral agent attempts to make themselves invisible. In the first case, this means making the categorial mistake of ascribing agency and responsibility directly toward the machine due to an erroneous anthropomorphization. In the second case, this entails that the system is falsely understood to operate without any intent because human judgment, agency, and responsibility, which the technological part of the collaboration is in need of, is ignored. Both situations are structured differently. While in the first case, there would be no need to ascribe responsibility toward any human agent, as the system itself is seen to be responsible, the second case is more complex. Here, the loss of responsibility is known but unaccounted for. While this problem might be solved juridically, for instance, by compiling a list of which agent involved with the system is responsible to what degree in which case, the moral problem that the system ceases to be under control at a given time stays in place. This is because if a person was targeted lethally in such a situation, nobody would acknowledge guilt.

The implications of these cases, however, can be intensified with respect to Bonhoeffer's insight that not shouldering responsibility leads to an even greater loss. In theological terms, this means that the person attempting to eschew their responsibility via technological means does in fact attempt to not become guilty.[259] This, however, does not simply lead to a situation where they can beware of becoming guilty: In eschewing responsibility, they incur precisely that, or do so in a more problematic manner, as the intentional failure to acknowledge guilt is added to the guilt incurred. In philosophical terms, the gist of this notion might be expressed as follows: In the attempt to evade responsibility, humans try to evade responsibility and humanity is lost. This is because in "simply pressing the 'fire' button,"[260] humans follow the system but do not make

259. This is very similar to Berman's argumentation. See Excursus 2 Assessments of Autoregulation in Weapons Technology Within Jewish Traditions.

260. Roff and Moyes, "Meaningful Human Control, Artificial Intelligence and Autonomous Weapons," 1.

An Ethical Evaluation of Lethal Functions in Autoregulative Weapons Systems

a judgment or a conscious decision and therefore do not act responsibly. Doing so, however, transfers agency and responsibility automatically to the machine at the cost of undermining the very same anthropological conceptions, so humans lose their own agency, responsibility, and autonomy in the process.

6.6.3 Autoregulative Functions in Weapons as a Means of Cheap Grace

To push things even further, this idea can be transferred to Bonhoeffer's differentiation between cheap and costly grace. Bonhoeffer elaborates on that difference in his book *The Cost of Discipleship* (1937), which he wrote prior to his *Ethics*.[261] He writes,

> Cheap grace means grace as bargain-basement goods, cut-rate forgiveness, cut-rate comfort, cut-rate sacrament [...]. Cheap grace means grace as doctrine, as principle, as system. [...] Cheap grace means justification of sin but not of the sinner.[262]

Costly grace instead means to be called into discipleship:

> Costly grace [...] is the call of Jesus Christ which causes a disciple to leave his nest and follow him. [...] It is costly, because it calls into discipleship; it is grace, because it calls us to follow *Jesus Christ*. It is costly, because it costs people their lives; it is grace, because it thereby makes them live. It is costly, because it condemns sin; it is grace, because it justifies the sinner.[263]

What Bonhoeffer refers to is the idea that forgiveness that does not demand anything from the person is cheap, as it gives rise to the possibility of dodging discipleship—and responsibility. It means that a person

---

261. This also entails that the terminology, and the gist of the two works, might not be coextensive, also due to the time they were written and the development of Bonhoeffer's thought over the course of time. I have made clear above that there is a development in his peace ethical thought when elaborating on Bonhoeffer's account of war and peace, where his peace ethics shifts more and more toward a progressing political stance. My reading of Bonhoeffer here therefore comes with the reservation that I interpret his prior work in the light of the later one. I do so because I think that this is very enlightening for the whole discussion concerning autoregulative functions in weapons systems, even though I am aware that an interpretation that focuses on the theological development of Bonhoeffer as a person might object to that approach.

262. *DBW* IV, 29.

263. *DBW* IV, 30–31. Emphasis original.

considers themselves to be exculpated no matter what. Costly grace, on the other hand, refers to the idea that in calling somebody into discipleship, Jesus urges them not to live their life as it is but to obey within a given situation.[264] Bonhoeffer refers to that in a bipartite statement that reads, "*Only the believers obey, and only the obedient believe.*"[265] What he means is that obedience and belief need to strike a balance and that in doing so, grace gains the meaning it is supposed to have. That way, Bonhoeffer opposes a simple justification by deeds, which would amount to being only obedient, as well as the dissipation of grace, which would be to believe without being obedient within certain circumstances because "you are given a situation in which you can have faith."[266]

These remarks reveal that grace is only experienced genuinely if it demands something from the person addressed. Or, put differently, the person can only hope for costly grace if they do not back away from the responsible position in which they are situated. On the other hand, to eschew responsibility means to resort to cheap grace. Applied to technology, the deployment of a system that enables the transfer of one's responsibility onto machines— thereby providing the possibility to evade responsibility—might be interpreted to be of such character. In such a case, autoregulation in weapons systems can be seen as a means of cheap grace: It enables the person to eschew their own responsibility because they can always put the blame onto the machine. This problem might still be in place even if juridical solutions might be found because the system is devoid of moral responsibility if a human operator solely follows the system's advice or because the system is indeed seen to be a moral agent. Therefore, these two cases need to be avoided. As I have argued above,[267] this might be the case if the possibility of exerting control is a given, due to sufficient time, resources, knowledge, and competence, and if the situation is relatively clear. The time factor might remain a fundamental problem, though, because as warfare accelerates, time frames close and it is hard to enable sufficient time.[268] Moreover, the general question of which time frame would be adequate is hard to answer. In addition, there is the open question of which phase of the decision-making loop automatization

---

264. See *DBW* IV, 51–52, 55–56.
265. *DBW* IV, 52.
266. *DBW* IV, 57–58.
267. See 6.5.5 Striking a Balance Between Responsibility and Risk.
268. See 4.4. Meaningful Human Control.

should take place in and to what extent.[269] At the very least, it would be important to allocate moral and deliberative judgment to humans. Killing is surely a situation that needs such judgment—and in real time, at that. This is because only humans can judge the situation as a whole, and only humans have an understanding of the world in which they live.[270] Only they can react to changing situations. To be fair, a very small time frame might be possible in that regard—the overall situation will hardly change within several seconds. But in such a case, the responsibility for using an autoregulative function needs to be accounted for as well.[271]

To put this thought in a nutshell, autoregulation in weapons systems is inherently problematic for theological reasons to the extent it can be seen as a means of renouncing the responsibility granted to and demanded from humans. This brings the crucial role of control to the fore because responsibility can only be maintained if control is exerted.[272] Accordingly, the ethical discussion needs to focus on how control can be maintained within these systems, especially in the light of closing time frames and decreasing scopes of human influence. To simply provide a technological solution toward these intricate ethical issues seems to be misguided at any rate, as the technological device with its means of reckoning cannot easily replace humans' capacity to judge. In other words, the autoregulative part of the overall human–machine system remains dependent on the autonomous one, which is per se a human being.

---

269. See 3.7.1 From OODA to F2T2EA.
270. See 3.3 Reckoning and Judgment.
271. See 6.5.3 Gaps or Diffusion of Responsibility?
272. See 6.5.3 Gaps or Diffusion of Responsibility?

7

Conclusion

THIS WORK HAS DISCUSSED the deployment of autoregulative functions within weapons systems from the peace ethical perspective of just peace. This approach stands out because ethical considerations of autoregulative functions in weapons systems have so far focused either on technological ethical questions or sidelined pacifist positions, usually analyzing the extent to which they exceed the regulations of IHL.[1] The research question I am focusing on here, however, is the issue of if, and to what degree, autoregulative functions within weapons systems might help or hinder the establishment of just peace. The question was elaborated on from a contingent pacifist stance, deeming the use of force exculpable only in cases of extraordinary need where it appears to be the lesser evil. I maintain that it is suitable because it emphasizes that answering violence with violence is a deeply precarious option, since peace can only be achieved by means of peace, while at the same time the use of force is not ruled out completely. Due to this, just peace theory is still plausible

---

1. There are exceptions, of course, and I refer to them in the course of this work. These are mainly the contributions provided by Bernhard Koch on philosophical grounds, but also the ideas proposed by Berman from a Jewish perspective. For Koch's account, see 5.3.4 Contingent Pacifism and Autoregulation in Weapons Systems. For Bermann, see Excursus 2 Assessments of Autoregulation in Weapons Technology Within Jewish Traditions. Furthermore, there are the peace ethical works provided by the Protestant theologian von Schubert and the Roman Catholic theologian Schockenhoff, who discuss autoregulative functions in weapons systems rather briefly within their overall approach toward peace ethics. There is also the memorandum of the Protestant church in Germany that discusses the ethics of digitization, thereby also turning toward autoregulative functions in weapons systems. For further information on these contributions, see 5.3.4 Contingent Pacifism and Autoregulation in Weapons Systems.

and appropriate.[2] The most convincing feature of just peace is that it does not focus on war alone but on the use of force in general, no matter who is using it. This is also why just peace suits the matter of technological crossover developments best. If expressed in terms of just war thinking, this is especially apparent when the classical framework of *jus ad bellum* and *jus in bello* is complemented and oriented toward a *jus post bellum* by emphasizing the *jus ad bellum* category of intention. Transferring this rationale toward a contingent pacifist frame by focusing not on war but on the use of force in general means that rather technological features, such as the problem of risk inflicted or the question how to maintain control thereby shouldering responsibility, can be conceptualized within a peace ethical frame. Especially taking account of the fact that the issue of responsibility concerns the question of whether a state of peace can be established in the aftermath of a conflict, it makes sense to ponder responsibility. This entails emphasizing the need to reconcile and to hold accountable the people responsible in the aftermath of a violent scenario (*jus post bellum*), and simultaneously the need to attune objective and intention of the use of force more to peace (*jus in bello*), as well as the need to highlight that the means resorted to in a violent scenario ought to promote rather than hinder the establishment of just peace in the aftermath of an armed conflict. Therefore, responsibility needs to be maintained in order to reconcile and to make peace, while not shouldering responsibility will hinder these processes and thus make it harder to achieve peace after armed conflict.

Before drawing my conclusion, I need to emphasize two findings that have come to the fore in the course of this assessment, one with respect to the technological systems, and the other pertaining to the langue we use. As for technology, the issues pertaining to autoregulative devices might not concentrate on a single system but rather on a complex network of devices, such as in a swarm or a system of systems It is highly plausible that an autoregulative robot should not be weaponized, since this would be too risky, at least with respect to the technology

---

2. I am aware that the international political institutions, such as the bodies of the UN, are de facto incapable of coming to one conclusion and even less able to act commonly. This, however, does not do away with the necessity of maintaining or (re-)building political bodies that operate on an international level. In that regard, it needs to be emphasized that international political bodies never had the same opportunities national political institutions have because international alliances cannot enforce their matters and laws. Whether or not a nation state conforms to certain international norm is up to them. This has not changed in recent times; it only becomes more apparent.

currently in use. This is also because means of war that cannot adhere to the demands of prevailing law, such as discrimination and proportionality, cannot be considered legitimate means of warfare.[3] These so-called out-of-the-loop devices are the devices that the political and especially the ethical debate focuses on—and for good reason, since a device that has means of reckoning but cannot judge a situation can hardly make the ethical decision of whether or not to target a person lethally.[4] In addition to these single out-of-the-loop devices, however, there is the development of swarms or systems of systems. Here, humans and machines collaborate more closely and in real time. In such a scenario, it is very likely and reasonable to resort to autoregulative functions because the processes within the system are so quick and complex that a human can hardly keep pace.[5] The issue here is rather that of whether humans will maintain control of the system or simply follow the suggestions made due to psychological effects such as automation bias.[6] If this were the case, the system would be out of control, and responsibility would be hard to establish. This is the reason why I do not focus on out-of-the-loop devices alone but consider contexts of human and machine collaborations as well. This is also because, even though a single out-of-the-loop device seems to operate without human engagement, humans provide the necessary data as well as the objective for a certain undertaking.[7] Accordingly, humans are still part of the collaboration, even if they are far more distanced. In any case, the military goal—to gain an advantage by accelerating the processes of decision-making—is in contrast to the ethical objective of maintaining control in a substantive sense. Therefore, the matter of time stands out in that regard.[8] By the same token, to automize single processes of the decision-making loop means to transfer control to the machine, so there is a danger that, in transferring single decisions, the control of the overall system is jeopardized.[9]

My second remark concerns the anthropomorphized language we use when talking about AI and autoregulative devices. As Frederike van

3. See 6.1 Legal Framework.
4. See 3.3 Reckoning and Judgment.
5. See 1.1.3 Future Combat Air System.
6. For this and other problems of human–machine interaction, see 4.2 Implications of Automatization.
7. See 3.8 Conclusion.
8. See 4.4 Meaningful Human Control.
9. See 4.7.1 From OODA to F2T2EA.

An Ethical Evaluation of Lethal Functions in Autoregulative Weapons Systems

Oorschot has shown, this is a kind of imitative imagination rather than something that mirrors the technological process within the systems.[10] Regardless of whether the subject is AI, technological "autonomy," or machine "learning," all of these terms indicate that humans are the role model and that the processes within the machines resemble the processes of humans. This, however, is not the case. Drawing on the differentiation between human judgment and technological reckoning Brain Cantwell Smith has proposed,[11] I maintain that the language we use when referring to technological devices in an anthropomorphized manner changes the way we interact with machines, running the risk that humans overtrust machines instead of resorting to their own ability to judge.[12] Yet, this jeopardizes the performance of the overall systems, risking to harm people in the case of weapons systems. This, however, does not mean that humans simply use tools when they interact with technology. I rather understand technology to be of transcendental nature, thereby co-shaping the worlds of life in which humans live. Therefore, the way we perceive and interact with technology changes these shared worlds of life, as it changes the way we perceive and interact with other humans.[13] Using the example of tele-technology, it makes a personal and societal difference in communication whether I send a letter, a telegram, or make a voice or video call. This is not only due to the form of communication influencing the people making use of it, but also because the time frame changes, thereby simultaneously changing societal structures. Similarly, transforming the means of using force can be expected to have an impact on warfare, self-defense, and policing. Accordingly, the advent of autoregulation in weapons technology can be expected to have ramifications for our forms of life that may not be contained to scenarios of violence alone but expand into daily life because of the transcendental character of technology.

Having made this clear, there are three major conclusions I want to draw here. The first pertains to the ongoing change from symmetrical scenarios of war toward more and more asymmetrical scenarios, which is, at least with respect to autoregulation, mainly connected to the issue of risk, thereby changing concomitantly the prevailing war paradigm to a police paradigm. Second, I demand that the human part of the

---

10. van Oorschot, "Alles Technik oder was?"; 3.4 Machines: Autoregulative, Not Autonomous.

11. See Smith, *TPromise of Artificial Intelligence*; 3.3 Reckoning and Judgment.

12. See 3.8 Conclusion.

13. See 2.1 Connecting Humans and Machines.

Conclusion

human–machine collaboration needs to maintain control, while third, I conceptualize these issues with respect to theological thinking, arguing that the attempt to eschew responsibility by means of autoregulative devices is an attempt to resort to cheap grace.

First, and with respect to risk, I hold that the risk inflicted by means of autoregulative devices changes the ethical assumptions for the use of force. This is closely connected to a trend already underway, and Herfried Münkler, for instance, has hinted toward the shift from symmetrical nation-state actors fighting each other to the current, stronger asymmetrical situation that merely resembles the situation of the Thirty Years' War.[14] By the same token, the precondition that war can be fought justly from both belligerent sides (*bellum iustum ex utraque partee*), as expressed by Grotius,[15] can hardly be upheld within such an asymmetrical scenario. As for risk, the asymmetrical infliction thereof can already be seen with respect to drone technology, but gains even more momentum with respect to autoregulative devices, since those weapons expose the opposing party, including civilians, to a high risk, while the side deploying the device fights virtually riskless—at least from a physical point of view. As Paul Kahn has argued persuasively, this constellation resembles a police rather than a war situation,[16] at least with respect to classical just war thinking. This is because, in war, both parties are imagined to be on an equal footing, each of them threatening the other and each of them a legitimate target. The police officer, on the other hand, is to be protected and must not be targeted lethally. They also have to treat an addressee not as their enemy but as a citizen with rights who is innocent until proven guilty. Accordingly, the protection these systems offer one-sidedly fits far better into a police situation. On these grounds, and given the revision of just war thinking, it might be plausible to argue in favor of autoregulative devices for the sake of the party that needs protection because they fight for legitimate reasons.[17] This idea, however, runs counter to contingent pacifist thought because the risk that a certain war might be only ostensibly legitimate—either because of flawed information or because the government deceives their citizens—is high. Therefore, the moral risk of partaking in such a violent undertaking, by whatever means, inflicts

---

14. See Münkler, *Die neuen Kriege*.
15. See 5.2.1 *Bellum iustum*: History of Ideas.
16. See Kahn, "Imagining Warfare"; 6.4.2 The Paradox of Riskless Warfare.
17. See Meireis, "Die Revisionist Just War Theory," 329.

moral risk on each person using force.[18] In cases of a sharp asymmetry in war, where the physical risk is put on the opposing side—including civilians—the moral risk (and responsibility) rests with the side deploying the device: They need to make sure that the reason they fight is worth taking that moral risk. This is the case generally because, within just peace, violent means are precarious in nature, as just peace thinking argues.[19] This is even more the case if a war paradigm no longer prevails but rather a kind of police paradigm. In this case, the addressee in question is no longer an enemy that can be a targeted lethally, but rather a suspect who is innocent until proven guilty, so the use of lethal force per se is problematic.

Second, and pertaining to moral agency and responsibility, my main argument is that in order to address these questions appropriately, the overall system must remain in the control of the human counterpart(s) collaborating with the machine because, within the overall system of humans and machines, it is the humans who provide agency and responsibility. To look at this from the reverse perspective, autoregulative functions might be deployed if humans decide to use them intentionally, as they also shoulder responsibility in this case.[20] In this context, two major misunderstandings need to be avoided, the first of which is that the machine itself is perceived to be a responsible agent. This would be an anthropomorphic misperception.[21] Second, the oversimplistic understanding of an autoregulative device—that is seen as an independent, distinct, and "autonomous" entity operating apart from humans—is to be averted.[22] What is more important is the focus on human control because it might not matter if humans are in-the-loop, on-the-loop, or out-of-the-loop if all they do is accomplish what the machine tells them to do.[23] It rather needs to be ensured technologically, by design, and by training that humans maintain control. One opportunity to address this issue is to consider the time frame given, the knowledge the human part(s) of the collaboration possess, the competence they prove to have, and the resources they are supplied with.[24] If these conditions are met,

18. See 6.4.3 Moral Risk.
19. See EKD, "Live from God's Peace," 103; 5.3.3.3 Just Peace Theory.
20. See 6.5.5 Striking a Balance Between Responsibility and Risk.
21. See 3.5 Artificial Entities as Moral Agents.
22. See 3.4 Machines: Autoregulative, Not Autonomous.
23. See 4.4 Meaningful Human Control.
24. See Hollnagel and Woods, *Joint Cognitive Systems*, 75. As described in 4.1 Joint Cognitive Systems.

Conclusion

humans are expected to hold control. While it is conceivable that at least the three latter requirements could be implemented in a comparatively uncomplicated way, the matter of time stands out. This is because the logic of accelerating procedures of decision-making with the help of machines runs counter to the ethical demand to maintain control.[25] Technological procedures, such as adaptive or adaptable automation, might mitigate that problem to some degree, but they cannot do away with it.[26] It finally comes down to the intricate question of what time frame would be appropriate to decide whether a person lives or dies—a question that seems hardly possible to answer.

Third, and more explicitly referring to Protestant theological thought, while following Bonhoeffer, I make the argument that deploying autoregulation in weapons systems might be a means of cheap grace because it is a way of avoiding the acknowledgement of guilt that may accompany acting responsibly.[27] Put in theological terms, this means that in attempting to eschew responsibility, humans incur even more guilt in changing costly grace into cheap grace. This means that the (costly) grace God offers to humans entails that they cannot continue living their lives as they did but are called into discipleship, which requires being responsive and living responsibly.[28] In doing so, humans follow Christ. As Bonhoeffer puts it, "Jesus takes the guilt of his brothers and sisters upon himself, and in carrying the burden of this guilt he proves himself as the sinless one. Now in this sinless guilty [*sündlos schuldig*] Jesus Christ all vicarious representative responsible action [*stellvertretend verantwortliches Handeln*] has its origin."[29] Just as Jesus became guilty in shouldering responsibility, humans can hope for costly grace if they follow his example. Yet, if they attempt to eschew responsibility and the guilt that comes with shouldering it, they lose this precious good.[30]

Against this backdrop, an autoregulative device wrongly depicted as making moral decisions, such as targeting people lethally, seems to be the attempt to do exactly that: to duck responsibility for ostensibly good reasons. The reasons given revolve around human failure but are confronted with a technology that cannot meet the legal and ethical

25. See 4.4 Meaningful Human Control.
26. See 4.3 Implementation of Automatization.
27. See 6.6 Waging War Without Guilt.
28. See 6.6.1 The Acceptance of Guilt in Responsible Action.
29. *DBW* VI, 275–76.
30. See 6.6.2 Eschewing Responsibility and Incurring an Even More Hopeless Guilt.

demands for combat, at least for the time being, not to mention the necessity of judging complex situations. Therefore, currently, there are no good reasons to transfer lethal, and therefore moral, control to machines. If it is done nonetheless, humans not only lose control but may no longer follow Christ in discipleship.[31] In more philosophical terms, this thought might be rephrased in the idea that by transferring the control to the system, humans concurrently try to get rid of their agency, autonomy, and responsibility, which entails losing their humanity in the process. This is because they freely hand over their very own characteristics to the machine, which cannot fulfil the necessary requirements. In that way, agency, autonomy, and responsibility are lost to the machine. This entails that, if control is not maintained and humans simply follow the machine, harm is done not only to the victims of the lethal attack but also to the humans collaborating with the system because they ultimately give away their humanity. Furthermore, it is very plausible to retransfer the essence of these terms after they have undergone a technologization back to humans, so humans are "machinized" in the process.[32]

The main question, therefore, is how control and therefore responsibility can be maintained. For this matter, I propose focusing on human control in the way the paradigm of joint cognitive systems proposes with respect to time, knowledge, competence, and resources.[33] If these conditions are met, humans are, in fact, in control of the system and they concomitantly shoulder responsibility.[34] In contrast, if these conditions are not met, control is lost and a gap in moral responsibility might indeed occur. This is because no human shoulders responsibility in real time. This, however, does not mean that every failure of the system needs to come back to the person(s) collaborating with the system, or that the problem might not be resolved in juridical terms.

Pertaining to the former, I can perceive of at least four elements that need to strike a balance, among them, clearly highlighted but not solely, the human part(s) of the collaboration. Next to them, the programmers of the algorithms and the companies they work for need to be addressed in terms of responsibility if the algorithms and the data the system is trained on is flawed, as well as the designers of the device and their companies in the case of an issue with the way the artificial entity

---

31. See 6.6.3 Autoregulative Functions in Weapons as a Means of Cheap Grace.
32. See Koch, "Maschinen, die uns von uns selbst entfremden."
33. See 4.1 Joint Cognitive Systems.
34. See 6.5.5 Striking a Balance Between Responsibility and Risk.

Conclusion

is designed.[35] For instance, if it facilitates the process of anthropomorphizing, that might lead to a misperception of the technology, such as outright anthropomorphic design.[36] Finally, within the context of war, the party deploying the device, such as the nation state, clearly needs to assume responsibility because they must justify the use of force altogether. If they are wrong in their assessment that a situation might indeed necessitate the use of force to avoid greater evil, such as genocide, then the use of any weapons system is wrong. In such a case, humans collaborating with the system are the most important entity that might hinder illegitimate deployment because the technological system itself will not refuse to operate for ethical reasons—it has no means to judge the situation morally. Against this backdrop, a fourpartite approach to address the diffusion of responsibility seems reasonable to me, referring to the human part(s) of the actual human–machine cooperation, the designers, the programmers, and the nation state.

As for finding juridical solutions, addressing autoregulation in weapons systems in such a fourpartite way might be a first answer. Within such networked approaches toward responsibility, the respective problem would need to be addressed in conjunction with the diverse parts of the network—to different degrees.[37] As far as the human collaborator(s) with the system are concerned, they ultimately bear the most risk by shouldering responsibility they cannot account for. This is reasonable with respect to forward-looking responsibility: The people collaborating with such systems know the risk this entails, including a failure of the system.[38] With respect to moral responsibility, however, the case seems to be more complicated because, if the system is no longer in control of the human part(s) of the collaboration, then an outright gap in moral responsibility might indeed occur. These people might then be made accountable afterward but, within the situation, there is no responsibility taken, no agency employed, and no person judging, hence there is a gap thereof.

One way to at least mitigate that problem might be to define situations where resorting to autoregulative functions might be more legitimate. As an example, I suggested deploying an autoregulative function within the deep sea, where machines fighting each other might pose

35. See 6.5.3 Gaps or Diffusion of Responsibility?
36. See 3.6 Artificial Entities as Moral Patients.
37. See 6.5.3 Gaps or Diffusion of Responsibility?
38. See 6.5.4 Forward-Looking Responsibility.

fewer moral problems than an urban fighting scenario due to the complexity of the situation.[39] Along these lines, it is also reasonable to argue that devices that do not target people lethally, such as devices for emergency medical services, as well as those that dispose of explosives, pose no considerable ethical concerns. Within the human–machine collaboration, the implementation of adaptive or adaptable automation might be considered as well. In doing so, cases that need the attention of a human are to be predefined, so it is ensured that lethal decisions within complex scenarios indeed rest with humans.[40] In any case, humans needs to maintain control, be it in terms of actually operating the system, in at least supervising it within a framework of sufficient time, resources, knowledge, and competence, or in clearly handing over the (lethal) operation to the machine, thereby concomitantly shouldering responsibility for its operations—a situation that is precarious in its ethical nature but that might be feasible in a very clear and distinct scenario. How this can be accomplished in a specific situation is a question that can only be answered within an interdisciplinary approach bringing together engineers, programmers, ethicists, and psychologists. The problem that the system might be devoid of control, however, as well as the crucial matter of time, are urgent topics that need further ethical and interdisciplinary pondering.

39. See 4.4 Meaningful Human Control.

40. See 4.3 Implementations of Automatization. It is, however, an open question whether adaptable or adaptive automation would be the appropriate technological means to do so. This is because in adaptive automation, it is the system rather than humans that influence the level of automatization, while it is the other way around in adaptable automation. Both procedures have advantages and disadvantages. In terms of control, adaptable automation would seem to be the better course of action because humans decide. If, however, this decision is made under too high a workload and the system is therefore in danger of failing, adaptive automation might be favored. I cannot decide here what should be preferred, but only hint at this question with the remark that this decision is inherently ethical and should be decided over not by engineers alone but in conjunction with ethicists and psychologists.

Bibliography

Abraham, Michael. "On Fear of Technology." https://mikyab.net/posts/60727.
———. "Q & A." https://mikyab.net.
Airbus. "FCAS." https://mediacentre.airbus.com/mediacentre/media?mediaTitle=title_FCAS+&mediaId=545950.
AlgorithmWatch, ed. "Automating Society: Taking Stock of Automated Decision Making in the EU." Berlin, 2019. https://algorithmwatch.org/en/automating-society-2019/.
Allen Institute for AI. "Ask Delphi." https://delphi.allenai.org/.
Allen, Colin, and Michael. Trestman "Animal Consciousness." *Stanford Encyclopedia of Philosophy* (2017). https://plato.stanford.edu/archives/win2017/entries/consciousness-animal/.
Allman, Mark J., and Tobias L. Winright. *After the Smoke Clears: The Just War Tradition and Post War Justice*. New York: Orbis, 2010.
Altmann, Jürgen, and Frank Sauer. "Autonomous Weapons Systems and Strategic Stability." *Survival* 59 (2019) 117–42.
Altmann, Jürgen. "Autonome Waffensysteme—der nächste Schritt im qualitativen Rüstungswettlauf?" In *Unbemannte Systeme und ihre ethische Legitimierung*, edited by Ines-Jacqueline Werkner et al., 111–36. Wiesbaden: Springer, 2010.
———. "Zur ethischen Beurteilung automatisierter und autonomer Waffensysteme." In *Handbuch Friedensethik*, edited by Ines-Jacqueline Werkner et al., 793–804. Wiesbaden: Springer, 2017.
Alwart, Dahlmann, et al. *First Steps Toward a Multidimensional Autonomy Risk Assessment (MARA) in Weapons Systems*. Berlin: Stiftung Wissenschaft und Politik, 2015.
Ameriks, Karl. "Kant on Freedom and Autonomy." In *Freiheit nach Kant. Tradition, Rezeption, Transformation, Aktualität*, edited by Saša Josifović et al., 95–116. Leiden: Brill, 2019.
Amoroso, Sauer, et al. "Autonomy in Weapon Systems: The Military Application of Artificial Intelligence as a Litmus Test for Germany's New Foreign and Security Policy." Publication Series on Democracy 49, edited by the Heinrich-Böll-Stiftung. Großbeeren: Arnold Group, 2018.
Antebi, Liran. "Who Will Stop the Robots?" *Military and Strategic Affairs* 2 (2013). https://www.inss.org.il/wp-content/uploads/systemfiles/MASA5-2Eng6_Antebi.pdf.
Aristotle. "Pol VII." http://www.perseus.tufts.edu/hopper/text?doc=Aristot.+Pol.+7.1333a&.

Bibliography

Arkin, Ronald C. "The Case for Ethical Autonomy in Unmanned Systems." *Journal of Military Ethics*, 4 (2010) 332–341.

———. "Ethics and Autonomous Systems: Perils and Promises." *Proceedings of the Institute of Electrical and Electronics Engineers (IEEE)* 10 (2016) 1779–881.

———. *Governing Lethal Behavior in Autonomous Robots*. Boca Raton: CRC, 2009.

———. "Governing Lethal Behavior: Embedding Ethics in a Hybrid Deliberative/Reactive Robot Architecture." http://www.cc.gatech.edu/ai/robot-lab/online-publications/formalizationv35.pdf.

Arnott, Stephen M. "A Jus Post Bellum Analysis of Lethal Autonomous Weapons: Assessing the Importance of Human Interaction and Moral Repair to Peace." https://etheses.whiterose.ac.uk/18547.

Asaro, Peter. "On Banning Autonomous Weapons Systems: Human Rights, Automation, and the Dehumanization of Lethal Decision-Making." *International Review of the Red Cross* 94 (2012) 687–709.

Assmann, Jan. *Totale Religion. Ursprünge und Formen puritanischer Verschärfung.* Vienna: Picus, 2016.

Augustine. "De civitae dei." https://phil.flet.keio.ac.jp/person/nakagawa/texts/august/cd/cd19.html.

Baer, Tobias. *Understand, Manage and Prevent Algorithmic Bias: A Guide for Business Users and Data Scientists*. Oxford: Oxford University Press, 2009.

Bahner, Jennifer Elin. "Übersteigertes Vertrauen in Automation: Der Einfluss von Fehlererfahrungen auf Complacency und Automation Bias." PhD diss., Technische Universität Berlin, 2008.

Bainbridge, Lisanne. "Ironies of Automation." *Automatica* 6 (1983) 775–79.

Barth, Friederike. "Widerstehende Gewalt. Das Beispiel Dietrich Bonhoeffer." In *Gewalt und Gewalten. Zur Ausübung, Legitimität und Ambivalenz rechtserhaltender Gewalt*, edited by Torsten Meireis, 269–86. Tübingen: Mohr Siebeck, 2012.

Baxter, Rooksby, et al. "The Ironies of Automation: Still Going Strong at 30?" Energy Conversion Congress and Exposition (ECCE), 2012.

Baxter, James Houston, trans. "Epistula 198." In *Augustine: Select Letters*, 323–33. London: 1930.

Bayertz, Kurt. "Eine kurze Geschichte der Herkunft der Verantwortung." In *Verantwortung. Prinzip oder Problem?* 3–72. Darmstadt: Wissenschaftliche Buchgesellschaft, 1995.

Beauchamp, Tom L., and James F. Childress. *Principals of Biomedical Ethics*. Oxford: Oxford University Press, 2001.

Beck, Ulrich. *Risikogesellschaft. Auf dem Weg in eine andere Moderne*. Frankfurt: Suhrkamp, 1986.

Becker, Ralf. "Die Zeichen der Zeit erkennen. Über christliche Verantwortungsethik und die Notwendigkeit, Möglichkeit und Wirksamkeit gewaltfreier Konfliktbewältigung." https://zeitzeichen.net/node/9624.

Bedford-Strohm, Heinrich. "Die Macht der Menschlichkeit." https://www.zeit.de/gesellschaft/zeitgeschehen/2022-03/ungarisch-ukrainische-grenze-fluechtlinge-ukraine-krieg-heinrich-bedford-strohm/komplettansicht.

Beestermöller, Gerhard. *Thomas von Aquin und der gerechte Krieg*. Cologne: Bachem, 1990.

Bibliography

Bellamy, Alex J., and Tim Dunne. "R2P in Theory and Practice." In *The Oxford Handbook of the Responsibility to Protect*, 3–17. Oxford: Oxford University Press, 2016.

Benbaji, Yitzhak, and Daniel Statman. *War by Agreement: A Contractarian Ethics of War*. Oxford: Oxford University Press, 2019.

Benbaji, Yitzhak. "A Defense of the Traditional War Convention." *Ethics* 3 (2008) 464–95.

———. "Distributive Justice, Human Rights, and Territorial Integrity: A Contractarian Account of the Crime of Aggression." In *The Morality of Defensive War*, edited by Cécile Fabre et al., 159–84. Oxford: Oxford University Press, 2014.

———. "The Moral Power of Soldiers to Undertake the Duty of Obedience." *Ethics* 1 (2011) 43–73.

Benjamin, Walter. "Critique of Violence." In *Selected Writings*, edited by Marcus Bullock et al., 1:236–52. Cambridge: Belknap, 2002.

Benvenisti, Eyal. "The Law on Asymmetric Warfare: Looking to the Future." In *Essays on International Law in Honor of W. Michael Reisman*, edited by Mahnoush H. Arsanjani et al., 931–50. Leiden: Martinus Nijhoff, 2010.

Berger, Butigan, et al. *Advancing Nonviolence and Just Peace in the Church and the World*. Brussels: Pax Christi International, 2020.

Berman, Nadav. "Jewish Law, Techno-Ethics, and Autonomous Weapon Systems: Ethical-Halakhic Perspectives." Jewish Law Association Studies 29 (2020) 91–124.

Beuth, Patrick. "Polizei von San Francisco darf künftig Roboter zum Töten einsetzen." https://www.spiegel.de/netzwelt/netzpolitik/san-francisco-polizei-darf-kuenftig-roboter-zum-toeten-einsetzen-a-7c2e3734-c272-4b99-b7f4-0f26958b5e5f.

Bierhoff, Hans-Werner, and Elke Rohmann. "Diffusion von Verantwortung." In *Handbuch Verantwortung*, edited by Ludger Heidbrink et al., 911–32. Wiesbaden: Springer, 2017.

Billings, Charles E. *Human-Centered Automation Aviation: Principles and Guidelines*. Moffett Field, 1996.

Birnbacher, Dieter. "Are Autonomous Weapons a Threat to Human Dignity?" In *Autonomous Weapons Systems: Law, Ethics, Policy*, edited by Nehal Bhuta et al., 105–21. Cambridge: Cambridge University Press, 2016.

Bleher, Hannah, and Matthias Braun. "Diffused Responsibility: Attributions of Responsibility in the Use of AI-Driven Clinical Decision Support Systems." *AI Ethics* 2 (2022) 747–61.

Bo, Brunn, et al. "Retaining Responsibility in the Development and Use of Autonomous Weapons Systems: On Accountability for Violations of International Humanitarian Law Involving AWS." Stockholm: SIPRI, 2022.

Bolivian Republic of Venezuela. "General Principles on Lethal Autonomous Weapons Systems." https://www.reachingcriticalwill.org/images/documents/Disarmament-fora/ccw/2018/gge/documents/GGE.1-WP1.pdf.

Bonacker, Thorsten, and Peter Imbusch. "Zentrale Begriffe der Friedens- und Konfliktforschung. Konflikt, Gewalt, Krieg, Frieden." In *Friedens- und Konfliktforschung. Eine Einführung*, edited by Peter Imbusch et al., 67–142. Wiesbaden: utb, 2010.

Bonhoeffer, Dietrich. "Discipleship." In *Dietreich Bonhoeffer Werke IV*. Minneapolis: Fortress, 2003.

———. "Ethics." In *Dietreich Bonhoeffer Werke VI*. Minneapolis: Fortress, 2005.

Bibliography

———. "Ethik." In *Dietrich Bonhoeffer Werke VI*. Munich: Chr. Kaiser, 1998.
———. *Ethik. Zusammengestellt und herausgegeben von Eberhardt Bethge*. Munich: Chr. Kaiser, 1956.
———. "London 1933–1935." In *Dietrich Bonhoeffer Werke XIII*. Munich: Chr. Kaiser, 1994.
———. "Nachfolge." In *Dietrich Bonhoeffer Werke IV*. Munich: Chr. Kaiser, 1989.
———. "Zur theologischen Begründung der Weltbundarbeit." In *Bonhoeffer-Auswahl I. Anfänge 1927–1933*, 128–43. Munich: Siebenstern, 1997.
Bostrom, Nick. "Ethical Issues in Advanced Artificial Intelligence." https://nickbostrom.com/ethics/ai.
———. *Superintelligence: Paths, Dangers, Strategies*. Oxford: Oxford University Press, 2014.
Boulanin, Vincent, and Maaike Verbruggen. *Article 36 Reviews: Dealing with the Challenges Posed by Emerging Technologies*. Solna: SIPRI, 2017.
———. *Mapping the Development of Autonomy in Weapon Systems*. Solna: SIPRI, 2017.
Brahms, Renke. "Heidelberger Thesen—ein Mythos. Warum sich seit 1959 viele Parameter geändert haben." https://zeitzeichen.net/node/10033.
Brändle, Claudia, and Arnim Grunwald. "Autonomes Fahren aus Sicht der Maschinenethik." In *Handbuch Maschinenethik*, edited by Oliver Bendel, 281–300. Wiesbaden: Springer, 2019.
Brayne, Sarah. "Big Data Surveillance: The Case of Policing." *American Sociological Review* 5 (2017) 977–1008.
Broggi, Zelinsky, et al. "Intelligent Vehicles." In *Springer Handbook of Robotics*, edited by Bruno Siciliano et al., 1175–98. Berlin: Springer, 2008.
Brown, Benjamin. "Art: Halacha E." In *Encyclopedia of the Bible and its Reception*, edited by Constance M. Furey et al., 11:20–27. Boston: De Gruyter, 2015.
Brücher, Gertrud. "Rechtspazifismus." In *Handbuch Friedensethik*, edited by Ines-Jacqueline Werkner et al., 433–449. Wiesbaden: Springer, 2017.
Brugman, Burgers, et al. "Metaphorical Framing in Political Discourse Through Words Vs. Concepts: A Meta-Analysis." *Language and Cognition* 1 (2019) 1–25.
Bundesverband der deutschen Luft- und Raumfahrtindustrie e.V. "Positionspapier zur deutsch-französischen Kooperation im Bereich Future Combat Air System, 6/2018." https://docplayer.org/99438663-Positionspapier-zur-deutsch-franzoesischen-kooperation-im-bereich-future-combat-air-system-6-2018.html.
Bunge, Kirstin, and Matthias Gillner. "Die Lehre vom gerechten Krieg in der Iberischen Spätscholastik. Francisco de Vitora und Bartolomé de Las Casas." In *Handbuch Friedensethik*, edited by Ines-Jacqueline Werkner et al., 251–63. Wiesbaden: Springer, 2017.
Bustamante, Damián Suárez. "Robotisierung der Kriegsführung und moralische Auswirkungen der tödlichen autonomen Roboter." In *Cyberwar @ Drohnenkrieg. Neue Kriegstechnologien philosophisch betrachtet*, edited by Michael Funk et al., 133–61. Würzburg: Königshausen & Neumann, 2017.
Butler, Judith. *The Force of Nonviolence: An Ethico-Political Bind*. London: Verso, 2020.
Campaign to Stop Killer Robots. "Retaining Human Control of Weapons Systems." http://reachingcriticalwill.org/images/documents/Disarmament-fora/ccw/2018/gge/documents/KRC_Briefing_eng.pdf.

Bibliography

———. "Statement by the Campaign to Stop Killer Robots to the Convention on Conventional Weapons." https://www.hrw.org/news/2019/11/14/statement-campaign-stop-killer-robots-convention-conventional-weapons.

Carpenter, Julie. *Culture and Human-Robot Interaction in Militarized Spaces: A War Story*. Dorchester: Ashgate, 2016.

Castoriades, Cornelius. *Gesellschaft als imaginäre Institution*. Frankfurt: Suhrkamp, 1984.

Caygill, Howard. "Autonomy." In *A Kant Dictionary*, 88. Malden: Blackwell, 1995.

———. "Person." In *A Kant Dictionary*, 315. Malden: Blackwell, 1995.

Charbonnier, Ralph. "Wahrnehmen, entscheiden, handeln—werden digitale Maschinen menschlich?" In *Daten als Rohstoff. Die Nutzung von Daten in Wirtschaft, Diakonie und Kirche aus ethischer Sicht*, edited by Björn Görder et al., 61–82. Münster: LIT, 2019.

Charters, Will. "Killing on Instinct." https://vce.usc.edu/volume-4-issue-1/killing-on-instinct-a-defense-of-autonomous-weapon-systems-for-offensive-combat.

Chengeta, Thompson. "Accountability Gap: Autonomous Weapon Systems and Modes of Responsibility in International Law." https://ssrn.com/abstract=2755211.

Chesterman, Simon. "Responsibility to Protect and Humanitarian Intervention: From Apology to Utopia and Back Again." In *The Oxford Handbook of the International Law of Global Security*, edited by Robin Geiß et al., 808–20. Oxford: Oxford University Press, 2021.

China. "Position Paper." https://www.reachingcriticalwill.org/images/documents/Disarmament-fora/ccw/2018/gge/documents/GGE.1-WP7.pdf.

Christman, John. "Autonomy in Moral and Political Philosophy." *Stanford Encyclopedia of Philosophy* (2018). https://plato.stanford.edu/archives/spr2018/entries/autonomy-moral/.

Cicero. "De officiis I." http://www.perseus.tufts.edu/hopper/text?doc=Perseus%3Atext%3A2007.01.0047%3Abook%3D1%3Asection%3D35.

———. "De republica III." http://www.perseus.tufts.edu/hopper/text?doc=Perseus:text:2007.01.0031:book=3:section=35&highlight=propulsandorum.

Coeckelbergh, Mark. *Green Leviathan or the Poetics of Political Liberty: Navigating Freedom in the Age of Climate Change and Artificial Intelligence*. New York: Routledge, 2021.

———. "Moral Appearances, Emotions, Robots and Human Morality." *Ethics and Information Technology* 12 (2010) 235–41.

———. *Using Words and Things: Language and Philosophy of Technology*. New York: Routledge, 2017.

Coeckelbergh, Mark, and Janina Loh. "Transformations of Responsibility in the Age of Automation: Being Answerable to Human and Non-Human Others." In *Technology, Anthropology, and Dimensions of Responsibility*, edited by Birgit Beck et al., 7–22. Stuttgart: J.B. Metzler, 2020.

Condliffe, Jamie. "The Week in Tech: Algorithmic Bias is Bad. Uncovering it is Good." https://www.nytimes.com/2019/11/15/technology/algorithmic-ai-bias.html.

Convention on Certain Conventional Weapons (CCW) Group of Governmental Experts. "Report of the 2018 Session of the Group of Governmental Experts on Emerging Technologies in the Area of Lethal Autonomous Weapons Systems." https://reachingcriticalwill.org/images/documents/Disarmament-fora/ccw/2018/gge/documents/final-report.pdf.

Bibliography

———. "Report of the 2022 Session of the Group of Governmental Experts on Emerging Technologies in the Area of Lethal Autonomous Weapons Systems." https://documents.unoda.org/wp-content/uploads/2022/08/CCW-GGE.1-2022-CRP.1-Rev.1-As-Adopted-on-20220729.pdf.

———. "Report of the 2014 Informal Meeting of Experts on Lethal Autonomous Weapons Systems." https://daccess-ods.un.org/access.nsf/Get?OpenAgent&DS=ccw/msp/2014/3&Lang=E.

Crootof, Rebecca. "A Meaningful Floor for 'Meaningful Human Control.'" *Temple International and Comparative Law Journal* 1 (2016) 53–62.

Daase, Abb, et al. "Frieden am Ende? Die Eskalation im Russland-Ukraine-Konflikt und die Rolle der Friedenspolitik." https://blog.prif.org/2022/02/24/frieden-am-ende-die-eskalation-im-russland-ukraine-konflikt-und-die-rolle-der-friedenspolitik/.

Dahlmann, Anja, and Marcel Dickow. *Preventive Regulation of Autonomous Weapon Systems: Need for Action by Germany at Various Levels*. Stiftung Wissenschaft und Politik Research Papers 3. Berlin: Deutsches Institut für Internationale Politik und Sicherheit, 2019.

Dahlmann, Anja. "Militärische Robotik als Herausforderung für das Verhältnis von menschlicher Kontrolle und maschineller Autonomie." *Zeitschrift für Evangelische Ethik* 3 (2017) 171–83.

Daniels, Norman. "Reflective Equilibrium." *Stanford Encyclopedia of Philosophy* (2020). https://plato.stanford.edu/archives/sum2020/entries/reflective-equilibrium/.

Dastin, Jeffrey. "Amazon Scraps Secret AI Recruiting Tool that Showed Bias Against Woman." https://www.reuters.com/article/us-amazon-com-jobs-automation-insight/amazon-scraps-secret-ai-recruiting-tool-that-showed-bias-against-women-idUSKCN1MK08G.

Davenport, Melander, et al. "Introduction." In *The Peace Continuum: What It Is and How to Study It*, 2–34. Oxford: Oxford University Press, 2018.

Davidson, Neil. "A Legal Perspective: Autonomous Weapon Systems Under International Humanitarian Law." *UNODA Occasional Papers* 30 (2017) 5–18.

de Greef, Tjerk. *ePartners for Dynamic Task Allocation and Coordination*. PhD diss., Delft University of Technology, 2012.

de Vitoria, Francisco. "De Bello." In *Kann Krieg erlaubt sein? Eine Quellensammlung zur politischen Ethik der Spanischen Spätscholastik*, edited by Heinz-Gerhard Justhoven et al., 78–107. Stuttgart: Kohlhammer, 2006.

———. "De Iure Belli." In *Vorlesungen II (Relectiones). Völkerrecht Politik Kirche*, edited by Ulrich Horst et al., 542–605. Stuttgart: Kohlhammer 1997.

Decker, Michael. "Robotik." In *Handbuch Bioethik*, edited by Dieter Sturma et al., 373–78. Stuttgart: J. B. Melzer, 2015.

DeJonge, Michael P. *Bonhoeffer's Reception of Luther*. Oxford: Oxford University Press, 2017.

Del Monte, Lois A. *Genius Weapons: Artificial Intelligence, Autonomous Weaponry, and the Future of Warfare*. Amherst: Prometheus, 2018.

Dickow, Marcel, and Daniel Jacob. "Das globale Ringen um die Zukunft der Künstlichen Intelligenz. Internationaler Regulierungsbedarf und Chancen für die deutsche Außenpolitik." Stiftung Wissenschaft und Politik Aktuell 24. Berlin: Deutsches Institut für Internationale Politik und Sicherheit, 2018.

Diel, Alexander, et al. "A Meta-Analysis of the Uncanny Valley's Independent and Dependent Variables." *Journal of Human-Robot Interaction* 1 (2021) 1–33.

Bibliography

Dignum, Virginia. *Responsible Artificial Intelligence: How to Develop and Use AI in a Responsible Way*. Cham: Springer, 2019.

Dildar, Akram, et al. "Skin Cancer Detection: A Review Using Deep Learning Techniques." *International Journal of Environmental Research and Public Health* 10 (2021) 1–22.

Dill, Janina, and Henry Shue. "Limiting the Killing in War: Military Necessity and the St Petersburg Assumption." In *Fighting Hurt: Rule and Exception in Torture and War*, edited by Henry Shue, 447–68. Oxford: Oxford University Press 2016.

Doorn, Neelke, and Sven Ove Hansson. "Design for the Value of Safety." In *Handbook of Ethics, Values, and Technological Design: Sources, Theory, Values and Application Domains*, edited by Jeroen van den Hoven et al., 491–511. Würzburg: Springer, 2015.

Dorff, Elliot N. "War and Peace: A Methodology to Formulate a Contemporary Jewish Approach." *Philosophia* 40 (2012) 643–61.

Dorlin, Elsa. *Selbstverteidigung. Eine Philosophie der Gewalt*. Berlin: Suhrkamp, 2022.

Düsing, Klaus. "Ethische Freiheit, Autonomie und Selbstbewusstsein bei Kant mit einem Ausblick auf Fichte." In *Freiheit nach Kant. Tradition, Rezeption, Transformation, Aktualität*, edited by Saša Josifović et al., 134–50. Leiden: Brill, 2019.

Emerton, Patrick, and Toby Handfield. "Order and Affray: Defensive Privileges in Warfare." *Philosophy and Public Affairs* 4 (2009) 382–414.

Endsley, Mica R., and Esin O. Kiris. "The Out-of-the-Loop Performance Problem and Level of Control in Automation." *Human Factors* 2 (1995) 381–94.

Epley, Waytz, et al. "On Seeing Human: A Three-Factor Theory of Anthropomorphism." *Psychological Review* 4 (2007) 864–86.

Ertel, Wolfgang. *Grundkurs Künstliche Intelligenz*. 5th ed. Wiesbaden: Springer, 2021.

Evangelische Kirche in Deutschland. *Aus Gottes Frieden leben—für gerechten Frieden sorgen*. Gütersloh: Gütersloher Verlagshaus, 2007.

———. *Das rechte Wort zur rechten Zeit*. Gütersloh: Gütersloher Verlagshaus, 2008.

———. *Freiheit digital. Die Zehn Gebote in Zeiten des digitalen Wandels*. Leipzig: EVA, 2021.

———. "Live from God's Peace—Care for Just Peace: A Memorandum of the Council of the Evangelical Church in Germany, 2007." https://archiv.ekd.de/live_from_gods_peace.html.

Evangelische Kirche in Mitteldeutschland. "Ökumenische Versammlung für Gerechtigkeit, Frieden und Bewahrung der Schöpfung." https://www.ekmd.de/attachment/aa234c91bdabf36adbf227d333e5305b/1e01a4aaf49f4e41a4a11e0bcbc61b47dbfc6d3c6d3/Texte_Oekumenische_Versammlung_1989.pdf.

Evangelische Landeskirche in Baden. "Richte unsere Füße auf den Weg des Friedens (Lk 1,79). Ein Diskussionsbeitrag aus der Evangelischen Landeskirche in Baden. 2013." https://www.ekiba.de/media/download/integration/83315/diskussionspapier_friedensethik_erweitert.pdf.

———. "Rethinking Security. From Military to Civil Security Toward 2040: A Trend Scenario (Abridged Version), 2019." https://sicherheitneudenken.eki-musterhausen.de/html/media/dl.html?v=186330.

Fabre, Cécile, and Seth Lazar. "Introduction." In *The Morality of Defensive War*, 1–8. Oxford: Oxford University Press, 2014.

Fabre, Cécile. *Cosmopolitan War*. Oxford: Oxford University Press, 2012.

Bibliography

Fiala, Andrew. "Pacifism." *Stanford Encyclopedia of Philosophy* (2018). https://plato.stanford.edu/archives/fall2018/entries/pacifism/.

Firestone, Reuven. *Holy War in Judaism: The Fall and Rise of a Controversial Idea*. Oxford: Oxford University Press, 2012.

Flemisch, Heesen, et al. "Toward a Dynamic Balance Between Humans and Automation: Authority, Ability, Responsibility and Control in Shared and Cooperative Control Situations." *Cognition, Technology and Work* 1 (2012) 3–18.

Floridi, Luciano, and J.W. Sanders. "On the Morality of Artificial Agents." *Minds and Machines* 3 (2004) 349–79.

Ford, Christopher M. "International Humanitarian Law, Article 36, and Autonomous Weapons Systems." In *Lethal Autonomous Weapons Systems: Technology, Definition, Ethics, Law and Security*, 76–84. Berlin: Federal Foreign Office of Germany, 2016.

Forschner, Maximilian. "Krieg und Frieden in der römischen Antike. Cicero und die Stoa." In *Handbuch Friedensethik*, edited by Ines-Jacqueline Werkner et al., 213–23. Wiesbaden: Springer, 2017.

Forst, Rainer. *Das Recht auf Rechtfertigung. Elemente einer konstruktivistischen Theorie der Gerechtigkeit*. Frankfurt: Suhrkamp, 2007.

Fox, Michael Allen. Understanding Peace: A Comprehensive Introduction. New York: Routledge, 2014.

Francis, Pope. "*Laudato Si.*" https://www.vatican.va/content/francesco/en/encyclicals/documents/papa-francesco_20150524_enciclica-laudato-si.html.

Franke, Ulrike E. "Automatisierte und autonome Systeme in der Militär- und Waffentechnik." *Aus Politik und Zeitgeschichte* 35–36 (2016) 28–32.

Frankfurt, Harry G. "Autonomy, Necessity and Love." In *Necessity, Volition and Love*, 129–45. Cambridge: Cambridge University Press, 1999.

———. "Freedom of the Will." In *The Importance of What We Care About*, 11–25. Cambridge: Cambridge University Press, 1990.

———. "What are We Morally Responsible For?" In *The Importance of What We Care About*, 95–113. Cambridge: Cambridge University Press, 1990.

Freedman, Lawrence. *The Future of War: A History*. New York: PublicAffairs, 2017.

Friedman, Batya, and Helen Nissenbaum. "Bias in Computer Systems." Association for Computing Machinery Transactions on Information Systems 3 (1996) 330–47.

Frowe, Helen. *Defensive Killing*. Oxford: Oxford University Press, 2014.

———. *The Ethics of War and Peace: An Introduction*. London: Routledge, 2015.

Fuchs, Marko J. "Die Lehre vom gerechten Krieg im Mittelalter. Thomas von Aquin." In *Handbuch Friedensethik*, edited by Ines-Jacqueline Werkner et al., 239–50. Wiesbaden: Springer, 2017.

Fuchs, Thomas. "Menschliche und Künstliche Intelligenz. Eine Klarstellung." In *Verteidigung des Menschen. Grundfragen einer verkörperten Anthropologie*, 21–70. Berlin: Springer, 2020.

Funk, Michael. "Drohnen und sogenannte 'autonom-intelligente' Technik im Kriegseinsatz. Philosophische und ethische Fragestellungen." In *Cyberwar @ Drohnenkrieg. Neue Kriegstechnologien philosophisch betrachtet*, edited by Michael Funk et al., 163–93. Würzburg: Königshausen & Neumann, 2017.

Galloit, Jai. "Lethal Autonomous Weapons Systems. Proliferation, Disengagement, and Disempowerment." In *Lethal Autonomous Weapons Systems: Technology,*

Bibliography

Definition, Ethics, Law and Security, 85–96. Berlin: Federal Foreign Office of Germany, 2016.

Galtung, Johan. "Violence, Peace, and Peace Research." *Journal of Peace Research* 3 (1969) 167–91.

Garcia, Denise. "Autonomous Weapon Systems and International Law: Consequences for the Future of International Peace and Security." In *Lethal Autonomous Weapons Systems: Technology, Definition, Ethics, Law and Security*, 97–108. Berlin: Federal Foreign Office of Germany, 2016.

Gašparević, Matija. "Die Lehre vom gerechten Krieg und die Risiken des 21. Jahrhunderts—der Präemptivkrieg und die militärische humanitäre Intervention. München 2010." https://edoc.ub.uni-muenchen.de/15885/.

Geiß, Robin, and Henning Lahmann. "Autonomous Weapons Systems: A Paradigm Shift for the Law of Armed Conflict?" In *Research Handbook on Remote Warfare*, edited by Jens David Ohlin, 371–404. Cheltenham: Elton, 2017.

Geiß, Robin. "Autonome Waffensysteme. Ethische und völkerrechtliche Problemstellungen." In *Unbemannte Systeme und ihre ethische Legitimierung*, edited by Ines-Jacqueline Werkner et al., 41–62. Wiesbaden: Springer, 2010.

———. "Die völkerrechtliche Dimension autonomer Waffensysteme. Friedrich-Ebert-Stiftung. Studien 2015." https://library.fes.de/pdf-files/id/ipa/11444-20150619.pdf.

German Bishops. "A Just Peace." https://www.dbk.de/fileadmin/redaktion/veroeffentlichungen/deutsche-bischoefe/DB66en.pdf.

Giubilini, Alberto. "Conscience." *Stanford Encyclopedia of Philosophy* (2022). https://plato.stanford.edu/archives/sum2022/entries/conscience/.

Goddard, Roudsari, et al. "Automation Bias: A Systematic Review of Frequency, Effect Mediators, and Mitigators." *Journal of the American Medical Informatics Association* 1 (2012) 121–27.

Graff, Bernhard. "Rassistischer Chat-Roboter. Mit falschen Werten bombardiert." https://www.sueddeutsche.de/digital/microsoft-programm-tay-rassistischer-chat-roboter-mit-falschen-werten-bombardiert-1.2928421.

Grudin, Jonathan. "A Moving Target: The Evolution of Human-Computer Interaction." In *Human Computer Interaction Handbook: Fundamentals, Evolving Technologies, and Emerging Applications*, edited by Julie A. Jacko, xxiii–lxi. London: Taylor & Francis Group, 2012.

Grünwald, Reinhard, and Christoph Kehl. *Autonome Waffensysteme. Endbericht zum TA-Projekt*. Karlsruher Institut für Technologie, 2020.

Gunkel, David. *Robot Rights*. Cambridge: Cambridge University Press, 2018.

Günther, Klaus. "Anerkannte Verantwortung—Verantwortete Anerkennung." In *Differenz und Dialog. Anerkennung als Strategie der Konfliktbewältigung?*, edited by Vera Flocke et al., 163–82. Berlin: Berliner Wissenschaftsverlag, 2011.

Gutmann, Thomas: *Würde und Autonomie. Überlegungen zur Kantischen Definition*. Münster: De Gruyter 2010.

Guyer, Paul. "Freedom, Will, Autonomy." In *Immanuel Kant: Key concepts*, edited by Will Dudley et al., 85–102. Durham: Acumen, 2011.

Habermas, Jürgen. *Auch eine Geschichte der Philosophie*. Berlin: Suhrkamp, 2019.

Hancock, Peter A. "Teleology for Technology." In *Human Performance in Automated and Autonomous Systems*, edited by Mustapha Mouloula et al., 265–300. Boca Raton: CRC, 2020.

Bibliography

Hanson, F. Allen. "Beyond the Skin Bag: On the Moral Responsibility of Extended Agencies." *Ethics and Information Technology* 11 (2009) 91–99.

Hanson Robotics. "Sophia." https://www.hansonrobotics.com/sophia/.

Hansson, Sven Ove. "Risk." *Stanford Encyclopedia of Philosophy* (2018). https://plato.stanford.edu/archives/fall2018/entries/risk/.

Haraway, Donna. "A Cyborg Manifesto: Science, Technology, and Socialist-Feminism in the Late Twentieth Century." In *Simians, Cyborgs and Women: The Reinvention of Nature*, 149–81. New York: Routledge, 1991.

Haspel, Michael. "Die Renaissance der Lehre vom gerechten Krieg in der anglo-amerikanischen Debatte: Michael Walzer." In *Handbuch Friedensethik*, edited by Ines-Jacqueline Werkner et al., 315–426. Wiesbaden: Springer, 2017.

Hauerwas, Stanley. *The Peaceable Kingdom: A Primer in Christian Ethics*. Notre Dame: University of Notre Dame Press, 1983.

———. *Performing the Faith: Bonhoeffer and the Practice of Nonviolence*. Eugene, OR: Wipf & Stock, 2015.

Hauerwas, Stanley, and Samuel Wells. "Breaking Bread: Peace and War." In *The Blackwell Companion to Christian Ethics*, 415–26. Chichester: Blackwell, 2001.

Haugeland, John. *Artificial Intelligence: The Very Idea*. Cambridge, MA: MIT Press, 1989.

Heidbrink, Ludger. "Definitionen und Voraussetzungen der Verantwortung." In *Handbuch Verantwortung*, edited by Ludger Heidbrink et al., 3–34. Wiesbaden: Springer, 2017.

———. *Kritik der Verantwortung. Zu den Grenzen verantwortlichen Handelns*. Weilerswist: Velbrück, 2003.

Heidbrink, Langbehn, et al., eds. *Handbuch Verantwortung*. Wiesbaden: Springer, 2017.

Helgeland, John. "Christians and the Roman Army A.D. 173–337." *Church History* 2 (1974) 149–63.

Henriksen, Anders, and Jens Ringsmose. "Drone Warfare and Morality in Riskless War." *Global Affairs* 1 (2015) 1–7.

Hertzberg, Joachim, and Raja Chatila. "AI Reasoning Methods for Robotics." In *Springer Handbook of Robotics*, edited by Bruno Siciliano et al., 207–27. Berlin: Springer, 2008.

Heylighen, Francis, and Cliff Joslynn. "Cybernetics and Second-Order Cybernetics." In *Encyclopedia of Physical Science and Technology*, edited by Robert A. Meyers, 4:115–70. New York: Academic, 2001.

Heyns, Christof. "A Human Rights Perspective on Autonomous Weapons in Armed Conflict: The Rights to Life and Dignity." In *Lethal Autonomous Weapons Systems: Technology, Definition, Ethics, Law and Security*, 148–59. Berlin: Federal Foreign Office of Germany, 2016.

Hoffberger-Pippan, Vohs, et al. *Autonomous Weapons Systems: UN Expert Talks Facing Failure*. Stiftung Wissenschaft und Politik Comment C43. Berlin: Deutsches Institut für Internationale Politik und Sicherheit, 2022.

Höffe, Otfried. "Menschenwürde als ethisches Prinzip." In *Gentechnik und Menschenwürde. An den Grenzen von Ethik und Recht*, edited by Otfried Höffe et al., 110–41. Cologne: Dumont, 2002.

Hofheinz, Marco. "Radikaler Pazifismus." In *Handbuch Friedensethik*, edited by Ines-Jacqueline Werkner et al., 213–431. Wiesbaden: Springer, 2017.

Bibliography

Höhne, Florian. "Bilder des Menschlichen. Theologisch-ethische Herausforderungen der Vorstellungswelten künstlicher Intelligenz." In *Framing KI. Narrative, Metaphern und Frames in Debatten über Künstliche Intelligenz*, edited by Frederike Oorschot et al., 111–36. Heidelberg: heiBOOKS, 2022.

———. "Darf ich vorstellen: Digitalisierung. Anmerkungen zu Narrativen und Imaginationen digitaler Kulturpraktiken in theologisch-ethischer Perspektive." In *Digitaler Strukturwandel der Öffentlichkeit. Interdisziplinäre Perspektiven auf politische Partizipation im Wandel*, edited by Jonas Bedford-Strohm et al., 23–46. Baden-Baden: Nomos, 2019.

Hollnagel, Erik, and David D. Woods. "Cognitive Systems Engineering: New Wine in New Bottles." *International Journal of Human-Computer Studies* 2 (1983) 339–56.

———. *Joint Cognitive Systems: Foundations of Cognitive Systems*. Boca Raton: CRC, 2005.

Holmes, Robert. *On War and Morality*. Princeton: Princeton University Press, 1989.

———. *Pacifism: A Philosophy of Nonviolence*. London: Bloomsbury, 2017.

Honnefelder, Ludger. "Die Frage nach dem moralischen Status des Embryos." In *Gentechnik und Menschenwürde. An den Grenzen von Ethik und Recht*, edited by Otfried Höffe et al., 79–110. Cologne: Dumont, 2002.

Honneth, Axel. "Zur Kritik der Gewalt." In *Benjamin Handbuch. Leben—Werk—Wirkung*, edited by Linder Burkhardt, 193–209. Stuttgart: J. B. Metzler, 2011.

Horowitz, Michael C. "The Ethics and Morality of Robotic Warfare: Assessing the Debate over Autonomous Weapons." Daedalus 4 (2016) 25–36.

Howard, Michael, and Peter Paret, eds. *Carl von Clausewitz: On War*. Princeton: Princeton University Press, 1976.

Huber, Wolfgang, and Hans-Richard Reuter. *Friedensethik*. Stuttgart: Kohlhammer, 1990.

Huber, Wolfgang. *Dietrich Bonhoeffer. Auf dem Weg zur Freiheit. Ein Portrait*. Munich: C.H. Beck, 2019.

———. *Ethik. Die Grundfragen unseres Lebens von der Geburt bis zum Tod*. Munich: C.H. Beck, 2016.

———. "Frieden V. Kirchengeschichtlich und ethisch." In *Theologische Realenzyklopädie*, 11:618–46. Berlin: de Gruyter, 1983.

———. *Gerechtigkeit und Recht. Grundlinien einer christlichen Rechtsethik*. Gütersloh: Gütersloher Verlagshaus, 1996.

———. "Legitimes Recht und legitime Rechtsgewalt in theologischer Perspektive." In *Gewalt und Gewalten. Zur Ausübung, Legitimität und Ambivalenz rechtserhaltender Gewalt*, edited by Torsten Meireis, 225–42. Tübingen: Mohr-Siebeck, 2012.

———. "Rechtsethik." In *Handbuch der Evangelischen Ethik*, edited by Wolfgang Huber et al., 125–94. Munich: C.H. Beck, 2015.

———. "Von der gemeinsamen Sicherheit zum gerechten Frieden. Die Friedensethik der EKD in den letzten 25 Jahren." In *Frieden—Einsichten für das 21. Jh. 12. Dietrich-Bonhoeffer-Vorlesung Juni 2008 in Münster*, edited by Hans-Richard Reuter, 146–70. Münster: LIT, 2008.

Human Rights Watch. "Killer Robots and the Concept of Meaningful Human Control." https://www.hrw.org/news/2016/04/11/killer-robots-and-concept-meaningful-human-control.

———. "Losing Humanity. The Case Against Killer Robots." https://www.hrw.org/report/2012/11/19/losing-humanity/case-against-killer-robots.

Bibliography

Israel Aerospace Industries. "Harpy." https://www.iai.co.il/p/harpy.

Institute of Electrical and Electronic Engineers. "Ethically Aligned Design, Version 1." https://standards.ieee.org/wp-content/uploads/import/documents/other/ead_v1.pdf.

International Humanitarian Law Databases. "Convention (II) with Respect to the Laws and Customs of War on Land and its Annex: Regulations Concerning the Laws and Customs of War on Land. The Hague 1899." https://ihl-databases.icrc.org/applic/ihl/ihl.nsf/Treaty.xsp?documentId=CD0F6C83F96FB459C12563CD002D66A1&action=openDocument.

———. "Protocol I Additional to the Geneva Conventions of 12 August 1949 and Relating to the Protection of Victims of International Armed Conflicts, 8 June 1977." https://ihl-databases.icrc.org/applic/ihl/ihl.nsf/Treaty.xsp?action=openDocument&documentId=D9E6B6264D7723C3C12563CD002D6CE4.

Inagaki, Toshiyuki. "Automation and the Cost of Authority." *International Journal of Industrial Ergonomics* 3 (2003) 169–74.

International Committee for Robot Arms Control. "Closing Statement to the 2016 UN CCW Expert Meeting." https://www.icrac.net/icrac-closing-statement-to-the-2015-un-ccw-expert-meeting/.

International Committee of the Red Cross. "Views of the ICRC on Autonomous Weapon System." https://www.icrc.org/en/download/file/21606/ccw-autonomous-weapons-icrc-april-2016.pdf.

———. "What is International Humanitarian Law?" https://www.icrc.org/en/doc/assets/files/other/what_is_ihl.pd.

International Ergonomics Association. "What is Ergonomics?" https://iea.cc/about/what-is-ergonomics/.

International Panel on the Regulation of Autonomous Weapons. *Focus on Computational Methods in the Context of LAWS*. Stiftung Wissenschaft und Politik "Focus on" Report 2. 2017. https://nbn-resolving.org/urn:nbn:de:0168-ssoar-77407-7.

———. *Focus on Ethical Implications for a Regulation of LAWS*. Stiftung Wissenschaft und Politik "Focus on" Report 4. 2018. https://nbn-resolving.org/urn:nbn:de:0168-ssoar-77409-3.

———. *Focus on Human Control*. Stiftung Wissenschaft und Politik "Focus on" Report 5. 2019. https://nbn-resolving.org/urn:nbn:de:0168-ssoar-77410-6.

———. *Focus on Technology and Application of Autonomous Weapons*. Stiftung Wissenschaft und Politik "Focus On" Report 1. 2017. https://nbn-resolving.org/urn:nbn:de:0168-ssoar-77399-0.

———. "Welcome." https://www.ipraw.org/.

Ipsos. "Global Survey Highlights Continued Opposition to Fully Autonomous Weapons." https://www.ipsos.com/en-us/global-survey-highlights-continued-opposition-fully-autonomous-weapons.

———. "Research Findings, 2019." https://www.ipsos.com/en-us/news-polls/human-rights-watch-six-in-ten-oppose-autonomous-weapons.

Isaacs, Alick. "The Concept of Peace in Judaism: A Vessel that Holds a Blessing." In *The Concept of Peace in Judaism, Christianity and Islam*, edited by Georges Tamer, 1–44. Berlin: de Gruyter, 2020.

Jäger, Sarah. "Frieden durch Recht. Eine Einführung." In *Frieden durch Recht. Rechtstraditionen und Verortungen*, edited by Sarah Jäger et al., 1–12. Wiesbaden: Springer, 2020.

Bibliography

———. "Gewalt in der Bibel und in kirchlichen Traditionen. Eine Einführung." In *Gewalt in der Bibel und in kirchlichen Traditionen*, edited by Sarah Jäger et al., 1–12. Wiesbaden: Springer 2018.
Jain, Neha. "Autonomous Weapons Systems: New Frameworks for Individual Responsibility." In *Autonomous Weapons Systems: Law, Ethics, Policy*, edited by Nehal Bhuta et al., 303–24. Cambridge: Cambridge University Press, 2016.
James, William. *The Principles of Psychology II*. New York: Henry Halt and Company, 1890.
Janik, Ralph. *International Law and the Use of Force: Cases and Materials*. New York: Routledge, 2020.
Jensen, Jessica. *Krieg um des Friedens willen. Zur Lehre vom gerechten Krieg*. Baden-Baden: Nomos, 2015.
Johnson, Deborah. "Computer Systems: Moral Entities but not Moral Agents." *Ethics and Information Technology* 8 (2006) 195–204.
Johnson, James Turner. *Can Modern War Be Just?* New Haven, CT: Yale University Press, 1986.
———. *Ideology, Reason, and the Limitation of War: Religious and Secular Concepts, 1200–1740*. Princeton: Princeton University Press, 1975.
Johnson, Mark. *Moral Imagination: Implications of Cognitive Science for Ethics*. London: The University of Chicago Press, 1993.
Johnson, Robert, and Adam Cureton. "Kant's Moral Philosophy." *Stanford Encyclopedia of Philosophy* (2019). https://plato.stanford.edu/archives/spr2019/entries/kant-moral/.
Jonas, Hans. *Das Prinzip Verantwortung. Versuch einer Ethik für die technologische Zivilisation*. Frankfurt: Suhrkamp, 1984.
Justenhoven, Heinz-Gerhard, and Rolf Schumacher, eds. *Gerechter Friede. Weltgemeinschaft in der Verantwortung. Zur Debatte um die Friedensschrift der deutschen Bischöfe*. Stuttgart: Kohlhammer, 2003.
Justenhoven, Heinz-Gerhard. "The Concept of Just War in Christianity." In *The Concept of Just War in Judaism, Christianity and Islam*, edited by Georges Tamer et al., 43–91. Berlin: de Gruyter, 2021.
———. "Friede durch Recht. Zur ethischen Forderung nach einer umfassenden und obligatorischen Gerichtsbarkeit." In *Christliche Friedensethik vor den Herausforderungen des 21. Jahrhunderts*, edited by Veronika Boch et al., 113–29. Münster: Nomos, 2015.
Kahn, Paul W. "Imagining Warfare." *European Journal of International Law* 1 (2003) 199–226.
———. "The Paradox of Riskless Warfare." *Philosophy and Public Policy Quarterly* 22 (2002) 2–7.
———. *Sacred Violence: Torture, Terror and Sovereignty*. Ann Arbor: Michigan University Press, 2008.
Kahneman, Daniel. *Thinking, Fast and Slow*. New York: Penguin, 2011.
Kant, Immanuel. *Gesammelte Schriften Vol. 4*. Berlin, 1900ff.
———. *Gesammelte Schriften Vol. 6*. Berlin, 1900ff.
———. *Gesammelte Schriften Vol. 7*. Berlin, 1900ff.
———. *Groundwork of the Metaphysics of Morals. A German–English Edition*. Edited and translated by Mary J. Gregor et al. Cambridge: Cambridge University Press, 2011.

Bibliography

———. "Metaphysics of Morals." In *Practical Philosophy*, edited and translated by Mary J. Gregor, 353–604. Cambridge: Cambridge University Press, 1996.

———. "Toward Perpetual Peace." In *Practical Philosophy*, edited and translated by Mary J. Gregor, 311–52. Cambridge: Cambridge University Press, 1996.

Kasher, Asa. *Military Ethics*. Tel Aviv: Ministry of Defense, 1996.

Käßmann, M. "Liebet eure Feinde. Das gilt doch auch im Krieg. Interview." *Christ Welt* 39 (2022) 2.

Kehl, Christoph, and Christopher Coenen. "Technologien und Visionen der Mensch-Maschine-Entgrenzung." *Büro für Technikfolgen-Abschätzung beim Deutschen Bundestag (TAB) Arbeitsbericht* 167 (2016).

Keisinger, Florian, and Wolfgang Koch. "Defence and Responsibility: How Can We Ensure that New Technologies Are Used Responsibly in a Future Combat Air System?" https://www.fcas-forum.eu/press/Op-ed-Keisinger-Koch-Behoerden-Spiegel-Defence-and-responsibility.pdf.

———. "Mission." https://www.fcas-forum.eu/en/mission.

Kemker, McClure, et al. "Measuring Catastrophic Forgetting in Neural Networks." *Thirty-Second Association for the Advancement of Artificial Intelligence (AAAI) Conference on Artificial Intelligence*, 2018.

Kernberg, Otto F. *Liebe und Aggression. Eine unzertrennliche Beziehung*. Stuttgart: Schattauer, 2014.

Ki-moon, Ban. "Responsible Sovereignty: International Cooperation for a Changed World." https://www.un.org/sg/en/content/sg/speeches/2008-07-15/address-event-responsible-sovereignty-international-cooperation.

Klaiber. Walter, and Manfred Marquardt. *Gelebte Gnade. Grundriss einer Theologie der Evangelisch-methodistischen Kirche*. Göttingen: Ruprecht, 2006.

Kleemeier, Ulrike. *Grundfragen einer philosophischen Theorie des Krieges. Platon—Hobbes—Clausewitz*. Berlin: de Gruyter, 2002.

Klein, Melanie. *Liebe, Schuldgefühl und Wiedergutmachung*. Munich: Fischer, 1983.

Koch, Bernhard, and Bernhard Rinke. *Ethische Fragestellungen im Kontext autonomer Waffensysteme. Gutachten*. Hamburg: ithf, 2018.

Koch, Bernhard. "Die kirchliche Friedensdebatte. Beobachtungen aus philosophischer Sicht." *Ethik und Gesellschaft* 2 (2021).

———. "Maschinen, die uns von uns selbst entfremden. Philosophische und ethische Anmerkungen zur gegenwärtigen Debatte um autonome Waffensysteme." *Militärseelsorge. Dokumentation* 54 (2016) 99–119.

Koch, Wolfgang. "FCAS—Herausforderungen für Sensordatenfusion und Ressourcenmanagement." *MPC Special Issue* (2019) 8–11.

———. "Künstliche Intelligenz—Technische Autonomie. Zur Vermenschlichung der Maschine und Maschinisierung des Menschen." *Kirchliche Umschau* (2019) 38–52.

Koh, Collin Swee Lean. "LAWS in the Maritime Domain: An Asia-Pacific Scenario." *Lethal Autonomous Weapons Systems: Technology, Definition, Ethics, Law and Security*, 201–16. Berlin: Federal Foreign Office of Germany, 2016.

Konrad, Raiser. "Rechtserhaltende Gewalt im ökumenischen Diskurs. Zwischen gerechtem Krieg und Pazifismus." In *Rechtserhaltende Gewalt—eine ethische Verortung*, edited by Ines-Jacqueline Werkner et al., 95–116. Wiesbaden: Springer, 2019.

Körtner, Ulrich H. J. "Flug in die Irre." *Christ Welt* 39 (2022) 1.

Bibliography

Krach, Hegel, et al. "Can Machines Think? Interaction and Perspective Taking with Robots Investigated via fMRI." *PLoS One* 3 (2008) 1–11.

Kramer, Friedrich, and Stephan Kosch. "Russland ist nicht unser Feind. Interview." *Zeitzeichen*. https://zeitzeichen.net/node/9602.

Krennmayr, Tina. "Metaphor and Parts-of-Speech." In *The Routledge Handbook of Metaphor and Language*, edited by Elena Semino et al., 165–77. Abingdon: Routledge, 2017.

Kunkel, Nicole. "Am Grab meines Roboters." In *Mensch und Maschine im Zeitalter "Künstlicher Intelligenz." Theologische Herausforderungen*, edited by Hermann Diebel-Fischer et al., 113–32. Münster: LIT, 2022.

———. "Programmierte Autonomie? Autoregulative Waffensysteme als anthropologische Anfrage." In *Digitale Transformation der Gesellschaft. Neubestimmung des Sozialen durch Technik*, edited by Sebastian Kistler et al., 165–80. Münster: Aschendorff, 2023.

Kutalev, Alexey. "Natural Way to Overcome the Catastrophic Forgetting in Neural Networks." https://arxiv.org/abs/2005.07107.

Kutz, Christopher. "The Difference Uniforms Make: Collective Violence in Criminal Law and War." *Philosophy and Public Affairs* 2 (2005) 148–80.

Labonte, Melissa. "R2P's Status as a Norm." In *The Oxford Handbook of the Responsibility to Protect*, edited by Alex Bellamy et al., 133–50. Oxford: Oxford University Press, 2016.

Lambrecht, Anja, and Catherine Tucker. "Algorithmic Bias? An Empirical Study of Apparent Gender-Based Discrimination in the Display of STEM Career Ads." *Management Science* 7 (2019) 2966–81.

Lango, John W. *The Ethics of Armed Conflict: A Cosmopolitan Just War Theory*. Edinburgh: Edinburgh University Press, 2014.

Last Stone, Suzanne. "The Jewish Law of War: The Turn to International Law and Ethics." In *Just Wars, Holy Wars, and Jihads: Christian, Jewish, and Muslim Encounters and Exchanges*, edited by Sohail H. Hashmi, 342–59. Oxford: Oxford University Press, 2012.

Latour, Bruno. *Pandora's Hope: Essays on the Reality of Science Studies*. Cambridge, MA: Harvard University Press, 1999.

———. *Reassembling the Social: An Introduction to Actor-Network-theory*. Oxford: Oxford University Press, 2005.

Lazar, Seth, and Laura Valentini. "Proxy Battles in Just War Theory: Jus In Bello, the Site of Justice, and Feasibility Constraints." In *Oxford Studies in Political Philosophy*, edited by David Sobel et al., 166–93. Oxford: Oxford University Press, 2016.

Lazar, Seth. "Necessity in Self-Defense and War." *Philosophy and Public Affairs* 40 (2012) 3–44.

———. *Sparing Civilians*. Oxford: Oxford University Press, 2015.

———. "War." *Stanford Encyclopedia of Philosophy* (2017). https://plato.stanford.edu/archives/spr2017/entries/war/.

Leavy, Susan. "Gender Bias in Artificial Intelligence: The Need for Diversity and Gender Theory in Machine Learning." In *Proceedings of the 1st International Workshop on Gender Equality in Software Engineering*, 14–16. New York: Association for Computing Machinery, 2018.

Leben, Derek. *Ethics for Robotics: How to Design a Moral Algorithm*. London: Routledge, 2019.

Bibliography

Lee, John D,. and Katrina A. See. "Trust in Automation: Designing for Appropriate Reliance." *Human Factors* 1 (2004) 50–80.

Legg, Shane, and Marcus Hutter. "A Collection of Definitions of Intelligence." In *Advances in Artificial General Intelligence. Concepts, Architectures and Algorithms*, edited by B. Gortzel et al., 1–12. Amsterdam: ios Press, 2007.

Leonhard, Nina. "Just Policing—eine Replik aus (militär-) soziologischer Sicht." In *Just Policing. Gerechter Frieden*, edited by Ines-Jacqueline Werkner et al., 77–97. Wiesbaden: Springer, 2019.

Leveringhaus, Alex: *Ethics and Autonomous Weapons*. London: Palgrave Pivot, 2016.

———. "Morally Repugnant Weaponry? Ethical Responses to the Prospect of Autonomous Weapons." In *The Cambridge Handbook of Responsible Artificial Intelligence: Interdisciplinary Perspectives*, edited by Silja Voeneky et al., 475–87. Cambridge: Cambridge University Press, 2022.

Lieblich, Eliav, and Eyal Benvenisti. "The Obligation to Exercise Discretion in Warfare: Why Autonomous Weapon Systems are Unlawful." In *Autonomous Weapons Systems. Law, Ethics, Policy*, edited by Nehal Bhuta et al., 245–83. Cambridge: Cambridge University Press, 2016.

Lieblich, Eliav. "Autonomous Weapons Systems and the Obligation to Exercise Discretion." https://ssrn.com/abstract=2834421.

Lienemann, Wolfgang. "Die Revision der Lehre vom gerechten Krieg angesichts der Erfahrungen der Weltkriege und der Atombewaffnung." In *Handbuch Friedensethik*, edited by Ines-Jacqueline Werkner et al., 301–14. Wiesbaden: Springer, 2017.

Loh, Janina. *Roboterethik. Eine Einführung*. Berlin: Suhrkamp, 2019.

———. *Trans- und Posthumanismus*. Hamburg: Junius, 2020.

Looney, Aaron. "Die Lehre vom gerechten Krieg im frühen Christentum: Augustinus." In *Handbuch Friedensethik*, edited by Ines-Jacqueline Werkner et al., 225–38. Wiesbaden: Springer, 2017.

Luther, Martin. "Die Freiheit des Christenmenschen." In *Martin Luther. Deutsch-Deutsche Studienausgabe,* edited by Dietrich Korsch, 1:277–315. Leipzig: EVA, 2012.

———. *On the Freedom of a Christian*, edited and translated by Tryntje Helfferich. Indianapolis: Fortress, 2013.

———. "Von der weltlichen Obrigkeit. Wie weit man ihr Gehorsam schuldet." In *Martin Luther. Deutsch-Deutsche Studienausgabe,* edited by Hellmut Zschoch, 3:217–90. Leipzig: EVA, 2016.

———. *Works of Martin Luther III*. Philadelphia: Castle, 1930.

Mamak, Kamil. "Should Criminal Law Protect Love Relation with Robots?" *AI and Society* 39 (2024) 573–82.

Marauhn, Thilo. "Meaningful Human Control and the Politics of International Law." In *Dehumanization of Warfare: Legal Implications of New Weapon Technologies*, edited by Wolff Heintschel et al., 207–18. Cham: Springer, 2018.

Maser, Peter. *Die Kirchen in der DDR*. Bonn: Bundeszentrale für politische Bildung, 2020.

Matthews, Gareth, and Amy Mullin. "The Philosophy of Childhood." *Stanford Encyclopedia of Philosophy* (2020). https://plato.stanford.edu/archives/fall2020/entries/childhood/.

Bibliography

May, Larry. *After War Ends: A Philosophical Perspective*. Cambridge: Cambridge University Press, 2012.

———. *Contingent Pacifism: Revisiting Just War Theory*. Cambridge: Cambridge University Press, 2015.

McMahan, Jeff. "Innocence, Self-Defense and Killing in War." *Journal of Political Philosophy* 2 (1994) 193–221.

———. *Killing in War*. Oxford: Oxford University Press, 2009.

———. "Moral Intuition." In *The Blackwell Guide to Ethical Theory*, edited by Hugh LaFolette et al., 103–20. Chichester: Blackwell, 2013.

Meireis, Torsten. "Berliner Realismus. Wolfgang Hubers Begründung der kritischen Funktion Öffentlicher Theologie." In *Kritische Öffentliche Theologie*, edited by Heinrich Bedford-Strohm et al., 13–30. Leipzig: EVA, 2022.

———. "Einleitung." In *Gewalt und Gewalten. Zur Ausübung, Legitimität und Ambivalenz rechtserhaltender Gewalt*, 1–7. Tübingen: Mohr-Siebeck, 2012.

———. "Ethik des Sozialen." In *Handbuch der Evangelischen Ethik*, edited byWolfgang Huber et al., 265–329. Munich: C.H. Beck, 2015.

———. "Evangelische Orientierung im öffentlichen Raum. Überlegungen zum Stand der protestantischen Ethik im deutschsprachigen Kontext." *Theologischen Literaturzeitung* 1 (2021) 3–20.

———. "Gerechter Frieden und Cybersicherheit. Wider die Rede vom Cyberwar." In *Cyberwar. Die Digitalisierung der Kriegsführung*, edited by Ines-Jacqueline Werkner et al., 105–20. Wiesbaden: Springer, 2019.

———. "Der gerechte Frieden und die Ambivalenz rechtswahrender Gewalt. Eine Synthese." In *Rechtserhaltende Gewalt. Eine ethische Verortung*, edited by Ines-Jacqueline Werkner et al., 149–60. Wiesbaden: Springer, 2019.

———. "Liebe und Gewalt. Hermeneutische Erwägungen zur Rekonstruktion eines theologischen Gewaltdiskurses." In *Gewalt in der Bibel und in kirchlichen Traditionen*, edited by Sarah Jäger et al., 35–51. Wiesbaden: Springer, 2018.

———. "Die Realität der Gewalt und die Hoffnung auf Frieden. Perspektiven des christlichen Umgangs mit Gewalt." In *Gewalt und Gewalten. Zur Ausübung, Legitimität und Ambivalenz rechtserhaltender Gewalt*, 184–95. Tübingen: Mohr-Siebeck, 2012.

———. "Die Revisionist Just War Theory: Jeff McMahan." In *Handbuch Friedensethik*, edited by Ines-Jacqueline Werkner et al., 327–39. Wiesbaden: Springer, 2017.

Merkl, Alexandr. "Das 'trügerische Gespenst des Krieges' (FT 260). Ein Umbruch in der kirchlichen Friedenslehre?" In *Unter Geschwistern? Die Sozialenzyklika Fratelli tutti. Perspektiven—Konsequenzen—Kontroversen*, edited by Ursula Nothelle-Wildfeuer et al., 193–206. Freiburg: Herder, 2021.

Mielke, Roger. "Frieden und Gerechtigkeit. Überlegungen zu ihrem Verweisungszusammenhang im Horizont der christlichen Tradition." In *Friede und Gerechtigkeit in der Bibel und in kirchlichen Traditionen. Politisch-ethische Herausforderungen*, edited by Sarah Jäger et al., 1:53–76. Wiesbaden: Springer, 2018.

Mikhail, John. *Elements of Moral Cognition: Rawls' Linguistic Analogy and the Cognitive Science of Moral and Legal Judgment*. Cambridge: Cambridge University Press, 2011.

Misselhorn, Catrin. *Grundfragen der Maschinenethik*. Ditzingen: reclam, 2018.

Bibliography

———. "Robots as Moral Agents." In *Ethics in Science and Society: German and Japanese Views*, edited by Frank Rövekamp et al., 30–24. Munich: iudicum, 2013.

Montag, Lachmann, et al. "Addictive Features of Social Media/Messenger Platforms and Freemium Games Against the Background of Psychological and Economic Theories." *International Journal of Environmental Research and Public Health* (2019) 14–16.

Montanari, Goh, et al. *The Brill Dictionary of Ancient Greek*. Leiden: Brill, 2015.

Moor, James H. "The Nature, Importance, and Difficulty of Machine Ethics." *Institute of Electrical and Electronics Engineers (IEEE) Intelligent Systems* 4 (2006) 18–21.

Mori, MacDorman, et al. "The Uncanny Valley [From the Field]." *Institute of Electrical and Electronics Engineers (IEEE) Roboticsa nd Automation Magazine* 2 (2012) 98–100.

Mosier, Kathleen, and Linda Skitka. "Human Decision Makers and Automated Decision Aids: Made for Each Other?" In *Automation and Human Performance: Theory and Applications*, edited by Raja Parasuraman et al., 1–25. Boca Raton: CRC, 1996.

Mouloua, Ferraro, et al. "Human Monitoring of Automated Systems." In *Human Performance in Automated and Autonomous Systems: Current Theory and Methods*, edited by Mustapha Mouloula et al., 1–25. Boca Raton: CRC, 2019.

Müller, Olaf L. "Pragmatischer Pazifismus." In *Handbuch Friedensethik*, edited by Ines-Jacqueline Werkner et al., 451–66. Wiesbaden: Springer, 2017.

Müller, Vincent C. "Autonomous Killer Robots Are Probably Good News." In *Drones and Responsibility: Legal, Philosophical and Sociotechnical Perspectives on the Use of Remotely Controlled Weapons*, edited by Ezio Di Nucci et al., 67–81. London: Ashgate, 2016.

Münkler, Herfried. *Die neuen Kriege*. Reinbek bei Hamburg: Rowohlt, 2003.

Narla, Kuprel, et al. "Automated Classification of Skin Lesions: From Pixels to Practice." *J Invest Dermatol* 10 (2018) 2108–10.

NASA. *Systems Engineering Handbook*. N.d.: CreateSpace, 2007.

Neerincx, Mark A., and Tim Grant. "Evolution of Electronic Partners: Human-Automation Operations and ePartners during Planetary Missions." *Journal of Cosmology* 12 (2010) 3825–33.

Nevins, Danny. "JTS Halakhic Responses to Artificial Intelligence and Autonomous Machines Responsum Approved by CJLS June 19, 2019." https://www.ramahdarom.org/wp-content/uploads/2020/04/Nevins-AI-and-Halakhah-Study-Sheet.pdf.

Newel, Allen, and Herbert A. Simon. "Computer-Science as Empirical Inquiry: Symbols and Search." *Communications of the Association for Computing Machinery* 3 (1976) 113–26.

Nida-Rümelin, Julian, and Johann Schulenburg. "Art.: Risiko." In *Handbuch Technikethik*, edited by Arnim Grunwald et al., 24–28. Heidelberg: Metzler, 2021.

Nida-Rümelin, Julian, and Nathalie Weidenfeld. *Digitaler Humanismus. Eine Ethik für das Zeitalter der Künstlichen Intelligenz*. Munich: Piper, 2018.

Niebuhr, Reinhold. *Moral Man and Immoral Society: A Study in Ethics and Politics*. New York: Charles Scribner's Sons, 1960.

Niewöhner, Sørensen, et al. "Einleitung." In *Science and Technology Studies. Eine sozialanthropologische Einführung*, 9–47. Bielefeld: Transcript, 2014.

Nissenbaum, Helen. "Accountability in a Computerized Society." *Science and Engineering Ethics* 2 (1996) 25–42.

Bibliography

Noble, Safija Umoja. *Algorithms of Oppression: How Search Engines Reinforce Racism.* New York: New York University Press, 2018.

Nussbaum, Martha C. *Creating Capabilities.* Cambridge, MA: Harvard University Press, 2011.

———. *Frontiers of Justice: Disability, Nationality, Species Membership.* Cambridge, MA: Harvard University Press, 2006.

Nyholm, Sven. *Humans and Robots. Ethics, Agency, and Anthropomorphism.* London: Rowman & Littlefield, 2020.

Oberdorfer, Bernd. "'Gerechter Frieden'—mehr als ein weißer Schimmel? Überlegungen zu einem Leitbegriff der neueren theologischen Friedensethik." In *Friede und Gerechtigkeit in der Bibel und in kirchlichen Traditionen. Politisch-ethische Herausforderungen Band 1*, edited by Sarah Jäger et al., 13–30. Wiesbaden: Springer, 2018.

O'Connor, Timothy, and Franklin, Christopher. "Free Will." *Stanford Encyclopedia of Philosophy* (2022). https://plato.stanford.edu/archives/sum2022/entries/freewill/.

O'Neil, Cathy. *Weapons of Math Destruction.* Harlow: Crown, 2017.

Open Roboethics Initiative. "The Ethics and Governance of Lethal Autonomous Weapons Systems: An International Public Opinion Poll." http://www.openroboethics.org/wp-content/uploads/2015/11/ORi_LAWS2015.pdf.

Orend, Brian. "Justice After War." *Ethics and International Affairs* 1 (2002) 43–56.

Pagel, Gerda. *Jaques Lacan. Zur Einführung.* Hamburg: Junius, 2019.

Parasuraman, Raja and Riley, Victor. "Humans and Automation: Use, Misuse, Disuse, Abuse." *Human Factors* 2 (1997) 230–53.

Parasuraman, Sheridan, et al. "A Model for Types and Levels of Human Interaction with Automation." In *Institute of Electrical and Electronics Engineers (IEEE) Transactions on Systems, Man, and Cybernetics—Part A: Systems and Humans* 3 (2000) 286–97.

Paul VI, Pope. "Pastoral Constitution of the Church in the Modern World *Gaudium et Spes.*" http://www.vatican.va/archive/hist_councils/ii_vatican_council/documents/vat-ii_const_19651207_gaudium-et-spes_en.html.

Pax Christi International. "Catholic Nonviolence Initiative." https://paxchristi.net/programmes/catholic-nonviolence-initiative.

———. "Our History." https://paxchristi.net/about-us/https-pcintlorg-files-wordpress-com-2019-10-timeline-posters-pdf.

Picht, Georg. "Der Begriff der Verantwortung." In *Wahrheit—Vernunft—Verantwortung. Philosophische Studien*, 318–42. Stuttgart: Klett, 1969.

Plato. "Nomoi I with an English Translation by G. Bury." http://www.perseus.tufts.edu/hopper/text;jsessionid=31093E2B708291FB30F6BB7CD1452320?doc=Plat.+Laws+1.628&fromdoc=Perseus%3Atext%3A1999.01.0165.

Polish, Daniel F. "Just War in Jewish Thought." In *The Concept of Just War in Judaism, Christianity and Islam*, edited by Georges Tamer, 1–42. Berlin: De Gruyter, 2021.

Potter, Ralph. *War and Moral Discourse.* Richmond: John Knox, 1969.

Preußger, Philipp. "'Drone Art' zwischen Anschauung und Vermittlung." https://wissenschaft-kunst.de/drone-art-zwischen-anschauung-und-vermittlung/.

Puzio, Anna. "Über-Menschen. Philosophische Auseinandersetzung mit der Anthropologie des Transhumanismus." Bielefeld: Transcript, 2022. https://www.transcript-verlag.de/978-3-8376-6305-1/ueber-menschen/?number=978-3-8394-6305-5.

Bibliography

———. "Zeig mir deine Technik und ich sag dir, wer du bist? Was Technikanthropologie ist und warum wir sie dringend brauchen." In *Mensch und Maschine im Zeitalter "Künstlicher Intelligenz." Theologische Herausforderungen*, edited by Hermann Diebel-Fischer et al., 9–28. Münster: LIT, 2023.

The Rabbinical Assembly. "Committee on Jewish Law and Standards." https://www.rabbinicalassembly.org/jewish-law/committee-jewish-law-and-standards.

Ramsey, Paul. *The Just War: Force and Political Responsibility*. New York: Charles Scribner's Sons, 1986.

———. *The Limits of Nuclear War*. New York: Council on Religion and International Affairs, 1963.

———. *War and the Christian Conscience: How Shall Modern War be Conducted Justly*. Durham: Duke University Press, 1961.

Rasborg, Klaus. *Ulrich Beck: A Critical Introduction to World Risk Society and Cosmopolitanism*. Cham: Springer, 2021.

Rauen, Verena. "Ethische Verantwortung." In *Handbuch Verantwortung*, edited by Ludger Heidbrink et al., 545–57. Wiesbaden: Springer, 2017.

Ravitzky, Aviezer: *AL DAÀT Ha-MaQom: Studies in the History of Jewish Philosophy*. Jerusalem: Maxwell-Macmillan-Keter, 1991.

———. "Prohibited Wars." In *Law, Politics, and Morality in Judaism*, edited by Michael Walzer, 169–82. Princeton: Princeton University Press, 2006.

Rawls, John. *A Theory of Justice*. Cambridge: Belknap Press, 1971.

Reeves, Shane and David A. Wallace. "Modern Weapons and the Law of Armed Conflict." In *U.S. Military Operations: Law, Policy, and Practice*, edited by Geoffrey S. Corn et al., 41–66. Oxford: Oxford University Press, 2015.

Reuter, Hans-Richard. *Botschaft und Ordnung. Beiträge zur Kirchentheorie*. Leipzig: EVA, 2009.

———. "Der international Rechtsfrieden zwischen Realismus und Idealismus." In *Kritische Öffentliche Theologie*, edited by Heinrich Bedford-Strohm et al., 149–58. Leipzig: EVA, 2022.

———. "Grundlagen und Methoden der Ethik." In *Handbuch der Evangelischen Ethik*, edited by Wolfgang Huber et al., 9–124. Munich: C.H. Beck, 2015.

———. "Kampfdrohnen als Mittel rechtswahrender militärischer Gewalt? Aspekte einer ethischen Bewertung." *epd-Dokumentationen* 49 (2014) 37–46.

———. *Recht und Frieden. Beiträge zur politischen Ethik*. Leipzig: EVA, 2012.

———. "Vom christlichen Pazifismus zum aktiven Widerstand. Dietrich Bonhoeffers (Denk-) Weg zwischen 1930 und 1943." In *Frieden—Einsichten für das 21. Jh. 12. Dietrich-Bonhoeffer-Vorlesung Juni 2008 in Münster*, 15–41. Münster: LIT 2008.

Ricken, Friedo. "Krieg und Frieden in der griechischen Antike. Platon und Aristoteles." In *Handbuch Friedensethik*, edited by Ines-Jacqueline Werner et al., 204–12. Wiesbaden: Springer, 2017.

Rodin, David. "The Moral Inequality of Soldiers: Why Jus In Bello Asymmetry is Half Right." In *Just and Unjust Warriors: The Moral and Legal Status of Soldiers*, edited by David Rodin et al., 44–68. Oxford: Oxford University Press, 2008.

———. "The Myth of National Self-Defence." In *The Morality of Defensive War*, edited by Cécile Fabre et al., 69–89. Oxford: Oxford University Press, 2014.

———. "Two Emerging Issues of Jus Post Bellum: War Termination and the Liability of Soldiers for Crimes of Aggression." In *Jus Post Bellum: Toward a Law of Transition*

Bibliography

from Conflict to Peace, edited by Carsten Stahn et al., 53–75. The Hague: TMC Asser, 2008.

———. *War and Self-Defence*. Oxford: Oxford University Press, 2002.

Roff, Heather M., and Richard Moyes. "Meaningful Human Control, Artificial Intelligence and Autonomous Weapons: Briefing Paper Prepared for the Informal Meeting of Experts on Lethal Autonomous Weapons Systems, UN Convention on Certain Conventional Weapons, April 2016." https://article36.org/wp-content/uploads/2016/04/MHC-AI-and-AWS-FINAL.pdf.

Rommel, Birgit. *Ekklesiologie und Ethik bei Stanley Hauerwas. Von der Bedeutung der Kirche für die Rede von Gott*. Münster: LIT, 2003.

Rosert, Elvira, and Frank Sauer. "Prohibiting Autonomous Weapons: Put Human Dignity First." *Global Policy* 3 (2019) 370–75.

Rudolf, Peter. *Zur Legitimität militärischer Gewalt*. Frankfurt: Zarbock, 2017.

Russel, Stuart, and Peter Norvig. *Artificial Intelligence: A Modern Approach*. Upper Saddle River, NJ: Pearson, 2016.

Russian Federation. "Potential Opportunities and Limitations of Military Uses of Lethal Autonomous Weapons Systems." https://reachingcriticalwill.org/images/documents/Disarmament-fora/ccw/2019/gge/Documents/GGE.2-WP1.pdf.

Santoni de Sio, Filippo, and Jeroen van den Hoven. "Meaningful Human Control Over Autonomous Systems: A Philosophical Account." *Frontiers in Robotics and AI* 5 (2018) 1–14.

Sarter, Woods, et al. "Automation Surprises." In *Handbook of Human Factors and Ergonomics*, edited by Gavriel Salvendry, 1926–43. New York: Wiley, 1997.

Scerbo, Mark W. "Theoretical Perspectives on Adaptive Automation." In *Human Performance in Automated and Autonomous Systems*, 1:103–25. Boca Raton: CRC, 2019.

Scharre, Paul, and Michael C. Horowitz. "An Introduction to Autonomy in Weapon Systems, Working Paper 2015." https://s3.us-east-1.amazonaws.com/files.cnas.org/documents/Ethical-Autonomy-Working-Paper_021015_v02.pdf?mtime=20160906082257&focal=none.

Scharre, Paul. *Army of None: Autonomous Weapons and the Future of War*. New York: Norton, 2018.

———. "Autonomous Weapons Systems and Operational Risk: Ethical Autonomy Project 2016." https://www.cnas.org/publications/reports/autonomous-weapons-and-operational-risk.

Schiffman, Lawrence H. "Art.: Halacha A." *Encyclopedia of the Bibel and its Reception*, edited by Constance M. Furey et al., 11:1–7. Boston: De Gruyter, 2015.

Schlosser, Markus. "Agency." *Stanford Encyclopedia of Philosophy* (2019). https://plato.stanford.edu/archives/win2019/entries/agency/.

Schmitt, Carl. *Political Theology: Four Chapters on the Concept of Sovereignty*. Translated by George Schwab. Chicago: University of Chicago Press, 2005.

Schockenhoff, Eberhard. *Kein Ende der Gewalt? Friedensethik für eine globalisierte Welt*. Freiburg: Herder, 2018.

Schörnig, Niklas. "Automatisierte Kriegsführung. Wie viel Entscheidungsraum bleibt dem Menschen?" *Aus Politik und Zeitgeschichte* 35–37 (2015) 27–34.

Schreiber, Wolfgang. "Innerstaatliche Kriege seit 1954." https://www.bpb.de/themen/kriege-konflikte/dossier-kriege-konflikte/54508/innerstaatliche-kriege-seit-1945/.

Bibliography

Schrey, Heinz-Horst. "Krieg IV Historisch/Ethisch." In *Theologische Realenzyklopädie Online.* https://www.degruyter.com/database/TRE/entry/tre.20_010_52/html.

Schwarke, Christian. "Technik und Technik und Theologie. Was ist der Gegenstand einer theologischen Technikethik?" *Zeitschrift für Evangelische Ethik* 49 (2005) 88–104.

Schwarz, Elke. "Autonomous Weapons Systems, Artificial Intelligence, and the Problem of Meaningful Human Control." *Philosophical Journal of Conflict and Violence* 5 (2021) 53–72.

Semino, Demjén, et al. "An Integrated Approach to Metaphor and Framing in Cognition, Discourse, and Practice, with an Application to Metaphors for Cancer." *Applied Linguistics* 5 (2018) 625–45.

Semino, Elena. *Metaphor in Discourse.* Cambridge: Cambridge University Press, 2008.

Sen, Amartya. *The Idea of Justice.* London: Allen Lane, 2009.

Sharkey, Noel. "Staying in the Loop. Human Supervisory Control of Weapons." In *Autonomous Weapons Systems: Law, Ethics, Policy,* edited by Nehal Bhuta et al., 23–38. Cambridge: Cambridge University Press, 2016.

Sheridan, Thomas B., and Raja Parasuraman. "Human-Automation Interaction." *Reviews of Human Factors and Ergonomics* 1 (2005) 89–129.

Shue, Henry. "Do We Need a Morality of War?" In *Just and Unjust Warriors: The Moral and Legal Status of Soldiers,* edited by David Rodin et al., 87–111. Oxford: Oxford University Press, 2008.

———. "War." In *Fighting Hurt: Rule and Exception in Torture and War,* 352–78. Oxford: Oxford University Press, 2016.

Sicherheitshalber Podcast. "Folge 33." https://sicherheitspod.de/2020/09/07/folge-33-feministische-ausenpolitik-flugabwehr-gegen-drohnen-fahigkeitslucke-short-range-air-defense/.

Siciliano, Bruno and Oussama Khatib. "Introduction." In *Springer Handbook of Robotics,* 1–7. Berlin: Springer, 2008.

Singer, Peter W., and August Cole. *Ghost Fleet: A Novel of the Next World War.* Boston: William Morrow, 2015.

Singer, Peter W. *Wired for War. The Robotics Revolution and Conflict in the 21st Century.* New York: Penguin, 2009.

Slenczka, Notger. "Gewissen und Gott. Überlegungen zur Phänomenologie der Gewissenserfahrung und ihrer Darstellung in der Rede vom Jüngsten Gericht." In *Das Gewissen,* edited by Stephan Schaede et al., 235–83. Tübingen: Mohr Siebeck, 2015.

———. "Die unvermeidliche Schuld. Der Normenkonflikt in der christlichen Ethik. Deutung einer Passage aus Bonhoeffers Ethik-Fragmenten." *Berliner Theologische Zeitschrift* 1 (1999) 97–119.

Smith, Brian Cantwell. *The Promise of Artificial Intelligence: Reckoning and Judgment.* Cambridge, MA: MIT Press, 2019.

Spaemann, Robert. "Menschenwürde und menschliche Natur." In *Normativität des Lebens—Normativität der Vernunft?,* edited by Markus Rothaar et al., 37–42. Berlin: De Gruyter, 2015.

Sparrow, Robert. "Killer Robots." *Journal of Applied Philosophy* 24 (2007) 62–77.

Sparrow, Robert J., and George Lucas. "When Robots Rule the Waves?" In *One Nation Under Drones: Legality, Morality, and Utility of Unmanned Combat Systems,* edited by J. E. Jackson, 75–98. Annapolis: Naval Institute Press, 2018.

Bibliography

Spiekermann, Sarah. *Digitale Ethik. Ein Wertesystem für das 21. Jahrhundert*. Munich: Droemer, 2019.

Stanford Law School. "International Human Rights and Conflict Resolution Clinic at Stanford Law School and Global Justice Clinic at NYU School of Law: Living Under Drones." https://www-cdn.law.stanford.edu/wp-content/uploads/2015/07/Stanford-NYU-LIVING-UNDER-DRONES.pdf.

Statman, Daniel. "Drohnen, Roboter und die Moral des Krieges." *Ethik und Militär* 1 (2014) 46–50.

———. "Drones and Robots: On the Changing Practice of Warfare." In *The Oxford Handbook of Ethics and War*, edited by Seth Lazar et al., 472–87. Oxford: Oxford University Press 2021.

Steil, Jochen. "Roboterlernen ohne Grenzen? Lernende Roboter und ethische Fragen." In *Roboter in der Gesellschaft. Technische Möglichkeiten und menschliche Verantwortung*, edited by Christiane Woopen et al., 15–33. Berlin: Springer, 2019.

Steinhoff, Uwe. "Jeff McMahan on the Moral Inequality of Combatants." Journal of Political Philosophy 2 (2008) 220–26.

Stop Killer Robots. "Less Autonomy. More Humanity." https://www.stopkillerrobots.org/.

Strawser, Bradley J. "Introduction: The Moral Landscape of Unmanned Warfare." In *Killing by Remote Control: The Ethics of an Unmanned Military*, 229–46. New York: Oxford University Press, 2013.

———. "Moral Predators: The Duty to Employ Uninhabited Aerial Vehicles." *Journal of Military Ethics* 4 (2010) 342–68.

———. "Revisionist Just War Theory and the Real World: A Cautiously Optimistic Proposal." In *Routledge Handbook of Ethics and War: Just War Theory in the Twenty-First Century*, edited by Fritz Allhoff et al., 76–90. London: Routledge, 2013.

Strohm, Christoph. "Realismus und Friedenssehnsucht. Radikaler Pazifismus kann sich nicht auf Luther berufen." https://zeitzeichen.net/node/9702.

Stüben, Joachim. "Die Kriegsethik der Spanischen Spätscholastik anhand ausgewählter Quellen. Einleitung des Übersetzers." In *Kann Krieg erlaubt sein? Eine Quellensammlung zur politischen Ethik der Spanischen Spätscholastik*, edited by Heinz-Gerhard Justhoven et al., 54–77. Stuttgart: Kohlhammer, 2006.

Stümke, Volker. "Gerechter Friede in der Debatte." *Theologische Rundschau* 4 (2020) 311–92.

———. "Religion und Gewalt. Ein Literaturbericht (Teil 2)." *Theologische Rundschau* 2 (2019) 105–57.

Suchman, Lucy, and Jutta Weber. "Human-Machine Autonomies." In *Autonomous Weapons Systems: Law, Ethics, Policy*, edited by Nehal Bhuta et al., 75–102. Cambridge: Cambridge University Press, 2016.

Talbert, Matthew. "Moral Responsibility." *Stanford Encyclopedia of Philosophy* (2022). https://plato.stanford.edu/archives/fall2022/entries/moral-responsibility/.

Taylor, Charles. "Kant's Theory of Freedom." In *Philosophy and Human Sciences*, 318–38. Cambridge: Cambridge University Press, 1985.

———. *Modern Social Imaginaries*. Durham: Duke University Press, 2004.

———. *Quellen des Selbst*. Frankfurt: Suhrkamp, 1996.

———. *Sources of the Self*. Cambridge: Cambridge University Press, 1989.

Bibliography

———. "What Is Human Agency?" In *Human Agency and Language: Philosophical Papers*, 15–44. Cambridge: Cambridge University Press, 1985.

Thomas Aquinas. "Summa Theologica Vol. 4." In *Summa Theologica*. Paris: Bloud & Barrel, 1885.

———. "Summa Theologica Vol. 17b." In *Die deutsche Thomas-Ausgabe*, edited by the Albertus-Magnus-Akademie bei Köln. Heidelberg: F. H. Kerle/Styra, 1966.

Ticehurst, Rupert. "The Martens Clause and the Laws of Armed Conflict." *International Review of the Red Cross* 317 (1997) 125–34. https://www.icrc.org/en/doc/resources/documents/article/other/57jnhy.htm.

Tirosh-Samuelson, Hava. "Jewish Philosophy and the Critique of AI Technology." In *Alexa, wie hast Du's mit der Religion?*, edited by Anna Puzio et al., 235–58. Darmstadt: wbg, 2023.

Tomasello, Michael. *A Natural History of Human Morality*. Cambridge, MA: Harvard University Press, 2018.

United Kingdom Ministry of Defence. *Joint Doctrine Publication 0-30.2—Unmanned Aircraft Systems*. HMSO: MOD Shrivenham, 2017.

United Nations. "A/RES/60/1." https://daccess-ods.un.org/tmp/785648.077726364.html.

———. "Charter." https://www.un.org/en/about-us/un-charter/chapter-1.

———. "Sustaining Peace." https://www.un.org/peacebuilding/tags/sustaining-peace.

United Nations Office for Disarmament Affairs. "Perspectives on Lethal Autonomous Weapons Systems." *UNODA Occasional Papers* 30 (2017). https://www.un.org/disarmament/publications/occasionalpapers/unoda-occasional-papers-no-30-november-2017/.

United Nations Panel of Experts on Libya. "Final report of the panel of experts on Libya established pursuant to Security Council resolution 1973 (2011) S/2021/229." https://documents.un.org/doc/undoc/gen/n21/037/72/pdf/n2103772.pdf.

United Nations Security Council. "Final Report of the Panel of Experts on Libya Established Pursuant to Security Council Resolution 1973 (2011) S/2021/229." https://documents.un.org/doc/undoc/gen/n21/037/72/pdf/n2103772.pdf.

United States Air Force. "Doctrinal Publication 3–60. Annex 3–60. Targeting: Dynamic Targeting and the Tasking Process." https://www.doctrine.af.mil/Doctrine-Publications/AFDP-3-60-Targeting/.

United States Department of Defense. "Directive 3000.09, 2012." https://irp.fas.org/doddir/dod/d3000_09.pdf.

———. "Summary of the 2018 Department of Defense Artificial Intelligence Strategy. Harnessing AI to Advance our Security and Prosperity." https://media.defense.gov/2019/Feb/12/2002088963/-1/-1/1/SUMMARY-OF-DOD-AI-STRATEGY.PDF.

———. "Unmanned Systems Integrated Roadmap. FY2017–2042, 2018." https://ntrl.ntis.gov/NTRL/dashboard/searchResults/titleDetail/AD1059546.xhtml#.

United States of America. "Human-Machine Interaction in the Development, Deployment, and Use of Emerging Technologies in the Area of Lethal Autonomous Weapons Systems." https://docs-library.unoda.org/Convention_on_Certain_Conventional_Weapons_-_Group_of_Governmental_Experts_(2018)/2018_GGE%2BLAWS_August_Working%2BPaper_US.pdf.

———. "Humanitarian Benefits of Emerging Technologies in the Area of Lethal Autonomous Weapon Systems." https://www.reachingcriticalwill.org/images/documents/Disarmament-fora/ccw/2018/gge/documents/GGE.1-WP4.pdf.

Bibliography

van de Poel, Ibo. "The Problem of the Many Hands." In *Moral Responsibility and the Problem of the Many Hands*, edited by Ibo van de Poel et al., 12–49. New York: Routledge, 2015.

van Oorschot, Frederike. "'Alles Technik oder was?' Ethische Perspektiven auf das Verhältnis von Mensch und Maschine im Kontext einer imaginationssensiblen Technikethik." In *Mensch und Maschine im Zeitalter "Künstlicher Intelligenz." Theologische Herausforderungen*, edited by Hermann Diebel-Fischer et al., 29–48. Münster: LIT, 2023.

———. "Einleitung." In *Framing KI. Narrative, Metaphern und Frames in Debatten über Künstliche Intelligenz*, edited by Frederike van Oorschot et al., 7–11. Heidelberg: heiBOOKS, 2022.

Vilone, Giulia, and Luca Longo. "Notions of Explainability and Evaluation Approaches for Explainable Artificial Intelligence." *Information Fusion* 76 (2021) 89–106.

Vogelmann, Frieder. *Im Bann der Verantwortung*. Frankfurt: Campus, 2014.

von Scheliha, Arnulf. *Protestantische Ethik des Politischen*. Tübingen: Mohr Siebeck, 2013.

von Schubert, Hartwig. "Das Reich Gottes, die Idee des Rechts und das Friedensvölkerrecht." In *Rechtserhaltende Gewalt. Eine ethische Verortung*, edited by Ines-Jacquline Werkner et al., 59–93. Wiesbaden: Springer, 2019.

———. "Ethische Herausforderungen digitalen Wandels in bewaffneten Konflikten. Einleitung" In *Ethische Herausforderungen digitalen Wandels in bewaffneten Konflikten*, edited by Matthias Rogg et al., 5–16. Hamburg: German Institute for Defence and Strategies, 2020.

———. "Jenseits von Eden." https://www.kas.de/documents/252038/16166715/Künstliche+Intelligenz+-+jenseits+von+Eden+Theologisch-ethische+Betrachtungen.pdf/6bf11744-154f-d33a-c7fd-2696bc5dc7c8.

———. *Nieder mit dem Krieg. Eine Ethik politischer Gewalt*. Leipzig: EVA, 2021.

Wagner, Johanna. *Künstliche Intelligenzen als moralisch verantwortliche Akteure?* Paderborn: Mentis, 2020.

Wallach, Wendell, and Colin Allen. *Moral Machines: Teaching Robots Right from Wrong*. Oxford: Oxford University Press, 2009.

Wallmann, Johannes. *Kirchengeschichte Deutschlands seit der Reformation*. Tübingen: Mohr Siebeck, 2012.

Walzer, Michael. "Commanded and Permitted Wars." In *Law, Politics, and Morality in Judaism*, edited by Michael Walzer, 149–68. Princeton: Princeton University Press, 2006.

———. "The Ethics of Warfare in the Jewish Tradition." *Philosophia* 40 (2012) 633–41.

———. *Just and Unjust Wars*. New York: Basic, 2015.

Weber, Max. *Politik als Beruf*. Munich: Duncker & Humblot, 1919.

Weissenberg, Tino J. *Die Friedenslehre des Augustinus. Theologische Grundlagen und ethische Entfaltung*. Stuttgart: Kohlhammer, 2005.

Weizenbaum, Joseph. *Computer Power and Human Reason: From Judgment to Calculation*. London: Penguin, 1987.

Wellbrink, Jörg. "Mein neuer Kamerad—Hauptgefreiter Roboter?" In *Ethik und Militär* 1 (2014) 52–55.

Werkner, Ines-Jacqueline, and Klaus Ebeling, eds. *Handbuch Friedensethik*. Wiesbaden: Springer, 2017.

Bibliography

Werkner, Ines-Jacqueline, and Hans-Joachim Heintze, eds. *Just Policing. Politisch-ethische Herausforderungen*. Wiesbaden: Springer, 2019.

Werkner, Ines-Jacqueline. "Diskurse um militärische Gewalt. Keine einfachen Antworten in der Bibel und den Konfessionen." In *Gewalt in der Bibel und in kirchlichen Traditionen*, edited by Sarah Jäger et al., 117–26. Wiesbaden: Springer, 2018.

———. "Just Policing. Eine Alternative zur militärischen Intervention?" *Epd-Dokumentation* 22 (2017) 4–86.

———. "Unbemannte Waffen. Humanisierung oder Entmenschlichung der Kriegsführung? Eine Einführung." In *Unbemannte Waffen und ihre ethische Legitimierung*, edited by Ines-Jacqueline Werkner et al., 1–12. Wiesbaden: Springer, 2019.

———. "Zum Friedensbegriff in der Friedensforschung." In *Handbuch Friedensethik*, edited by Ines-Jacqueline Werkner et al., 19–32. Wiesbaden: Springer, 2017.

———. "Zur Aktualität der Heidelberger Thesen." *Ethik und Militär* 1 (2021). http://www.ethikundmilitaer.de/de/themenueberblick/20201-nukleare-abschreckung/werkner-zur-aktualitaet-der-heidelberger-thesen/.

Wiechmann, Jan Ole. *Sicherheit neu denken. Die christliche Friedensbewegung in der Nachrüstungsdebatte 1977–1984*. Baden-Baden: Nomos, 2017.

Williams, Garrath. "Kant's Account of Reason." *Stanford Encyclopedia of Philosophy* (2018). https://plato.stanford.edu/archives/sum2018/entries/kant-reason/.

Winright, Tobias, and Nathaniel Hibner. "The Costs of *jus ante bellum* and *jus post bellum*." In *The Business of War: Theological and Ethical Reflections on the Military-Industrial Complex*, edited by James McCarty et al., 193–206. Eugene, OR: Cascade, 2020.

Wood, Allen W. "How a Kantian Decides What to Do." In *The Palgrave Kant Handbook*, edited by Matthew C. Altman, 263–84. Ellensburg: Palgrave, 2017.

World Council of Churches. "Statement on the Way of Just Peace." https://www.oikoumene.org/resources/documents/statement-on-the-way-of-just-peace.

Yeh, Michelle, and Christopher D. Wickens. "Display Signaling in Augmented Reality: Effects of Cue Reliability and Image Realism on Attention Allocation and Trust Calibration." *Human Factors* 3 (2001) 355–65.

Yoreh, Tanhum S. *Waste Not: A Jewish Environmental Ethics*. New York: State University of New York, 2019.

Zawieska, Karolina. "An Ethical Perspective on Lethal Autonomous Weapon Systems." *Perspectives on Lethal Autonomous Weapons Systems* 30 (2017) 49–56.

Zenke, Poole, et al. "Continual Learning Through Synaptic Intelligence." *Proceedings of Machine Learning Research* 70 (2017) 3987–95.

Zeyher-Quattlener, Julian. *Du sollst nicht töten (lassen)? Eine Rekonstruktion der Friedensethik Dietrich Bonhoeffers aus der Perspektive Öffentlicher Theologie in aktueller Absicht*. Leipzig: EVA, 2021.

Zohar, Noam J. "Collective War and Individualistic Ethics. Against the Conscription of 'Self-Defense.'" *Political Theory* 4 (1993) 606–22.

Zuckier, Shlomo. "A Halakhic-Philosophic Account of Justified Self-Defense." *The Torah U-Madda Journal* 16 (2012) 21–51.

Zycha, Joseph, ed. "Contra Faustum Manicheum." In *Corpus Scriptorum Ecclesiaticorum Latinorum* 25.1, 251–797. Vienna: Tempsky, 1891.

www.ingramcontent.com/pod-product-compliance
Lightning Source LLC
Chambersburg PA
CBHW071142300426
44113CB00009B/1060